LOCAL HISTORY

ROCKFORD PUBLIC LIBRARY

3 1112 018337754

W9-AOM-043

WITHDRAWN

R 929.3715 P984E V. 1
Punch, Terrence M.
Erin's sons :
Irish arrivals in Atlantic Canada /

ERIN'S SONS:

Irish Arrivals in Atlantic Canada
1761-1853

Rockford
Public
Library

This item does not circulate.

ERIN'S SONS:
Irish Arrivals in Atlantic Canada

1761-1853

Terrence M. Punch, FRSAI

Genealogical Publishing Company

ROCKFORD PUBLIC LIBRARY

Copyright © 2008
Terrence M.Punch
All Rights Reserved. No part of this publication may be reproduced
in any form or by any means, including electronic reproduction or
reproduction via the Internet, except by permission of the author
and the publisher.

Published by Genealogical Publishing Company
3600 Clipper Mill Rd., Suite 260
Baltimore, MD 21211-1953
Second printing, April 2008
Third printing, June 2008
Fourth printing, April 2009

Library of Congress Catalogue Card Number 2007935045
ISBN 978-0-8063-1782-3
Made in the United States of America

CONTENTS

♣   ♣   ♣   ♣   ♣

INTRODUCTION

On 17 April 2007 a Halifax newspaper, *The Chronicle-Herald*, reported the discovery of an ancient hemlock in western mainland Nova Scotia. Surrounded by old-growth forest, this particular tree provided a core sample with a verified age of 418 years. A seed from the parent tree fell to the earth about the time the Spanish Armada failed in its attempt to invade England. In the spring of 1589 that seed began a growth that has continued for more than four centuries, thus predating Québec and Jamestown, the senior surviving earliest settlements by Europeans north of the Gulf of Mexico.

This hemlock is not a tree of huge girth. Its modest circumference has probably saved it from the woodsman's axe over the centuries. There is a metaphor for the presence of the Irish in Atlantic Canada herein. From the earliest settlements by Europeans, there have been Irish people here, fishing the rich banks off these coastlines. Although the Irish in the nineteenth century were often regarded as intruders, their countrymen and women have been here for a very long time indeed.

Like that tree, they have not loomed as large as others, but they have survived. Some left, but others established roots here. This book celebrates that persistence by attempting to put names to some of those pioneers and telling, when possible, where they came from in the old country. Bridging the Atlantic to find the homes of our Irish forebears is among the most daunting tasks confronting North American genealogists. Most of the Irish were humble folk, and until well into the nineteenth century many could neither write their names nor correct errors entered in records by people who knew neither Irish Gaelic nor the names of the places which these people called home.

Viewed from Atlantic Canada, North America is a funnel, its spout resting here, its bowl opening ever wider into the continent beyond. Atlantic Canada's early records are fewer and less informative than those of New England and New York from the same period. Genealogists in eastern Canada search records in the adjacent seaboard of the United States in pursuit of information lacking nearer to home. Yet, poor as Atlantic Canada's colonial documentation may be, it often contains details about people in Ireland that cannot be found in Irish records, where few census returns survived from before 1901, and whose Catholic records began a generation or more *after* their counterparts in Atlantic Canada.

Given the flood of Irish through Atlantic Canada, where Saint John or Halifax and a score of lesser ports witnessed the arrival and departure of Irish immigrants, the record left here even by transients may contain the vital clue that links a modern American Irish family to its homeland in the old country. These considerations should recommend this collection of names and places to researchers within and beyond these four provinces.

Terrence M. Punch   Halifax, August 2007

ABBREVIATIONS USED FOR SOURCES

AR - *Acadian Recorder*, a Halifax newspaper, 1813 - 1930

C.O. - Colonial Office (Great Britain)

HJ - *Halifax Journal*, a Halifax newspaper,1819 - 1854

mfm - microfilm

NAC - National Archives of Canada

NS - *Novascotian*, also *Nova Scotian*, a Halifax newspaper, 1824 - 1892

NSARM - Nova Scotia Archives and records Management (formerly the Public
    Archives of Nova Scotia)

PRO - The Public records Office (Great Britain)

RG - Record Group (used to distinguish government-generated documents from those
    created by private agencies, e.g., churches, individuals, businesses)

StM - St. Mary's Roman Catholic Basilica, Halifax, formerly St. Peter's Catholic Church

W.O. - War Office (Great Britain)

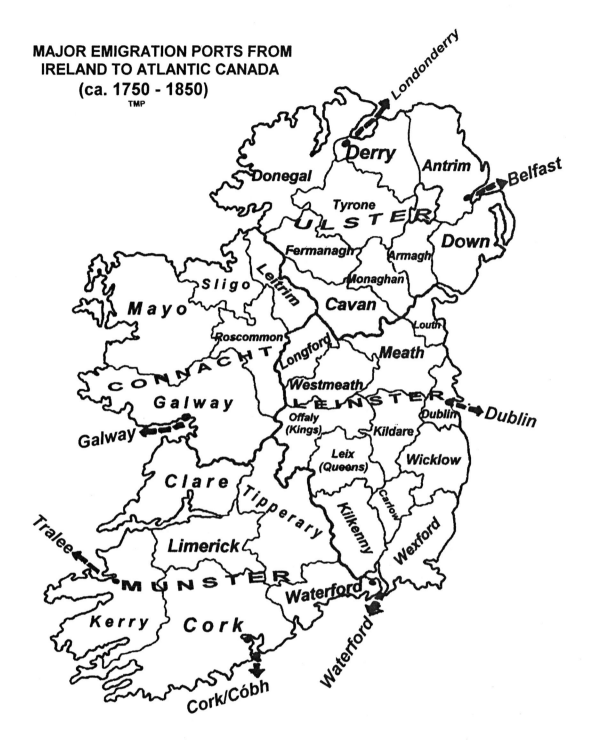

**MAJOR EMIGRATION PORTS FROM
IRELAND TO ATLANTIC CANADA
(ca. 1750 - 1850)**
TMP

Irish emigrants coming to Atlantic Canada departed from one of seven major ports for the most part. Tralee, County Kerry; Cork and Cóbh, County Cork; and Waterford Harbour served the southern counties from which the majority of Catholic Irish came. Galway was the main port of departure in the west of Ireland, as was Dublin on the eastern side. The Ulster Irish left Ireland via Londonderry and Belfast in the north. In two cases, the emigration port stood where a river hinterland reached the sea, namely Waterford and Londonderry. The following maps show the areas served by those ports by way of the river systems reaching inland behind them.

HINTERLAND OF THE PORT OF (LONDON)DERRY

LONDONDERRY

Londonderry, or simply Derry, stood on the River Foyle, the principal stream in a system reaching into the western Ulster counties of Derry, Donegal and Tyrone. The rivers and streams carried small boats towards the sea, and emigrants could follow the waterways on foot towards their destination. This hinterland had long formed a coherent and natural economic and social area. By the mid-nineteenth century Londonderry was connected by regular shipping service with ports in Atlantic Canada, especially with Saint John, New Brunswick.

WATERFORD

The harbour at the city of Waterford was sometimes known as 'the confluence' because three major streams, the Suir from the west and the Nore and the Barrow from the north, converged opposite the city and then flowed east and south into the Atlantic. Intending emigrants from Tipperary, Kilkenny, Leix, Carlow and Wexford, as well as Waterford itself, would use this port because it could be reached relatively easily from its riparian hinterland. Waterford, along with Youghal and Cork, further west along the Irish coast, were the heartland of the Grand Banks fishery which carried thousands of Irish annually to the coasts of Newfoundland,

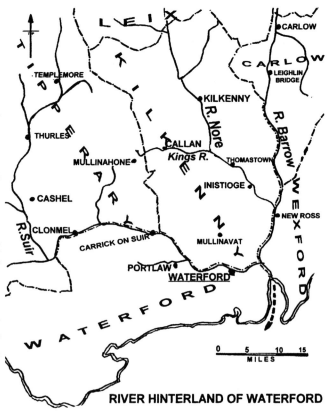

RIVER HINTERLAND OF WATERFORD

ERIN'S SONS COME TO ATLANTIC CANADA

Atlantic Canada consists of the four provinces of Newfoundland and Labrador, Prince Edward Island, New Brunswick and Nova Scotia. A useful approach for present purposes is to discuss the island of Newfoundland first, as it received the earliest Irish settlers, then to examine Prince Edward Island, which for a brief moment almost came to be dubbed 'New Ireland'. I have treated the two mainland provinces together, since they shared much, though not all, of their Irish settlement history. By presenting some idea of the Irish arrival in the region within the broader story of settlement by people of European stock it is possible to note some of the economic, logistical influences at work, rather than merely to deal in politics and religion which, while important, were not the decisive factors in the settlement of Atlantic Canada that earlier writers and some more recent ethnic and sectarian partisans have alleged.

Newfoundland

Until the Treaty of Utrecht was signed in 1713, Newfoundland was virtually uncolonized despite over two centuries of sustained European contact and the banks fishery offshore. No successful settlement scheme had planted British people there. Newfoundland offered little to permanent inhabitants in an age when people had to be self-sufficient in food if they proposed to live remote from sources of supply. The ocean posed a nearly insurmountable barrier. Europeans required considerable stores of grain, or the local ability to produce this staple food. The poor soil and damp climate of Newfoundland ruled out such agricultural efforts.

Newfoundland's main attraction was to provide a shoreline where seasonal fishermen built stages to dry their fish each summer, but as late as 1713 fewer than a thousand people could be said to live there permanently. This suited official policy, because the English government did not want large numbers of experienced seamen living far from home should they be needed to man naval vessels in the event of war. Captain Wheeler of the Navy attempted to dispel official fears by observing that in Newfoundland "soe long as there comes noe women they are not fixed."[1]

Two circumstances altered the situation after mid century and did encourage some permanent settlement. Firstly, the potato was introduced into Newfoundland in the 1750s. It had been cultivated in Ireland for about a century, but had for many decades served to augment, rather than replace, oats, barley and milk products as the dietary staple. It was becoming the main source of nourishment for the Irish and had begun to win wide acceptance among the English, which probably explains its introduction into Newfoundland. Potatoes can thrive in poor soil and a damp climate, so that its easy cultivation in quantity on small plots was tremendously significant for Newfoundland settlement. Secondly, the British conquest of Canada opened a major trade route between Great Britain and the St. Lawrence after 1760. Shipowners had hesitated to send their vessels to St. John's in hopes of finding either an assured market or a return cargo. Now, ships travelling between Québec and Britain found it profitable to put into St. John's in order to complete a cargo or to deliver a consignment. This further stabilized the town.

---

[1] C.O. I/55: 241 (1684), Report of Captain Wheeler.

By 1783 mercantile activity and strength at St. John's enabled its merchants to take advantage of the American loss of the West Indies trade after their Revolution. Newfoundland's cheap salt fish was attractive to planters in the West Indies as food for the slaves on the large estates. Returning ships sailed with holds stored with rum, sugar and molasses . This further strengthened Newfoundland and, by 1800 nearly 19,000 people, mainly fishermen and people in associated trades, such as box and barrel makers, lived there.[2]

Despite a sprinkling of Irish, most of that earlier population derived from south-western England. During the1790s numbers of Irish were attracted by the wages paid in the Newfoundland fishery, and quickly became a major component in the population. Wages were high during the long Napoleonic wars between France and Britain because Newfoundland enjoyed a monopoly of salt fish production at a time of high demand. By 1810 the price of fish in Spain and Portugal had risen 400% above pre-war levels.[3]

The Irish arrival was concentrated in time, mainly falling between 1785 and 1835. They were drawn there from Waterford, Kilkenny, Wexford, Tipperary and east Cork. Though they came out as servants and hands on fishing ships, many Irish became independent fishermen once the fishery changed to a more family-oriented enterprise later in the 1800s. The development of the truck system, wherein a merchant advanced goods on credit against a man's anticipated seasonal catch, facilitated this tendency even as it reduced most fishermen to permanent debt and dependence on a merchant who enjoyed a local monopoly.

Thanks to the increased opportunities for earning a living (however meagre and near subsistence we might consider it), Newfoundland's population trebled between 1814 and 1850, to about 105,000. This doubled again by 1900. West country English and southern Irish formed the backbone of the population.

Newfoundland's advantage ended with the return of peace in 1815 and a brief but serious demographic crisis which continued until the opening of the seal hunt enabled fishermen to remain in Newfoundland. The Industrial Revolution in Britain created a rapidly growing demand for grease and oil. Seal oil and fat were the major sources of those necessities for over thirty years. A seasonal pattern evolved in Newfoundland which served the fishermen well during that period.[4]

A major transformation occurred at mid-century, once James Young discovered that oil could be distilled from cannel (bituminous or soft coal). A Nova Scotian, Dr. Abraham Gesner, evolved a process to extract kerosene from coal tars and shales in 1846 and patented his *petroleum* in the United States in 1853. The new product quickly superseded seal oil as the

---

[2] Michael Staveley, "Population Dynamics in Newfoundland: The Regional Patterns," in John J. Mannion, ed., *The Peopling of Newfoundland* (St. John's: Memorial University of Newfoundland, 1977), p. 53.

[3] Shannon Ryan, "Introduction to Newfoundland History," in Elsa Hochwald, ed., *Family History Seminar 1987* (St. John's: Newfoundland and Labrador Genealogical Society, 1988), p. 12.

[4] Chesley Sanger, "The Evolution of Sealing and the Spread of Permanent Settlement in Northeastern Newfoundland," in Mannion, *op. cit.*, pp. 136-151, discusses this development.

standard industrial lubricant, and Newfoundland's economy suffered accordingly. The diminishing demand for labour at mid century ended large-scale immigration from the British Isles to Newfoundland.

John Mannion, a historical geographer, believed it "unlikely that any other province or state in contemporary North America drew such an overwhelming proportion of its immigrants from such localized source areas in the European homeland over so substantial a period of time" as had Newfoundland.[5] Consequently, Newfoundlanders tracing ancestry in Britain have a fairly limited number of places in which to seek records. So close was the connexion between people in Newfoundland and their places of origin that one may read notices of Newfoundland property offered for sale, and estates being settled, in older newspapers in England and Ireland.

Prince Edward Island

Prince Edward (until 1799 St. John) Island came under British rule only in 1763, and was legally part of Nova Scotia in 1765 when Samuel Holland surveyed it into 67 large lots of between sixteen and twenty-seven thousand acres each. Two years later the British government determined title to the entire island outside the three shire town sites or royalties by lottery. The new proprietors were gentlemen whom A. H. Clark termed "the worthiest names on the list" of retired officers and prominent office-seekers.[6] Each proprietor was expected to settle one hundred Protestants on his lot within ten years. St. John Island made slow progress as a distinct colony after 1769. By 1797 one-third of the lots were uninhabited and ten others averaged three settlers apiece. If the proprietors hoped to establish an old-world farm tenantry in America, Prince Edward Island's example proved conclusively that once people reached North America they expected to own land in freehold and not serve an absentee landlord.

Prince Edward Island received few settlers before 1775. Presbyterian Scots mainly came from Argyllshire, Galloway and Perthshire, as well as Catholic Highlanders from the MacDonald estates. Several hundred Loyalist families later reached the Island from the central colonies of New York, New Jersey and Pennsylvania.[7]

Like Newfoundland, but unlike the mainland provinces, Prince Edward Island derived more of its population directly from the British Isles than from other parts of North America. In 1798, 3700 Islanders were of British origins: 2100 Scots, about 200 Irish, and 700 English, meaning that 700 of British origins had come from elsewhere in America, or were discharged servicemen.[8]

---

[5] John J. Mannion, "Introduction," in Mannion, *op. cit.*, p. 7.

[6] Andrew Hill Clark, *Three Centuries and the Island* (Toronto: University of Toronto Press, 1959), p. 42.

[7] *Ibid.*, p. 58. *An Island Refuge; Loyalists and Disbanded Troops on the Island of Saint John* (Charlottetown: Abegweit Branch of the United Empire Loyalist Association of Canada, 1983), *passim*.

[8] Clark, pp. 58-61.

The basic population patterns of the Island were established early in the nineteenth century, as immigration raised the numbers of people from 5,000 in 1800, to 23,000 by 1827, and 47,000 in 1841. Some Channel Islanders from Guernsey arrived in 1806, Scots from Oban and Clydesdale a little later, west country English in the 1820s, about the same time that County Monaghan Irish arrived via the port of Dundalk, and Wexford and Waterford Irish from the latter port.

Significant immigration to Prince Edward Island from the British Isles ended after 1850. In the Island, the Scots predominated in over half the sixty-seven lots, and the Irish and English in about half a dozen each. The Scots tended to become relatively fewer in the western and northern districts, and the Irish the opposite. The Island had scarcely seen the end of immigration when the combination of attractive work opportunities in the United States and the narrow economic base of the Island produced emigration. Despite a healthy birthrate, the Island suffered a 25% net loss in population between 1881 and 1931.

The Mainland Provinces

New Brunswick was once part of Nova Scotia, as Sunbury County which, together with Sackville Township, returned members to the Assembly in Halifax until 1784, when the British government established New Brunswick at the behest of certain Loyalists.

Other than a handful of English families at Annapolis Royal after 1713, British settlement in the mainland provinces began with the founding of Halifax in 1749. Halifax commenced with 2500 colonists, but wholesale desertion, personal unsuitability of many individuals, and a high mortality rate cut their numbers in half within eighteen months. A few hundred Irish fisherfolk, New England joiners, carpenters and masons replaced some of the attrition. John Dick was hired by the British government to recruit and ship 'Foreign Protestants' from the Rhine, Switzerland and Montbéliard to Nova Scotia.[9] By this means, 2700 people were brought to the region, though the lure of more settled colonies elsewhere and an epidemic soon reduced their numbers. The politically-motivated insistence of the British on the settlers being Protestants did not help, and many of the foreign recruits were turned away as suspected 'Papists'

The need for a reliable English-speaking population in Nova Scotia was plain. The expulsion and flight of the Acadians in the later 1750s made arable land available for such newcomers. In 1758 Governor Charles Lawrence issued a proclamation offering 100 acres to each Protestant settler, with a further 50 acres for each dependent. Advertising was directed towards New England, which was becoming overpopulated due to natural increase and an emerging shortage of arable land. Nova Scotia offered an eastern frontier to New England Planters from 1759 until the outbreak of the American Revolutionary War.

---

[9] Winthrop P. Bell, *The 'Foreign Protestants' and the Settlement of Nova Scotia* (Toronto: University of Toronto Press, 1961).

Mainland Nova Scotia was greatly affected by the arrival of the New England Planters. Over 8,000 Planters came to fish and farm by 1775. By comparison, few settlers arrived directly from Britain in that decade. New England townships sprouted up all around the western seaboard and neighbouring tracts of good soil. Coastal trading and fishing were the major activities and some form of Congregationalism the main religious tradition. Fishing remained important, but Congregationalism largely disintegrated when its clergy, almost to a man, decamped to New England during the American Revolution.

At the head of Fundy, Amherst, Londonderry and Truro townships attracted Ulster Irish either by way of New Hampshire or directly out from the port of Derry.[10] Other Irish, usually Protestant, appeared in significant numbers at Granville, New Dublin and New Donegall (now Pictou) by 1770. The *Hector* deposited about 180 Scots from Ross and Loch Broom in Pictou in 1773. Several hundred Yorkshire people settled between 1772 and 1775 on the Chignecto Isthmus where Nova Scotia and New Brunswick adjoin, and at Granville, in Annapolis County.[11]

In 1775, greater Nova Scotia had a population of whom nearly 60% were natives of New England or their children. Direct settlers from the British Isles consisted in the Yorkshire folk, the Ulster Irish, two hundred Scots, and the growing southern Irish community around Halifax. When next the British element grew rapidly the influx was of the Loyalists from this side of the Atlantic.

The Loyalists were, according to some, the heroic ancestors and true founding fathers of English Canada. Another opinion would term them war refugees who supported a losing cause. That was simple fact to a "Neutral Yankee", as Brebner termed the Nova Scotia Planters who refused to take sides in the Revolutionary War.[12] Viewed dispassionately, the Loyalists were a cross-section of Americans of that day who for a variety of reasons did not support the Revolution. Both during and after the war many Loyalists could not or would not remain in their former homes, but removed to the remaining parts of British America. Nova Scotia was a major destination for the Loyalists, thanks to proximity and the availability of shipping for their transport.

Between 1776 and 1784, 35,000 to 40,000 Loyalists more than doubled greater Nova Scotia's population. The influx necessitated a major adjustment and drastic measures in a short time. In 1784, Britain split off New Brunswick and Cape Breton from Nova Scotia as separate colonies. The 15,000 Loyalists in New Brunswick swamped the Planter population and came to dominate the political and economic life of the new colony. Nova Scotia proper received about 20,000 Loyalists. Many of them soon removed to Britain, Upper Canada, or returned to the new United States after a few years.

---

[10] About two-thirds of the population of those three townships had origins in Ireland, if we judge by the 1770 census.

[11] Peter Wilson Coldham, *Emigrants from England to the American Colonies, 1773-1776* (Baltimore: Genealogical Publishing, 1988), pp. 13-19, 21-22, 135-137.

[12] L. F. S. Upton, ed., *The United Empire Loyalists: Men and Myths* (Toronto: The Copp Clark Publishing Company, 1967), pp. 1-9.

British Isles immigration was thin between 1792 and 1815. Several ships from Scotland arrived during the 1790s with settlers for the future Antigonish and Pictou counties . Southern Irish appeared on the Atlantic coastline and Halifax, many by way of Placentia or St. John's, Newfoundland. During the war years before 1815 very few immigrant ships landed here. The Scots are chronicled by Jack Bumsted and Lucille Campey, while the Irish are covered in several accounts by Toner, MacKenzie, O'Grady, and Punch.[13]

After 1815 British immigration to the Maritimes dramatically increased. Scots predominated in Nova Scotia by a ratio of 7:2 over the Irish in second place.[14] The other ten percent came from England, Wales, the Isle of Man and Channel Islands. The Irish made more impression in New Brunswick where they arrived in strength. This was not entirely direct migration from Ireland, since many had come via Newfoundland while others had been discharged from the armed forces and received land grants. Between 1819 and 1826, New Brunswick gained 12,000 Irish settlers whose preferred destinations included Westmorland and Northumberland counties, the City of Saint John and its adjacent coastline. The flow continued into the 1840s. A glance at the advertisements for lost relatives in the *Boston Pilot* of that period reveals that Irish were streaming through New Brunswick toward American cities in search of relatives, townsmen and opportunities for work.[15]

Nova Scotia had a substantial Irish influx between 1815 and 1845, but they were outnumbered by the Highland Scots.[16] The Irish who reached Nova Scotia and eastern New Brunswick came from a band of southern Irish counties: Cork, Wexford, Kilkenny, Waterford, Tipperary, and Kerry, with the more easterly prevalent before 1835, the others thereafter. Prince Edward Island's Irish arrivals of that era came mainly from Monaghan in the north and Wexford in the south.

The Great Famine boosted the flow into a flood in the later 1840s, mainly in Saint John. In the decade of 1840 New Brunswick received 59,000 Irish, one-third of whom died or left within a

---

[13] J.M. Bumsted, *The People's Clearance 1770-1815* (Edinburgh: Edinburgh University Press, 1982); Lucille H. Campey, *After the Hector; The Scottish Pioneers of Nova Scotia and Cape Breton 1773-1852* (Toronto: Natural Heritage Books, 2004). For the Irish, see P.M. Toner, ed., *New Ireland Remembered* (Fredericton: New Ireland Press, 1988); A.A. MacKenzie, *The Irish in Cape Breton* (Antigonish: Formac Publishing, 1979); Brendan O'Grady, *Exiles and Islanders; The Irish Settlers of Prince Edward Island* (Montréal and Kingston: McGill-Queen's University Press, 2004); and Terrence M. Punch, *Irish Halifax: The Immigrant Generation, 1815-1859* (Halifax: St. Mary's University, 1981), and "'Gentle as the Snow on a Rooftop': the Irish in Nova Scotia to 1830," in *The Untold Story: the Irish in Canada*, Vol. I (Toronto: Celtic Arts of Canada, 1988), pp. 215-229.

[14] Figures based on land grant applications, ca. 1800-1840 (NSARM, RG 20, Series "A").

[15] Daniel F. Johnson, *Irish Emigration to New England Through the Port of Saint John, New Brunswick, Canada, 1841 to 1849* (Baltimore: Clearfield, 1997).

[16] J. S. Martell, *Immigration to and Emigration from Nova Scotia 1815-1838* (Halifax: Public Archives of Nova Scotia, 1942), p. 95.

year or two. Western Ireland and Louth were strongly represented among this group.[17] The landing of famine Irish in Saint John was not typical of Irish immigration into Atlantic Canada. It remains a persistent piece of folk memory that the Irish here were fleeing the 'Potato Famine'.[18]

New Scotland was translated *Nova Scotia* by Jacobean clerks who seemed unaware that *Nova Scotia* really meant *New Ireland*. Nova Scotia was not particularly Scottish until after 1800, when Highlanders filled up the eastern counties and then Cape Breton. Research on Nova Scotia surnames reveals that eleven of the top thirteen family names in the province are of Scots Highland provenance.[19]

From 1815 to 1851 the population of Nova Scotia and New Brunswick grew rapidly, thanks largely to the immigration of the Scots and Irish. There were fewer than 150,000 inhabitants in the two mainland provinces in 1815 on the eve of that mass migration. By 1851 the two counted half a million people. When we consider that half of the Irish and one-quarter of the Scots had scarcely reached this region before they migrated onward, the growth of population amounted to a demographic revolution for the region.

From 1836, Thomas Chandler Haliburton wrote the popular series, *The Clockmaker*. His principal character, Sam Slick, was a Yankee clockmaker and shrewd salesman who usually gets the better of his Bluenose customers. Sam gives a fair description of Nova Scotia in his day: "If you want to know all about us and the Bluenoses (a pretty considerable share of Yankee blood in them too, I tell you; the old stock comes from New England and the breed is tolerable pure yet, near about one half applesauce and t'other molasses, all except to the Easterd, where there's a cross of the Scotch), jist ax me and I'll tell you candidly."[20] Had Haliburton's Sam mentioned the Irish he would have captured the major components of the British population over a century and a half ago.

Conclusion

An American visitor two decades later remarked "the complete isolation of the people of these colonies; the divisions among them; the separate pursuits, prejudices, languages; they seem to have nothing in common; . . . existence without nationality; . . . a mere exotic life with not a fibre rooted firmly in the soil. The colonists are English, Irish, Scotch, French, for generation after

---

[17] Mary McDevitt, "The Enduring Testimony: St. Mary's Cemetery, Saint John," in Michael Toner, ed., *New Ireland Remembered (Fredericton, 1988)*, pp. 155-156.

[18] Terrence M. Punch, *Irish Halifax: The Immigrant Generation, 1815-1859* (Halifax: Saint Mary's University, 1981), p. 11.

[19] Terrence M. Punch, *In Which County? Nova Scotia's Surnames from Birth Registers, 1864 to 1877* (Halifax: Genealogical Association of Nova Scotia, 1982), p. 8.

[20] Walter S. Avis, ed., *The Sam Slick Anthology* (Toronto: Clarke, Irwin & Company, 1969), p. 23.

generation."[21]

Eventually those parochial walls began to fall, and a more regional character developed. The genealogists of our later age have some cause to appreciate the former survival of particularism, for to it we owe the strong awareness of ancestry and the highly developed sense of identity which distinguishes Atlantic Canada.

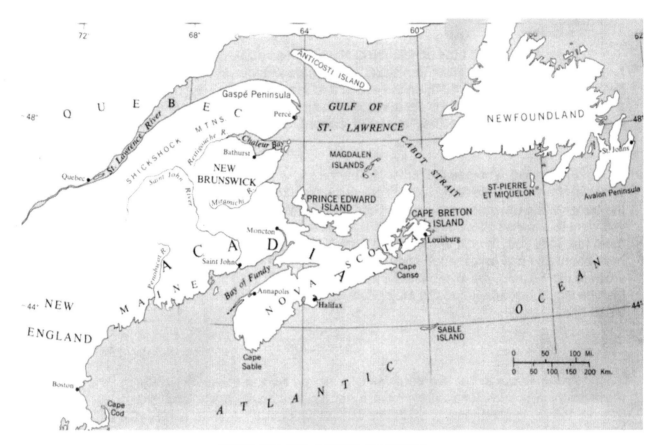

MAP OF ATLANTIC CANADA

---

[21] Frederic S. Cozzens, *Acadia; or, a Month with the Blue Noses* (New York: Derby & Jackson, 1859), p. 90.

BIBLIOGRAPHY

Bell, Winthrop P. *The 'Foreign Protestants' and the Settlement of Nova Scotia.* Toronto: University of Toronto Press, 1961.

Brebner, John Bartlet. *New England's Outpost; Acadia before the Conquest of Canada.* New York: Columbia University Press, 1927.

Buckner, Phillip A., and John G. Reid, ed. *The Atlantic Region to Confederation: A History.* Toronto: University of Toronto Press, 1994.

Bumsted, J.M. *The People's Clearance 1770-1815.* Edinburgh. Edinburgh University Press, 1982.

Campey, Lucille H. *After the Hector; The Scottish Pioneers of Nova Scotia and Cape Breton 1773-1852.* Toronto. Natural Heritage Books, 2004.

Clark, Andrew Hill. *Acadia; The Geography of Early Nova Scotia to 1760.* Madison: The University of Wisconsin Press, 1968.

_____. *Three Centuries and the Island.* Toronto. University of Toronto Press, 1959.

Coldham, Peter Wilson. *Emigrants from England to the American Colonies.* Baltimore: Genealogical Publishing, 1988.

Crowder, Norman K. *British Army Pensioners Abroad, 1772-1899.* Baltimore: Genealogical Publishing, 1995.

Dobson, David. *Ships from Scotland to America 1628-1828.* Baltimore: Genealogical Publishing, 1998.

Fischer, David Hackett. *Albion's Seed; Four British Folkways in America.* New York: Oxford University Press, 1989.

Gilroy, Marion. *Loyalists and Land Settlement in Nova Scotia.* Halifax: Public Archives of Nova Scotia, 1937.

Houston, Cecil J. and William J. Smyth. *Irish Emigration and Canadian Settlement; Patterns, Links & Letters.* Toronto: University of Toronto Press, 1990.

Johnson, Daniel F. *Irish Emigration to New England Through the Port of Saint John, New Brunswick, Canada, 1841 to 1849.* Baltimore: Clearfield, 1997.

MacKenzie, A.A. *The Irish in Cape Breton.* Antigonish, NS.: Formac Publishing, 1979.

Mannion, John J., ed. *The Peopling of Newfoundland.* St. John's: Memorial University of Newfoundland, 1977.

Martell, J. S. *Immigration to and Emigration from Nova Scotia 1815-1838*. Halifax. Public Archives of Nova Scotia, 1942.

O'Grady, Brendan. *Exiles and Islanders; The Irish Settlers of Prince Edward Island*. Montréal and Kingston: McGill-Queen's University Press, 2004.

Power, Thomas P., ed. *The Irish in Atlantic Canada 1780-1900*. Fredericton: New Ireland Press, 1991.

Punch, Terrence M. *Irish Halifax: The Immigrant Generation, 1815-1859*. Halifax. Saint Mary's University, 1981.

Toner, P.M. ed. *New Ireland Remembered*. Fredericton. New Ireland Press, 1988.

Whyte, Donald. *A Dictionary of Scottish Emigrants to Canada before Confederation*, 3 vols. Toronto: Ontario Genealogical Society, 1986, 1995, 2002.

1 - ULSTER SCOTS TO NOVA SCOTIA IN 1761

The *Belfast Newsletter* of 11 March 1762 published a declaration dated at Halifax, Nova Scotia, on 16 November 1761, by a committee chosen from among the natives of Ireland who had gone to Nova Scotia the preceding summer[1] to view lands at Minas Basin and Cobequid that had been advertised by Colonel Alexander McNutt and his associates in Londonderry on 21 April 1761, and found that the lands were good and the inhabitants helpful.[2] Sixteen men signed this testimonial and gave their place of origin in Ireland.

Andrew ROSS, Parish Belroshain, C. Antrim [Parish of Ballyrashane, County Antrim]
William MOORE, Parish of Faun [Fahan], Co. Donegal[3]
William HENDERSON, Ruthmillon, C. ditto [Town of Rathmullan, County Donegal]
William McNUTT, Parish of Mavagh, C. ditto [Parish of Mevagh, Co. Donegal]
John MAHON, Russes, ditto [Rosses Quarter, Parish of Drumhome, Co. Donegal]
Joseph CRAWFORD, near Rathmalton, C. ditto [Town of Rathmelton, Co. Donegal]
Robert SPENCER, Clanda Horky, C. ditto [Parish of Clondahorky, Co. Donegal]
John MORRISON, P. Ry Tollegbebegly, ditto [Parish of Tullaghobegly, Co. Donegal]
Benjamin McNUTT, P. Mavagh, Bar. Killnacrenen, ditto [Mevagh, Kilnacrenan Barony, Co.
      Donegal]
Mark PATTON, P. Forghan Vael, C. Derry [Parish of Faughanvale, Co. Derry] [4]
John McNUTT, Tullyachnish, C. ditto [Parish of Ballynascreen, Co. Derry]
Daniel COCHRAN, Derrykrychen, C. Antrim [Parish of Derrykeighan, Co. Antrim]
Robert SMITH, of Cahery, Parish of Drummsoose and County of Londonderry
      [Cahery, Parish of Drumachose, Co. Derry]
John BARNHILL, P. Lake, C. Don. [Parish of Leck, Co. Donegal. [5]
Anthony McCLEAN, near Letter Kenny, C. Don[egal].[6]
John CLARK, P. Tamlaughtsmleggan, [Parish of Tamlaght Finlagan], Co. Derry.

---

[1] The *Hopewell* reached Halifax on 6 October 1761, carrying about 300 people from the north of Ireland.

[2] *Belfast News-Letter and General Advertiser,* 21 April 1761, sought "industrious farmers and useful mechanics" to emigrate to Nova Scotia. Heads of family were promised a grant of 200 acres, plus 50 additional acres for each dependent family member.

[3] Patton lived at Cumberland, NS, and had children: Dorothy, Letitia, Mary, and Mark, Jr.

[4] "Clean Billy" Moor(e), a wheelwright at Shubenacadie, NS, and his wife Susannah Long had 9 children: Elizabeth, Janet, Robert, Sarah, Hugh, William, Daniel, Charles, Susannah.

[5] John was a son of Robert Barnhill, patriarch of a large progeny, some of whom accompanied him to Nova Scotia in the *Hopewell* in 1761, including his daughter Margaret and her husband, Thomas BAIRD, from Saintjohnstown, Co., Donegal, daughter Esther and her husband ,Joseph CROWE, from the Parish of Tamlaghtard, Co. Derry, daughter Sarah, and son John with his wife, Letitia DEYARMOND from Letterkenny, Co. Donegal, and their issue.

[6] Anthony McClean of Creeve Glebe, Parish of Leck, Co. Donegal, settled in Londonderry Township, Nova Scotia. He and his wife Margaret were parents of John and Mary.

2 - THE *POLLY*: SEEKING UNITED IRISHMEN, 1799

In1798 the rebellion of the United Irishmen convulsed Ireland A Royal Proclamation was made on 15 March 1799 "to prevent all persons engaged in such treasonable designs from passing out of the said Kingdom of Ireland into this kingdom..." On 30 April the ban was extended to British America, including Nova Scotia. Any ship entering the province from an Irish port or believed likely to be carrying Irish people became subject to investigation before its passengers could disembark.

When the brig *Polly*, Capt. Kellar, arrived from either Belfast or Greenock (sources do not agree on its point of clearing), the Quarter Sessions of Halifax County boarded the vessel to interrogate Irish passengers. Evidently all was in order because the *Royal Gazette* (Halifax newspaper) of 7 May 1799 reported the departure from Halifax of the *Polly* en route for Québec. The record is repeated *in toto* because of its informative nature.

"The Examination of the following Persons Passengers on board of the brig Polly, Capt. Kellar—

DAVID ROBINSON – says that he is aged 27 years – that he came from the north of Ireland in the County of Entrim – that his intention was of proceeding to the United States – but that he will remain in Halifax provided he can obtain a living – he produces a Certificate from Samuel Allen Esqre of Larn – stating that he had taken the Oath of Allegiance 22nd Nov. 1798 and had abjured any connexion with the United Irishmen – and also produced a Certificate of J. Casement acting Collector of the Customs at Larn stating that he had permission to depart from Ireland.

WILLIAM BOYCE, a Merchants Clerk aged 30 years, has a wife and 3 children – is bound for the United States – is a native of Entrim – produces a Certificate dated 29th Dec. 1798 from Edward Jones Esqre and William Montgomery Gentlemen resident near Larn – stating that he bore a good Character during his residence at that place.

WILLIAM CLARK – has relations at Charlestown, South Carolina, to which place he intends going and produces a Certificate from Alderman James of Dublin dated 10th Nov. 1798 stating he has permission to depart from Ireland.

EDWARD FITZGERALD, a single man aged 22 years, says he is a native of Ireland and intends to proceed to New York – produces a Certificate from Charles Jackson and Laurence Smith two Gentlemen who state that FitzGerald is of a good Character and that he had leave to depart from Ireland.

ANDREW GAFNEY, a single man aged 21 years, says he is a native of Ireland, Co. of Cavan– that he intends to remain in Halifax – that he is by Trade a Tanner and Currier, and is at present engaged with Mr. Major, has no Certificate but Mr Koch the owner of the Brig vouches to his being examined and passed and thinks a Certificate was given him which is now lost.[Frederick MAJOR of Dublin was a tanner in Halifax for many years and died in Nova Scotia in 1847.]

SAMUEL JACK, a single man aged 19 years, says he is a Native of Ireland, by trade a Shoemaker – that he intends to remain in Halifax and produces two Certificates, One from his parish Minister of his good Character, and the other from the Deputy Collector of Customs stating he had leave to depart from Ireland.

THOMAS MILLER, a single man, aged 32 years – says he is a native of Ireland and intends to remain in Halifax, produces a Certificate from Samuel Allan a Magistrate, stating that he had liberty to depart from Ireland.

THOMAS THORNTON, a single man aged 29 years – says he is a Native of Ireland and intends to remain a short time in Halifax and finally to proceed to South Carolina, produces a Certificate from J. Casement and Samuel Allen, stating that he had taken the Oath of Allegiance and had permission to leave Ireland.

JEREMIAH HALL, a single Man, aged 30 years, says that he is a Native of Ireland and intends to remain a short time in Halifax and finally to proceed to South Carolina, produces a Certificate from J. Casement and Samuel Allan, stating that he had taken the Oath of Allegiance and had permission to leave Ireland."

From the tenor of the Foregoing Examination and the parties being all willing to take the necessary oaths, the Court can have no objections to their being admitted to Land in this Province, and which the Court submit to his Excellency's consideration." Governor Sir John Wentworth, Baronet, gave Royal Assent to the findings.

(Source: NSARM, RG 34, Series "P", Vol. I,)

3 - IRISH IMMIGRANT BURIALS, HALIFAX, NS, 1800 - 1842

The penal acts restricting the civil rights of Roman Catholics began to be relaxed in Nova Scotia in the early 1780s. There was a resident priest, James Jones, from 1785. The earliest Catholic parish of St. Peter's Church, which became St. Mary's Basilica, had an adjacent burial ground. The records of burials only began in 1800 and, the cemetery having been closed in 1843 and paved over as a schoolyard in the twentieth century, there is no physical evidence to be seen of the resting place of three thousand people, many of them natives of Ireland.

This is a collection of gleanings from the records of those early immigrant burials. The information is presented in the sequence: Burial date, identity of the decedent, age, birthplace, other information in the register. Added information appears within square parentheses "[ ]". The contemporary Halifax newspapers, Acadian Recorder [AR], Novascotian [Ns], and Halifax Journal [HJ] have supplied additional information. The source used in each instance is indicated. Marriages of a couple in the same church are indicated as [StM, Hfx].

3 Sep 1828 John **AHERAN**, 67, husband of Mary **O'BRIEN**, Waterford.
25 Oct 1824 Michael **AHERN**, carpenter, 38, Cork [AR, 30 Oct 1824, reported an inquest held on 24 October on the body of Michael HERRON.]
24 Jul 1824 Eleanor, 34, wife of James **ARCHARD,** Tipperary
27 Sep 1840 Bartholomew **AST**, mason, 40, born Ireland [AR, 26 Sep 1840: died 24 Sep. Ast came from Clonmel, Tipperary.]
22 Sep 1833 Bridget **KEHOE**, 40, wife of John **AST**, shoemaker [She died on 22 Sep 1833; married 9 May 1822: John, son of Robert & Margaret (**WATSON**) **AST** of Clonmel, Tipperary, to Bridget, dau of John & Bridget (**KEATING**) **KEHOE** of Tintern, Wexford. [StM, Hfx]
21 Jan 1841 Margaret [**WATSON**], 84, born Clonmel, Tipperary [widow of Robert] **AST**.

12 Mar 1837   Robert **AST**, stonemason, 44, born Ireland [Married 21 Apr 1837: Robert son of Robert & Margaret (**WATSON**) **AST** of Clonmel, Tipperary, to Mary, dau of John & Elanor (**FLINN**) **HUNT** of Waterford. [StM, Hfx]

16 Aug 1834   Walter **ATKINS**, 40, Cork, husband of Jane **NASH**.

28 Jan 1839   Margaret, 86, born Waterford, widow of Richard **AYRES**.

17 Mar 1835   Richard **AYRES**, 87, Waterford.

1 Oct 1831   Catherine **BYRNS**, 32, Longford, wife of Christopher **BANNAN**.

5 Nov 1832   Christopher, 2 mos, born Cork, son of John & Honora (**CONNORS**) **BARRETT**.

2 Apr 1837   Eleanor **POWER**, 25, wife of William **BARRON** [AR, 1 Apr 1837: Ellen, 23, died 31 March. Married 17 May 1832: William, son of Walter & Margaret (**WALSH**) **BARRON** of Inistiogue, Kilkenny, to Eleanor, dau of Michael & Eleanor (**POWER**) **POWER** of Waterford. [StM, Hfx]

28 Jan 1836   John **BARRON**, stonecutter, 45, born Ireland [Married 4 July 1818: John, son of Lawrence & Catherine **BARRON** of Waterford City, to Bridget, dau of John & Mary (**DWYER**) **RYAN** of Newfoundland. [StM, Hfx]

28 Aug 1834   Peter **BARRON**, 45, born Ireland, husband of Elizabeth **McGRATH** [AR, 30 Aug 1834: died 26 Aug; Married 1 June 1828: Peter, son of Patrick & Catherine (**MURPHY**) **BARRON** of St. James, Wexford, to Elizabeth, dau of David & Lydia (**STOBO**) **McGRATH** of Halifax. [StM, Hfx]

11 Aug 1827   Thomas **BARRON**, 37, Borris, Carlow, left a widow, had lived "for many years" at Lower Prospect, NS

8 May 1835   Eleanor, 3, born Cork, dau of William & Judith (**SULLIVAN**) **BARRY**.

3 Dec 1820   Robert **BARRY**, 60, Cork

24 Apr 1828   Thomas **BARRY**, 37, Ireland

1 Mar 1829   Ann **PHELAN**, 28, Ballymo[r]e, Tipperary, wife of William **BATES**, truckman

6 Jun 1818   Anthony **BEECHAM**, 46, husband of Catherine **CORCORAN**, Cork

2 Feb 1822   Pvte. John **BELL**, 62nd. Regt., 25, Stradbally, Leix

23 Feb 1819   John, son of John & Anne **BENNETT**, 39, Mount Uniacke, Cork

23 Aug 1834   Pvte. John **BERGIN**, Rifle Brigade, born Ireland, no age shown.

5 Feb 1829   Catherine **DOYLE**, 31, Ballinglas [Baltinglass], Carlow, wife of Henry **BIGGS**, Rifles

29 Mar 1826   William **BLAKE**, truckman, 28, Ballyhooly, Cork

15 Jun 1833   Mary **BLANEY**, 74, born Belfast [Mrs. Blaney died 13 June, age 73.]

4 Mar 1826   Richard **BOURKE**, 82, Ireland, 40 years at Manchester, NS [AR, 11 Mar 1826, has the death of Richard **BURK**, 85, of Guysborough, NS, on 3 March, at the Blue Bell (a small inn on the Windsor Road, in Halifax).]

15 Jun 1827   Pierce **BOWE**, 17, "died 4 days after arrival here", Comeragh, Waterford

19 Jun 1827   Pierce **BOWE**, 63, "here 8 days", Comeragh, Waterford. [The Bowes arrived in the *Cherub*, whose arrival was reported in *Ns*, 14 June 1827.]

11 Apr 1833   John **BRADLY**, 50, Derry.

23 Oct 1836   Thomas **BRADY**, 45, born Ireland.

20 Feb 1834   William **BRAWDER**, 50, Kilkenny.

13 Apr 1828   James **BRAWDERS**, 56, husband of Margaret **POWER**, Cork City

3 Jul 1826   Mary **BREMNER**, 24, "from Ireland this spring"

10 Feb 1824   Edward **BRENNAN**, truckman, 38, husband of [Ann **SCANLAN**] widow **BURNS**, Arklow, Wicklow [AR, 14 Feb 1824: died 8 Feb 1824]

24 Mar 1820   Mary, wife of John **BRENNAN**, 39, Carrick-on-Suir, Tipperary, and dau of Richard & Anastasia (**NEIL**) **SHORTIS**

3 Jul 1827	Charles, 13, son of John & Anne (BYRNE) BRIAN, Ireland, "here a few days ago"
4 Apr 1825	Mary, 30, wife of Pvte. John BROADHOUSE, 74th. Regiment, Down
8 Jan 1838	Eleanor, 29, Leix, wife of Sgt. Robert BROBSON, 65th Regt.
30 Sep 1826	Mary BROPHY, 27, Roscrea, Tipperary
28 Jan 1840	William BROTHERS, 45, Kilkenny.
23 Aug 1834	Pvte. Daniel BROWN, Rifle Brigade, born Ireland, no age shown.
9 Sep 1828	Patrick BRUN, 52nd. Regiment, 26, Tipperary
10 Nov 1839	Daniel BUCKLEY, 54, Cork [AR, 9 Nov 1839: Buckley died 8 Nov, age 55, leaving a widow and three children. Married 19 Sep 1819: Daniel BUCKLEY of Cork, to Eleanor, dau of Lawrence & Catherine POWER of Kilmacthomas, Waterford. [StM, Hfx]
29 Feb 1836	Elizabeth MURPHY, 36, born Cork, wife of William BUCKLEY.
12 Aug 1827	John BUGGY, 64, Castlecomer, Kilkenny
10 Jul 1827	Mary, 2, dau of late John & Mary (CRAWLEY) BUGGY, Ireland [Leix]; "father died 3 days from Halifax"
25 Jul 1827	Mary CANFILL, 63, wife of John BUGGY, Castlecomber, Kilkenny.
2 Jul 1827	John, 1 day, son of John & Mary (CRAWLEY) BUGGY. His father died at sea 4 days ago on passage from [Leix] Ireland [in either the Bolivar or the Cherub.]
10 Jul 1827	Mary, 2, born Ireland [Leix], dau of late John & Mary (CRAWLEY) BUGGY; "Father died 3 days from Halifax" [in either the Bolivar or the Cherub.]
27 Aug 1834	Ann MANNING, Galway, widow of Sgt. [David] BURKE, Rifle Brigade.
31 Mar 1834	Sgt. David BURKE, Rifle Brigade, 34, Sligo.
2 Dec 1820	Rt Rev Dr Edmund BURKE, Titular Bishop of Sion, and Vicar Apostolic of NS, 78, Kildare [Died 29 Nov 1820; born at Portlaoighise, Leix.]
1 Dec 1832	Edmund BURKE, 45, Tipperary.
18 Feb 1824	James BURKE, 29, former Sgt. in the 62nd. Regiment, Macroom, Cork
26 Jan 1827	James BURKE, 75, Cashel, Tipperary
9 Mar 1822	Pvte. Jeremiah BURKE, 60th. Regt., 20, Co. Kerry
9 Nov 1827	Mary CURTIN, –, widow of Sgt. BURKE, 62nd. Regt., Mallow, Cork.
12 Jul 1835	Mary WALSH, 23, Waterford, wife of John BURKE.
2 May 1829	John BURNS, 30, Leix
8 Apr 1829	Pvte. James BUTLER, 52nd. Regiment, 25, Golden, Tipperary
18 Nov 1829	Richard BUTLER, 29, Kilkenny
30 Jul 1816	Sgt. Richard BUTLER, 98th. Regt., 32, Thomastown, Kilkenny, and husband of Mary WHELAN. [Died 29 July 1816.]
4 Apr 1832	Walter BUTLER, 70, born Ireland.
29 Dec 1840	Anne, 64, born Ireland, widow of Patrick BYRNE [Morning Post, 31 Dec 1840: Ann BYRNS died 29 Dec.]
7 Mar 1837	Francis BYRNE, 30, Carlow [AR, 11 Mar 1837: died 5 March, Francis BYRNES, 24.]
6 Jun 1836	James BYRNE, 35, Tipperary.
17 Aug 1834	Lawrence BYRNE, 35, born Ireland, husband of Charlotte KAVENAGH.
11 May 1833	Letitia CAREW, 31, Wexford, wife of James BYRNE [Married 16 Oct 1831: James, son of John & Elizabeth (CODY) BYRNES of Wexford, to Letitia, dau of Robert & Anne (CONNELL) CAREW of Waterford (sic). [StM, Hfx]
14 Jul 1823	Margaret, 25, wife of Garrett BYRNE, Ballymurphy Parish, Cork
19 Sep 1834	Martin BYRNE, carpenter, 30, Carlow.

9 Oct 1827	Michael **BYRNE**, 58, Shillelagh, Wexford [*recte* Wicklow]; "kept a Grocery store In this town for many years" [*AR*, 13 Oct 1827: *Patrick* Byrne died 7 Oct, age 54]
1 Feb 1833	Patrick **BYRNE**, 26, Leix.
27 Oct 1832	Thomas, 1 yr., born Longford, son of William & Mary (**ROGERS**) **BYRNE**.
3 Dec 1821	Edward **BYRNES**, 45, Revilla [Rathvilly], Carlow.
16 May 1837	Margaret **COLLINS**, 36, Carlow, wife of Patrick **BYRNES**.
29 Jun 1824	Thomas **BYRNES**, servant, 30, Wexford, "drowned in Harbour" on 7 June.
8 Sep 1833	William **BYRNES**, 32, Longford, husband of Mary **ROGERS**.
11 Jun 1828	Catherine **KENEDY**, 43, wife of William **CAHILL**, Killenaule, Tipperary
31 Jul 1827	Michael **CAHILL**, 40, Kilmaganny, Kilkenny
2 May 1827	Patrick **CAHILL**, 42, Knocktopher, Kilkenny
25 Jan 1826	Pvte. Thomas **CAHILL**, 74th. Regiment, 40 [Longford]
21 Sep 1831	Michael **CAMMELL**, 26, Wicklow, husband of Bridget **KIRWAN**.
14 Sep 1841	Pvte. Martin **CAMPION**, 37th Regt., born Ireland.
29 Nov 1821	Patrick, son of John & Mary (**KAVANAGH**) **CAMPION**, Parish of Freshard [Freshford], Kilkenny.
8 Sep 1834	Joseph **CAREY**, 35, Kilkenny.
9 Jul 1833	Patrick **CARRIGAN**, 25, Waterford, husband of Mary **DENIFFE**.
5 Feb 1832	Mrs. .... **CARROLL**, 66, born Ireland.
27 Nov 1840	Jane **CARROLL**, 51, born Ireland.
17 Jul 1827	John **CARROLL**, 23, cooper, New Ross, Wexford, "here a few days"
23 Nov 1826	John, 56, son of Lawrence & Elenor (**LAWLER**) **CARROLL**, Muckalee Parish, Kilkenny.
15 Feb 1823	Pvte. Owen **CARROLL**, 62nd. Regiment, 33, Carlow Town
14 Sep 1837	Catherine **CARSON**, 30, Leitrim.
7 Jun 1833	Eleanor **FLINN**, 35, Waterford, wife of John **CASEY**.
8 Nov 1833	James, 4, born Waterford, son of John & Eleanor (**FLINN**) **CASEY**.
25 Oct 1827	John **CASEY**, 70, Tipperary
2 May 1817	Michael **CASEY**, 28, Ireland.
10 Sep 1834	Michael **CASEY**, 49, Cork.
5 Nov 1840	Joanna **CASHIN**, 54, born Ireland.
7 Jul 1816	John **CAULFIELD**, truckman, 35, Ireland.
14 Oct 1840	Michael **CAYLEY**, shoemaker, 52, born Ireland.
12 Jul 1824	John **CEASY**, "professor on the Anion pipes", 48, Kilkenny, "has not left after him a single Minstrel to make the sad strains of a mournful dirge to his immortal memory. Requiescat in pace."
27 Oct 1837	James **CHARLES**, shoemaker, 44, Meath [*AR*, 28 Oct 1837: died 25 Oct, age 43, native of Kells, Meath.]
12 Feb 1827	Francis **CHERRY**, 60, Armagh.
22 Sep 1834	Mary **MOORE**, 35, Westmeath, widow of Thomas **CLARKE**.
13 Sep 1834	Thomas **CLARKE**, 35, Westmeath, husband of Mary **MOORE**.
14 Jan 1828	Peter **CLARY**, 60, Tipperary.
9 Oct 1835	Deborah **ROACHE**, 60, Cork, widow of Hugh **CLEARY** [*AR*, 10 Oct 1835: died 7 Oct, age 59.]
29 Jun 1834	Hugh **CLEARY**, 77, Tipperary, "for many years in Halifax" [*AR*, 28 June 1834: Capt. Hugh Cleary died 27 June.
25 Nov 1822	Pvte. John **CLEARY**, 81st. Regt., 27, Ballinasloe, Galway [*Free Press*, 26 Nov 1822, reported that an inquest on 24 Nov found he had died of natural causes.]

16 Sep 1834   John **CLOWNEY**, cooper, 40, Wexford, husband of Mary **GLODY**.
26 Sep 1836   Abbey **DRUHAN**, 35, Waterford, wife of Michael **COADY**.
14 Jan 1829   Catherine **CULLIN**, 65, Carrick, Tipperary, wife of John **CODY**
5 Apr 1827   Edward **COADY**, 35, Glenmore, Kilkenny
12 Jan 1837   John **COADY**, 54, Kildare, husband of Dorothy **O'BRIEN**.
21 Feb 1820   Mary, wife of William **CODY**, fisherman, -, Parish of Ballylooby, Tipperary, and
              dau of Andrew & Margaret (**LONERGAN**) **ENGLISH**.
27 May 1834   Daniel **COCHRAN**, 45, Cork, husband of Catherine **DONOHOE**.
31 Mar 1824   Nicholas **COLBERT**, 66, Dungarvan,Waterford
2 Jun 1818   Philip **COLFORD**, 60, Wexford [*HJ*, 2 June 1828, died 1 June; he was a truckman
              and husband of Mary **MURPHY**.]
1 Feb 1825   Margaret **COLLINS**, 16, Affidown [Aghadown], Cork.
21 Aug 1834   Pvte. William **COLLINS**, Rifle Brigade, 30, born Ireland.
8 Aug 1834   Nicholas **COLWELL**, 60, born Ireland.
3 Sep 1837   Mrs. **CONDON**, 74, born Ireland [*AR*, 2 Sep 1837, names her Bridget.]
4 May 1816   James **CONDON**, labourer, 50, Ireland [Died 3 May 1816]
5 Mar 1828   William **CONDON**, 38, husband of Ann **RYAN**, Kilrohan [Kilruane] Parish,
              Tipperary [*AR*, 4 Mar 1828 reported his death on 3 March.]
4 Jul 1839   William **CONDON**, 40, Cork [Married 9 Nov 1829: William, son of John & Margaret
              (**DULING**) **CONDON** of Youghal, Cork, to Anne **RYAN** of Tipperary. Halifax record.]
6 Sep 1829   Catherine, 40, Kilcash, Tipperary, wife of Patrick **CONNELL**
31 Jul 1823   Pvte.Patrick **CONNELL**, 20, 81ˢᵗ. Regiment, Dungarvan, Waterford
2 Aug 1830   Terrence **CONNELL**, 44, Ireland.
14 Apr 1837   Sgt. Terrence **CONNERTY**, 85ᵗʰ Regt., 33, born Limerick.
21 Nov 1838   Barnaby **CONOLLY**, 38, born Ireland.
24 Feb 1839   Mary **PHELAN**, 30, born Ireland [Tipperary], wife of Anthony **CONNOLLY**.
18 Jan 1820   Bartholomew **CONNOR**, husband of Margaret, 50, Middleton, Cork,
              [and son of Jeremiah & Eleanor (**KEEFF**) **CONNOR**.]
8 May 1818   Constantine **CONNOR**, militia officer, 74, Ireland, widower of Margaret **CODY**
              [Born Co. Waterford, died 7 May 1818.]
29 Sep 1834   John **CONNOR**, tinsmith, 26, Kilkenny.
6 Sep 1841   John **CONNOR**, stonemason, 45, Cork [*Morning Herald*, 10 Sep 1841: died
              4 Sep., Mr. **CONNORS**, mason, age 43.]
2 Sep 1833   Margaret **SOWEN** [?], 35, Tipperary, wife of John **CONNORS**.
9 Jan 1801   Margaret **CODY**, wife of Constantine **O'CONNOR**, 40, Waterford [Died 8 Jan]
17 Feb 1827   John **CONRAN** of Dartmouth, NS, 30, Castlecomer, Kilkenny
20 Oct 1840   Thomas **CONROY**, 57, born Ireland [*AR*, 24 Oct 1840: died 19 Oct.]
1 Apr 1841   Pvte. John **COONEY**, 37ᵗʰ Regt., 25, born Ireland.
22 Jun 1827   Bridget **CORBETT**, 21, Ballyneil, Carrick [on Suir], Tipperary
22 Dec 1829   Pvte. Thomas **CORBET**, 52ⁿᵈ Regiment, 25, [Clonulty], Tipperary
27 Jan 1833   Mary Anne **CORCORAN**, 23, Wexford.
7 Jul 1833   Michael **CORMACK**, 25, Kilkenny.
1 Jun 1835   Murtagh **CORNYN** [CORNEEN], 64, Leitrim.
3 Jun 1841   Pvte. Michael **COSKER**, 8ᵗʰ Regt., 35, born Ireland.
11 Jan 1822   Sgt. Thomas **COSSER** [or **CAPPER**], 62ⁿᵈ. Regt., 30, Hackettstown, Carlow
14 Jun 1837   Richard **COTTER**, 40, Midleton, Cork.
17 Sep 1834   Kieran **COTTON**, stonemason, 40, Kilkenny.
29 Oct 1828   Pvte. Michael **COUGHLIN**, 96ᵗʰ. Regiment, 23, Clonmel, Tipperary

22 May 1825	Margaret, 30, wife of Thomas **CRAWLEY**, Cork, servant to Mr. **PIERS**
2 Sep 1834	Timothy **CRAWLEY**, 54, Cork.
14 Apr 1840	Michael **CREAMER**, ship's carpenter, 72, born Ireland [Married 5 Sep 1831: Michael **CREAMER** of Cork, widower of Mary **TURNER**, to Rebecca **PETERS** of Halifax, widow of John **FOLEY**. [StM, Hfx]
29 Oct 1837	Thomas **CROAK**, 68, Waterford
12 Jul 1840	Thomas **CROAK**, tailor, 32, Tipperary [*AR*, 11 July 1840: died 11 July, age 31, leaving a widow and five children.]
18 Jan 1820	Pvte. Timothy **CROWLEY**, 67th. Regt., 28, Dunmanway, Cork
21 Feb 1827	John **CULLY**, 30, Ballymahon, Longford [*AR*, 24 Feb 1827, says that Cully "died as the result of a quarrel", on 19 February.
6 Jun 1833	Thomas **CUMMERFORD**, 30, Kilkenny.
5 Sep 1825	Elizabeth **CUMMINS**, *alias* **POWER**, 30, Kilkenny [not a criminal; merely a way of stating her maiden name as well as her married one.]
4 Mar 1841	Joanna **CUMMINGS**, 66, Kilkenny.
13 Aug 1833	Maria, 3, born Tipperary, dau of Thomas & Bridget (**SULLIVAN**) **CUNARD**.
23 Jan 1835	Bridget **SULLIVAN**, 50, born Ireland [Tipperary], wife of Thomas **CUNARD**.
20 Feb 1833	Matthew **CURLEY**, 23, Galway.
10 Jan 1829	Denis **CURRAN**, 60, Ireland, at the Poor House.
1 Jul 1833	Eliza **CARR**, 26, born Tipperary, wife of Michael **CURRAN** [Married 15 Apr 1833: Michael, son of Thomas & Judith (**BERRANS**) **CURRAN** of Kildare, to Eliza, dau of John & Eliza (**AUSTIN**) **CARR** of Tipperary, and widow of William **ANDERSON**. [StM, Hfx]
7 Feb 1837	Michael, 11, born Kerry, son of Dennis & Mary (**BOWLER**) **CURRAN**.
3 Jun 1821	Samuel **CURROLL**, 38, Belfast.
14 Feb 1837	Bridget, 18 mos., born Cork, dau of Patrick & Jane (**GEERAN**) **CURTIN**.
16 Apr 1839	Elizabeth **FITZMAURICE**, 71, Ireland [Cork], widow of John **CURTIN** [*Ns*, 18 Apr 1839: died on 14 April.]
27 Nov 1830	John **CURTIN**, 72, Clare, husband of Elizabeth **FITZMAURICE** [*AR*, 27 Nov 1830, gives his death date as 24 November.]
28 Dec 1828	James **CUSHEN**, 52nd. Regiment, 25, Clonmel, Tipperary
24 Sep 1823	Thomas **DADY**, 76, Ballyporeen, Tipperary
3 Aug 1832	Charles **DALEY**, mason, 46, Tipperary [*AR*, 4 Aug 1832: Charles **DAILEY** died 1 August, age 44.]
28 Oct 1839	Daniel **DALY**, baker, 34, born Ireland.
5 Apr 1829	David **DALEY**, 59, [shipwright], Wexford, husband of Catherine **MADDOX** [*AR*, 4 Apr 1829, gives a death date of 30 March].
14 Jan 1816	William **DALEY**, husband of Mary..., -, Waterford.
25 Jun 1826	John, 1 day, son of William & Margaret (**DAILY**) **DALTON**, "lately from Ireland"
6 Apr 1827	Margaret **HALLY**, 27, wife of Thomas **DALTON**, tailor, Waterford City [died in consequence of childbirth; Eliza, 5 days old, child of this couple, was baptised in the Catholic church at Halifax on 3 April.]
9 Dec 1835	Mary **KINSELA**, 47, Leix, widow of Thomas **DARCY**.
8 Apr 1834	Ann **SCANLON**, 38, Tipperary, wife of Richard **DAVIS**.
9 Oct 1835	Catherine **LONERGAN**, 26, Tipperary, wife of Sgt. Manning **DAVY**, 83rd Regt.
24 Sep 1827	Laughlin **DEAGAN**, 19, Ballycolla [Aghaboe Parish], Abbeyleix, Leix.
30 Jan 1821	John **DEALY**, 80, husband of Sara **STEPHENS**, Ireland.
10 Sep 1834	Garret **DeCOURSEY**, 48, Cork, husband of Mary **MULLANY**.

5 Apr 1816	Michael, seaman, son of Maurice & Mary **DELANEY**, 31, Wexford
14 Aug 1820	Thomas **DELANEY**, 63, Pilltown, Kilkenny
20 Jan 1820	Philip **DENNY**, tailor, husband of Eleanor **FLINN**, 50, Middleton, Cork [*AR*, 22 Jan 1820, mentioned an inquest into his death. The inquest found that death was caused by a pair of scissors thrown at his head during an argument with his son, John **DENNY**, on Sunday morning, 16 Jan. Denny died Tuesday evening, 18 Jan, leaving a widow and 6 children.]
12 Mar 1833	Pvte. Peter **DEVIT**, Rifle Brigade, 23, Westmeath
14 Sep 1834	Daniel **DILLON**, 35, Wexford, husband of Mary **NEWMAN**
8 Aug 1841	Edward **DILLON**, tailor, 36, born Ireland
8 Jul 1837	Mary **DILLON**, 35, Tipperary
17 Aug 1837	Pvte. Patrick **DOBBINS**, 85th Regt., 28, born Ireland.
4 Jun 1829	James **DOLLARD**, 29, Kilkenny, husband of Mary **ENRIGHT**
10 Jul 1829	Thomas **DOLLARD**, 28, Mooncoin, Kilkenny [*AR*, 11 July 1829: died 6 July, age 25]
27 Jun 1838	Catherine **CAFFERY**, 28, Dublin, wife of James **DONNELLY**
28 Dec 1832	Eliza, 3 yrs., born Tyrone, dau of Peter & Mary (**GRAHAM**) **DONELLY**
27 May 1822	Ex-Sgt. Hugh **DONELLY**, 64th. Regt., 36, Co. Tyrone [husband of Mary **ROSS**]
9 Sep 1834	James **DONNELLY**, 44, Longford, husband of Bridget **DOWNS**.
18 Jan 1836	Michael, 9, Waterford, son of the late James & Bridget (**DOWNS**) **DONNELLY**.
2 Sep 1829	Peter **DONNELLY**, cabinetmaker, 23, Ireland, husband of Mary **GORMALLY** [The *HJ*, 31 Aug 1829 says that he died that day from the effects of a stone thrown by Andrew **WAUGH**.]
28 Dec 1826	Mary, 40, widow of William **DONOHOE**, Ireland
7 Jul 1840	Pvte. John **DONOVAN**, 37th Regt., 23, born Ireland.
1 Oct 1823	Thomas **DONOVAN**, 15, "a few months from Ireland" [*Free Press*, 30 Sep 1823, gives the date of death as 29 Sep 1823]
27 Jul 1824	William **DONOVAN**, shopkeeper, 34, Parish of Carrig, Monaghan
29 Jul 1833	William **DONOVAN**, 45, Waterford, husband of Catherine **ALMAN**.
29 Aug 1829	Richard **DORMODY**, 60, Ireland [probably Kilkenny], at the Poor House
9 Jul 1827	Eleanor **MULHALL**, 40, wife of James **DOWLING**, St. John's Parish, Kilkenny Town; "here a few days on ship *Cumberland*".
12 Dec 1833	James **DOWLING**, 23, Carlow, husband of Margaret **McDONALD** [*AR*, 21 Dec 1833: died 9 Dec, age 22; married 18 Apr 1833: James, son of Michael & Winnifred (**PHELAN**) **DOWLING** of Carlow, to Margaret, dau of John & Alice (**CORCORAN**) **McDONALD** of Newfoundland. [StM, Hfx]
28 Jul 1827	Patrick **DOWLING**, 27, Inistioge Parish, Kilkenny
15 Jul 1827	Thomas **DOWLING**, 57, Thomastown Parish, Kilkenny, "a few days here".
1 Jun 1833	Honora **FENTON**, 25, Cork, widow of John **DOWNEY** [Married 11 Sep 1831: John, son of James & Elizabeth (**HENESSY**) **DOWNEY** of Kilkenny, to Honora, dau of John & Mary (**KINNON**) **FENTON** of Cork. [StM, Hfx]
26 Jan 1832	John **DOWNEY**, 24, born [Kilkenny] Ireland, husband of Honora **FENTON**.
21 Dec 1841	Margaret **DOWNEY**, 60, born Ireland [*Times*, 21 Dec 1841, gives her age as 53.]
21 Apr 1828	James **DOYLE**, 89, Kilkenny.
12 May 1839	John **DOYLE**, ship carpenter, 45, born Ireland, husband of Mary **RYAN**.
2 Jun 1840	Pvte. John **DOYLE**, 37th Regt., 35, born Ireland.
2 Jun 1835	Lawrence **DOYLE**, 63, Carlow.
30 Jan 1818	Michael, son of Garret & Eleanor (**BURKE**) **DOYLE**, 17, Clonmel, Tipperary
6 Dec 1825	Michael **DOYLE**, 56, tailor, Wexford.

24 Mar 1837   Sarah **DOYLE**, 26, Wexford.
13 Feb 1836   Thomas **DOYLE**, 46, Waterford, husband of Johanna **O'BRIEN** [*AR*, 12 Feb
                1836: died 10 Feb, age 45. Married 26 Nov 1831: Thomas, son of John & Catherine
                DOYLE, to Johanna, dau of Jeremiah & Mary (**WARD**) **O'BRIEN**, all of Wexford.
                [StM, Hfx]
 5 Mar 1829   Augustine **DRAPER**, 28, painter, Waterford
17 May 1837   Elizabeth **DRAY**, 25, Kilkenny.
26 Nov 1835   Michael **DREENAN** [**DRENNAN**], 60, Carlow
19 Jan 1826   John **DRISCOLL**, 35, Whitechurch Parish, Waterford.
29 May 1836   Francis **DUFFY**, 40, Monaghan, husband of Elizabeth **McGEE**.
15 Mar 1835   James **DUFFY**, Dublin, husband of Eleanor **DOYLE**.
17 Mar 1836   David **DUGGAN**, Rifle Brigade, 28, Derry
 1 Sep 1825   Richard **DULHANTY**, 36, Kilkenny
26 Jan 1831   Thomas **DULLEHANTY**, "long of Halifax," 76, born Ireland [*AR*, 5 Feb 1831, has
                Thomas **DULHANTY** died 24 Jan, age 75.]
12 Jan 1842   Pvte. J. ... **DUNNE**, 30th Regt., 35, Dublin.
28 Feb 1821   James **DUNN**, 57, husband of Mary **CAREW**, Ireland
 – Dec 1841   Pvte. James **DUNNE**, 8th Regt., 24, born Ireland.
29 Nov 1837   John **DUNNE**, 35, born Ireland [Callan, Kilkenny], widower of Martha **KELLY**.
28 Jul 1827   Malachy **DUNN**, 47, Ballinakill [Dysertgallen Parish], Leix, leaving a widow
                and six children
29 Jan 1837   Martha **KELLY**, 30, wife of John **DUNNE** [Married 10 July 1834: John, son of
                Michael & Ann (**HAMMON**) **DUNN** of Callan, Kilkenny, to Martha, dau of James &
                Mary (**WALSH**) **KELLY** of Kilkenny. [StM, Hfx]
14 Apr 1829   Mary **CAREY**, 59, Parish of Miham[?], Tipperary, widow of James **DUNN**, carpenter
                [*Acadian Recorder*, 18 Apr 1829, reports the death date as 12 April]
 4 Sep 1829   Patrick **DUNN**, 60, Cappoquin, Waterford
 6 Jul 1829   Richard **DUNN**, 71, Kilkenny [*AR*, 11 July 1829, died 4 July, age 69.]
20 Sep 1837   Richard **DUNNE**, 56, Waterford
20 Nov 1826   Mary **DUNPHY**, widow, 72, Dunmore, [Killea Parish], Waterford.
27 May 1835   Patrick **DURGAN**, 83rd Regt., 27, born Ireland
21 Jul 1827   Nicholas **DURGAN**, 70, Leixlip, Kildare
23 Jan 1828   Cornelius **DWYER**, 60, Ireland
 2 Aug 1829   James **DWYER**, 32, Tipperary
 8 Jan 1835   Thomas **DWYER**, 40, Kilkenny, husband of Mary **TRACY**.
 2 Aug 1822   Patrick **EARLE**, 60th. Regt., 22, Liberties of Dublin.
18 Jun 1839   William **EGAN**, musician, 37th Regt., 22, Carlow.
25 Apr 1825   James **ENGLISH**, 86, Clonmel, Tipperary
29 Jun 1822   Michael **ENGLISH**, stonemason, 38, Rayell, Tipperary [Bridget **KEHOE's** husband]
23 Nov 1825   Michael **ENGLISH**, truckman, 38, Tipperary (here many years).
17 Jan 1841   Thomas **FAHIE**, 50, Waterford [Married 14 May 1828: Thomas, son of Matthew &
                Mary (**MOONEY**) **FAHY** of Kilrossanty, Waterford, to Honora, dau of John & Mary
                (**GRANT**) **WALSH** of Owning, Kilkenny. [StM, Hfx]
 9 Sep 1834   Edward **FALVEY**, 38, Kerry, husband of Margaret **STEWART** [*AR*, 13 Sep 1834:
                died 7 Sep, a grocer, leaving widow and a child. Married 25 Oct 1832: Edward, son
                of John & Honora (**FERRIS**) **FALVEY** of Lisvan (Lissavane, Parish of Kilbonane),
                Kerry, to Margaret, dau of James & Anne (**MOONEY**) **STEWART** of Halifax.[StM,
                Hfx]

11 Jul 1836	Mary **MIHAN**, 27, Kilkenny, wife of Dennis **FALVEY** [*NS Royal Gazette*, 13 Jul 1836: died 10 July. Married 21 Nov 1832: Dennis, son of John & Honora (**FERRIS**) **FALVEY** of Lissavane, Kerry, to Mary, dau of William & Alice (**MORISSY**) **MIHAN** of Kilkenny. [StM, Hfx]
6 Apr 1830	John **FANNING**, 86, Ireland, "many years at Blandford [NS]"
6 Aug 1828	Michael **FANNING**, 50, Raheen, Leix
4 Jul 1826	Denis, 14, son of Michael & Johanna (**TOBIN**) **FARRELL**, "lately from Ireland"
30 Dec 1824	Mary, 52, widow of Michael **FARRELL**, tailor, Killenaule, Tipperary
18 Jan 1823	Michael **FARRELL**, 73, Tipperary
16 May 1826	Michael **FARRELL**, 44, Ballynakill, Kilkenny [*AR*, 20 May 1826: died 13 May, age 40.]
7 Dec 1832	William **FARRELL**, 40 [born Waterford], husband of Eleanor **FLINN**.
31 Aug 1827	Thomas **FENNESSEY**, 35, Tipperary
16 Mar 1823	James **FERGUSON**, 32, Kinsale, Cork
22 Feb 1830	Jeremiah **FERGUSON**, 45, Cork, husband of Eleanor **DONOVAN**
17 Sep 1834	Dennis **FINLEN**, 35, Carlow, husband of Mary **MURPHY**.
26 Aug 1834	Anthony **FINN**, 85, Wexford.
14 Sep 1834	Daniel **FINN**, 27, Wexford.
— Jun 1836	John **FINN**, 40, born Ireland, husband of Mary **GRACE** [Married 20 Jun 1829: John, son of Richard & Margaret (**HENDRICK**) **FINN** of Kilkenny, to Mary, dau of William & Abigail (**LANDRIGAN**) **GRACE** of Mount Uniacke, NS. [StM, Hfx]
14 Feb 1840	John **FINN**, tailor, 35, born Ireland. [Married 22 May 1832: John, son of John & Bridget (**POWER**) **FINN** of Wexford, to Bridget, dau of Patrick & Mary (**RYAN**) **SHEEHAN** of Kilkenny. [StM, Hfx]
3 Dec 1822	Pvte. John **FINTON**, 81st. Regt., 35, Midleton, Cork.
19 Jan 1842	Edward **FITZGERALD**, 45, born Ireland.
17 Apr 1838	John **FITZGERALD**, 35, Cork, husband of Margaret **GEARY** [Married 15 Sep 1830: John, son of John & Mary (**KNOWLES**) **FITZGERALD**, to Margaret, dau of David & Margaret (**MURPHY**) **GEARY**, all of Cork. [StM, Hfx].
12 Jul 1841	Robert **FITZGERALD**, cooper, born Ireland.
13 Aug 1831	Nicholas **FITZHENRY**, 28, Wexford, husband of Anastasia **O'BRIEN** [*AR*, 13 Aug 1831: died 10 Aug, age 30, leaving widow and a child.]
28 Sep 1834	Eleanor **SKERRY**, 35, Kilkenny, wife of Edward **FITZMAURICE**.
30 May 1837	John **FITZMAURICE**, "many years in Nova Scotia," 63, born Ireland [*HJ*, 29 May 1837: died at Windsor Road 28 May, leaving widow and 6 children. Married 22 Jan 1801: John, son of John & Mary (**O'KEEFE**) **FITZMAURICE** of Limerick, to Mary (dau of Armistead) **FIELDING**, Windsor Road, NS. [StM, Hfx]
22 Apr 1822	Arthur **FITZPATRICK**, 68, Parish of Ardemine [Artramon?], Wexford
31 Dec 1837	James **FITZPATRICK**, 65, Cavan.
24 Jul 1840	Kieran **FITZPATRICK**, 63, Kilkenny [*AR*, 25 Jul 1840: died 22 July, age 62, "for the last 23 years a resident of Halifax."]
9 Sep 1834	Mary **BRENNAN**, 35, Kerry, wife of Michael **FITZPATRICK**, 96th Regt.
29 Jul 1834	Michael **FITZPATRICK**, 37, Meath.
20 Oct 1836	Daniel **FLAHERTY**, 40, born Ireland.
27 Aug 1834	Mary **DILLON**, 27, Waterford, wife of Manus **FLANNELLY** [Married 25 Jun 1834: Manus, son of Manus & Bridget (**BALLARD**) **FLANELLY** of Sligo, to Mary, dau of Patrick & Ann (**THOMPSON**) **DILLON** of Coloughmore, Waterford. [StM, Hfx]
24 Jul 1825	James, 2, son of Christopher & Honora [**McDONOUGH**] **FLANNIGAN**, Mayo

30 Mar 1827	John **FLEMMING**, 65, Clonmel, Tipperary.
6 Feb 1834	Ann **MULLONEY**, 37, wife of William **FLINN** [Married 30 Jul 1829: William, son of Philip & Mary (**MARR**) **FLINN** of Mothel, Waterford, to Ann, dau of Andrew & Honora (**DORAN**) **MOLONY** of Columbkille, Kilkenny. [StM, Hfx]
6 Jul 1833	Bridget **FLINN**, 22, Waterford.
8 Mar 1829	Jeremiah **FLINN**, 72, Waterford City [AR, 7 Mar 1829: *Jeffery* Flinn died 5 March.]
11 Feb 1829	John **FLINN**, mason, 46, Cashel, Tipperary, husband of Catherine **KERAN** [Ns, 19 Feb 1829, says Flinn died on 9 Feb]
12 Jan 1830	John **FLINN**, 41, Cork.
8 Feb 1840	John **FLINN**, 45, born Ireland.
4 Oct 1836	Patrick **FLINN**, 40, Waterford.
5 Jul 1841	Patrick **FLINN**, 36, born Ireland, husband of Catherine **McFARLANE**.
6 Mar 1825	Thomas **FLINN**, servant to Mr. **SKERRY** at Dartmouth, NS, 66, Ireland
4 May 1828	Thomas **FLINN**, 76, Carrick-on-Suir, Tipperary, "He had been a resident of Musquodoboit these 30 years past" [AR, 3 May 1828: died 1 May.]
4 May 1835	Thomas, 3, born Wexford, son of Thomas & Eleanor (**BRENNAN**) **FLINN**.
11 Dec 1833	Valentine **FLINN**, 35, Carlow, husband of Judith **DOYLE** [Married 15 Jul 1823: Valentine, son of Arthur & Bridget (**TROY**) **FLINN** of Myshall, Carlow, to Judith, dau of James & Catherine (**GORMAN**) **DOYLE** of Dunleckney, Carlow. [StM, Hfx]
18 Apr 1822	William **FLINN**, mason, 70, Cashel, Tipperary.
14 Mar 1838	Michael **FLYN**, 40, Leitrim [AR, 17 Mar 1838: Michael **FLYNN**, 36, died 13 Mar]
20 Jun 1828	Joanna, 66, Cork, wife of James **FOGARTY**
4 May 1821	Martin **FOGARTY**, 63, Co. Kilkenny.
27 Aug 1834	John **FOLEY**, 44, Waterford.
18 Sep 1840	John **FOLEY**, 38, Cork
14 Nov 1827	Nicholas **FOLEY**, cooper, 69, Cork
8 Nov 1828	Timothy **FOLY**, 67, Ireland
12 Jun 1828	Elizabeth **WINTER**, 42, wife of Timothy **FORAN**, Churchtown, Cork
1 May 1827	John **FORAN**, 32, Tipperary
20 Jun 1822	Pvte. Michael **FORD**, 81st. Regt., 28, Co. Mayo.
19 Jul 1841	Daniel **FOWLER**, shoemaker, 24, Cork [NS Royal Gazette: died 17 July.]
16 Dec 1835	Dennis **FOWLER**, 60, Kilkenny.
24 Sep 1826	Daniel, 13, son of James **FOX**, "lately from Ireland"
6 Nov 1832	James, 6 mos., son of Francis & Bridget (**SCULLY**) **FOX**, Longford.
14 Nov 1823	Pvte. John **FOX**, 81st. Regt., "died suddenly", 45, Dublin.
17 Apr 1831	Thomas **FOX**, 60, born Ireland.
14 Jul 1827	Judith **SALLY**, 50, wife of Thomas **FOYLE**, Castlecomer Parish, Kilkenny, "a few days here"
15 Jul 1840	Pvte. Thomas **GALVIN**, 36th Regt., 24, born Ireland.
4 Aug 1821	John **GAUL**, 38, Thomastown, Kilkenny
30 Oct 1827	Patrick **GAUL**, 56, Wexford
24 Mar 1827	John **GIBSON**, drummer, 74th. Regt., 27, Ireland.
3 Oct 1833	Eleanor **GILASPY**, 48, Donegal.
25 Sep 1839	Patrick **GILFOYLE**, 38, Leix, husband of Judith **TOBIN** [Married 18 Aug 1828: Patrick, son of Thomas & Judith (**EGAN**) **GILFOY**, to Judith, dau of Michael & Mary (**POWER**) **TOBIN** of Kilkenny. [StM, Hfx]
29 Jun 1827	James **GITON**, 26, Killenaule Parish, Tipperary, left a wife and 2 children.
22 Jul 1827	Bridget **GLEESON**, 30, Kilkenny

22 Apr 1830	John **GLEESON**, carpenter, 66, Ireland, "Old resident of Halifax."
5 Feb 1840	John **GOGINS**, 72, Cork.
11 Jul 1832	Catherine **PARKER**, 25, wife of Denis **GORMAN**, blacksmith, Innistioge, Kilkenny "here a few days ago."
15 Oct 1833	Michael **GORMAN**, 35, Tipperary, husband of Eleanor **MAGHER**.
28 Aug 1822	William **GORMAN**, –, Holy Cross, Tipperary
16 Aug 1815	Thomas **GOW[H]EEN**, 22, Ireland [Kilronan Parish, Roscommon.]
28 Nov 1828	Margaret **KEATING**, 39, wife of Timothy **GRADY**, Tipperary.
23 Feb 1834	James **GRAHAM**, 45, Tipperary, husband of Johanna **GREEN**.
9 Feb 1837	Pvte. John **GRAHAM**, 85th Regt., 24, Kilkenny.
12 Sep 1835	Johannah **FITZPATRICK**, 69, Kilkenny, wife of John **GRANGEL**.
26 Jul 1837	John **GRANGEL**, 70, born Ireland [Kilkenny], widower of Johana **FITZPATRICK**.
3 Oct 1830	Alice, 36, Kilkenny, dau of Nicholas & Ann (**LYONS**) **BYRNES**, wife of Patrick **GREEN**.
10 Aug 1829	Pvte. James **GREEN**, 96th. Regiment, 25, Carlow.
22 Dec 1834	James **GREEN**, 40, Tipperary.
20 May 1836	James **GREEN**, stonemason, 27, born Ireland.
23 Aug 1834	Mary **CRANE**, 40, Waterford, wife of James **GRENDALL**.
10 Mar 1828	Charles **GRENNELL**, 34, Cork; "Sexton of this church for many years"
3 Feb 1829	Anne **PURCELL**, 55, Kilkenny, wife of James **GRIFFIN**.
24 Feb 1831	Elizabeth **GRIFFIN**, 35, Kilkenny, wife of William **BRUCE**.
17 Nov 1830	James **GRIFFIN**, 70, Ireland.
29 Nov 1821	Lawrence **GRIFFIN**, Clonmel, Tipperary; "convicted for the murder of Henry **FERGUSON**." [*NS Royal Gazette*, 18 Apr 1821, reported the murder, the previous day on the street, of Mr. Henry **FERGUSON**, Jr., 22, a cooper. The miniature lake in the centre of Halifax Public Gardens was long known as *Griffin's Pond*, that having been the scene of Griffin's public hanging.]
3 Dec 1819	Thomas **GRIFFIN**, shoemaker, husband of Mary **LACEY**, Carlow; son of John & Mary (**MOORE**) **GRIFFIN**.
16 Oct 1820	Cpl. William **GRIFFIN**, 82nd. Regt., 27, Kerry, son of John & Mary (**MOORE**).
17 May 1829	Catherine **MURPHY**, 34, Carlow, wife of John **GUIHAN**
23 Jul 1823	Thomas **GUINAN**, 33, Kilmacow, Kilkenny.
17 Nov 1829	Philip **GUINAN**, carpenter, 37, Tipperary, husband of Margaret **QUINLAN** [Married, 16 Apr 1825: Philip, son of Timothy & Margaret (**O'BRIEN**) Guinan of Cashel, Tipperary, to Margaret, dau of Edmund & Susan **QUILLINAN**, Sheet Harbour, NS.]
17 Jul 1831	Richard **HABBERLIN**, 65, born [Glenmore, Kilkenny] Ireland [*AR*, 16 Jul 1831, Capt. Richard **HABERLIN** died 15 July.]
22 Dec 1833	Catherine **SMIGEAN**, 55, Tipperary, wife of Michael **HACKET**.
1 Feb 1835	Mrs. Mary **HACKET**, 86, Tipperary [*AR*, 31 Jan 1835: died 30 Jan, age 87.]
25 May 1828	Bartholomew **HACKETT**, 34, Coolnamuck, Cork; in margin: "Uniacke" [If Coolnamuck is correct, it must be in either Waterford or Kilkenny. He was the husband of Mary **BRITT**. Their son became Sir William Hackett, Chief Justice of Ceylon, *circa* 1877.]
25 Apr 1820	Nicholas **HACKETT**, 34, Tipperary.
16 Sep 1834	Terrence **HALES**, painter, 40, Dublin [*Times*, 16 Sep 1834, calls him **HAIL**.]
13 Apr 1823	Edward **HALL**, carpenter, 37, Clonmel Town, Tipperary
25 Feb 1818	Michael, son of Edmund & Bridget (**MAGEE**) **HALL**, 13 mos, Clonmel, Tipperary.

21 Mar 1838   Pvte. James **HALPENNY**, 65th Regt., 45, Carlow.

15 Jul 1823   Henry **HAMMON**, 60, blacksmith, Gowran, Kilkenny, "a few days here."

13 Mar 1841   Darby **HANAVAN**, 56, Kerry.

1 Feb 1835   Mary **McGRATH**, Waterford, widow of Thomas **HANIGAN**.

18 Jan 1838   William **HANIGAN**, 38, Waterford, husband of Catherine **DOWNEY**.

21 Jan 1835   Thomas **HANNIGAN**, 22, Waterford, husband of Katherine **KEARNEY** [AR, 24 Jan 1835: died 19 Jan, age 21. Married 5 Nov 1833: Thomas, son of Thomas & Mary (**McGRATH**) **HANNIGAN** of Waterford, to Catherine, dau of Patrick & Catherine (**POWER**) **KEARNEY** of "Ballyhan Parish" (Ballyhane townland in either the parish of Affane or of Whitechurch), Waterford.][StM, Hfx]

1 Jul 1833   Thomas **HANRAHAN**, 45, Wexford, husband of Bridget **CONWAY**.

12 Nov 1834   Richard **HARNEY** [Sr.], "long resident of this town," 74, Tipperary [AR, 15 Nov 1834: died 10 Nov, age 73.]

7 Jan 1842   Elenor **BARRY**, 65, Cork, widow of Andrew **HARRIGAN**.

25 Oct 1824   Denis **HARRINGTON**, 25, Kerry.

17 May 1835   Michael **HARRISON**, 70, born New Ross, Wexford [AR, 16 May 1835: died 14 May, age 69.]

30 May 1838   William **HAUGHNEY**, shoemaker, 30, Carlow.

26 Nov 1832   Eleanor, 4 yrs., Tipperary, dau of Maurice & Eleanor (**LAHEY**) **HARTERY**.

25 Feb 1827   Samuel **HAWKSWORTH**, carpenter, 40, Limerick City [Married 29 Jan 1822: Samuel, son of Samuel & Bridget (**CLANSEY**) **HAWKSWORTH** of Limerick, to Bridget, dau of Moses & Mary (**MURRY**) **NOWLAN**, Wexford. [StM, Hfx]

10 Feb 1825   Denis **HAYS**, drowned, 49, Kilshane, Tipperary [AR, 12 Feb 1825, reported an inquest, on 9 February, on the bodies of Dennis **HAYS** and Edward **RYAN**, found drowned.]

19 Aug 1833   Dorothy **HAYES**, 60, Tipperary.

29 May 1821   Edward **HAYES**, 71, Ireland [AR, 2 June 1821: died 29 May.]

21 Apr 1828   Michael **HAYS**, 40, Ireland

6 Jun 1827   Thomas **HAYES**, died at Shubenacadie, NS, 41, Carlow

30 Sep 1821   William **HAYES**, 27, husband of Eleanor **FLINN**, Waterford.

6 Sep 1828   Cpl. William **HAYS**, in the Rifle Brigade, Limerick.

30 Nov 1829   Elizabeth **LEARY**, 32, New Ross, Wexford, wife of Patrick **HEADEN**.

23 Jan 1838   John **HEALY**, 60, born Ireland.

13 Apr 1837   Patrick **HEALY**, 50, born Ireland [Married: Patrick, son of James & Mary (**SULLIVAN**) **HEALY** of Castlemaine, Kerry, to Anne, dau of Hugh & Jeroth (**DRISKELL**) **FRASER** of Harrietsfield, NS. [StM, Hfx]

17 Dec 1827   Jeffrey **HEARN**, 40, Passage, Waterford

15 May 1824   Philip **HEARN**, 74, Ireland, "here twenty years."

7 Feb 1838   David **HEFFEY**, 30, Cork, husband of Margaret **DORNEY**.

23 Sep 1820   Ellen, dau of John & Catherine (**McGRATH**) **HENEBERY**, 24, Carrick-on-Suir, Tipperary.

8 Oct 1837   Anne **WALSH**, 38, born Ireland, wife of John **HENESSY** [Married 8 Feb 1829: John, son of Maurice & Julia (**KEEFE**) **HENISSY** of Cloyne, Cork, widower of Margaret **MURPHY**, to Anne, dau of Maurice & Margaret (**TIBIS**) **WALSH** of Cappoquin, Waterford. [StM, Hfx]

21 Jul 1840   Pvte. Cornelius **HENESSY**, 37th Regt., 24, born Ireland.

17 Jan 1837   Patrick **HENESSY**, 30, Tipperary, husband of Mary **DWYER**.

2 Sep 1834   John **HENNESSY**, 35, Kilkenny, husband of Mary **CUTT** [Married 20 Apr 1830: John, son of Thomas & Bridget (**MORISSY**) **HENISSEY**, Kilkenny, to Mary, dau of Thomas & Margaret (**POWER**) **CUTT** of Waterford.[StM, Hfx]

23 Dec 1818   William **HENNETHY** or **HANRATTY**, 62nd. Regt., 26, Monaghan

27 May 1821   Daniel **HENSHELL**, 62, husband of Mary **FOLEY**, Cork

11 Mar 1829   Michael **HERBERT,** 86, Fedamore, Limerick [AR, 14 Mar 1829: died on 9 9 March at Dartmouth, NS.]

26 Dec 1833   Elizabeth **DREW**, 51, Limerick, wife of George **HEWSON** [Died 24 Dec. She was a sister of Dr. John **DREW**, Royal Navy - *Free Press*, 31 Dec 1833.]

18 Feb 1840   George **HEWSON**, 61 [AR, 22 Feb 1840: died 16 Feb, age 60, from Limerick.]

16 Jul 1827   Margaret **HICKEY**, 30, Cashel, Tipperary, "here a few days"

25 Nov 1824   Pvte. William **HICKEY**, 74th. Regiment, 36, Limerick

28 Sep 1820   Patrick **HIGGINS**, 38, Waterford

14 Apr 1823   Jane **CHERRY**, 25, Co. Meath, wife of Pvte. William **HILL** or **HALL**, 62nd. Regt.

 5 Apr 1830   John **HINISSY**, 65, Ireland.

 6 Sep 1840   Patrick **HOARE**, 50, Kerry.

25 Aug 1828   Mary **HOCTOR**, 30, Ireland; "A passenger in the *Penelope*."

25 May 1840   John **HOGAN**, 40, born Ireland.

 8 Dec 1826   Philip **HOGAN**, 66, Inistiogue, Kilkenny.

16 Jan 1821   Eleanor, 9 mos., dau of Philip & Mary (**DUNPHY**) **HOLDEN**, Kilkenny

12 Sep 1825   Mary **DUNPHY**, 28, wife of Philip **HOLDEN**, Ireland [Kilkenny]

12 Sep 1834   Mary **HICKEY**, 35, Waterford, wife of William **HOLFIELD**.

24 Feb 1840   Andrew **HOLLIGAN**, 67, born Ireland.

 8 Nov 1829   Daniel **HOLLIHAN**, tailor, 38, Ireland.

23 Aug 1839   Michael **HOLLOHAN**, "many years a resident," 80 [AR, 24 Aug 1839: **HOLOHAN**, born Ireland, died 20 Aug, age 80.]

23 Jul 1822   Thomas **HOLLOHAN**, 60 [Ireland; AR, 27 July 1822: died on 21 July, age 59.]

12 Jun 1837   Mary **DOWNEY**, 24, Kerry, wife of Pvte. Thomas **HOPE**, 34th Regt.

31 Jul 1833   Catherine **HERBERT**, 48 [born Fedamore, Limerick, dau of Michael **HOWARD**], wife of Benjamin **HORN**, Eastern Passage, NS.]

23 Jan 1828   William **HOULIHAN**, 40, Ireland.

 6 Nov 1833   Ann **HOWARD**, 72, Carlow.

27 Mar 1820   William, son of Michael & Catherine (**CAFFERY**) **HOWARD**, 50, Dublin [AR, 1 April: died 25 Mar, age 54.]

 6 Jul 1817   John **HOWE**, 56, Ireland

 4 Aug 1830   James **HOWLEY**, 46, Kilkenny.

31 May 1841   Mrs. **HOYNES**, born Ireland.

21 Oct 1839   John **HUNT**, 56, Kilkenny.

 2 Jan 1824   Martin **HUNT**, shopkeeper, 62, Ireland [Waterford] [AR, 3 Jan 1824: died 1 Jan.]

23 Jan 1835   Daniel **HURLEY**, 40, Cork, husband of Mary **SHEA**.

23 Jan 1839   James **HURLEY**, 60, Waterford.

 6 Dec 1816   Roger **HURLEY**, labourer, husband of Bridget..., 76, Ireland.

 5 Oct 1841   Thomas **HURLEY**, 55, Cork.

18 Aug 1833   Michael **HYDE**, 50, Waterford.

29 Jun 1837   Robert **JOYCE**, stonemason, 30, Kilkenny [AR, 22 Jul 1837: died 28 June, a native of Inistiogue, Kilkenny.]

13 Feb 1822   Pvte. Edward **KANDLE**, 60th. Regt., –, Wicklow.

 2 Oct 1832   Denis **KARNEY**, shoemaker, born [Cashel], Tipperary.

24 Dec 1820	George, son of John & Eleanor (**ELWORTH**) **KAVANAGH**, 30, Duncormick Parish, Wexford.
24 Sep 1837	Mary **CARY**, 35, born Ireland, wife of Edward **KAVANAH** [Married 10 Oct 1834: Edward, son of Morgan & Margaret (**DULHANTY**) **KAVANAGH,** to Mary, dau of Edmund & Mary (**CANTFIELD**) **CAREY**, all of Kilkenny.
12 Oct 1825	Pvte. Michael **KAVANAH**, 81st. Regiment, 36, Wexford Town.
10 Mar 1841	Mary **KEANE**, 25, Lismore, Waterford.
14 Sep 1838	Dennis **KEARNEY**, 20, born Ireland.
30 Nov 1836	Elizabeth **BUCKLEY**, 28, Cork, wife of Simon **KEARNEY** [Married 23 Oct 1834: Simon, son of James & Ann (**ROACHE**) **KARNEY** of Carlow, to Elizabeth, dau of Daniel & Catherine (**LINEHAN**) **BUCKLEY** of Cork. [StM, Hfx]
9 Oct 1835	Elizabeth **LEWIS**, 30, Waterford, wife of Thomas **KEARNY**.
21 Feb 1835	Joseph **KEARNY**, 35, born Ireland, husband of Bridget **FLINN**.
15 Aug 1839	Elizabeth, 45, born Ireland, wife of Nicholas **KEARNS**.
18 Aug 1827	Rose, 8 yrs. 6 mos., dau of Patrick & Margaret (**HICKEY**) **KEARNS**, Ireland; "passengers who arrived here a few months ago"
23 Jul 1827	William **KEATING**, 50, Mothel[l] Parish, Kilkenny, "a few days here." [*Ns,* 5 July 1827, reported the arrival that week of the ship *Cumberland* out of Waterford, with "350 passengers."]
2 Sep 1840	J..... **KEEFFE**, Poor Asylum 65, born Ireland.
18 Dec 1840	Michael **KEEFFE**, 63, born Ireland.
28 Jul 1837	Mary **KEEGAN**, "died on board of a ship in this harbour," 20, born Ireland [*Nova-Scotian,* 3 Aug 1837, reported the arrival that week of the brig *Clitus,* out of Cork, with "106 passengers."]
3 Jun 1821	Humphrey **KEERANS**, 35 [husband of Margaret **MURPHY**], Bandon, Cork
24 May 1822	Pvte. James **KEERNAN**, 81st. Regt., 22, Fermanagh
16 Aug 1820	Thomas, son of Alexander & Mary **KEIFF**, 72, Castlelyons, Cork, and husband of Mary **SCANNEL**.
20 Dec 1832	Daniel **KEILY**, 40, Cork, husband of Eleanor **HANIGAN**.
18 Aug 1827	Andrew **KELLY**, 40, born Parish "Patts" [St Patrick's], Kilkenny; left widow and family.
9 Jan 1837	Ann **QUIN**, 56, Roscommon , wife of Owen **KELLY**.
9 Feb 1833	Edward **KELLY**, 34, born Ireland, husband of .... [Married 5 Aug 1826: Edward, son of Edward & Eliza (**RYLANDS**) **KELLY** of Clonmel, Tipperary, to Bridget, dau of Edward & Mary (**MUNDAY**) **LAFFIN** of Halifax. [StM, Hfx]
9 Sep 1828	James **KELLY**, 55, Ireland.
24 Nov 1836	James **KELLY**, 28, Kilkenny, husband of Joanna **DeYOUNG** [Married 18 Feb 1833: James, son of Edward & Catherine (**WHITE**) **KELLY** of Kilkenny, to Joanna, dau of John & Barbara (**BALDIN**) **DeYOUNG**, Eastern Passage, NS. [StM, Hfx]
25 Apr 1841	Joana **KELLY**, 20, Cork.
24 Aug 1840	Maurice **KELLY**, late of the Rifle Brigade, 40, born Ireland.
10 Oct 1801	Patrick **KELLY**, 47, Ardfinnan, Tipperary
27 Sep 1816	Thomas **KELLY**, 87, Ireland
9 Jan 1829	Pvte. Thomas **KELLY**, Rifles, 24, Wexford.
20 Dec 1833	Thomas **KELLY**, 35, husband of Mary **DREEDY** [*AR,* 21 Dec 1833: died 18 Dec, age 32; Married 26 Nov 1826: Thomas, son of Richard & Mary (**MAGUIGAN**) **KELLY** of Dromore Parish, Tyrone, to Margaret, dau of James & Mary (**McGRATH**) **DREDY**, Musquodoboit, NS. [StM, Hfx]

26 Aug 1834   Sgt. Dennis **KENNEDY**, Rifle Brigade, 31, born Ireland.

20 Jan 1832   James **KENNEDY**, 50, born Ireland [*HJ*, 6 Feb 1832: died 18 Jan, age 48, born in Wexford.]

30 Sep 1829   Mary **KENNEDY**, 17, Kerry.

3 Jan 1840   Mary **KENNEDY**, 64, Waterford [*NS Royal Gazette*, 8 Jan 1840: died 1 Jan, Mrs. Mary **KENNEDY**, age 60.]

17 Sep 1827   Timothy **KENNEDY**, 25, Dingle, Kerry, "killed by lightning at the Shubenacadie."

26 Oct 1841   Timothy **KENNEDY**, 45, Kerry [*Halifax Morning Post*, 26 Oct 1841: died 24 Oct.]

12 Jul 1827   Catherine **BRENNAN**, 45, wife of Nicholas **KENNY**, Kilkenny, "here a few days" [*Ns*, 5 July 1827, reported the arrival that week of the ship *Cumberland* out of Waterford, with "350 passengers."]

20 Jul 1827   Nicholas **KENNY**, –, Ireland [Kilkenny], "here a few days." [*Ns*, 5 July 1827, reported the arrival that week of the ship *Cumberland* out of Waterford, with "350 passengers."]

16 Jul 1841   Patrick **KENT**, 32, Wexford [*AR*, 17 Jul 1841: died 15 July, leaving widow and 2 children. Married 24 Apr 1836: Patrick, son of Mark & Margaret (**MILLER**) **KENT** of Wexford, to Sophia, dau of James & Ann (**KLINE**) **ANDERSON** of Halifax. [StM, Hfx]

20 Apr 1830   Nicholas **KERWAN**, 30, Waterford

12 Jul 1827   Thomas **KERWIN**, tailor, 40, leaving a wife in Ireland, Waterford, "a few days here" [*Ns*, 5 July 1827, reported the arrival that week of the ship *Cumberland* out of Waterford, with "350 passengers."]

19 Nov 1822   Patrick **KIELY**, chandler, 34, Clonmel, Tipperary.

3 Apr 1832   James **KIHOE**, 46, born Ireland.

23 Dec 1832   Thomas **KIHOE**, 40, Waterford.

3 Oct 1830   Maurice **KILEY**, 50, Cork, husband of Bridget **BURKE**.

3 Apr 1840   Peter **KILLARNEY**, 65, Longford.

7 Nov 1826   Eleanor **MEAGHER**, 32, wife of William **KILPATRICK**, 74th. Regt., Donegal.

12 Feb 1837   Mary **ROURKE**, 40, born Ross, Wexford, wife of Joseph **KINGSTON**.

8 Jan 1833   Pvte. Patrick **KINNA**, 8th Regt., 34, Meath.

3 Mar 1819   Pvte. Francis **KINREAVY**, 15th. Regt., 41, Ireland

19 Sep 1819   Daniel **KINSELLA**, 64, Carlow

12 Mar 1823   Daniel **KINSELA**, 50, Graiguenamana, Kilkenny

25 Mar 1828   Mary **BURKE**, 30, wife of Michael **KINSELLA**, Killglass Parish, Longford.

18 Oct 1837   Catherine **SHEEDY**, 53, Waterford, wife of Michael **KIRIVAN**.

29 Dec 1817   Francis, son of Thomas & Margaret (**BIBLE**) **KIRK**, 33, Waterford

4 Jun 1828   Henry **KIRK**, 74th. Regt., 28, [illegible], Ireland.

12 Sep 1834   Michael **KIRWICK**, 72, Kilkenny.

25 Mar 1838   Bridget **LACEY**, 30, born Ireland.

7 Jul 1833   Edward **LAFFAN**, 56, born [Kilkenny], husband of Catherine **ROAST**. [He died on 4 July 1833, age 55, and was a son of Michael & Bridget (**GLANDON**) **LAFFIN**.]

15 Oct 1824   Bridget [**GLANDON**], 74 [Kilkenny], wife of Michael **LAFFIN** [*AR*, 16 Oct 1824: died 14 Oct.]

16 Jan 1820   Bartholomew **LAHEY**, tailor, -, Pilltown, Kilkenny.

1 Jul 1833   Catherine **BUCHER**, 39, Cork, wife of Patrick **LAHY**.

12 Dec 1834   Catherine **SULLIVAN**, 30, Cork, wife of Patrick **LAHEY**.

30 Nov 1840   David **LAHEY**, 35, born Ireland, husband of Mary **IRVIN** [*NS Royal Gazette*, 9 Dec 1840: David **LAHEE** died 28 Nov, age 36.]

19 Aug 1834   Thomas **LAHEY**, 35, born Ireland.

12 Sep 1834   Mary **DUFFY**, 25, Monaghan, wife of Thomas **LAMASNEY**.

16 Nov 1834   Mary **LEYCID**, 80, Monaghan, widow of Thomas **LAMASNEY**.

14 Sep 1834   Catherine **COUGHLIN**, 39, Clare, wife of Sgt. **LANDER**, Rifle Brigade.

31 Oct 1832   John **LANDRIGAN**, 40, Cork.

27 Nov 1830   Ann **FITZMAURICE**, 50, Cork [wife of William **LANGLEY**; *AR*, 27 Nov 1830: died 24 Nov, age 49.]

21 Aug 1831   Eleanor **LANIGAN**, 54, Kilkenny, wife of James **TOBIN**, Esq.

29 Mar 1828   Thomas **LANIGAN**, 30, Callan Parish, Kilkenny

 1 Oct 1827   Patrick **LANNAN**, 52, Kilkenny

17 Aug 1826   John **LANNIGAN**, 55, Ireland "here many years" [*AR*, 19 Aug 1826: died 15 Aug, age 54.]

12 Mar 1838   William **LARASCY**, 40, born Ireland [*AR*, 17 Mar 1838: died 10 March, William **LARICY**, 38, leaving widow and 3 children. Married 5 Feb 1831: William, son of William & Honora (**DREW**) **LARISSY** of Kilkenny, to Mary Anne, dau of William & Ellen (**MADOX**) **CASHIN** of Halifax.   [StM, Hfx]

 7 Jan 1833   John **LARISSY**, 45, Kilkenny, husband of Mary **KIERAN**.

28 Oct 1834   Patrick **LAUGHNAN**, 71, Tyrone.

18 Mar 1835   Edward **LAWLER**, cooper, 49, Carlow.

12 Apr 1835   John **LAWLER**, "here many years", 72, Limerick [*AR*, 11 Apr 1835: died 8 Apr, age 71.]

16 Feb 1838   William **LAWLER,** 45, Kildare.

16 Mar 1821   Hanney, 3, dau of William & Ann (**BUCKLEY**) **LAWLOR**, Ireland.

18 Feb 1834   John **LAWLOR**, 30, Leix, husband of Mary **DEWIRE**.

 2 Apr 1824   Edmond **LAWRENCE**, 30, Ballypatrick Parish, Tipperary.

 7 Jun 1840   Helena, 50, born Ireland, widow of S. **LAWRENCE** [*AR*, 6 Jun 1840: Ellen, 44, widow of Samuel **LAWRENCE**, died 5 June, leaving 7 children. Married 30 May 1824: Samuel, son of John & Elizabeth (**LEE**) **LAWRENCE** of Wiltshire, England, to Eleanor, dau of Michael & Honor (**COUGHLAN**) **SULLIVAN** of Buttevant, Cork.

13 Mar 1820   John, son of James & Eleanor **LEAMY**, 40, Thurles, Tipperary.

15 Aug 1827   Patrick **LEANE**, tailor, 33, Watergrasshill, Cork

14 May 1828   Patrick **LEARY**, 35, Wexford; "He died suddenly at the Canal."

15 Mar 1821   Mathew **LEE**, 28, Red Gap, Kildare [*recte* Redgap, Kilkenny.]

20 Nov 1833   Mary **BARTON**, 40, Kerry, wife of Timothy **LINEHAN**.

25 May 1824   John **LISTER**, servant, 64, Ireland.

26 Mar 1836   Charles **LONERGAN**, tailor, 53, born Ireland [*AR*, 2 Apr 1836: Charles **LANIGAN**, age 54, died on 24 March.]

13 Mar 1835   Edward **LONERGAN**, carpenter, 45, Waterford, husband of Elizabeth **KELLY** [*AR*, 14 Mar 1835: died 11 March, age 44.]

 2 Sep 1834   Pierce **LONERGAN**, 17, Tipperary.

27 Feb 1839   William **LONERGAN**, 68, Tipperary.

13 Feb 1822   Thomas **LONWORTH**, 81st. Regt., 27, Inniskillen, Fermanagh.

12 Jul 1827   John **LOUGNAN**, 34, Carlow, "here a few days" [*Ns*, 5 July 1827, reported the arrival that week of the ship *Cumberland* out of Waterford, with "350 passengers."]

 8 Jul 1827   Michael, 8, son of John & Catherine (**MYERS**) **LOWREY**, Ireland, "arrived a short time ago" [*Ns*, 5 July 1827, reported the arrival that week of the ship *Cumberland* out of Waterford, with "350 passengers."]

6 Nov 1829	Thomas **LUCAS**, 35, Waterford [Married 9 May 1823: Thomas, son of John and Margaret **LUCAS** of Aglish, Waterford, to Johanna, dau of James and Hanna (**LARKEY**) **MacKENSY**, Manchester, NS. [StM, Hfx]]
13 Jul 1831	Daniel **LYNARD**, 58, Cork.
12 Nov 1826	John **LYNCH**, 36, Cork
26 Feb 1826	Matthew **LYNCH**, 73, Ireland, 25 years at Ferguson's Cove, NS [*AR*, 5 Feb 1826: died 23 February, leaving a widow and five children.]
27 Oct 1832	Jean **LYNNOX**, 80, Sligo.
9 Oct 1829	Catherine **WHITE**, 43, Kilkenny, wife of Thomas **LYONS** [[Married 21 June 1824: Thomas, son of Patrick and Honora (**MULLOWNEY**) **LYONS** of Newtownhunt [?], Kilkenny, to Catherine, dau of James and Catherine (**PURCELL**) **WHITE** of Callan, Kilkenny, and widow of Thomas **GUINAN**, Halifax. [StM, Hfx]
23 Jan 1830	James **LYONS**, 52, Waterford, husband of Mary **WALSH**.
9 Aug 1837	James **LYONS**, shoemaker, 47, Waterford [*HJ*, 15 Aug 1837: died 7 August.]
5 Mar 1840	Jane **WARREN**, 52, Cork, wife of Thomas **LYONS**.
11 Jul 1826	John **LYONS**, 28, Cork.
20 Oct 1816	John **MacCAFFREY**, seaman, 31, Ireland.
20 Dec 1835	Florence **McCARTHY**, 40, Waterford.
3 Sep 1834	John **McCARTHY**, 40, Cork [*Ns*, 3 Sep 1834: inquest that day on the body of John McCarthy.]
16 Oct 1838	John **McCARTHY**, 45, Cork.
27 Mar 1840	John **McCARTHY**, 45, Cork.
31 May 1834	John, 10, Limerick, son of Pvte. John & Honora **MACLEW**, Rifle Brigade.
23 Aug 1834	Pvte. John **McCLUE**, Rifle Brigade, born Ireland, no age stated.
2 Aug 1837	Anne **McCLUSKY**, "died on ship in the harbour," 30, Armagh. [*Ns*, 3 Aug 1837, reported the arrival that week of the brig *Clitus* from Cork with "106 passengers."]
26 Feb 1838	Elenor **McCORMACK**, 34, Limerick.
7 Jan 1840	Richard **McCORMACK**, 60, Longford.
7 Jan 1822	Pvte. Michael **MacCARTY**, 60th. Regt., 19, Templemore, Cork.
29 Jan 1822	Patrick Peter **MacCARTHY**, tobacconist, 26, Waterford.
30 Oct 1827	John **McCUSKER**, 25, Five Mile Town [Fivemiletown, Clogher Parish], Tyrone; "Came passenger in the brig *Kate*, Webb master, from Barbadoes."
6 Aug 1838	John **McDONALD**, 100, Leix.
18 Jul 1829	Pvte. Michael **MacDONALD**, 96th. Regiment, from Dublin.
7 Oct 1822	Michael **McDONALD**, 36, Kilkenny Town [*AR*: died 5 Oct 1822.]
4 Sep 1827	Patrick **McDONNELL**, 34, Ardmore Parish, Waterford.
26 Oct 1832	Bridget, 2 mos., born Kilkenny, dau of John & Bridget **McEVOY**.
14 May 1835	Nicholas **McEVOY**, 31, born Ireland [*AR*, 16 May 1835: died 12 May, age 27.]
13 Jun 1839	Pvte. James **McGINNIS**, 23rd Regt., 30, Dublin.
8 Aug 1820	Bernard, son of Daniel & Catherine (**DONAHERTY**) **McGORY**, 56, Magherafelt, Derry, and husband of Mary **McKEIVER**. [Died 7 August 1820.]
8 Mar 1837	Andrew **McGOWAN**, carpenter, 21, Sligo [*HJ*, 13 Mar 1837: Andrew **McOWEN**, 20, died on 6 March.]
25 Dec 1839	Andrew **McGOWEN**, 68, Sligo.
2 Apr 1836	Mary **McGOWAN**, 67, Donegal.
18 Sep 1837	Mary Ann, 4, born Ireland [Sligo], dau of Roger & Jane (**ROWLET**) **McGOWAN**.
4 Apr 1828	David **McGRATH**, 30, Ireland.
13 Oct 1830	David **MAGRATH**, 70, Ireland [*AR*, 23 Oct 1830, died 12 Oct.]

13 Apr 1840   David **McGRATH**, 60, Ireland.

20 Oct 1816   Denis **McGRATH**, labourer, 30, Ireland

15 Jan 1822   Edward **McGRATH**, 32, Tipperary

23 Jan 1830   John **McGRATH**, 30, Kilkenny

30 Mar 1830   John **MAGRATH**, 40, Waterford.

4 Jan 1841   Mary **DEVLIN**, 41, born Ireland, widow of John **McGRATH**.

10 Jun 1836   Owen **McGRATH**, 54, Limerick, husband of Eleanor **McCORMACK**.

29 Jan 1837   Patrick, 6, born Cork, son of Dennis & Catherine (**BARRETT**) **McGRATH**.

8 Jan 1837   Philip **McGRATH**, 52, born Ireland [Married 15 July 1821: Philip, son of Philip & Abigail (**CONNOR**) **McGRATH** of Dungarvan, Waterford, to Bridget, dau of Patrick & Catherine (**TATE**) **BARRON** of "Skellins', Wexford. [StM, Hfx] Note by TMP: Tate and Barron are surnames found in Fethard Parish, Wexford.

29 Sep 1827   Thomas **McGRATH**, 47, Thomastown, Kilkenny

31 Oct 1827   Mary **McGUIRE**, 36, Cork.

24 Sep 1834   Michael **McGUIRK**, 40, born Ireland, husband of ... **FINN** [AR, 27 Sep 1834: died 24 Sep. Married 11 Jan 1831: Michael, son of Edward & Catherine (**ROACH**) **McQUIRK**, to Margaret, dau of Anthony & Bridget (**DORAN**) **FINN**, all of Wexford. [StM, Hfx]

14 May 1836   Margaret **BURKE**, Tipperary, widow of Daniel **McINTOSH**.

31 Aug 1830   Thomas **MacIVER**, sailor, 27, Belfast.

26 Jan 1838   William **MACKAY**, 44, Waterford.

6 Jul 1837   Abigail **FALVEY**, 32, Kerry, wife of Michael **McKENNA** [AR, 8 July 1837: died 4 July, age 31, leaving husband and 3 children. Married 24 Sep 1829: Michael, son of James & Margaret (**BLANY**) **McKENNA** of Tralee, Kerry, to Abigail, dau of John & Honora (**FERRIS**) **FALVEY** of Lissavane, (Parish of Kilbonane), Kerry.][StM, Hfx]

9 Aug 1834   Pvte, John **McKENNA**, 9rth Regt., 30, born Ireland.

23 Dec 1832   Lewis **McLOUGHLIN**, 23, born Ireland [AR, 22 Dec 1832: died 21 Dec, age 22.]

19 Dec 1836   Pvte. John **McMAHON**, 85th Regt, 25, Meath.

11 Sep 1839   Mary **MOONEY**, 33, born Ireland [Waterford], wife of Michael **McMAHON**.

8 May 1817   Lt. Terrence **McMAHON**, 60th. Regt., -, Ireland

4 May 1828   James **McNAMARA**, 35, Waterford; 'He died on his passage from Newfoundland.'

18 Oct 1822   Patrick **MacNISBOTH**, drummer, 62nd. Regt., 27, Donegal.

20 Feb 1833   Anne, 4, born Mayo, dau of Roger & Mary (**EARLY**) **McNULTY**.

16 Sep 1829   Michael **McNULTY**, 20, Rosemore [Ross More], Leitrim.

12 Apr 1840   Daniel **McSWEENY**, 45, born Ireland [AR, 11 Apr 1840: died 10 April, age 40. Married 15 Jun 1825: Daniel, son of Terence **McSWINEY** of Parish of Farlavis (Fanlobbus?), Cork, to Jane, dau of Henry & Jane (**REED**) **MacGILPIN** of Drownmore (Dromore, Parish of Layd), Antrim, and widow of James **O'RATH** (**O'RAW**). [StM, Hfx]

26 Dec 1822   James **MACKEY**, 60, Ross, Wexford [Halifax Free Press, 31 Dec 1822: died 24 Dec, leaving a widow and four small children, and that he had long been a resident of Halifax, NS.]

25 May 1840   John **MACKEY**, 37, Waterford [NS Royal Gazette, 27 May 1840: died 23 May, age 36, born in the Parish of Windgap, Kilkenny (sic).]

3 Oct 1834   Mary, 6, born Kilkenny, dau of Patrick & Eleanor (**DENIEF**) **MACKEY**.

19 Feb 1836   Patrick **MACKEY**, 45, Kilkenny, husband of Elenor **DENIEFE**.

20 Jan 1821   Mary, 28 [wife of William] **MAGHER**, dau of John & Mary [**FINN**] **CUMMINGS**, [Tipperary.]

24 Feb 1832   Michael **MAGHER**, Dartmouth, 40, born Ireland.

27 May 1825   Pvte. Henry, 38, 81st. Regiment, son of Henry **MAGILL**, gardener to Lord **O'NEIL**, Change Castle, Antrim.

16 Feb 1819   Anne **RYAN**, wife of Cornelius **MAGNION**, 37, Lismore, Waterford.

9 Sep 1834   Catherine **NOLAN**, 40, Kilkenny, widow of Michael **MAHER** [AR, 13 Sep 1834: died 9 Sep, age 42, leaving 4 children.]

5 Oct 1828   John **MAHER**, constable, 38, Castlecomer, Kilkenny [AR, 4 Oct 1828: died 2 Oct.]

18 Sep 1825   Michael **MAHER**, 33, Killenaule, Tipperary.

8 Nov 1841   Michael **MAHER**, baker, 36, Kilkenny [Married 5 Oct 1833: Michael, son of Andrew & Bridget (**PURCELL**) **MAGHER** of Tipperary, to Catherine, dau of ...... & Joanna (**WALSH**) **MORISSY** of Kilkenny. [StM, Hfx]

20 Sep 1838   Patrick **MAHER**, 50, Carlow, husband of Catherine **PHELAN** [AR, 22 Sep 1838: Patrick **MAHAR**, age 58.]

7 Feb 1842   Patrick **MAHER**, seafarer, 62, Kilkenny.

11 Dec 1839   Thomas **MAHER**, tailor, 80, born Ireland.

27 Jan 1842   John **MAHONEY**, 45, born Ireland.

7 Sep 1820   Edward **MAHONY**, 50, Tipperary

5 Oct 1829   Mary, 7, Cork, dau of William & Honora (**HARRINGTON**) **MAHONY**

23 Dec 1832   Mary **MAHONY**, 56, Cork.

5 Sep 1837   Mary **MAHONY**, 30, Waterford.

18 Nov 1841   Mary **MAHONY**, 82, born Ireland.

21 Jun 1827   Michael **MAHONEY**, 28, Waterford City

29 Oct 1827   Michael **MAHONY**, 17, Innishannon Parish, Cork

19 Apr 1825   Thomas **MAHONY**, 60, Dingle, Kerry.

2- Dec 1818   William **MALLEN**, 70, Ireland. [AR, 26 Dec 1818: James **MALLAN** died 25 Dec.]

4 Sep 1834   Sgt. Mjr. Charles B. **MALLOY**, 96th Regt., 44, Longford.

15 Nov 1837   George **MALLOY**, carpenter, 65, Wexford [HJ, 13 Nov 1837: died 13 Nov.]

4 Dec 1826   Pvte. Patrick **MALOWNEY**, 52nd. Regiment, 32, Roscommon Town.

28 Jan 1840   Eleanor **MANNING**, 35, Cork [Married 22 Nov 1824: John, son of William & Mary (**HARRINGTON**) **MANNING** of Cloyne, Cork, to Eleanor, dau of James & Mary (**WALSH**) **LYONS** of Halifax. [StM, Hfx]

8 Jan 1840   Mrs. .... **MANNING**, 70, Cork.

6 Mar 1834   Peter **MANNING**, 30, Cork, husband of Mary **FITZGERALD** [AR, 8 Mar 1834: died 1 March, age 39.]

11 Aug 1819   Thomas **MARA**, 33, Tipperary   [a coach maker], husband of Ann **DALTON**.

4 Apr 1832   Thomas **MARLIN**, 72, Tipperary.

20 Mar 1821   Edward **MARRAGH**, 86, husband of Elizabeth **WILLIAMS**, Ireland [HJ 19 Mar 1821: died 17 March, E. **MARA**, 49]

27 Aug 1826   Margaret **MARTIN**, 76, Ireland; here many years

18 Nov 1829   Catherine **RILEY**, 40, Cork, wife of John **MATHIAS**

7 Aug 1828   John **MAY**, 44, Longford, husband of Jane **DONNELLY**

12 Jul 1827   John **MEANEY**, 40, husband of Mary **CARROLL**, Brownstown, Kilkenny.

12 Jul 1827   Richard, 13, son of John & Mary (**CARROLL**) **MEANEY**, Brownstown, Kilkenny.

23 Aug 1835   David **MEEHAN**, carpenter, 45, Tipperary.

8 Nov 1840   Catherine **MIHAN**, 36, Kilkenny [AR, 7 Nov 1840: Miss **MIHAN** died 6 Nov, age 33.]

9 Apr 1802   John **MILLER**, 45, Top [?], Wexford

10 Jan 1830   Pierce **MINNS**, 30, Ireland, at the Poor House.

5 Dec 1831   James **MOLONY**, mason, 40, born Ireland.

22 Aug 1834   Pvte. Michael **MONTAGUE**, Rifle Brigade, 30, born Ireland.
27 Dec 1829   Edward **MOORE**, shoemaker, 23, Edgeworthtown, Longford.
16 Jun 1826   Edmond, 3, son of John & Margaret (**ROWNAN**) **MORRIS**, "lately from Ireland."
14 Jun 1826   Johanna **CREAMER**, 36, wife of Richard **MORRISEY**, Ireland [Cork] [*AR*, 17 Jun 1826, says that she died on 13 June, age 35, and was formerly Mrs. **HOLLAHAN**, and left four children.
22 May 1816   James, 32, son of John **MORRISSEY**, Waterford.
2 Sep 1834   Mary **RUTHLEDGE,** 45, Waterford, wife of Robert **MOUNTAIN**.
24 Nov 1835   Margaret **WASHINGTON**, 33, Kilkenny, wife of Thomas **MULCAHY** [Married 31 Aug 1827: Thomas, son of Thomas & Joanna (**FORD**) **MULCAHY** of Waterford City, to Margaret, dau of Patrick & Mary (**RICE**) **WASHINGTON** of Poorstown [Powerstown], Kilkenny.   [StM, Hfx]
16 Sep 1831   Thomas **MULHALL**, 35, Kilbeacon, Kildare.
21 Aug 1834   Pvte. James **MULHOLLAND**, Rifle Brigade, 40, born Ireland.
2 Feb 1837   Pvte. Michael **MULLIGAN**, 85th Regt., 30, Leitrim.
26 Dec 1800   - - - - **MULLINS**, 95, Ireland.
11 Jul 1822   John **MULLOY** of Mahone Bay, NS, 37, Wexford [husband of Eliza **ANKNEY**]
20 Jan 1827   Robert **MURDOCH**, 80, Sligo
9 Apr 1825   Andrew **MURPHY**, truckman, 45, Wexford
26 Mar 1830   Bridget, 35, Cóbh, Cork, wife of John **MURPHY**
26 Apr 1829   Catherine **CASEY**, 41, Kilkenny, wife of Patrick **MURPHY**.
8 Aug 1839   Catherine **MURPHY**, 18, Cork.
6 Jan 1828   Gerald **MURPHY**, 49, Limerick
15 Aug 1824   Henry **MURPHY** of Shubenacadie River, NS, 33, Carlow; "was killed by a bull on 13 August."
1 Nov 1837   Henry **MURPHY**, 22, born Ireland [*Times*, 31 Oct 1837: died 30 Oct.]
22 Nov 1817   James **MURPHY**, 32, Ross, Wexford
8 Aug 1821   James **MURPHY**, 52, Timahoe, Leix
24 Jul 1830   James **MURPHY**, 56, Cork, husband of Juliana **SULLIVAN**
5 Oct 1829   John **MURPHY**, carpenter, 45, Wexford
30 Dec 1829   John **MURPHY**, 45, Wexford, husband of Susanna **BOWEN** [Married, 25 Nov 1823: John, cooper, son of Daniel & Bridget (**COADY**) **MURPHY** of Rosegarland, Wexford, to Susanna, dau of Richard & Susanna (**GLEESON**) **BOWEN** of Chester, NS. [StM, Hfx]
6 Dec 1835   John **MURPHY**, 50, waterford, husband of Mary **POWER**.
20 Mar 1816   Mark **MURPHY**, innkeeper, 66, husband of Anne **SMITH**, Ireland [*AR*, 23 Mar 1816: died 18 March, age 63, leaving 9 children.]
4 Jan 1833   Mary **BRADY**, 40, Cork, wife of Maurice **MURPHY**.
4 Sep 1837   Mary **POWER**, 54, Wexford, widow of John **MURPHY**.
25 Mar 1840   Maurice **MURPHY**, 40, Cork.
30 Jun 1821   Michael **MURPHY**, Ordnance Dept., 50, Wexford.
29 Jun 1835   Michael **MURPHY**, 30, Wexford, drowned at Dartmouth [*HJ*, 29 June 1835: drowned on 27 June.]
23 May 1838   Pvte. Michael **MURPHY**, 65th Regt., 32, Meath.
20 Apr 1831   Patrick **MURPHY**, 50, Carlow.
8 Dec 1822   Simon **MURPHY**, 32, Ballyhail, Kilkenny
2 Oct 1827   Thomas **MURPHY**, truckman, 35, Kilkenny; here many years.
28 Jul 1840   William **MURPHY**, 40, born Ireland.

12 Oct 1820	Catherine **MURRAY**, 49, Wexford.
22 Sep 1834	Jane **GRIFFIN**, 76, Offaly, widow of Mathew **MURRAY** [*Times*, 23 Sep 1834: died 21 Sep, age 75.]
9 Mar 1837	Johanna **GLEESON**, 35, Limerick, wife of Patrick **MURRAY**, 85th Regt.
12 May 1840	Benjamin **MURTAGH**, pensioner of 8th Regt., 68, born Ireland.
9 Jan 1828	Patrick **MYLONE**, about 50, Wexford
23 Jun 1828	John **NEAGH**, about 40, Clo[g]heen, Tipperary, husband of Mary **WHITE**
4 Jan 1819	Richard **NEIL**, 35, Carlow
7 Nov 1829	Patrick **NEWMAN**, carpenter, 32, Cork [*AR*, 7 Nov 1829, reported this death on 5 Nov, and gives his age as 37.]
15 Mar 1820	Patrick, son of Stephen & Mary **(MYLAN) NEWPORT**, 27, New Ross, Wexford.
2 Jan 1837	Margaret **WALSH**, 31, Wexford, wife of Isaac **NEWTON**.
3 Jan 1830	Catherine **NOLAN**, "long of Halifax", 99 [*AR*, 2 Jan 1830, says she came from Ireland, and died on 2 January.]
3 Oct 1827	Thomas **NORRISS**, 25, Caher, Tipperary, "found drowned in this Harbour."
30 Jan 1823	Patrick **NORTON**, 47, Dublin [*AR*, 1 Feb 1823, reported an inquest held 29 Jan 1823 on Norton's body, at Preston, NS. Ruled accidental death.]
8 Jul 1838	Edward **NOWLAN**, 31, Wicklow, husband of Elizabeth **KAVENAH** [Married 12 Oct 1828: Edward, son of John & Elenor **(BURNS) NOWLAN,** to Elizabeth, dau of Denis & Mary **KAVANAH** of Carlow. Halifax Catholic record.]
19 Jul 1841	Patrick **NOWLAN**, 32, Carlow, husband of Elenor **BROPHY** [*AR*, 24 Jul 1841: died 18 July, leaving a widow and small family. Married 18 June 1834: Patrick, son of Garret & Anastasia **(HENISSY) NOLAN**, to Ellen, dau of Michael & Ellen **(McSWEENEY) BROPHY**, all of Carlow. [StM, Hfx]
22 Aug 1834	Bridget **RUSSELL**, 33, Tipperary, wife of John **O'BRIEN** [*AR*, 23 Aug 1834: died 21 Aug, age 32, leaving husband and 5 children. Married 25 Aug 1823: John, son of Michael & Mary **(WALSH) O'BRIEN**, to Bridget, dau of Philip & Margaret **(GORMAN) O'BRIEN**, all of "Templetrim" (?), Tipperary. [StM, Hfx]
12 Jan 1836	John **O'BRIEN**, 40, Tipperary, widower of Bridget **RUSSELL** [*AR*, 16 Jan 1836: died 10 Jan, age 37, "left five children without a relative in America."]
17 Feb 1834	Daniel **O'BRIEN**, 40, Cork, husband of Mary **GARRIGAN**.
11 Sep 1834	Daniel, 7, born Cork, son of Daniel & Bridget **(McCARTHY) O'BRIEN**.
6 Sep 1834	Elenor **HAYES**, 35, Kilkenny, wife of Michael **O'BRIEN**, 96th Regt.
13 Oct 1820	Elizabeth **O'BRIEN**, 18, Cork.
2 May 1831	Grace [**RYAN**], 34, Tipperary, wife of John **O'BRIEN**, Work House [*AR*, 30 Apr 1831: died 30 April, age 33.]
12 Jan 1833	John **O'BRIEN**, 27, husband of Eliza **MURPHY** [*AR*, 11 Jan 1833: hairdresser, died 9 Jan. Married 17 Apr 1831: John, son of Timothy & Julia **(BROWN) O'BRIEN** of Youghal, Cork, to Eliza, dau of Arthur & Rebecca **(McCARTHY) MURPHY** of Killigrew (?), Wexford. [StM, Hfx]
3 Mar 1834	John **O'BRIEN**, 45, [Cork], husband of Juliana **BROWN,** and widower of Grace **RYAN** [*AR*, 8 Mar 1834: died 1 March, age 44. Married 19 Feb 1833: John, son of John **O'BRIEN** & Mary **EVANS**, Co. Cork, and widower of Grace RYAN, Halifax, to Johanna **BROWN**, Youghal, Co. Cork, widow of Timothy **O'BRIEN**, Saint John, NB. [StM, Hfx]
23 Aug 1821	Joseph **O'BRIEN**, 39, Clare
15 Jan 1828	Mary **DOYLE**, 33, wife of James **O'BRIEN**, Thomastown Parish, Kilkenny.
9 May 1840	Mary **TAPPAN**, 45, born Ireland, wife of [John] **O'BRIEN**.

8 Nov 1833   Owen **O'BRIEN**, 75, Tipperary.

29 Apr 1834   William **O'BRIEN**, 24, Waterford.

2 Apr 1834   Bridget **BROWN**, 35, Kilkenny, wife of Hugh **O'CONNOR**.

17 Jul 1835   Bridget **WHELAN**, 37, Kilkenny, wife of Michael **O'CONNOR**.

30 Apr 1826   Denis **O'CONNORS**, tailor, 76, [Abbeyfail?] Wexford [*AR*, 29 Apr 1826, reported the death, on 27 April, of Dennis **O'CONNOR**, age 75]

10 Nov 1828   John **O'CONNOR**, schoolmaster, 30, Limerick.

1 Sep 1834   John **O'CONNOR**, 60, Tipperary.

3 Nov 1839   Thomas **O'CONNOR**, pilot in the harbour, 55, born Ireland.

30 Apr 1837   John **O'DELL**, 72, Waterford [*AR*, 29 Apr 1837: died 28 April, age 79.]

29 Jun 1837   Bridget **O'BRIEN**, 40, Carlow, wife of John **O'DONNELL**.

23 Aug 1834   John **O'DONNELL**, 27, born Ireland.

29 Aug 1834   Pierce **O'DONNEL**, 37, Tipperary, husband of Mary **MANDEVILLE**.

10 Jul 1833   Rose **MAGUIRE**, 35, Donegal, wife of Anthony **O'DONNELL**.

21 Nov 1824   Margaret, 50, wife of Patrick **O'HERE**, Northern Ireland

18 Dec 1828   Patrick **O'HARE**, 54, Down [*AR*, 20 Dec 1828: died 16 December]

21 Apr 1825   Pvte. Thomas **OLLIVE**, 81st. Regiment, 30, Dublin City.

1 Sep 1834   Peter **O'MEALY**, 25, Mayo, husband of Mary **McALLY**.

28 Sep 1824   Elizabeth [**BUTLER**], 33, [Kilkenny], wife of Henry **O'NEIL** [*AR*, 2 Oct 1824: died 27 Sep.]

24 Aug 1824   Ann [**DARCY**], 40, Leix, wife of James **O'ROURKE** [*AR*, 28 Aug 1824: died 23 Aug]

3 Oct 1834   Bridget **O'ROURKE**, 20, Carlow.

6 Feb 1834   Felix **O'ROURKE**, 30, Sligo, husband of Joanna **MULONY**.

5 Oct 1834   John **O'ROURKE**, carpenter, 45, Carlow.

22 Mar 1837   Pvte, John **ORRIGAN** [O'Regan?], 85th Regt., 30, Limerick.

27 Mar 1833   Francis **OSBORN**, 24, Waterford.

28 Jul 1833   Sarah **CURRAN**, 22, Kildare, wife of James **OWENES**.

6 Jan 1828   Mary **PARRY**, 52, Wexford

21 Sep 1826   Eleanor, 61, wife of John **PATTERSON**, Cóbh, Cork [*AR*, 23 Sep 1826: Mrs. Ellen Patterson died 19 September, age 59.]

29 Oct 1836   Catherine **POWER**, 31, Waterford, wife of John **PAYNE** [Married 8 Nov 1835: John, son of James & Margaret (**FLANIGAN**) **PAINE**, of Tara, Meath, to Catherine, dau of Richard & Mary **POWER** of Waterford. [StM, Hfx]

27 Jul 1832   Mary [**RYAN**], "50 yrs. in Halifax" [born Waterford], widow of Capt. [Thomas] **PEMBERTON**.

23 Aug 1838   Anne **O'NEIL**, 30, Carlow, wife of Michael **PENDERGAST** [*AR*, 24 Aug 1838: died 22 Aug, Ann, 26, wife of Michael **PENDER**, leaving husband and 2 children.]

10 May 1821   Lawrence **PENDER**, brewer, 40, Carlow [*AR*, 12 May 1821: died 8 May, age 39.]

15 Jul 1831   John **PENDERGAST**, 48, Wexford [*AR*, 16 July 1831: died 13 July, age 46.]

11 May 1831   Michael **PENDERGAST**, 64, Kilkenny [*AR*, 14 May 1831, age 67.]

5 Jul 1829   Redmond **PHARISY**, 46, Youghal, Cork

8 May 1824   James **PHELAN**, 28, Waterford City, nephew of John **PHELAN** of the Town   6 Kilkenny, who educated him.

16 Jan 1840   Mary **PHELAN**, 60, Carlow.

28 May 1837   Maurice **PHELAN**, 65, Kilkenny.

16 Jun 1836   William **PHELAN**, 46, Tipperary, husband of Mary **WALL** [*AR*, 25 June 1836: died 16 June, age 45.]

14 Jan 1831   Thomas **PIERCE**, 30, Wexford.

25 Nov 1839	Catherine **POWELE**, 45, Tipperary [*Times*, 26 Nov 1839: widow of Thomas **POWELL**, died 24 Nov, leaving 7 children.]
7 Mar 1829	Ann, 16, Kilmacthomas, Waterford, dau of Lawrence & Catherine **POWER**, sister of Mrs. Philip **RYAN** of Halifax [*Ns*, 12 Mar 1829: died 4 Mar, age 15]
8 Oct 1826	Catherine, 63, died on 7 October, wife of Richard **POWER**, 75, who died on morning of 7 October, both of Kilkenny [*cf., AR,* 14 Oct 1826]
31 Aug 1830	Eleanor **TOBIN**, 30, Kilkenny, wife of Nicholas **POWER**.
24 Dec 1818	George **POWER**, husband of Johanna **POWER**, 49, Ireland [He died on 22 Dec 1818, and came from Kill St. Lawrence, Waterford.]
7 May 1833	James **POWER**, 40, Kilkenny.
13 Jan 1840	Mary **DWYER**, 30, Tipperary, wife of John **POWER** [Married 12 Dec 1837: John, son of James & Mary **POWER,** of Waterford, to Mary, dau of James & Judith (**CUMMINS**) **DWYER**, of Tipperary, widow of Patrick **HINESSY**. Halifax record.]
12 Dec 1841	John **POWER**, seafarer, 30 [*AR*, 18 Dec 1841: Capt. John **POWER** died 11 Dec, age 29. His wife, Sarah, 29, buried 5 Dec 1841. Married 7 Jan 1832: Capt John son of George & Joanna (**POWER**) **POWER**, of [Kill St. Lawrence], Waterford, to Sarah, dau of Henry & Anne (**BURRIDGE**) **BURDETT**, of Plymouth, England. [StM, Hfx]
14 Nov 1820	Martin, son of John & Margaret **POWER**, 27, Waterford
25 Jul 1824	Michael **POWER**, 70, Waterford.
22 Sep 1841	Michael **POWER**, 40, Waterford, husband of Anne **LONERGAN**.
15 Mar 1820	Patrick, son of James & Margaret (**EGAN**) **POWER**, 29, Templeorum, Kilkenny.
3 Jan 1834	Patrick **POWER**, 44, Waterford, husband of Eleanor **VALE**.
3 Dec 1816	Peter **POWER**, husband of Eleanor . . ., 30, Ireland.
1 Jan 1825	Pierce **POWER**, 27, Passage, Waterford
23 Sep 1825	Richard **POWER**, 85, Waterford
6 Jan 1830	Thomas **POWER**, 30, Waterford, husband of Abigail **DROGHAN**.
17 Dec 1832	Thomas **POWER**, 38, Waterford [*HJ*, 17 Dec 1832: Power left widow, 6 children.]
16 Sep 1834	Thomas **POWER**, carpenter, 45, Waterford.
22 Nov 1823	Capt. William **POWER**, 59, [Waterford] [*AR*, 27 Nov 1824: died 20 Nov, leaving 7 children.]
2 Oct 1836	Mary **PURCELL**, 36, Tipperary.
10 Jul 1827	Philip **PURCELL**, 65, Tipperary [*AR*, 14 July 1827: died 8 July. Married 5 Oct 1800: Philip Purcell, to Sophia J. **KIDDY** (dau of William & Magdalena {**HALTER**} **KEDDY** of Lunenburg), Nova Scotia. [StM, Hfx]
30 Jun 1825	Michael **QUHOE [KEHOE]**, 36, St. Mary's, New Ross, Wexford
17 Mar 1828	Thomas **QUIGLEY**, 35, Ireland.
29 Apr 1841	James **QUINLAN**, 60, Waterford [*AR*, 1 May 1841: died 27 April, age 59.]
4 Sep 1830	Edward **QUINN**, 61, Kilkenny, husband of Mary **MESSER**.
1 Dec 1833	Edward C. **QUINN**, born Ireland [*AR*, 30 Nov 1833: died 29 Nov, age 48.]
25 Oct 1829	Michael **QUINN**, 23, Kilkenny.
30 Jan 1820	Michael, son of Jeremiah & Anne (**DEE**) **QUIRK**, 32, Rose Green [Tullamain Parish], Tipperary.
11 Dec 1834	Mary **BRADY**, 34, Meath, wife of Richard **REA**.
25 Jan 1840	Catherine **DREA**, 44, Kilkenny, wife of Michael **REID**.
11 Apr 1837	Bridget **READE, 24,** Kilkenny.
5 Jul 1822	Daniel **READY** of Preston, NS, 75, Kilkenny.
1 Feb 1826	Edward **REARDON**, police constable in Halifax for 4 years, 30, Thurles, Tipperary.
20 Apr 1830	Catherine **POWER**, 67, Waterford, wife of Thomas **REDIGAN**.

13 Jul 1827	Eliza, 10 mos, dau of Thomas & Margaret (**NARY**) **REED**, Ireland, "here a few days" [*Ns*, 5 July 1827, reported the arrival that week of the ship *Cumberland* out of Waterford, with "350 passengers."]
21 Sep 1837	John **REGAN**, 34, Cork.
7 Oct 1827	Michael **REILY**, 78, Ireland, "many years in this town" [husband of Mary **UHLMAN**.]
15 Sep 1834	Christopher **REYNOLDS**, 38, Sligo, husband of Alice **DUNPHY**.
18 Aug 1837	Henry **RICHARDSON**, 20, Tipperary.
10 Sep 1837	John **RICHARDSON**, 50, Tipperary.
16 Oct 1833	John **RIVELL**, 25, Wexford.
29 Dec 1828	Pvte. Patrick **ROBBINS**, 96th. Regiment, 24, Leix.
8 Dec 1841	Michael **ROBINSON**, carpenter, 69, Leix [*HJ*, 13 Dec 1841: *Nicholas* **ROBINSON** *died 5 Dec, age 66*.]
21 Oct 1820	Moses **ROCH**, 60, Wexford.
29 May 1837	Francis **ROCHE**, 22, born Ireland.
5 Nov 1837	Thomas **ROCHE**, ship carpenter, 45, Cork.
21 Jan 1837	Mary **QUINN**, 32, Waterford, wife of Patrick **RONAYNE** [Married 10 Feb 1831: Patrick, son of Michael & Mary (**McCARTHY**) **RONAYNE**, to Mary, dau of Michael & Catherine (**WALSH**) **QUINN** , all of Waterford. [StM, Hfx]
25 Jun 1840	Catherine **SLATTERY**, 45, Limerick, wife of James **RORKE**.
21 Jan 1827	Edward **ROURKE**, 40, Wexford [His wife was Mary **McCALLUM**, Dartmouth.]
31 Aug 1827	Francis **ROURKE,** 60, Carlow.
6 Aug 1834	Mary **ROSEMAN**, 60, Westmeath.
7 May 1840	Anne **ELWARD**, 30, Kilkenny, wife of John **RYAN** [Married 19 Sep 1829: John, son of Thomas & Joanna (**RYAN**) **RYAN**, to Anastasia, dau of John & Mary (**MAGRATH**) **ELWART**, all of Kilkenny. [StM, Hfx]
31 Jul 1833	Catherine **NOLAN**, 44, Kilkenny, wife of Richard **RYAN**.
3 Jun 1840	Catherine, 30, born Ireland, wife of William **RYAN**.
10 Feb 1825	Edward **RYAN**, drowned, 38, Roseborough [?], Tipperary [*AR*, 12 Feb 1825: inquest, 9 February, on the bodies of Dennis **HAYS** and Edward **RYAN**, found drowned.]
30 Sep 1833	Edward **RYAN**, 100, Tipperary [*AR*, 28 Sep 1833: died 28 Sep.]
27 Apr 1833	Ellen, 1 yr., born Tipperary, dau of Michael & Mary (**RICE**) **RYAN**.
2 Sep 1825	James **RYAN**, 44, Templemichael, Waterford.
11 Dec 1832	James **RYAN**, 27, Kilkenny, husband of Margaret **MAGRATH**.
9 Jan 1819	John **RYAN**, 35, Kilkenny
16 Jan 1823	John, 28, son of Rodger & Mary (**HALLERAN**) **RYAN**, Parish of Clerehen [Curraheen, Ballymurreen Parish], Tipperary [*AR*, 20 Jan 1823: died 14 Jan, age 27]
30 Jun 1823	John **RYAN**, 52, Thurles, Tipperary
14 Jun 1816	Martin **RYAN**, 55, Waterford
5 Feb 1824	Mary [**CULLEN**], 24, wife of Pierce **RYAN**, tailor, [Carlow]
3 Mar 1839	Margaret **PEMBROKE**, 40, Kilkenny, wife of John **RYAN**.
3 Jul 1826	Michael **RYAN**, 26, Passage, Waterford.
21 Jan 1831	Patrick **RYAN**, 45, Cork.
28 Aug 1832	Thomas **RYAN**, mason [Kilkenny], husband of Elizabeth **EEDS** [This entry is repeated with date 10 March 1833, with the same details, but no explanation.]
2 Dec 1839	Timothy **RYAN**, victualler, 44, Tipperary.
1 Mar 1819	Charles **RYLY**, husband of Elizabeth **GRANT**, 37, Cavan

26 Sep 1820   Andrew **RYNE**, 32, Kilkenny.

22 Jun 1834   Bernard **SAUL**, butcher, 46, born [Clonmel], Tipperary [*AR*, 21 Jun 1834: *Barnaby* **SAUL** died 21 June, age 45.]

22 Feb 1832   John **SCALLION**, 40, Wexford.

21 Aug 1826   Robert **SCANDLAN**, 46 Galway Town, drowned at Dartmouth, NS [*AR*, 26 Aug 1826, refers to the inquest on the body of Robert **SCANDLING** on 20 August.]

12 Mar 1837   Margaret, 12, born Ireland, dau of John & Bridget **SCULLY**.

30 Mar 1824   John **SCURY** [**SKERRY**], 63, Ireland.

21 Aug 1824   Peter **SCURY** , 28, died at Dartmouth, NS, born Knocktopher, Kilkenny, but raised in Waterford [*AR*, 21 Aug 1824, reported an inquest held on the body of Peter **SKERRY** on 20 Aug.]

25 Jun 1833   Margaret **BYRNE**, 25, Tipperary, wife of Michael **SHANIHAN**.

30 Sep 1836   Mary, 8, born Waterford, dau of Michael & Margaret (**BYRNES**) **SHANAHAN**.

13 Feb 1839   Pvte. J. **SHAUGHNESSY**, 36th Regt., born Ireland.

23 Apr 1838   David **SHEA**, 54, Tipperary, husband of Mary Ann **McGRATH**.

9 Jan 1842   Joanna, 44, wife of William **SHEA** and widow of Thomas **POWER** [Married 31 Oct 1833: William, son of Richard & Bridget (**HEFFERNAN**) **SHEA** of Mullinahone, Tipperary, to Joanna, dau of Richard & Catherine (**DELANEY**) **WALSH** of Windgap, Kilkenny, and widow of Thomas **POWER** of Halifax. [StM, Hfx]

29 May 1839   Mary Ann **McGRATH**, 50, born Ireland [Tipperary], widow of David **SHEA**.

2 Sep 1834   Patrick **SHEA**, 35, Cork, husband of Mary **O'BRIEN**.

20 Dec 1826   Catherine, 32, wife of William **SHEEHAN**, Cóbh, Cork

5 Mar 1824   Edmond **SHEHAN**, 38, Kilcash, Tipperary

12 Apr 1824   Edmond **SHEEHAN**, 30, Ireland, "here four years"

4 Oct 1825   Bridget **KEHOE**, 36, wife of Philip **SHELLY**, Thomastown, Kilkenny

27 Jun 1828   Philip **SHELLY**, 40, Waterford, husband of the late Bridget **KEHOE**.

28 Aug 1834   Martin **SHINE**, 40, Tipperary, husband of Margaret **O'CONNOR**.

27 May 1829   William **SHORTLE**, 35, Thomastown, Kilkenny, husband of Mary **MAGHER** [*AR*, 30 May 1829: died 25 May.]

23 Sep 1822   James **SKALLY**, 26, Churchtown Parish, Westmeath.

26 Feb 1840   Pvte. J. **SLATTERY**, 37th Regt., born Ireland.

2 Nov 1823   Francis **SMITH**, "dead of intoxication", 45, Dublin.

4 Nov 1832   Margaret, 10 wks., born Kilkenny, dau of John & Catherine (**WHELAN**) **SMITH**.

15 Jun 1836   Margaret **LEARY**, 35, born Ireland, wife of Michael **SMITH**, 83rd Regt.

29 Feb 1836   Michael **SMITH**, 52, Fermanagh.

27 Dec 1836   Thomas **SMITH**, 32, Wexford [*AR*, 31 Dec 1836: died 25 Dec, age 31.]

8 Aug 1825   Judy, 6 months, dau of Charles **SOLOVAN**, Bantry Bay, Kerry.

6 Apr 1834   Thomas **SPENCE**, 50, Waterford.

29 May 1821   William **SPENCE**, 70, Ireland [Waterford.]

2 Feb 1830   Honora **O'DONOHOE**, 29, Ireland, wife of [Cpl] William **SPIERS**, Royal Artillery.

22 Dec 1820   Michael **SPROUGHAN**, 35, Thomastown, Kilkenny.

12 Jan 1831   Mary **SPRUGHEN**, 19, Kilkenny.

25 Aug 1836   Edward **SPRUHAN**, 36, Kilkenny, husband of Margaret **DUNNE** [Married 22 Jan 1829: Edward, son of Thomas & Mary (**CODY**) **SPRUHAN** of Thomastown, Kilkenny, to Margaret, dau of Michael & Ann (**HAMMON**) **DUNN** of Gowran, Kilkenny. [StM, Hfx]

9 Jun 1839   James **SPRUHAN**, 50, Kilkenny, husband of Mary **RYAN** [*AR*, 8 Jun 1839: died 7 June, age 48, leaving a widow and 5 children. He had been 13 years in Halifax.]

29 Mar 1834	Walter **SPRUHAN**, 40, husband of Bridget **McLEAN** [Married 21 Feb 1830: Walter, son of Thomas & Mary (**WHELAN**) **SPRUHAN** of Kilkenny, to Bridget, dau of Michael & Bridget (**NEILL**) **McLEAN** of Wexford. [StM, Hfx]
3 Feb 1819	Eleanor, widow of James **STACK**, 30, dau. of Thomas & Mary [**SCANNEL**] **KEEFE** [Castlelyons, Cork]
13 Sep 1818	James **STACK**, innkeeper, husband of Eleanor **KEEFE**, 46, [Tralee, Kerry]
23 Jun 1829	Mathew **STACK**, pedlar, 52, Ballygiblin [Parish of Castlemagner], Cork.
11 Sep 1836	Thomas **STAFFORD**, 32, Cork, husband of Mary [Married 30 July 1833: Thomas, son of John & Juliana (**MANNING**) **STAFFORD**, of Cork, to Mary, dau of Patrick & Joanna (**POWER**) **WARD**, of Waterford. [StM, Hfx]
25 Mar 1816	Thomas **STAPLETON,** mason, 75, Ireland [Tipperary]
7 Nov 1827	Thomas **STAPLETON**, 65, Mullinahone Parish, Tipperary
6 Jul 1827	William **STAPLETON**, 32, Ballynakill, Leix.
17 Aug 1825	James **STEPHENSON**, 27, Mountfadd [Monfad, All Saints], Donegal.
15 Mar 1841	William **STONE**, 39, born Ireland [Kilkenny], husband of Mary Ann **BASELY**.
19 Sep 1837	Mary **McCLUSKEY**, 35, Derry, wife of John **STUART**.
31 Aug 1834	Anne, 8, Cork, dau of Dennis & Anne **SULLIVAN**.
16 Jul 1827	Cornelius **SULLIVAN**, 35, Bantry, Cork, two years at Dartmouth, NS, and left a wife and two children [married, 22 June 1824, at St. Paul's Anglican Church, Cornelius Sullivan and Jane **HALL**.]
24 Jan 1841	Pvte. Daniel **SULLIVAN**, 37th Regt., 23, born Ireland.
27 Aug 1834	James **SULLIVAN**, 23, Cork.
2 Jun 1828	John **SULLIVAN**, 40, Cork.
22 Jul 1838	John **SULLIVAN**, 95, Cork.
15 Oct 1839	John **SULLIVAN**, pensioner, 50, Ireland [*Times*, 15 Oct 1839: died 14 Oct, age 69.]
24 Aug 1829	Margaret **HARRINGTON**, 26, Cork, wife of James **SULLIVAN**, pedlar.
12 Sep 1834	Mary **McDONALD**, 27, Kilkenny, wife of John **SULLIVAN**.
30 Aug 1834	Michael, 10, Tipperary, son of John & Mary (**HARDY**) **SULLIVAN**.
27 Mar 1822	Patrick, 5 yrs., son of Robert & Anne (**GEARY**) **SULLIVAN**, Waterford.
28 Oct 1838	Thomas **SULLIVAN**, 52, born Ireland, husband of ....
26 Sep 1840	Timothy **SULLIVAN**, painter, 25 [Married 20 Oct 1839: Timothy, son of Bartholomew & Catherine (**DONEGAN**) **SULLIVAN**, of Cork, to Catherine, dau of Patrick & Joanna (**McCARTHY**) **O'NEILL**. [StM, Hfx]
4 Jan 1837	Thomas **SUTTON**, 79 [*AR*, 7 Jan 1837: Thomas **SUTTON**, Sr. died 2 Jan. He was born in Wexford, and came to Halifax from Newfoundland.]
17 Oct 1828	Timothy **SWEENY**, 30, husband of Bridget **DRISCOLL**, Cork.
10 Aug 1823	William **SWEENEY**, formerly a soldier, 34, Dublin
4 Oct 1828	John **SYNNETT**, 40, husband of Margaret **SANDERS**, Kilkenny.
3 Aug 1835	Margaret **KEATING**, 30, Cork, wife of Charles **TAYLOR**, 34th Regt.
7 Jun 1824	Charles **THOMPSON**, servant to Col. **GORE**, 19, Ireland.
3 Feb 1837	Hugh **TIERNEY**, at the Asylum, 60, born Ireland.
9 May 1835	Mary **CURRAN**, 35, Kildare, wife of William **TIERNY**.
22 Sep 1824	Philip **TIERNEY**, tailor, 40, Tullamore, Offaly
10 Jan 1830	James **TIMSSY**, 22, Kilkenny.
27 Aug 1827	Elenor, 26, wife of Thomas **TINAN**, Curraghmore, Waterford.
15 May 1838	Anne **MELAY**, 60, Kilkenny, widow of Thomas **TOBIN**.
24 Apr 1835	Catherine **JACKMAN**, 77, Callan, Kilkenny, widow of Thomas **TOBIN**.

21 Aug 1831	Eleanor **LANIGAN**, 54, born [Callan], Kilkenny, wife of James **TOBIN**, Esq. [*AR*, 20 Aug 1831: died 19 Aug, age 53.]
26 May 1837	Elenor, 9, born Waterford, dau of Patrick & Eleanor **TOBIN**.
6 Mar 1828	Richard **TOBIN**, 30, Ireland.
13 Aug 1834	Thomas **TOBIN**, 52, Kilkenny.
11 Sep 1834	Thomas **TOBIN**, blacksmith, 50, Kilkenny.
2 Aug 1840	James **TOOHILL**, 43, Tipperary [Married 12 June 1835: James, son of Owen & Eleanor (**BENNET**) **TOOHILL** of Tipperary, widower of Mary **DWYER**, to Joanna, dau of James & Frances (**HAYES**) **ROCHE**, of Ross, Wexford. [StM, Hfx]
15 Nov 1837	Mrs. **TOOLE**, 68, born Ireland [*AR*, 18 Nov 1837: died 14 Nov, age 74.]
29 Feb 1820	Richard **TOOMEY**, 50, Ireland.
8 Jul 1821	Michael **TRACY**, 43, husband of Bridget **MAHER**, Kilmallock, Limerick
1 Sep 1828	Thomas, 21, son of Patrick & Catherine (**BURKE**) **TROY**, Waterford.
26 Aug 1834	William **TWOMY**, 35, Cork, husband of Sarah **WILLIAMS**.
21 Feb 1841	James **WALL**, 45, born Ireland.
14 Jun 1829	John **WALL**, 70, Clonmel, Tipperary [*AR*, 13 June 1829: died 12 June, age 69.]
2 Apr 1840	Patrick **WALL**, 56, Tipperary [*AR*, 4 Apr 1840: died 1 April, age 55.]
30 Jun 1828	William **WALL**, about 40, Tipperary.
10 May 1839	James **WALLACE**, shoemaker, 35, Cork.
20 Sep 1834	William **WALLACE**, 82, Kilkenny.
23 Jan 1833	Bridget **WALSH**, 23, Wexford.
5 Sep 1834	Catherine **LEARY**, 32, Wexford, wife of James **WALSH**.
20 Mar 1828	Eleanor **WALSH**, 60, Ireland
5 Jul 1839	Eleanor **WALSH**, 89, born [Lismore], Waterford.
19 May 1829	Elizabeth **WALKER**, alias **WALSH**, 83, Newcastle, Limerick, in the Poor House.
30 Aug 1830	Honora **MURAN**, 37, Cork, wife of Thomas **WALSH**.
10 Feb 1842	James **WALSH**, Cork [The last entry in this register.]
31 Dec 1822	Pvte. John **WALSH**, 81st. Regt., 32, Castlebar, Mayo.
8 Jan 1827	John **WALSH**, 72, Waterford.
27 Jun 1827	Pvte. John **WALSH**, 74th. Regt., drowned in the Northwest Arm, 31, Kilkenny.
4 Sep 1834	John **WALSH**, 35, Cork, husband of Eleanor **CRAWLEY**.
11 Sep 1829	Margaret **CARTHY**, 51, Wexford, wife of James **WALSH.**
28 Aug 1829	Mary **HALEY**, 34, Fethard, Tipperary, wife of John **WALSH**.
8 Oct 1832	Mary **WALSH**, 40, Kilkenny.
1 Apr 1822	Patrick **WALSH**, 60, Mullinavat, Kilkenny, servant to John **SKERRY**, Dartmouth.
14 Jul 1827	Patrick **WALSH**, 58, left wife and 7 children, Cashel, Tipperary, "a few days here".
16 Feb 1839	Patrick **WALSH,** cooper, 41, Carlow.
19 Feb 1840	Pvte. Patrick **WALSH**, 37th Regt., 20, born Ireland.
6 Sep 1834	Thomas **WALSH**, 84, Waterford.
6 May 1833	Timothy **WALSH**, 50, Cork.
6 Sep 1828	Walter **WALSH**, about 69, Kilkenny.
7 Sep 1834	William **WALSH**, shoemaker, 27, Cork.
11 Aug 1840	William **WALSH**, carpenter, 60, born Ireland.
26 Jul 1823	Pvte. Cornelius **WARD**, 27, 62nd. Regiment, Ireland.
24 Mar 1832	Catherine **WARREN**, 50, born Ireland.
21 May 1830	Michael, 4, Tyrone, son of Martin & Bridget (**MacBROWRY**) **WATERS**
30 Apr 1818	Simon **WATSON**, 50, Waterford.
2 Feb 1830	Mary **WELDON**, 70, Wicklow

9 Jul 1827   Francis **WHELAN**, 35, Kilkenny Town, "here a few days" [*Ns*, 5 July 1827, reported arrival that week of the ship *Cumberland* from Waterford, with "350 passengers."]

29 Sep 1837   Honora **BRAWDERS**, 36, born Ireland, wife of Patrick **WHELAN**.

27 Mar 1827   John **WHELAN**, 60, Tintern Parish, Wexford.

4 Sep 1827   Patrick **WHELAN**, 40, Kilkenny.

2 Jun 1840   William **WHELAN**, 24, born Ireland, husband of Mrs. **WALL** [*AR*, 6 June 1840: died 31 May, Edward **PHELAN**, age 34. Married 16 Aug 1832: Edward, son of Maurice & Ellen (**MURPHY**) **WHELAN**, to Mary, dau of Matthew & Anastasia (**SHELLY**) **FINLEY**, all of Kilkenny, and widow of Thomas **WALL**, carpenter. [StM, Hfx]

18 Mar 1840   Joseph **WHITE**, 26, Dublin.

2 Jun 1837   Patrick **WHITE**, 35, Waterford.

11 May 1831   Thomas **WHITE**, 29, Waterford, husband of Catherine **HALEY**.

19 Sep 1834   Thomas **WHITE**, 40, Kilkenny, husband of Catherine **GLODY**.

15 Jun 1836   Alice, 64, Limerick, wife of Theophilus **WILSON**.

14 May 1836   Mary **SULLIVAN**, 23, Tipperary, wife of Thomas **WRIGHT**.

7 Feb 1829   Margaret **ROWLY**, 50, Hospital, Limerick, wife of James **WOODS**

27 Dec 1829   Denis **WRIN**, 80, Limerick [*AR*, 26 Dec 1829, died 25 Dec, age 86.]

13 Jul 1831   Anastasia **ALLEN**, 42, Kinsale, Cork, wife of William **YOUNG**.

4 - THE IRISH-BORN IN NEW BRUNSWICK IN 1851

New Brunswick alone among the Atlantic Provinces had a nominal (rather than head-of-household) census taken earlier than 1871 for the entire province. The 1851 census asked those not born in the province to state their year of entry. The surviving census returns are incomplete. Two counties (Gloucester and Kent) are missing, and only a small part of Wickham Parish sur- vives from Queens Co. Only one-third of the return exists for Saint John. Also lacking are the town but not the township of Moncton and three of ten parishes in York County. Subject to these limitations, the balance of New Brunswick in 1851 exhibited about 20,750 Irish-born residents.

This listing consists of the names of 109 natives of Ireland who had been in the province from 1812 or earlier. Seventeen had resided in the province since 1800 or earlier. Sixty-five lived in the coastal counties (39 along the Bay of Fundy and 26 on the Gulf of St. Lawrence), forty-four in landlocked counties. By religion, 29 were Catholic, 15 Anglican, 6 Presbyterian, 5 Baptist, four Methodist, one "Other". That information does not appear for the remaining fifty people.

The list is arranged alphabetically, in the sequence: name, year of entry, age in 1851, religion, parish and county, Irish origin if specified. I have compared my reading of certain unusual-seeming names with that in Peter M. Toner, *An Index to Irish Immigrants in the New Brunswick Census of 1851,* and other secondary sources.

ANDERSON, Thomas	1810 63 Bapt.	Dumfries, York	Ireland
BARRY, James	1811 74	Sussex, Kings	Wexford
BARRY, Mary	1794 72	Fredericton, York	Ireland
BARRY, Peter	1807 66 RC	Newcastle, Northumberland	Cork
BELL, John	1812 58 Angl.	Shediac, Westmorland	Ireland
BELL, Letitia	1783 83 Angl.	Burton, Sunbury	Ireland [widow of John]
BELL, William	1812 57 Angl.	Shediac, Westmorland	Ireland
BLANCH, James	1810 56	Westmorland, Westmorland	Ireland
BLEAKNEY, William	1784 79	Coverdale, Albert	Ireland

BOYLE, John	1812 56 RC	St. Andrews, Charlotte	Ireland
BRITT, Patrick	1810 67 RC	Sussex, Kings	Ireland
BROWN, Patrick	1802 90	Burton, Sunbury	Ireland
BURNS, John	1806 65	St. David, Charlotte	Ireland
BURNS, Lewis	1810 60	Kings Ward, Saint John	Ireland
CAMERON, Peter	1783 72	Queensbury, York	Ireland [son of Peter]
CAMPBELL, Ann	1808 63 Pres.	Sussex, Kings	Ireland [Donegal]
CARNEY, William	1812 68 RC	Durham, Restigouche	Ireland
CARSON, James	1802 51 Meth.	Salisbury, Westmorland	Ireland [Ulster]
CARSON, William	1812 45 Angl.	St. Patrick, Charlotte	Armagh
CHAMBERS, Ephraim	1812 40	Sussex, Kings	Tyrone
CHAMBERS, Moses	1812 53	Sussex, Kings	Tyrone
COCHRANE, Thomas	1811 50	Moncton Twp., Westmorland	Ireland
CONNOLLY, John	1810 70	Lincoln, Sunbury	Ireland
CRANY, Ann	1796 55 RC	Chatham, Northumberland	Wexford [CRANNEY]
CRONIN, Michael	1803 65 RC	St. Andrews, Charlotte	Carlow
CULLEN, Ellen	1810 70	Nelson, Northumberland	Ireland
CULLEN, Francis	1811 55 RC	Chatham, Northumberland	Ireland
CULLEN, John	1796 65	Nelson, Northumberland	Ireland
CURRAN, Timothy	1810 65	Hampton, Kings	Ireland
CUSACK, James	1811 60	Studholm, Kings	Ireland
DALEY, Catherine	1810 63 RC	Dukes/Queens, Saint John	Ireland
DALEY, John	1810 60	St. Andrews, Charlotte	Westmeath
DELAHUNT, Catherine	1812 46 RC	Moncton, Westmorland	Ireland
DENNISON, Ann	1810 65	Norton, Kings	Ireland
DOCKRILL, Benjamin	1812 64	Saint Mary's, York	Ireland [died 1870]
DONAHEY, Patrick	1812 40	Dukes/Queens, Saint John	Ireland
DOOLY, Daniel	1811 66 RC	Kent, Carleton	Offaly
DUNN, Bridget	1810 60 RC	Blackville, Northumberland	Cork
EAGLE, Henry	1811 58	Alnwick, Northumberland	Ireland
FLANIGAN, John	1780 90 Bapt.	Simonds Parish, Carleton	Ireland
FLYNN, James	1811 60 RC	Chatham, Northumberland	Waterford
FLYNN, James	1812 50	Fredericton, York	Ireland
FOX, Martin	1809 66 RC	Alnwick, Northumberland	Ireland
GORDON, William	1800 78 Meth.	Burton, Sunbury	Antrim
GRANT, John	1812 60 RC	Wakefield, Carleton	Ireland
HAYES, James	1811 60 RC	Douglas, York	Ireland
HENNEBERRY, John	1812 55	Campobello, Charlotte	Ireland
HENNESSEY, John	1812 66 RC	St. Patrick, Charlotte	Ireland
HILL, John	1801 65 RC	St. George, Charlotte	Ireland
HILLY, Michael	1800 55 RC	Woodstock, Carleton	Donegal
HOWARD, William	1781 70 Bapt.	Upham, Kings	Ireland
JELLISON, Hannah	1798 59 Angl.	Nelson, Northumberland	Ireland
JOHNSTON, Ann	1811 42	St. Patrick, Charlotte	Ireland
KELLY, Edward	1810 55	Wakefield, Carleton	Ireland
KENNEDY, John	1804 70	Nelson, Northumberland	Donegal
LARKEN, Catherine	1811 55 RC	Douglas, York	Ireland
LINTON, John	1802 84	Sussex, Kings	Ireland
LYNCH, Peter	1808 70	Sackville, Westmorland	Ireland
McALISTER, William	1812 59 Pres.	Fredericton, York	Tipperary

McCANN, Rodney	1802 72	St. David, Charlotte	Ireland
McCOURT, John	1800 68 Angl.	Campobello, Charlotte	Waterford
McCULLAM, Mary	1788 82 Pres.	Newcastle, Northumberland	Ireland [Antrim]
McDOWELL, William	1810 57 Bapt.	St. Marys, York	Ireland [Ulster]
McFADDEN, Thomas	1811 85 Angl.	Wicklow, Carleton	Fermanagh [Ulster]
McLAUGHLAN, Henry	1812 75	St. Stephen, Charlotte	Ireland
McLEAN, James	1810 50	Perth, Victoria	Ireland
McPEAKE, James	1810 70	Kings Ward, Saint John	Ireland [Derry]
McTAVISH, Elizabeth	1806 60 Pres.	Northesk, Northumberland	Ireland
MORAN, Patrick	1810 63	St. George, Charlotte	Ireland
MURPHY, Edward	1811 61 RC	Durham, Restigouche	Ireland
MURRAY, Elizabeth	1811 71 Angl.	Wicklow, Carleton	Ireland
MURRAY, John	1811 76 Angl.	Wicklow, Carleton	Ireland
NELSON, William	1809 55 Angl.	Sussex, Kings	Ireland
NERVEY, Thomas	1810 80	St. Marys, York	Ireland [labourer]
O'ROURKE, Margaret	1812 50 RC	Moncton, Westmorland	Ireland
ORR, James	1811 62 Pres.	St. Patrick, Charlotte	Antrim
ORR, Martha	1811 57 Pres.	St. Patrick, Charlotte	Antrim
PAYNE, John	1783 80 Other	Fredericton, York	Tipperary
POND, Eve	1783 83	St. Marys[New Durham].York	Ireland [Mrs.John]
POWER, Capt. Edmund	1811 70 RC	Woodstock, Carleton	Waterford
POWER, Martin	1810 60 RC	Nelson, Northumberland	Ireland
POWER, Patrick	1811 62 RC	Nelson, Northumberland	Ireland
POWER, Richard	1811 80 RC	Woodstock, Carleton	Waterford
POWER, Thomas	1809 67 RC	Nelson, Northumberland	Ireland
POWER, Thomas	1810 60	Duke/Queens, Saint John	Ireland
PURCY, Thomas	1810 64	Springfield, Kings	Ireland
QUILTY, David	1811 57	Kings Ward, Saint John	Ireland
RICHARDSON, Joseph	1811 52 Angl.	Sussex, Kings	Ireland
ROACH, Nicholas	1809 57	Sussex, Kings	Ireland
ROSITER, John	1810 65	Harvey, Albert	Ireland [Wexford]
SHAUGHNESSEY, Sarah	1808 50 Angl.	Hillsborough, Albert	Ireland
SHAUGHNESSEY, Wm.	1808 55 RC	Hillsborough, Albert	Ireland
SHAW, Elizabeth	1810 64	Duke/Queens, Saint John	Ireland
SLATTERWAY, Patrick	1802 68	Sussex, Kings	Ireland
SLOAN, James	1809 65 Meth.	Duke/Queens, Saint John	Tyrone
SLOAN, Mary	1809 50 Meth.	Duke/Queens, Saint John	Tyrone
SPLANE, James	1810 50	West Isles, Charlotte	Ireland [Cork]
SULLIVAN, Michael	1805 65 Angl.	Blackville, Northumberland	Ireland
SUTHERLAND, Ann	1782 94	Nelson, Northumberland	Ireland
TAPLEY, John	1794 68 Bapt.	Sheffield, Sunbury	Ireland [Cork]
THOMPSON, Archibald	1808 61 Angl.	St. Stephen, Charlotte	Antrim
THOMPSON, William	1810 61	Blackville, Northumberland	Donegal [age 51]
WALSH, Edmund	1809 73 RC	St. Stephen, Charlotte	Ireland
WHELAN, Michael	1810 65	Nelson, Northumberland	Ireland
WHITE, Frances	1810 46	Simonds Parish, Saint John	Ireland
WHITHEAD, Margaret	1783 75	Perth, Victoria	Ireland
WILSON, Harper	1786 65 Angl.	Hillsborough, Albert	Ireland [teacher]
WILSON, Jane	1783 75	Kings Ward, Saint John	Ireland

5 -MILITARY ATTRITION IN BRITISH AMERICA:

(A) THE 98 /99TH REGIMENT, 1813-1818

The 99th (Prince of Wales) Regiment carried 1,044 men on its rolls between 1813 and 1818. Of these, 530 other ranks were taken off strength in the four Atlantic colonies/provinces of New Brunswick, Newfoundland, Nova Scotia and Prince Edward Island. Most (376 men) were "located" - i.e., settled on the land. In addition, five were discharged without mention of settling on the land, one was invalided due to illness and one was released to general service. Eighty-seven men were marked "Ran", i.e., that they had deserted or gone AWOL. Another fifty-six died while on duty in the region, two were claimed as deserters from other units, and two were struck off strength in the region for reasons not recorded. Many of the men later were awarded pensions, and reference to them will be found in Norman K. Crowder, *British Army Pensioners Abroad, 1772-1899* (Baltimore: Genealogical Publishing Co., Inc., 1995), 58-62, 223-6. Due to renumbering, this regiment changed from 99th to 98th in the Army list.

The regimental depot description books supply considerable detail about each man. One reason for their careful detailing each of the "Non Commissioned Officers, Drummers & Private Men" was the usefulness of such information in any advertising required should a man desert. The regimental description book which opened in September 1813 contains thirteen columns: I. date of enlistment in the regiment; 2. whether enlisted for limited or unlimited term; 3. where received from; 4. age; 5. size [height], 6. description (see *infra*); 7. where born (parish, county); 8. trade or occupation; 9. former military service; 10. period of service in the Indies; 11. how disposed of (place, date, reason); 12, total service; and 13. remarks.

Typical descriptive terms in column 6 were these:

Make - stout, slender	Head - large, long, oval, round, small
Face - high, long, oval, round	Eyes - blue, brown, dark, grey, "hazle"
Shoulders - square, round	Arms - long, slender, stout
Hands - large, long, small	Thighs & legs - slender, stout
Mouth - large, long, small	Neck - long, short, thick

Eyebrows - black, brown, dark, dark brown, fair, heavy, light, very light, long
Nose - "cocked", large, proportionate, long, short, slender, small, thick
Hair - black, brown, dark, dark brown, fair, light brown, red
Feet - large, long, small

By trade or occupation, 300 (56.6%) were labourers, then follow 49 weavers, 34 shoemakers, 29 tailors, 16 servants. 11 carpenters, 9 no stated trade, 7 coopers, 6 each of butchers, gardeners and nailers, 5 each of blacksmiths and masons, 4 hatters, 3 calling themselves farmers, or painter/glaziers, a pair each of chandlers, colliers, dyers, hosiers, miners, stonecutters, tobacconists and watchmakers. Soloists were a baker, bookbinder, cabinetmaker, clerk, cloth dresser, crofter, cotton printer, currier, cutler, drummer, glassblower, hairdresser, "lawyer", maltster, potter, rope maker, saddler, sailmaker, spinner, watchman and wheelwright.

Since the purpose was genealogical, the information taken down for each man was his age, birthplace, and occupation; when, where and why he was taken off strength. Reference to PRO London, W.O. 25, Vol. 548, or the microfilm copy at the National Archives of Canada, in Ottawa, will enable a researcher to obtain the full information for any man on the list.

The largest number of men left the regiment in New Brunswick: Fredericton 186, Saint John 23, Moose Island 8, St. Andrew's 5, Fort Cumberland on the Nova Scotia border 2, 224 in all. Newfoundland accounted for 77 men, all but 36 at St. John's being at no specific location, Forty-five men left the regiment at Halifax, Nova Scotia, and seven men drowned in the Annapolis River, NS, for a provincial total of 52 men. One hundred and forty men left strength as "St John", which could refer to either Saint John, New Brunswick (more likely), or to St. John's, Newfoundland. For thirty men the description book omits this information. One man died at sea and one left to go to Chatham Depot in England. The remaining five ran (deserted) at Penobscot. This recalls the British occupation of eastern Maine from September 1814 into the late spring of 1815. The five desertions occurred between 17 and 25 March 1815.

The birthplaces given for the 530 men listed here reflect the fact that this was a heavily Irish regiment: 449 (84.7%) were born in Ireland compared to 58 (10.9%) in England. For six no birthplace is given. The remaining seventeen included nine from British North America (4 Newfoundland, 2 Nova Scotia, 2 Québec, 1 Upper Canada), three Scotland, two United States, one each from Barbados, Channel Islands and Germany. All 32 Irish counties are represented and it may be helpful to observe the geographical distribution of the soldiers' birthplaces in Ireland:

Tipperary	64	Waterford	23	Antrim	9	Cavan	5
Kilkenny	37	Dublin	17	Mayo	9	Longford	5
Limerick	32	Carlow	13	Wicklow	8	Meath	3
Roscommon	30	Galway	12	Offaly /Kings	7	Donegal	2
Armagh	25	Leitrim	12	Tyrone	7	Fermanagh	2
Wexford	25	Leix/Queens	12	Kerry	6	Kildare	2
Clare	23	Sligo	11	Monaghan	6	Derry/Londonderry	1
Cork	23	Down	10	Westmeath	6	Louth	1

The information concerning the 530 men is presented in the sequence: (A)Miscellaneous departures 11; (B) Died 56; (C)"Ran" 87; (D) "Located" 376.

A - MISCELLANEOUS DEPARTURES (11 men)

BAIRD, Henry, 21, "Killevatee", Antrim, labourer, joined on 10 Feb 1817, but was claimed by the Royal Navy as a deserter at Halifax, NS.

BOAM, John, 28, "Mauhel", Lancashire, England, weaver, discharged at Halifax, 2 Nov 1816.

BROWNE, Ignatius, 33, Thurles, Tipperary, tobacconist, joined on 3 Apr 1804. and was released for General Service at Halifax, 24 Nov 1817.

DONNELLAN, Patrick, 34 yrs. 6 mos., Strokestown, Roscommon, weaver, joined on 16 June 1804. [Although sent to Chatham Depot in England, 25 Sep 1818 (the latest date in this record), he received a land grant, and was located, with a wife and child, on lot 164 South, in Dalhousie Settlement, NS, on 16 Oct 1820. He appears in the 1827 census as a farmer in Annapolis Township, with a household of twelve. Pension, NS, 3 May 1820.]

DOWD, Patrick, 24, "Taunagh" [Tawnagh], Sligo, labourer, joined in June 1813 and was present in the Regiment at Halifax in July 1815. His later disposal is not recorded here.

FLOHR, John [Johann Heinrich Flohr], 46, Marburg, Hessen, labourer. He served in the 60th Foot from 7 Jan 1787 to July 1795, mostly in the West Indies, then in various units until he joined the 99th on 24 May 1805. He settled in Halifax, NS, where he died, 24 Aug 1844 age 75. His widow Martha died in Halifax a few years later.

McGILL, Robert, 51, Kingan [Kinagha, Annagh Parish], Cavan, weaver, served in the 33rd Regiment from 6 Nov 1787 to 31 Mar 1793, and joined the 99th Regiment on 10 May 1804; discharged at Halifax, 24 Nov 1815. [He was awarded a pension at Halifax, 15 Dec 1819, and was said to be living in Mauritius (*Cf.*, Crowder, 63).]

MAHER, Martin, 30, "Carrackeshor" [Carrick-on-Suir], Tipperary, labourer, discharged at Halifax, 9 Dec 1816.

THOMAS, William, 19, Suffolk, England, labourer, joined on 30 Jan 1817, but was claimed by the 15th Regiment of Foot at Halifax, as a deserter.

WILSON, William, 27, Manchester, England, weaver, discharged at Halifax, 2 Nov 1816.

B - DEATHS (56 men)

BEASLEY, John, 17, Bampton, Oxfordshire, England, labourer. He joined the Regiment on 1 April 1814, but died at Halifax, 28 Sep 1814.

BRAITHWITH, Thomas, 26 yrs. 8 mos., St. Patrick's, Waterford, labourer. He died at Saint John, NB, 4 Apr 1814. [Sgt. "Breatwith" married at St. Paul's Anglican, Halifax, 19 Nov 1811, Eleanor Belshaw, a widow.]

BUTLER, Richard, 32, Thomastown, Kilkenny, nailer, died at Halifax, 29 July 1816. He had joined the Regiment on 18 June 1804. [His burial record gives his age as 32.]

CASEY, John, 29, Longwall [Longueville, Parish Ballyclough], Cork, died at Halifax, 7 Feb 1814. He had enlisted on 28 Sep 1804.

CHRISTY, James, 27, Manchester, England, weaver, died at Fort Cumberland, 27 Mar 1814.

CLEARY, Henry, 27 yrs. 8 mos., Nenagh, Tipperary, servant, died at Halifax, 4 Sep 1815.

CONLAN, Michael, 24, Hill [Parish Kilturk], Sligo, labourer, died at Halifax, 13 Jan 1817.

CORDWELL, Giles, 26, Manchester, England, dyer, died at Halifax, 1 Feb 1814.

CROWE, Michael, 26, Gorth [Gort], Galway, labourer, died Newfoundland, March 1817.

CUMMINS, Patrick, 24 yrs. 6 mos., Emly, Tipperary, labourer, died on shipboard in the harbour of Saint John, NB, 13 June 1815.

CUNDY, Nicholas, 24, St. Stephen, Cornwall, labourer, died St. John's, NL, 20 Nov 1816.

DAVIS, James, 26, Ripley, Derbyshire, England, labourer, died at Halifax, 16 Jan 1817.

DUFFE, Terence. 26, Errigal [Keerogue], Tyrone, weaver, died in Newfoundland, no date.

DUKE, William, 27, Fingall [Finglas], Dublin, farmer, died at Halifax, 16 Apr 1814.

DUNN, John, 25, Dublin, painter, died at Halifax, 15 Dec 1815.

DWYER, Anthony, 26, Thurles, Tipperary, labourer, died at Halifax, 8 Nov 1815.

EGERTON, Peter, 42, Handley, Cheshire, labourer, died at Moose Island, NB, 21 Jan 1818.

EVANS, William, died at Fredericton, NB, no details.

FARRELL, James, 27, Goree [Gowran?], Kilkenny, labourer, died at :St John", 28 Mar 1815.

FITZGIBBON, Thomas, 32 yrs. 4 mos., St. Patrick's, Limerick, saddler, died NL, March 1817.

GARDNER, William, 20, Mortimer, Berkshire, labourer, died at Halifax, 3 May 1815.

GEE, William, 28, Cullumkill [Columbkille], Kilkenny, hairdresser, died Halifax, 12 Nov 1815.

GREEN, William, 34, Thurles, Tipperary, labourer, drowned at St. John's, NL, 22 Nov 1816.

HARDY, William, 40, Killard [Killora], Galway, labourer, died at Halifax, 4 Sep 1815. [His widow Bridget married, 25 Nov 1815, Cpl. William WILEY, of the same Regiment.]

HINES, Patrick, 26, Phelepo [Philipston?], Tipperary, labourer, died at Halifax, 24 Nov 1813.

HOGAN, Edward, 19, St. John's, waterford, shoemaker, died at "St John", 16 Mar 1815.

KELLY, James, 17, Newport, Tipperary, labourer, died at Halifax, 7 July 1815.

KELLY, Michael, 22, St. Nickets [Nicholas], Galway, labourer, drowned in the St. John River, NB, 12 July 1816. He had joined on 16 May 1804 [Married with a family].

LYONS, Robert, 26, St. Mary's, Kilkenny, nailer, died at Fredericton, NB, 15 Mar 1815.

McADDEN, John, 26, Wolley [Wooly, Parish of Drumhome], Donegal, tailor, died in NL, n.d.
McCOY, James, 51, Kilmore, Armagh, weaver, died at Halifax, 12 Nov 1815.
McCUE, James, 29, "Landeek" [?], Leitrim, labourer, died at Halifax, 20 Sep 1815.
McDONOUGH, Thomas, 23, Cullagh [Parish of Drumcliff], Galway, died at Moose Island, NB. in
        October 1814. He had joined in July 1804.
McKEONE, Patrick, 24, Killoran, Sligo, labourer, died at Fort Cumberland, 22 Mar 1818.
MALONY, Edward, "Preton" [?], Limerick, labourer, died at "St John", 22 Jan 1818.
MEALIE, Lawrence, 35, Loughrea, Galway, tailor, died at "St John", 15 May 1815.
MERCIER, James, 27, Harrod, Lancashire, labourer, died at Moose Island, NB, 7 Mar 1815.
MOONEY, Michael, 26, Moyne, Tipperary, labourer, died at Halifax, 2 Feb 1814.
MURPHY, Daniel, 31, St. John's, Dublin, tailor, died at Halifax, 16 July 1816.
NOCTON, Thomas, 30, Loughrea, Galway, labourer, died at Halifax, 31 July 1817.
O'NEILL, Hugh, 37, Tringhelly [Donaghedy], Tyrone, died at "St John", 2 Mar 1815.
PATTERSON, Mark, 26, "Ildwind", Lanarkshire, Scotland, shoemaker, died at Fredericton, NB, 3
        May 1818.
PIGGOT, Peter, 34 yrs. 6 mos., Thurles, Tipperary, nailer, died at "St John", 28 Dec 1817. He
        served in the 18th Regiment from 2 Jan 1799 to 5 July 1802, joined the 99th in June 1804.
POE, Thomas, 35, Nenagh, Tipperary, carpenter, died at Halifax in August 1816.
REAVY, Daniel, 26 yrs. 11 mos., Drum [Drumbo], Down, weaver, died at Halifax, 18 Aug 1815
RYAN, John, 28 yrs. 2 mos., Cashel, Tipperary, labourer, died at Halifax, 25 Jan 1814.
SHAUGHNESSY, Thomas, 20, Inchicronan, Clare, labourer, died at "St John", no date.
        He had joined the Regiment in Feb 1817.
WARD, Richard, 25, Liscole [Lisgoold], Cork, drowned at sea on 27 May 1818.
WILLIAMS, Stephen, 33, Mollowy [Molough], Tipperary, labourer, committed suicide at
        Halifax, 3 Sep 1816. He had joined on 12 Aug 1804.

        Seven men drowned in the Annapolis River, Nova Scotia, on 13 December 1813:
CONNER, Michael, 27, Kilglass, Roscommon, labourer
DILLON, Thomas, 28 yrs. 7 mos., Kilglass, Roscommon, carpenter
GARRATY, Charles, 30, Glenmore [Parish Lackagh], Galway, carpenter
McGUIRE, James, 29, St. Mary's, Dublin, nailer
OWENS, Dominick, 19, St. John's, Leitrim, labourer
SHEEHAN, John, 19, Clonmel, Tipperary, labourer
WILKINS, Samuel, 28, Magheross, Monaghan, weaver

(C) "RAN" (87 men)

        There is considerable lore in Atlantic Canada about ancestors who "jumped ship" or otherwise dismissed themselves from the armed forces of Great Britain in the early part of the nineteenth century. At least some of the men listed in this section went to earth somewhere in North America, whether in the United States or one of the British colonies – possibly using an assumed name – and may be ancestors of some modern North Americans.

BEDDING, John, 22 Cowley, Oxfordshire, labourer, at Halifax, 22 Aug 1816
BLACKHATCH, George, 19, Newcastle, Northumberland, labourer, at Halifax, no date
BUCKLEY, John, 28, Drummon[Dromin], Cork, carpenter, from Moose Island, NB, no date
BUNNY, Thomas, 18, "Lordanstown" [?], Kildare, labourer, from Fredericton, NB, no date

COCKER, Abraham, 30, Oldham, Lancashire, spinner, from Moose Island, NB, 9 June 1818 [He made his peace with the Army, as he was granted 100 acres on the Annapolis Road, NS, and was located on lot 87 South in Dalhousie Settlement, NS, on 16 Oct 1820.]

COLLINS, James, 26, St. Michael's, Limerick, carpenter, at Halifax, 20 Nov 1813, but returned, 20 Feb 1814 [*cf.*, Isaac Ryer, *infra*]

CONDON, John, "Templelegan" [Templeludigan], Wexford, labourer, at Fredericton, no date

CONNORS, James, 28, Strokestown, Roscommon, labourer, at St. Andrews, NB, 16 May 1813

CONNORS, Thomas, 21, "Ballynaly" [Ballyneill], Tipperary, labourer, at Fredericton, no date

CORCORAN, Owen, 19, Burris, Carlow, labourer, at Moose Island, NB, 9 June 1818

COYLE, Richard, 21, Street, Longford, labourer, no details

CRAWLEY, John, 19, Arless, Leix, labourer, no details

CRAWLEY, Thomas, 17, Annaduff, Leitrim, weaver, at "St John", 5 June 1818

CROSS, Barnabas, 28, Newburyport, MA., carpenter, at "St John", no date. Served in the New Brunswick Fencibles before joining the Regiment in June 1816 [Almost certainly the "St John" in this instance is the one in New Brunswick.]

CURTISS. Thomas, 29, Tymon [Taghmon], Wexford, labourer, in Newfoundland, 20 Nov 1817

DALY, William, 27, Down, Down, butcher, no details

DARCY, John, 21, New Ross, Wexford, labourer, no details

DAY, James, 28, Templemore, Tipperary, labourer, at St. Andrew's, NB, 8 Aug 1814

DOHERTY, Patrick, 28 yrs. 4 mos., Ballyduff, Leitrim [*sic*], labourer, at "St John", 5 July 1818

DONNELY, Martin, 25, Waterford City, labourer, no details

DORAN, Denis, 25, Killann, Wexford, labourer, at Saint John, NB, no date

DOYLE, John, 22, Rosegarland [Parish Ballylannan], Waterford, labourer, at "St John", no date

DOYLE, Michael, 19, Hook, Wexford, labourer, at "St John", no date

DUNN, Edward, 19, Mooncoin, Kilkenny, labourer, no details

DUNN, Patrick, 18, Drumcullen, Offaly, labourer, no details

DWYER, James, 17, Newport, Tipperary, labourer, no details

EATON, Abel, 23, Omey [Omagh], Tyrone, labourer, at Saint John, NB, 20 May 1815

ELLIS, George, 35, "Tipley", Derbyshire, weaver, at St. Andrew's, NB, 16 Oct 1817

FOLEY, Bartholomew, 23, Keel, Kerry, clerk, no details

FUNCHEON, Patrick, 20, Dunmannion [Dunnamaggan], Kilkenny, labourer, at "St John", no date

GALLAGHER, John, 31, Lurgy, Leitrim, labourer, at "St John", 15 July 1818

GREER, George, 28, Omagh, Tyrone, labourer, at "St John", in 1815

GREY, Edward, 17, Greenock, Scotland, labourer, at Fredericton, NB, no date

HANLEY, Francis. 20, St. John's, Limerick, tailor, no details

HANLEY, Peter, 29, "Darly Hill" [?], Tipperary, butcher, at Halifax, no date

HARRINGTON, John, 30 yrs. 5 mos., Tipperary, Tipperary, at St. Andrew's, NB, 27 Aug 1817

HARVEY, Thomas, 18, St. Michael's, Limerick, tailor, no details

HEANY, John, 27, Trim, Westmeath, victualler, at "St John", 5 Nov 1817

HOLMAN, Henry, 25, Guernsey, Channel Islands, labourer, no details

HOWARD, John, 20, Québec City, labourer, no details

INGLEBERTH, Jonas, 30, Hull, Yorkshire, sailmaker, at "St John", no date. He served from 5 Oct 1810 to 24 June 1816 in the Nova Scotia Fencibles, then joined the 99th Regt.

KELLY, Bernard, 20, Portarlington, Leix, labourer, no details

KENNARD, James, 19, [St.] Minver, Cornwall, tailor, at Moose Island, NB, 16 Dec 1817

KENNEDY, John, 27, Mountsea [Monsea], Tipperary, gardener, at Fredericton, NB, no date

KILMARTIN, William, 24 yrs. 6 mos., Mine [Moyne], Tipperary, labourer, st "St John" [Saint John, NB, in this instance], 12 June 1815

LAWLESS, Michael, 20, Bectiff [Bective], Meath, baker, no details

LAWLESS, Peter, 19, Clara, Kilkenny, labourer, at Fredericton, NB, no date
LORM, Charles, 22, Newton, Devonshire, labourer, no details
LUCAS, Robert, 23, Pallace [Pallis], Limerick, weaver, at Saint John, NB, 12 June 1815
LYNCH, James, 23, Leighlinbridge, Carlow, labourer, at "St John", no date
McCARRICK, James, 24, Clooncare, Leitrim, labourer, at Fredericton, NB, no date
McCORMICK, James, 20, Mullingar, Westneath, labourer, no details
McOWEN, Peter, Desertmartin, Derry, weaver, no details. He joined the Regiment in 1816
McWIGGAN, Edward, Armagh Town, labourer, no details [presumably McGUIGAN]
MACKARELL, Patrick, 25, Tantarren, Wexford, labourer, at "St John", no date
MARGINSON, John, 20, Coleraine, Derry, rope maker, at Fredericton, NB, 13 Mar 1818
MARTIN, Barney, 20, Mullingar, Westmeath, labourer, no details
MAY, James, 36, Drumore [Dromore], Sligo, labourer, at Moose Island, NB, 21 May 1818
MILLER, William, 18, Upper Canada, labourer, no details. He joined the 99th Regiment in 1816.
MOLLOY, William, 21, New Ross, Wexford, cooper, no details. He joined the 99th in Feb 1817.
MULROONEY, Michael, 26, Killaloe, Kilkenny, labourer, no details. He joined the 99th in 1816.
MURPHY, John, 27, Rossbarragan [Rosbercon], Kilkenny, labourer, at Fredericton, NB, no date
O'BRIEN, Michael, 22, Gowran, Kilkenny, labouirer, no details. He joined the 99th in 1816.
O'FLYNN, Peter, 29, Nenagh, Tipperary, labourer, at Halifax, 5 Nov 1815.
O'NEIL, Denis, 21, Castletown, Cork, labourer, at Halifax, no date. He joined on 24 Jan 1817.
PARKER, William, 25, "Magalean" [Maglin, Parish St. Nicholas], Cork, at Halifax, no date.
          He joined the 99th Regiment in Feb 1817.
PEYZANT, Thomas, 25, "Blochester"[?], Gloucestershire, shoemaker, at Halifax, no date.
          He joined the 99th Regiment on 29 July 1816.
ROWE, Thomas, 22, deserted at Halifax, no date
RUSSELL, Michael, 17, Ballinascully [Ballynacally], Clare, blacksmith, no details. Joined in 1816.
RUSSELL, William, 16, Newry, Armagh, carpenter, no details. He joined in 1817.
RYAN, James, 23, Galway Town, labourer, at "St John", 5 Oct 1817
RYER, Isaac, 23, Skethon [Skelton], Cumberland, tailor, at "St John", 20 Nov 1813. He joined in
          1809, ran in Nov 1813, but rejoined 20 Feb 1814. [cf., James Collins, supra]
SCALLION, Peter, 25, Cloyne, Cork, shoemaker, at Halifax, no date. He joined on 24 Jan 1817.
SHAW, Robert, 28, Tymon [Taghmon], Wexford, labourer, at St. Andrew's, NB, 27 Aug 1817
STOKES, William, 18, Creggan, Armagh, labourer, no details
THOMSON, John, 20, deserted at Halifax, no date
TONER, Patrick, 32, "Cnockwerly" [Knock . . .?], Cavan, labourer, at Halifax, 14 Mar 1814
TOWNSHEND, John, 20, Killealy [Killaloe], Clare, labourer, no details
TRESCOTT, Thomas, 27, St. Stephen's, Cornwall, malster, 8 Jan 1814, no location shown
WALSH, John, 34, St. Patrick's, Waterford, mason, at "St John", 21 May 1818
WESTON, John, 24, Bredon, Berkshire, labourer, at Halifax, 7 June 1818
WILLIAMS, Joseph, 25, Gumsly, Lanarkshire, Scotland, cabinetmaker, at Fredericton, no date.
          He joined the 99th Regiment in 1817.

          Most desertions were solitary affairs, although four cases appear above where two men
ran on the same date and same location: Cocker and Corcoran in 1818, Harrington and Shaw in
1817, Kilmartin and Lucas in 1815, Collins and Ryer in 1813. The five that follow deserted while
the Regiment was occupying the area around Penobscot Bay, Maine, during the war of 1812. It
would be logical to assume that they fled from recapture to the safety of American-held areas.

BODKIN, Michael, 26, Cartenan [Cartoon, Parish Cashel], Longford, tailor, 17 March 1815.
HANNON, John, 18, Kilmallock, Limerick, labourer, 25 March 1815.
MORETON, Thomas, 21, Killaghant [Killaghan and Gort], Roscommon, tailor, 21 March 1815.
SMITHWICK, James, 24, Callan, Kilkenny, labourer, 25 March 1815.
TIGHE, John, 21, Killogenst [Killasnet], Leitrim, labourer, in March 1815.

(D) LOCATED (376 men)

These have been arranged by the location where the man was taken off strength in the Regiment. Comparison with various records (and Norman K. Crowder's book, *British Pensioners Abroad, 1772-1899*) suggests that the men did not necessarily remain in the vicinity of the place where they were discharged. Those awarded pensions are indicated by an asterisk *. Genealogists might expect to find that some of these men came to live in an assortment of communities across North America. The arrangement being adopted here is meant to facilitate the process of trac(k)ing these veterans by suggesting a place at which to begin that search. In several instances I have been able to discover where a man settled. In such cases, you will find that information is supplied.

FREDERICTON, NEW BRUNSWICK, 24 June 1818 (160 men)

AURTHOR, John, 16, St. Mary's, Devonshire, labourer
AUSTEN, Patrick, 17, Killalue [Killaloe], Clare, labourer
BAILY, David, 18, Drumbo, Down, labourer
BENSON, Samuel, 20, Tipperary Town, shoemaker
*BILBY, Joseph, 27, Halifax, Nova Scotia, labourer [served 24 Mar 1805-24 July 1816 in the Nova Scotia Fencibles, then joined the 99th Regiment. He was awarded a Chelsea pension from the 15th Regiment at Halifax, on 19 July 1826, and was employed in the Barrack Dept. of the British Army in Halifax as late as 1873, according to the City Directory.]
BOURK, Richard, 25, Fethard, Tipperary, painter
BOYLAN, Philip, 18, Trim, Meath, labourer
BRADY, John, 17, Lara[h], Cavan, labourer.
BRIDGE, Samuel, 19, Tottington, Lancashire, crofter
BRIEN, James, 23, Thurles, Tipperary, labourer
BROWNRIGG, George, 19, Templeorum, Kilkenny, labourer
BRYAN, James. 24, Hospital, Limerick, shoemaker
BRYAN, Philip, 22, Suttons, Wexford, labourer
BRYANT, John, 24, Exeter, Devon, labourer
CAHILL, Michael, 21, Killealy [Killaloe], Clare, labourer
CARMODY, Michael, 22, Feddimore [Fedamore], Limerick, labourer
CASEY, William, 21, Mitchelstown, Cork, labourer
CASSADY, John, 24, Kilmurry, Clare, labourer
CAULFIELD, James, 18, Burriskean [Borrisokane], Tipperary, labourer
CHERRY, Joseph, 21, Blaris, Down, labourer
CLANCEY, Patrick, 20, Killaloe, Clare, tailor
COADY, Edward, 28, Glenmore, Kilkenny, labourer
COADY, John, 21, Glenmore, Kilkenny, labourer
COIN, Neil, 18, Disecreate [Desertcreat], Tyrone, tailor
COLLINGS, Timothy, 21, Tralee, Kerry, labourer
COLLINS, James, 17, Antrim Town, labourer
CONAVY, Joseph, 23, Maryborough, Leix, smith

CONNELLY, James, 28, Roscommon Town, farmer
CONNELLY, Thomas, 23, St. James, Dublin, weaver
CONNERS, Charles, 18, Templeboyle [Templeboy], Sligo, labourer
CONRON, Patrick, 19, Mayo [Parish Killabban], Leix, collier
CORBETT, John, 20, St. Mary's, Dublin, servant
CORBOY, Patrick, 23, Tipperary Town, labourer
CROCKER, Richard, 18, "St. John's, Middlesex. labourer
CRONEEN, Richard, 26, "Munister", Cork, labourer [ork, in Munster, was intended.]
CULLEN, Michael, 24, Ninemilehouse, Tipperary, labourer
CULLIN, Patrick, 16, Newmarket, Clare, servant
DALTON, Robert, 28, Rossbaragan [Rosbercon], Kilkenny, labourer
DARRIGAN, John, 21, Paulstown, Carlow, butcher [Paulstown is in Kilkenny]
DELANEY, Michael, 28, Tuam, Galway, labourer
DILLON, Daniel, New Ross, Wexford, tailor
DONNELLY, Edward, 22, Castlepollard, Westmeath, cooper
DONNELSON, James, 19, Tynan, Armagh, weaver
DONOHOE, Michael, 22, Kilbeggan, Westmeath, labourer
DOODSON, Paul, 17, West Hooton, Lancashire, mason
DOWDEN, Moses, 27, [Bonavista], NL, labourer [He served 11 Aug 1803 - 24 May 1810 in the Royal Newfoundland Fencibles.]
DUFFEY, Patrick, 23, Creive [Creeve], Roscommon, labourer [He joined on 18 Aug 1813. With a wife and child he lived on lot 93 South, Dalhousie Settlement, NS, in 1820. The Census of 1827 lists him in Annapolis Township, NS, as a farmer with a household of four.]
DUGGAN, Denis, 19, Stradbally, Waterford, labourer
FARRELL, Francis, 21, Cashel, Tipperary, weaver
FITZGERALD, James, 23, Affane, Waterford, servant
FLING, James, 16, Kilkenny City, labourer
FLINN, Richard. 21. Cashel, Tipperary, weaver
GORMAN, Daniel, 18, "Morough", Limerick, labourer [The Catholic parish of Murroe and Boher approximates the civil parish of Abington.]
GORMAN, Richard, 29, Mooncoin, Kilkenny, labourer
GRIER, Samuel, 17, Killead, Antrim, gardener
GRIER, William, 19, Killead, Antrim, tailor
GRIMMISON, William, 18, Kilmore, Armagh, weaver
HACKETT, Thomas, 24, Egless [Aglish], Offaly, cutler [He joined on 29 Oct 1816. He was granted 150 acres on the Annapolis Road, NS, and was on lot 88 North, Dalhousie Settlement, NS, on 16 Oct 1820.]
HANLY, John, 23, St. Andrew's, Dublin, shoemaker [He joined on 23 Jan 1817. He was granted 200 acres on the Annapolis Road, NS, and was on lot 6 North, Dalhousie Settlement, NS, on 16 Oct 1820. The 1827 Census 1827 lists him in Annapolis Township, NS, as a labourer with a household of six.]
HARDEN, Patrick, 18, Derelossory [Derrylossory], Wicklow, labourer
HARRINGTON, James, 27, New Ross, Wexford, chandler
HAWTHORNE, David, 21, Drumbo, Down, weaver
HAYES, Peter, 27, Poulpaiste [Poulpeasty, Parish Whitechurchglynn], Wexford, tailor
HEALY, Patrick, 17, Tipperary Town, labourer
HENRY, Samuel, 18, "Kircubber"[Kircubbin, Parish Inishargy], Down, weaver
HICKEY, Daniel, 24, Waterford City, labourer
HIGGINS, John, 18, Hacketstown, Wicklow, labourer

HILL, John, 26, Linkingharn [Linkinhorne], Cornwall, tailor
HINES, Felix, 23, St. Marys, Wexford
HOLAHAN, John, 16, Kilfinan [Kilfintinan], Clare, labourer
JOHNSON, William, 24, Ballyclare, Antrim, tailor [Ballyclare in either Ballynure or Doagh Grange
      Parish.]
KEATING, Patrick, 18, Feakle, Clare, labourer
KEEFE, Mathew, 21, Castleconnor [Castlecomer], Kilkenny, labourer
KELLY, Edward, no details
KELLY, John, 19, Gowran, Kilkenny, shoemaker
KILBY, George, 18, Moate, Offaly, servant
LAFFIN, John, 19, Callan, Kilkenny, labourer
LARKIN, Patrick, 17, Belfast, Antrim, shoemaker
LEAHY, William, 19, Carrick on Suir, Tipperary, labourer
LEARY, Moses, 20, Clegney [Killegney], Wexford, labourer
LESLEY, Edward, 16, Ennis, Clare, labourer [He received 100 acres on the Annapolis Road, NS,
      in 1821. He appears in the 1838 Census in Clements Township as a mechanic with a
      household of six.]
LESLEY, Patrick, 13, Ennis, Clare, labourer [recall that this was his age in 1813, not in 1818.]
*LONERGAN, William, 25, Cashel, Tipperary, tailor [pension awarded, 24 Oct 1821, at Halifax, after
      service in 98th Regiment. He joined on 27 Oct 1804. Wm." Lundergan", farmer, appears in
      1827 Census of Annapolis Township, NS, with a household of 9.]
LYNCH, Michael, 17, St. John's, Limerick, labourer
LYNCH, Patrick, 23, Castlemartyr, Cork, labourer
*LYONS, James, 27, Kilbride, Roscommon, labourer [pension awarded, 24 Oct 1821, at Halifax
      after service in 98th Regiment. He died 12 Aug 1847 in Nova Scotia (Cf., Crowder, 224).]
McCARRICK, John, 25, Cloonclare, Leitrim, "lawyer" [surely sawyer was intended.]
*McCARTHY, John, 30, Trinity, Waterford City, labourer [He served in the Nova Scotia Fencibles
      from 24 Nov 1805 to 24 June 1816. He was awarded a pension, 9 May 1823, at Halifax,
      after service in the 98th Regiment.]
McCAULAY, George, 17, Kayde [Keady], Armagh, carpenter
McGAGOY, Terence, 24, Armagh Town, weaver [perhaps his name was McCaghey]
McGILL, James, 21, Shantenaven [Shantemon, Parich Castleterra], Cavan, labourer [He joined on
      25 Sep 1805. He was granted 200 acres on the Annapolis Road, NS, in 1821, and appears
      in the 1838 Census in Wilmot Township, NS, as a farmer with a household of ten.]
McKENNA, Daniel, 17, Drynoose [Derrynoose], Armagh, labourer
McKER, George, 17, Shankey [Shankill], Armagh, weaver
McLAUGHLIN, Michael, 17, Killoran, Clare, weaver
McWIGGAN, James, 17, Armagh Town, labourer [this would be properly McGuigan]
McWILLIAM, Bernard, 19, Artrea, Derry, weaver
MADDIGAN, William, 23, St. John's, Limerick, tailor
MARKEY, Stephen, Drumand, Monaghan, labourer
*MEARA, William, 29, Geashill, Offaly, labourer [pension awarded 24 Oct 1821, Nova Scotia.]
MOORE, Christopher, 21, Rathmore, farmer
MORRISON, Mathew, 17, Tartarshun [Tartaraghan], Armagh, weaver
MULCAHY, Thomas, 17, Kilmurry, Kilkenny, labourer
MURPHY, David, 29, Tor Bay, NL, labourer
MURPHY, Thomas, 22, Butlerstown, waterford, labourer
MURRAY, David, 19, Kill, Waterford, labourer
NASH, Thomas, 17, St. Mary's, Limerick, cooper

NEAL, Philip, 15, St. Philip's, Barbados, labourer

NEILL, John, 20, Clonick [Catholic parish of Clonegal?], Wexford, painter and glazier

NELSON, Thomas, 18, Québec City, labourer

NESBIT, John, 27, Glenavy, Armagh, hosier [Glenavy is in Antrim. Nesbit served in the Nova Scotia
    Fencibles from 24 Dec 1805 to 24 July 1816.]

NEWELL, Thomas, 19, Loughgilly, Armagh, weaver

NORRIS, Thomas, 21, Vollard [Ullid], Kilkenny, labourer

NOWLAN, William, 19, Waterford City, labourer

NOWLAN, William, 18, St. Barry's [St. Finbar's, locally called St. Finbarry's], Cork, stonecutter

O'DOUGHERTY, William, 19, Tipperary Town, servant

O'NEAL, John, 15, Muckney [Muckno], Monaghan, labourer

O'NEILL, Patrick, 15, Clogher, Tipperary, labourer [He joined 29 June 1812 age 15. He received
    100 acres on the Annapolis Road in 1821, and appears in the 1827 Census in Clements
    Township with a household of five.]

PICKSTOCK, John, 20, Ashley, Staffordshire, labourer

POOLE, John, 24, Wigan, Lancashire, miner

*QUILTY, Thomas, 27, Rathkeale, Limerick, hatter [pension awarded 24 Oct 1821, Nova Scotia]

QUINN, John, no details.

REDDIGAN, Edward, 21, Kilmacow, Kilkenny, labourer

REDMOND, John, 18, Ballynahinch, Down, labourer

*REILLY, Patrick, 24, Ross, Wexford, labourer [He served in the Royal Newfoundland Fencibles
    from 1 Oct 1815 to 24 June 1816, then joined this Regiment. He was awarded a pension on
    23 Sep 1818, and was later near Richmond, Ontario (Cf., Crowder, 227).]

REYNOLD, John, 18, Granard, Longford, carpenter

RIMMER, Thomas, 23, Crosby, Lancashire, shoemaker

RINGROSE, William, 18, Durras [Dorrus, Parish Killuran], Clare, gardener

ROCHE, Patrick, 23, Mavain [Monaughrim, Parish Moyacomb], Carlow, labourer [He and his wife,
    Mary EDWARDS, buried a son, John, at Halifax, 30 Jan 1816. - Catholic record]

RYAN, Thomas, 20, Newbawn, Wexford, labourer

RYAN, William, 23, Grange, Kilkenny, labourer

SAUL, John, 25, St. Mary's [Clonmel], Tipperary, shoemaker

SCURRY, Peter, 23, Waterford City, labourer [The name is SKERRY]

SHAUGHNESSY, Michael, 24, St. John's, Limerick, labourer

SHERRY, Francis, 18, Donough [Donagh], Monaghan, labourer

STARKS, John, 22, Newport, Isle of Wight, carpenter [He was granted 200 acres on Annapolis
    Road, and is listed at lot 157 South, Dalhousie Settlement, NS, on 16 Oct 1820. John
    "Sterk", labourer, with wife, appears in the 1838 Census of Annapolis Township.]

STENSON, Thomas, 20, Donaghenry, Tyrone, weaver

STEWART, Hugh, 22, Keady, Armagh, labourer

STEWART, John, 21, Cashel, Tipperary, labourer

*STODDORS, Robert, 35, Longford Town, carpenter [He was awarded a pension at Halifax, on 24
    Oct 1821, after service in the 98th Regiment. "Robart Studders", farmer, appears in the 1838
    Census of Dalhousie Settlement as a farmer, with a household of eleven.]

SULLIVAN, John, 17, Rathkeale, Limerick, labourer

SULLIVAN, Maurice, 25, Dingle, Kerry, servant

*TAYLOR, George, 26, Wicklow Town, smith. He was awarded a pension at Halifax, on 24 Oct
    1821, after service in the 98th Regiment.]

TIERNEY, Timothy, 24, Graig[uenamanagh], Kilkenny, labourer

TOBIN, Darby, 18, Ballymackey [Ballymackensy, Parish Chapel], Wexford, cooper

TOBIN, William, 12 [*sic*], Waterford City, labourer; joined on 7 Sep 1815 [granted 100 acres on the Annapolis Road, and listed at lot 23 South, Dalhousie Settlement, NS, 16 Oct 1820]

*TOOLE, Edward, 27, Armagh Town, stonecutter [He served in the Royal Artillery from 1 Mar 1808 to 31 July 1814, and joined this Regiment on 17 July 1816. Granted 200 acres on the Annapolis Road, NS, and was listed at lot 127 South, Dalhousie Settlement, NS, on 16 Oct 1820. He was awarded a pension at Halifax, on 9 Nov 1831].

TOOLE, William, 13, Halifax, Nova Scotia, drummer

TORPEY, James, 19, Castleconnell, Limerick, labourer

TURLEY, Peter. 27, Creggan, Armagh, weaver [He served in the Royal Scots from 28 May 1808 to 26 Aug 1815, and joined this Regiment in 1816.]

TURVEY, Michael, 18, St. James, Dublin, labourer

*WALKER, Francis, 26 yrs. 1 mo., St. Catherine's, Dublin, labourer [He enlisted 23 May 1804; on lot 165 North, Dalhousie Settlement, NS, 16 Oct 1820, with wife and 2 children; awarded a pension at Halifax, 24 Oct 1821. He died in Apr 1851.(*Cf.*, Crowder, 225, "Fred[k] Walker")

WALSH, Edward, 23, Oney [Owning], Kilkenny, labourer

WALSH, John, 18, Mullingar, Westmeath, shoemaker

WALSH, John, 20, Templane [?], Kilkenny, labourer

WALSH, Thomas, 24, Butts, Kilkenny [The Butts, City of Kilkenny], labourer

WILLIAMS, Thomas, 18, Liverpool, Lancashire, watchmaker

WILSON, John, 19, Glenavy, Antrim, labourer

WOODS, James, 30, Woolridge [?], Dorset, labourer [He served in the Royal Newfoundland Fencibles from 25 May 1804 to 24 May 1816, and joined this Regiment in Feb 1817.]

----NLY, George, 17, St Michael's, Limerick, labourer

----NOR, Patrick, 20, Mullaghbrack, Armagh, labourer [He served in the Royal Horse Artillery from May 1812 to 30 Mar 1816. These last two surnames are completely illegible except for the last three letters.]

FREDERICTON, NEW BRUNSWICK, 24 July 1818 (13 men)

AUSTEN, Richard, 26, Rosenalls [Rosenallis], Leix, weaver

DINN, Richard, 22, Cushinstown, Wexford, labourer

*DUNN, John, 28, Stradbally, Leix, gardener [He joined on 15 May 1804. Sgt. Dunn married Sarah Buckler. He and his wife and two children were on lots 12 South & 13 North, Dalhousie Settlement, NS, on 16 Oct 1820, and was granted 200 acres on the Annapolis Road in 1821. The 1838 Census reports him at Dalhousie Settlement, with a household of twelve. He was awarded a pension at Halifax, 24 Oct 1821.]

HENNESSY, William, 21, Carlow Town, servant

IRWIN, William, 19, Down, Down, potter

LACEY, Nicholas, 18, Crooke, Waterford, labourer

MURPHY, Cornelius, 21, Kilbrogan, Cork, labourer [He joined on 19 Oct 1813. He was located on lot 126 South, Dalhousie Settlement, NS, on 16 Oct 1820, and was granted 100 acres on the Annapolis Road in 1821.]

*RUTH, Patrick, 35, Cullen [Callan], Kilkenny. mason [He was awarded a pension at "St Johns", 24 Oct 1821, after service in the 98th Regiment.]

*RYAN, John, 37 yrs. 2 mos., Killora, Galway, labourer [He joined on 10 May 1804. He was on lot 168 North, Dalhousie Settlement, NS, 16 Oct 1820. He was granted 100 acres on the Annapolis Road, NS, in 1821.[He was awarded a pension at Halifax on 24 Oct 1821, after service in the 98th Regiment.]

TOBIN, Richard. 30, Bantry, Cork, labourer [He was born at Kilmocomogue, adjacent to Bantry. He joined on 17 Aug 1813, and lived with his wife and two children on lot 28 North in Dalhousie Settlement, NS. on 16 Oct 1820. He is listed with a household of seven in the Census of 1827 in Annapolis Township.]

TOOLE, James, 21, Ballytoher, Kildare, servant [He may have been born at Crookstown, Parish Narraghmore and enlisted on 20 Oct 1813. he was living on lot 164 North, Dalhousie Settlement, NS, on 16 Oct 1820. The 1827 Census reported him in Annapolis Township, while that of 1838 placed him as a labourer in Clements Township, with a family of five. He had a wife and 8 children when he was assisted by the Poor Commissioners ion 1854 (*Cf.*, NSARM, RG 5, Series "P", Vol. 86 #64).]

WARD, Thomas, 18, Newcastle, Limerick, labourer

WARE, Thomas, 18, Kilmacow, Kilkenny, weaver

SAINT JOHN, NEW BRUNSWICK, 24 July 1818 (17 men)

*ADAMS, John, 30, Philadelphia, Pennsylvania, labourer [pension awarded, 19 June 1822]

AUSTIN, Henry, 15, Tipperary Town, no trade stated

BUTLER, David, 25, Dunmore, Kilkenny, labourer

HANDCOCK, William, 38, Tewkesbury, Gloucestershire, labourer

*HAWTHORN, John, 30, Emlyford [Emlaghfad], Sligo, weaver [pension awarded, 24 Oct 1821]

HAYES, Martin, 26, Finloe [Fennagh?], Clare, labourer

*HUTCHINSON, Hugh, 31, Cady [Keady], Armagh, weaver [pension at Halifax, 24 Oct 1821]

LAVELL, Thomas, 27, Aglass [Aglish], Mayo, shoemaker

LEARA [LEARY], John, 31, Mallow, Cork, tailor

*McCONNELLY, Bernard, 28, Louth Town, shoemaker [Barney McConnell joined on 4 May 1805. He was granted 100 acres on the Annapolis Road, NS, and was located on lot 123 North, Dalhousie Settlement, NS, on 16 Oct 1820. He appears in the 1827 Census in Annapolis Township, as Barnabas McColley, with a household of seven. He was awarded a pension at Halifax, 24 Oct 1821. He died on 16 July 1851 (*Cf.*, Crowder, 224).]

MORAN, Peter, 28, Kilglass, Roscommon, labourer [Peter MOREN, farmer with a household of four, appears in the 1838 Census of Sherbrooke Settlement (now New Ross, NS).]

NUGENT, Thomas, no details

*O'NEILL, William, 31, Hurlingford, Kilkenny, weaver [He joined on 22 Feb 1805, and was granted 100 acres on the Annapolis Road, NS, in 1821. Pension awarded, 26 Aug 1819.]

ROE, Michael, 23, Kilbride, Offaly, tobacconist

WALSH, James, 19, St. John's, NL, labourer

WALSH, John, 25, Cork City, shoemaker

WILLIAMS, John, 41, Birr, Offaly, shoemaker

"ST. JOHN'S", 24 July 1818 (34 men)

Modern usage spells the Newfoundland city thus to distinguish it from Saint John, New Brunswick. My division among those entered as *St. John's, Saint John*, and *St John* is necessary, but the city in New Brunswick is most probably the place of discharge.

*BELL, George, 24, St. Mary's [Clonmel], Tipperary, shoemaker [pension in NS, 26 Aug 1819]

BRAHEL, James, 28, Stonyvalter, Dublin, labourer [perhaps Stonybatter, Wexford, was intended]

BURKE, Michael, 28, Croome [Croom], Limerick, labourer

CAHILL, John, 18, Dungarvan, Waterford, shoemaker [Received a military land grant at Andover, New Brunswick, in 1825. His sons by his first wife were born in Newfoundland, while his later children were born in New Brunswick.]

CAHILL, John, 22, Cloghrenan [Clogrenan, Parish Cloydagh], Carlow, servant

CARTER, Michael, 19, Elphin, Roscommon, labourer

*CUMMINS, Thomas, 28, Enniskillen, Fermanagh, nailer [pension in NS, 28 Mar 1821]

*DELAHUNT, Denis, Cashel, Tipperary, labourer [He enlisted on 18 Feb 1809, and was granted 100 acres on the Annapolis Road, NS, being located on lot 120 North, in Dalhousie Settlement, on 16 Oct 1820; pension in NS, 9 Nov 1831]

DICKINS, John, 22, Swinton, Lancashire, dyer [Swinton was in Yorkshire]

*ELLIOT, William, 27, Bonaw [?], Wicklow, butcher [pension in NS, 26 Aug 1819, lived near Fredericton, New Brunswick]

FLANNERY, Thomas, 20, Kilnagry [Kilkeary?], Tipperary, labourer {Flannery and his wife, Bridget Carroll, had a daughter, Anne, baptised in Halifax, 1 Jan 1816 (Catholic record).]

GREENWOOD, James, 24, Huntington, England, servant

HANNON, Michael, 17, Goresbridge, Kilkenny, shoemaker.

HARDING, Michael, 17, Ballyhigran, Limerick, tailor [The Catholic parish of Ballyagran]

HOGAN, Patrick, 20, Ballybricken, Waterford, gardener

*KEARNEY, Patrick, 29, Doonass [Parish Kiltemanlea], Clare, labourer

*KEARNY, Patrick, 29, Ennis, Clare, labourer

[One of these Kearneys was given a pension, 23 Sep 1818, the other, 26 Aug 1819]

KILLEENY, Patrick, 22, Clonclare, Leitrim, labourer

*KNOX, Robert, 39, Skreen, Sligo, labourer [granted 100 acres on the Annapolis Road, NS, in 1821; pension awarded in NS, 26 Aug 1819. Died 6 Mar 1853 (Cf., Crowder, 224).] *LEE, Cornelius, 26, Cavan Town, labourer [enlisted on 7 Feb 1811; granted 200 acres on the Annapolis Road, NS, in 1821; located on lot 126 North, Dalhousie Settlement, NS, on 16 Oct 1820. He appears in the 1827 Census in Annapolis Township, NS, as a farmer with a household of three. He was awarded a pension in NS, 8 Aug 1827.]

LENAGHAN, James, 25, Killrustin [Kiltrustan], Roscommon, weaver [Granted 100 acres on the Annapolis Road, being located on lot 161 South, Dalhousie Settlement, NS, 16 Oct 1820. James Lennehan, farmer with wife, appears in the 1827 Census of Annapolis Township. In 1858 he sought poor relief at Annapolis (NSARM, RG 5, Series "P", Vol. 87 # 110).

McGUIRE, Michael, 20, Killeghart [Catholic parish of Killargue, which approximates the civil parish of Killarga], Leitrim, labourer

McMAHON, Francis, 20, Brides [St. Bridget's], Dublin, watchman [Enlisted on 10 Aug 1811, following service in the 8th Regiment. He was a Sergeant, and son of Arthur and Mary (CANON) McMahon, and married in Halifax, 22 Jan 1817 (Catholic record), Eliza Elenor CANN of Sydney, NS. He was granted 200 acres on the Annapolis Road, NS, in 1821.]

MADDEN, Timothy, 17, Ballingarry, Limerick, labourer

MAHON, Patrick, 29, Lucan [Lackan], Mayo, labourer

*MALONY, Thomas, 49, Newmarket, Clare, labourer [pension in NS, 26 Aug 1819; resided near Fredericton, New Brunswick]

MYLES, Patrick, 17, Kilnaboy [Killinaboy], Clare, labourer

PELLEY, John, 30, Bude, Worcestershire, tailor

QUIGLEY, Denis, 20, Kilcomman [Kilcolman, near Nenagh], Tipperary, labourer

STOKES, Edward, 23, Creggan, Armagh, shoemaker

TRAFFORD, William, 19, Handborough, Oxfordshire, mason

TRAVERS, Michael, 24, Kilkenny Town, labourer

*WILEY, William, 38, Hamford [?], Gloucestershire, mason [pension, 26 Aug 1819, died at Halifax in 1846 (*Cf.*, Crowder, 225).He enlisted on 6 Jan 1805. As a widower, Cpl. Wylie married 25 Nov 1815 at St Paul's Anglican, Halifax, Bridget, widow of William HARDY, of the same Regiment (for his death, *supra*). He was granted 200 acres on the Annapolis Road in 1821, and was located on lot 118 in Dalhousie Settlement, NS, on 16 Oct 1820.]

WILSON, John, 18, Armagh Town, labourer.

NEWFOUNDLAND, 24 July 1818 (34 men)

*ANDERSON, William, 33, Elseton [Elston], Nottinghamshire, shoemaker [Cpl. Anderson married, 9 Jan 1815 (St. Matthew's Presbyterian, Halifax), Margaret McENNELY, widow. He was awarded a pension in Nova Scotia, 26 Aug 1819.]

BARTLEY, John, 27, Ballysaber [Ballysaggart, Parish Kilaghtee], Donegal, labourer

BECKER, William, 31, St. Michael's, Dublin, cotton printer

*BOYLE, John, 20, Waterford City, labourer [pension awarded in Nova Scotia, 5 July 1820; he lived near Fredericton, NB.]

*BROWN, Daniel, 29, Rosgrey [Roscrea], Leix, shoemaker [granted 100 acres on the Annapolis Road, NS; located at lot 156 North, Dalhousie Settlement, NS, with his wife and child, on 16 Oct 1820. He was awarded a pension in Nova Scotia, 26 Aug 1819.]

*BURKE, John, 31, Drum [Drom], Tipperary, no trade shown [pension award in Nova Scotia, 26 Aug 1819; he lived near Fredericton, NB.]

*CODD, Francis, 47, Tram[or]e, Waterford, glassblower [pension, Nova Scotia, 26 Aug 1819.]

*COLLINS, Michael, 27, Nenagh, Tipperary [pension, Nova Scotia, 26 Aug 1819.]

*COLMAN, Timothy, 38, Cloronan, Waterford, labourer [pension, Nova Scotia, 26 Aug 1819.]

*COTT, Cpl. Michael, 21, Fethard, Tipperary, shoemaker [pension, Nova Scotia, 26 Aug 1819.]

*DARGIN, Patrick, 27, Clonmel, Tipperary, labourer [pension, Nova Scotia, 5 July 1820.]

*DILLON, Patrick, 23, Minchen [?], Tipperary, labourer [Dillon enlisted on 16 June 1804. He was granted 200 acres on the Annapolis Road, and was living on lots 3 and 164 South, in Dalhousie Settlement, NS, on 16 Oct 1820. Pension awarded, Nova Scotia, 26 Aug 1819. He died at Halifax, 29 May 1845 (*Acadian Recorder*, 31 May 1845, says aged 70).]

*DYER, Mathew, 20, Kilgarvan, Mayo, labourer [on lot 157 North, Dalhousie Settlement, NS, on 16 Oct 1820; pension awarded, Nova Scotia, 26 Aug 1819.]

*EARS [AYERS], William, 16, Termanagh [?], Wicklow, servant [pension, Nova Scotia, 26 Aug 1819. (*Cf.*, Crowder, 58).]

FARRELL, James, 20, Clonmel, Tipperary, labourer

FENNELL, Martin, 20, Clonmore, [Parish of Killeshin], Leix, labourer

*FLANAGAN, John, 38, Boyle, Roscommon, weaver [He enlisted in Aug 1804, and was granted 100 acres on the Annapolis Road, NS, and was located on lot 121 South, in Dalhousie Settlement, NS, on 16 Oct 1810. Service pension in Nova Scotia, 26 Aug 1819.]

*GARVEY, Cornelius, 28, Knocklong, Limerick, cooper [Pension, Nova Scotia, 26 Aug 1819.]

*GRIMES, William, 31, Fana [Fenagh], Leitrim, labourer [Pension, Nova Scotia, 26 Aug 1819; lived near Fredericton, NB, and died 5 May 1851 (*Cf.*, Crowder, 224).]

KELLY, Edward, 21, Bunnycarry [Bunnagurragh, Parish Barragh], Carlow, labourer

KILLEEN, John, 29, Tohill [?], Galway, weaver

KNOX, William, 13, Skreen, Sligo, labourer

LANNON, William, 27, Ballintober, Roscommon, servant

LARKIN, Daniel, 29 yrs. 7 mos., Tipperary Town, labourer

*LELAND, Thomas, 27 yrs. 8 mos., Strokestown, Roscommon, nailer [pension, NS, 28 Mar 1821]

*LONG, James, 29, Drom, Tipperary, shoemaker [He enlisted on 13 Apr 1805, and had a grant of 100 acres on the Annapolis Road, NS, and was located on lot 158 North, in Dalhousie Settlement, NS, on 16 Oct 1820. He is listed as a farmer in Annapolis Township with a household of three in the 1827 Census. Pension in Nova Scotia, 26 Aug 1819.]

McCANNA [McKENNA], James, 29 yrs. 9 mos., Ennismore, Leitrim, labourer [No place of this name noted in Leitrim. Possibly Inishmean was intended.]

*MULLEN, John, 36 yrs. 7 mos., Kiltevin [Kilteevan], Roscommon, labourer [Pension in Nova Scotia, 26 Aug 1819. (Cf., Crowder, 58).]

MULVEY, Hugh, 33, Killareghte [Kiltoghert], Roscommon, labourer

*O'BRYAN, John, 27, Kilconnel, Mayo, labourer [probably an error for Kilconnell, Galway; awarded a pension, Nova Scotia, 24 Oct 1821. (Cf., Crowder, 60).]

*ROCHFORD, Thomas, 28, Gorey, Wexford, shoemaker [granted 200 acres on the Annapolis Road, NS, and located on lot 124 South, in Dalhousie Settlement, NS, on 16 Oct 1820, with a wife. Pension in Nova Scotia, 26 Aug 1819. (Cf., Crowder, 59).]

SILK, Patrick, 24, Glenthern [?], Galway, labourer

TREACY, Francis, 25, Thurles, Tipperary, labourer [He enlisted on 17 May 1804, and was granted 100 acres on the Annapolis Road, NS, and was located on lot 25 South, in Dalhousie Settlement, on 16 Oct 1820; Joanna, wife of Francis Tracey, died at Annapolis, NS, on 2 Aug 1843, age 50 (headstone in RC cemetery); pension in Nova Scotia, 26 Aug 1819.]

WHITE, John, 27, Kilglass, Roscommon, labourer [pension in Nova Scotia, 26 Aug 1819.]

NEWFOUNDLAND, other dates in 1818 (2 men)

*BROWN, John, 24, Roscrea, Tipperary, labourer, discharged on 24 Sep 1818. [He seems to have re-enlisted and only received a pension, at Fredericton, NB, on 10 Aug 1836.]

*HANNON, Anthony, 28 yrs, 4 mos., Hospital, Limerick, labourer [He joined on 14 Aug 1804, and was granted 390 acres on the Annapolis Road, NS, and was located on lot 98 South, in Dalhousie Settlement, on 16 Oct 1820, with his wife. The couple appear, without children, as farmers in Annapolis Township in the 1827 Census. He received a service pension in Nova Scotia, from 26 Aug 1819. He died at Annapolis, 14 Oct 1836, age 57 (Yarmouth Herald, 4 Nov 1836), and his widow, Martha, died 6 Oct 1842 at Annapolis, age 52 (Halifax Times, 8 Oct 1842).]

"ST JOHN" (116 men)

This placename is ambiguous due to the lack of a standardized spelling ca 1818 for St. John's, Newfoundland, and Saint John in New Brunswick. In cases where other records enable a confident identification of which "St John" was intended, I have noted the fact.

BRYANT, John, 20, Bilton [?], Gloucestershire, collier, discharged on 21 Jan 1817.

McGUIRE, Bryan, 32, Enniskillen, Fermanagh, shoemaker, discharged on 24 Nov 1817.

Seventeen men were discharged on 24 June 1818:

ABBOTT, Stephen, 21, Bonavista, NL, labourer [He served in the Newfoundland Fencibles from 18 Mar 1814 until 24 June 1816. In this case St. John's, NL is the location.]

*BATES, Thomas, 34, Tipperary Town, labourer [He enlisted on 19 Nov 1804, and was granted 100 acres on the Annapolis Road, NS, and was located, a single man, on lot 163 North, in Dalhousie Settlement, NS. Awarded a pension in NS, 24 Oct 1821.]

*BURKE, John, 28, Duhill [Donohill], Tipperary, butcher [Pension in NS, 24 Oct 1821.]

*CONNELL, Patrick, 28, Fauban [Feaghmaan, Parish Valencia], Kerry, tailor [He joined on 18 Sep 1804, and was granted 100 acres on the Annapolis Road, NS, and was located on lot 89 North, at Dalhousie Settlement, NS, on 16 Oct 1820, with wife and two children. Pension in NS, 24 Oct 1821; died 17 July 1872 (*Cf.*, Crowder, 224).]

*COX, John, 20, Twyenon [Tibohine], Roscommon, tailor [Pension in NS, 24 Oct 1821; died in 1848 (*Cf.*, Crowder, 224).]

DAILY, Robert, Donogall [?], Down, labourer [He enlisted on 29 July 1812, and was located on lot 161 North, in Dalhousie Settlement, NS, on 16 Oct 1820.]

DOOLY, Daniel, 27, Graig[uenamanagh], Kilkenny, labourer

FARDY, Patrick, 20, New Ross, Wexford, labourer

*HARRIS, George, 28, Cork City, labourer [He served in the Nova Scotia Fencibles from 1 Nov 1803 to 24 July 1816. Pension in NS, 24 Oct 1821.

*HORNER, Alexander. 26, Templepatrick, Antrim, weaver [He enlisted on 4 Nov 1804, and was granted 200 acres on the Annapolis Road, NS. He was located with his wife and three children on lots 97 North and South, at Dalhousie Settlement, NS, on 16 Oct 1820. Pension in NS, 24 Oct 1821.]

KEEFFE, Laughlin, 22, Old Leighlin, Carlow, labourer

*KELLY, Thomas, 36, Quin, Clare, weaver [He enlisted on 24 Nov 1804, and was granted 100 acres on the Annapolis Road, NS, and was located with his wife, Eleanor, and two children on lot 119 North, Dalhousie Settlement, NS, on 16 Oct 1820. Pension in NS, 26 Aug 1819]

*LONERGAN, Michael, 28, Cashel, Tipperary, shoemaker [He enlisted on 28 June 1804, amd was granted100 acres on the Annapolis Road, NS, and was located on lot 165 South, Dalhousie Settlement, on 16 Oct 1820. Pension in NS, 24 Oct 1821.]

*LONERGAN, William, 28, St. Nicholas, Cork, labourer [He enlisted on 1 Mar 1805, and was granted 100 acres on the Annapolis Road, NS, and was located on lot 155 North, in Dalhousie Settlement, NS, on 16 Oct 1820. Pension in NS, 24 Oct 1821.]

*QUILTY, John, 29, An[n]agh, Limerick, labourer [He enlisted on 13 Oct 1804, and was granted 200 acres on the Annapolis Road, NS; located on lot 95 North, in Dalhousie Settlement, on 16 Oct 1820, with his wife. Pension in NS, 24 Oct 1821.]

RIEDE [sic], Caleb, 26, Stelargan [Stillorgan], Dublin, shoemaker [He enlisted on 25 Aug 1804, and was awarded a pension in Nova Scotia, 24 Oct 1821.]

RYAN, James, 25, Powerstown, Kilkenny, labourer.

The remaining ninety-six men were discharged on 24 July 1818:

ALMOND, William, 25, Northern [Northen], Cheshire, smith

AUSTEN, Mathew, 24, Rosenaglass [Rosenallis], Leix, weaver

*BANNON, Patrick, 26, Killisheen [Kilteasheen, Parish Kilbryan], Roscommon, labourer [Awarded a pension in NS, 7 Feb 1822 (*Cf.*, Crowder, 62).]

BARRY, Stephen, 20, St. John's, Limerick, hatter

*BARRY, Thomas, 27, St. John's, Limerick, labourer [He served in the 89th Regiment from 15 Aug 1806 to 2 Dec 1814; pension in NS, 30 Aug 1826 (*Cf.*, Crowder, 62).]

BAYLEY, Henry, 21, Portstock [?], Dorset, labourer

BURKE, Patrick, 30, Hospital, Limerick, labourer

BUTLER, Edward, 24, Laughlinbridge [Leighglinbridge], Carlow, currier

*BUTLER, John, 28 yrs. 6 mos., Clonbegg [Clonbeg], Tipperary, labourer [He enlisted on 14 Mar 1804, and married in Halifax, 14 Aug 1816 (Catholic record), Catherine BURKE. He was granted 290 acres on the Annapolis Road, NS, and was located on lot 98 North, in Dalhousie Settlement, NS, on 16 Oct 1820, with his wife and three children. Pension awarded in NS, 24 Oct 1821 (*Cf.*, Crowder, 60).]

BUTLER, John, 18, Portlaw, Waterford, labourer

COADY, James, 22, Rossbarcon [Rosbercon], Kilkenny, labourer

COADY, Joseph, 20, Waterford City, cooper

*CONNORS, Edward, 33, Dormaul [?], Cork, labourer [Pension in NS, 24 Oct 1821.]

*COSGROVE, Edward, 28, Arklow, Wicklow, labourer. Pension in NS, 30 Aug 1826.]

*COSGROVE, Francis, 36 yrs. 5 mos., Birr, Offaly, shoemaker [He enlisted on 6 Sep 1804, and was granted 200 acres on the Annapolis Road, NS, being located on 16 Oct 1820 on lot 94 South, in Dalhousie Settlement, NS, with two children. In the 1827 Census, he is listed in Annapolis Township as a farmer, with a household of seven. Awarded a pension in NS, 24 Oct 1821.]

*COYLE, Owen, 29 yrs. 3 mos., Armagh Town, weaver [Pension awarded in NS, 24 Oct 1821].

CRIMON, Patrick, 17, Charle[s]field, Cork, labourer

*DAWSON, Michael, 27 yrs. 5 mos., Stonehill [Stonehall, Parish Kilcornan], Limerick, labourer [Pension awarded in NS, 24 Oct 1821 (*Cf.*, Crowder, 61).]

DELANY, Kierans, Galwey [?], Kilkenny, labourer

DIFFELY, James, 25, Nockenlay [Knocknacloy, Parish Boyle], Roscommon, servant [He enlisted in Dec 1814, and was granted 100 acres on the Annapolis Road, NS, being located on lot 121 North, in Dalhousie Settlement, NS., on 16 Oct 1820,]

DOHERTY, Edward, 18, Elphin, Roscommon, labourer

DUFFAY, Michael, 18, Kilcolman, Mayo, labourer.

*DUNN, John, 25, Mountmellick, Leix, labourer [Pension awarded in NS, 24 Oct 1821.]

FANNON, Michael, 19, Cloontuskert, Roscommon, labourer

FARRELL, John, 17, Strokestown, Roscommon, labourer

FARRELL, Patrick, 19, Carlow Town, labourer

*FINNEGAN, Patrick, 25, St. John's, Roscommon, labourer [Pension in NS, 26 Aug 1819.]

FLANAGHAN, James, 23, Dundrum, Tipperary, labourer

FORSTER, Thomas, 19, St. James, Cork, labourer

FRANCIS, Thomas, 15, Innistutroud [Inishtubbrid, Parish Killadysert], Clare, bookbinder

GALAGHER, Martin, 17, Crossmaline, Mayo, labourer

GRAHAM, Joseph, 17, Kilmore, Monaghan, weaver

GREENHALGH, John, 18, Tottington, Lancashire, weaver

*HENNESSY, John, 28, Emly, Tipperary, labourer [Pension in NS, 24 Oct 1821; resident of "St Johns".]

HINDE, Richard, Brinton, Berkshire, labourer

*HOGAN, Michael, 24, St. John's, Limerick, labourer [He enlisted on 14 July 1804; granted 100 acres on the Annapolis Road, NS,.and was located on lot 175 in Dalhousie Settlement on 16 Oct 1820, with his wife, Julia BRIEN, and two children. He appears in the 1827 Census in Annapolis Township as a farmer, with a household of six. Pension in NS, 24 Oct 1821].

HOLLINGSWORTH, George, 28, Almondbury, Yorkshire, cloth dresser

*HOLMES, Patrick, 26, Wexford Town, labourer [He enlisted on 26 Nov 1804. His widow, Diana, granted 100 acres on the Annapolis Road, NS, and was located, with three children, at lot 6 South, in Dalhousie Settlement, NS, 16 Oct 1820. Holmes was killed by an accident while felling a tree (*Cf.*, Calnek, *History of the County of Annapolis*, 263). He died before his pension was awarded, 23 May 1821.]

*HOME, James, 23, Worsley, Lancashire, weaver [John Home, or Hulme, served 2½ years in the 33rd Regiment before joining this unit in 1815.. Pension awarded in NS, 24 Oct 1821.]

HOPKINS, George, 24, Glenairn [Gleninagh], Clare, labourer

*HUDSON, James, 39 yrs. 6 mos., Tipperary Town, shoemaker [Enlisted, 31 Aug 1804, after serving from 18 Oct 1799 to 19 Mar 1802 in the 15th Regiment. He was granted 100 acres on Dalhousie Road, NS, being located on 16 Oct 1820 at lot 94 North, in Dalhousie Settlement, NS. Pension awarded in NS, 24 Oct 1821 (Cf., Crowder, 61).]

ISLES, William, 18, Brescoll [?], Berkshire, labourer [Enlisted, 23 Mar 1814, granted 100 acres on the Annapolis Road, NS, being located on lot 156 South, in Dalhousie Settlement, on 16 Oct 1820. In a petition made at Clements, NS, on 26 Jan 1853, he says that he had been born at Farringdon, Berkshire, and was 57 years of age (NSARM, RG 5, Series "P", Vol. 85 # 106).]

*JONES, Thomas, 35, Longford Town, labourer [Pension in NS, 24 Oct 1821.]

KEATING, Michael, 17, Loughlin [Leighlinbridge], Carlow, labourer

*KELLY, John, 28, Kilronan [Killoran], Galway, tailor [Pension in NS, 24 Oct 1821.]

KELLY, Michael, 16, Loughgall, Armagh, weaver

*KELLY, Patrick, 29, Thomastown, Kilkenny, watchmaker [He enlisted in Aug 1804. He and his wife, Catherine HORAN, had a son, John, baptised at Halifax, 19 Jan 1815 (Catholic record). Pension in NS, 24 Oct 1821 (Cf., Crowder, 61).]

*KELLY, Robert, 28, St. James, Dublin, tailor [Pension in NS, 24 Oct 1821 (Crowder, 60).]

KINESTON, Edward, 21, Coppington [?], Salopshire, miner

*LANE, James, 28, Roscommon Town, servant [Pension in NS, 24 Oct 1821.]

*LINNON [LENNON], John, 27, Baltinglass, Wicklow, labourer [Pension in NS, 23 May 1821.]

LIPSETT, William, 30, Ballydone [Ballindoon, Parish Killadoon], Sligo, weaver

LOCKEY, Joseph, 24, Hampstead, Berkshire, labourer [He enlisted on 5 Sep 1812. In 1850, age 62, he was in Clements Township, NS, and again in 1853, when he received relief (NSARM, RG 5, Series "P", Vol. 85 # 47, 106).]

LOURY [LOWRY], Robert, 28, Ballindery [Ballinderry, Antrim?], weaver [Pension in NS, 31 July 1822 (Crowder, 62).]

McCAN, Edward, 17, Kilmore, Armagh, weaver

*McCARTHY, Denis, 30, Dublin City, labourer [Pension in NS, 24 Oct 1821.]

*McCRATE, Denis, 30 yrs. 6 mos., Monaghan Town, wheelwright [Pension in NS, 24 Oct 1821.]

McGILL, Robert, 18, Ballanagilla [Ballynagilly], Tyrone, smith [He enlisted on 15 Nov 1813, and was granted 100 acres on the Annapolis Road, NS, being located on lot 1 on the Liverpool Rd., at Dalhousie Settlement, NS, on 16 Oct 1820, with a wife and two children. He was listed in the 1827 Census as a farmer in Annapolis Township with a household of six.]

*McGOWN, Thomas, 27, Kilmore, Armagh, labourer [He enlisted on 2 Mar 1805; granted 100 acres on the Annapolis Road, being located at lot 169 South, Dalhousie Settlement, on 16 Oct 1820. He was listed as a farmer in the 1827 Census in Annapolis Township with a household of four. Pension in NS, 24 Oct 1821 (Cf., Crowder, 61).]

MAHON, James, 11, Geneva [Barracks, St. Nicholas Parish], Waterford, labourer

*MAHONY, Frederick, 27 yrs. 4 mos., Ardfinan, Tipperary, chandler [He enlisted on 24 May 1804. He was granted 100 acres on the Annapolis Road, NS, being located at lot 122 North, in Dalhousie Settlement, NS, on 16 Oct 1820. Pension in NS, 24 Oct 1821.]

MATHEWS, Richard, 24, Lancaster, Lancashire, servant

*MEARA, John, 36, Skirk, Leix, labourer [Pension in NS, 24 Oct 1821 (Cf., Crowder, 60).]

*MEARA, Sgt. Patrick, 27 yrs. 6 mos., Skirk, Leix, labourer [Enlisted, 16 May 1804; married 7 Nov 1814 at Menzies Manor, New Brunswick, Ann O'NEILL of Dipper Harbour, NB. Their daughter Eleanor was baptised at Halifax, 29 Jan 1816 (Catholic record). Pension in NS, 24 Oct 1821 (*Cf.*, Crowder, 60).]

MERRITT, Henry, 18, Stanton, Wiltshire, labourer

MILES, Robert, 16, Athleague, Roscommon, shoemaker

MITCHELL, Thomas, 21, Kiltegan, Wicklow, weaver

MORAN, Jerry, 29, Tralee, Kerry, hatter

*NOCTON, Patrick, 32, Dublin City, labourer [Pension in NS, 24 Oct 1821.]

*O'BRYAN, James, 29, Farmon [Termonbarry], Roscommon, labourer [He enlisted on 18 May 1804, and was awarded a pension in NS, 24 Oct 1821. The 1838 Census lists James "Obrine" near Sydney, Cape Breton, with a household of seven.]

*O'BRYAN, John, 29, Harbourstown [Herbertstown, Parish Kilcullane], Limerick, cooper [He enlisted on 3 May 1804, and was awarded a pension in NS, 26 Aug 1819.]

*O'BRYAN, John, 26, Kilcullen [perhaps Kilcummin intended?], Mayo, labourer [Pension in NS, 24 Oct 1821 (*Cf.*, Crowder, 60).]

O'LAUGHLIN, Thomas, 22, Killeily [Killaloe], Clare, labourer

PARR, Thomas, 28, Windle [Hindley?], Lancashire, tailor

PATTEN, Maurice, 24, St. John's, Sligo, tailor

PHILLIPS, Thomas, 18, Ballyheden [Ballyhean], Mayo, labourer

POWER, Edward. 26, Cloyne, Cork, labourer

*POWER, John, 32, Golden, Tipperary, hatter [Pension in NS, 24 Oct 1821.]

*QUADE, Thomas, 33, Kilmurry, Limerick, labourer [Pension in NS, 24 Oct 1821.]

*QUIRK, William, 29, Kilburn [Kilbarron], Tipperary, labourer [Pension in NS, 24 Oct 1821.]

RIELLY, James, 20, Rushwat [Rushwarp], Yorkshire, labourer [Enlisted in 1812.]

RIELLY, James, 21, Kilglass, Roscommon, labourer

RODGERS, Patrick, 20, Ballintubber [Ballintober], Roscommon, labourer

RYAN, Edward, 28, Carrick, Tipperary, labourer

RYAN, Francis, 20, Ballintober, Roscommon, labourer

*RYAN, James, 28, Fethard, Tipperary, tailor [Pension in NS, 24 Oct 1821.]

RYAN, William, 22, Burrowsoleigh [Borrisoleigh], Tipperary, shoemaker [Enlisted Nov 1813]

*SLATTERY, Thomas, 28, Kilcommon, Mayo, labourer [Pension in NS, 16 Aug 1825.]

SUMMERS, Michael, 23, Templedegan [Templeludigan], Wexford, tailor [He enlisted in Feb 1817. He married at St. Paul's Anglican, Halifax, 14 Jan 1823, Sarah EADES.]

SWEET, John, 24, S. Austle [St. Austell], Cornwall, labourer [He enlisted, 7 Apr 1813; granted 100 acres on the Annapolis Road, being located with his wife and child on lot 127 South, in Dalhousie Settlement, NS, on 16 Oct 1820. He appears in the 1827 Census in Annapolis Township as a farmer with a household of five.]

THOMAS, Jeremiah, 30, St. Michael's, Dublin, shoemaker

WALDERS, David, 31, Woodchurch, Bedfordshire, labourer [almost certainly an error. Both Walders as a surname and Woodchurch as a place name are found in Kent]

WALSH, Thomas, 32 yrs. 5 mos., Glenbaun [Parish Kilmoylan], Limerick, labourer

WALSH, William, 27, Carlow Town, hozier [He enlisted,31 Dec 1813; granted 100 acres on the Annapolis Road, and located on lot 169 North, in Dalhousie Settlement, NS, 16 Oct 1820]

WHITE, Daniel, 30, Dungarvan, Waterford, labourer

WYATT, Joseph, 17, Whitney, Oxfordshire, labourer.

<u>HALIFAX, NOVA SCOTIA</u>, 24 July 1818 (1 man)

HENNESSY, James, 23, Bonnykerry [Bunnagurragh, Parish Barragh], Carlow, labourer [He enlisted on 31 Dec 1813, and was granted 100 acres on the Annapolis Road, NS, being located on lot 96 North, in Dalhousie Settlement, on 16 Oct 1820.]

<u>Note</u>: There are many references to grants on the Annapolis Road. A word of explanation is necessary for those unacquainted with colonial Nova Scotia. The first British capital of Nova Scotia was Annapolis Royal, the French capital, Port Royal, having been renamed in 1713 to honour Queen Anne. Halifax was founded as the new capital in 1749. Annapolis remained important and a garrison was maintained there well into the nineteenth century.

After the Napoleonic wars and the War of 1812, the British military establishment was reduced, and the idea of developing a major road to connect the old and new capitals was advanced. By settling groups of discharged soldiers at various points along the proposed route, not only would a labour force be put in place to construct and maintain the proposed road, but the presence of inhabitants would attract settlement and development to the western interior of Nova Scotia.

The road was not completed. Had it been, the present drive of 206 km (128 miles) from Halifax to Annapolis would be about 160 km (100 miles). A series of disconnected communities allows its route to be traced on a modern map: Halifax>Hammonds Plains> Pockwock (Wellington Settlement)>Sherwood>New Ross [Sherbrooke Settlement] >Dalhousie Road>East Dalhousie> Albany Cross>West Dalhousie>Annapolis Royal.

(B) THE 64th REGIMENT, 1813-1815

The 64th was the Second Staffordshire Regiment of Foot, sometimes known by the name of their colonel as Wynyard's Regiment, and nicknamed "The Black Knots". Between August 1813 and June 1815, forty-nine of its men died at Halifax, Nova Scotia, one deserted, and a further twenty-four were discharged there. The War of 1812 had ended and - it must have seemed at the time - Napoleon's career had finished. Ironically, even as the 64th Regiment was thinning its ranks, Bonaparte was plotting his escape from Elba and the celebrated "Hundred Days" lay ahead, with the dramatic conclusion at the near run Battle of Waterloo in June 1815.

Since all deaths, discharges and desertions occurred at Halifax that information is notgiven in individual cases. Fifty-five of the men were Irish and fifteen English. Of the remainder there was one each from Poland, Scotland and Wales. One man's origin is not stated, but his name - Hugh McInness - could have been either Scottish or Ulster Irish.

DISCHARGED

21 Feb 1815: Samuel BLAIR, 26 in 1808, weaver from Finmoy [Finvoy], Antrim (married at St. Matthew's Presbyterian, Halifax, NS, 24 Sep 1819, to Catherine MOODY.]
1 June 1815: John BOLTON, 20 in 1803, tailor from Donain [Doonan in the Parish of Tickmacrevan], Antrim.
30 Aug 1813: Henry BOYCE, 19 in 1809, labourer from Rye [Ryelands], Donegal

24 Feb 1815: Thomas COOPER, 19 in 1807, painter from Birmingham, Warwickshire

24 Feb 1815: Samuel CUNNINGHAM, 24 in 1807, weaver from Shankill, Antrim

24 Feb 1815: Sgt. Hugh DONNELLY, 20 in 1807, weaver from Killiman [Killyman], Tyrone [He married Mary ROSS and had several children. He was a police constable at Halifax from 1815 to 1818 and then kept an inn. He received a land grant at Chezzetcook, east of Halifax, NS, and was buried 27 May 1822, age 36 (Halifax Catholic record)]

24 Feb 1815: John DONNELLY, 34 in 1807, weaver from Marafelt [Magherafelt], Derry

24 Feb 1815: John DONOUGHY, 18 in 1807, labourer from Donakehan [?], Antrim

24 May 1815: Patrick DREW, 22 in 1807, cordwainer from Belfast

24 Feb 1815: James FARRELL, 19 in 1807, labourer from Teboyne [Taughboyne], Donegal [He married at St. Paul's Anglican, Halifax, on 5 Oct 1815, Mary DIEREN, widow]

24 Feb 1815: Stephen GRINDY, 23 in 1807, potter from Stoke [on Trent], Staffordshire

24 Feb 1815: William HAMILTON, 18 in 1807, weaver from Lifford, Donegal

24 Feb 1815: Peter HILL, 29 in 1807, mason from Kingsling [Kingsley], Staffordshire

24 May 1815: Thomas KEAN, 20 in 1807, tailor from Drumall [Drummaul], Antrim

20 Feb 1815: William KITSON, 26 in 1807, ropemaker from Antrim Town

24 Feb 1815: Maurice LOONEY, 30 in 1807, labourer from Car[n]money, Antrim

24 Feb 1815: Daniel McALLEAR, 20 in 1807, labourer from Longfield, Tyrone

24 Feb 1815: Philip McGROARTY, 24 in 1807, weaver from Dromhome [Drumhome], Donegal

24 Feb 1815: Hugh McINNESS, 19 in 1807....

24 Feb 1815: Adam MOORE, 32 in 1807, blacksmith from Linegarvy [Lisnagarvy, Parish of Blaris], Antrim.

24 Apr 1815: John O'NEILL, 21 in 1807, weaver from Belfast

24 Feb 1815: Cpl. Samuel SHOOTER, 20 in 1807, cloth lapper from Coner [Connor], Antrim

24 Feb 1815: James STRANGE, 20 in 1807, labourer from Ballyeaston, Antrim

24 Feb 1815: Joseph WARTON, 20 in 1807, tailor from Womborn [Wombourne], Staffordshire

DESERTED

7 Sep 1813: Timothy CONNAHAN, 25 in 1810, weaver from Fenis [Fenit], Kerry. Did not   return.

DEATHS

13 Jun 1813: Hugh McCOY, 20 in 1800, weaver from Coleraine, Derry

24 Aug 1813: Robert McGRATH, 20 in 1799, weaver from Annahill[Annahilt], Down

 3 Oct 1813: Isaac LANKEY, 21 in 1812, weaver from Saego [Seagoe], Armagh

 8 Oct 1813: William JOHNSTONE, 30 in 1800, currier from Lisburn, Antrim

13 Oct 1813: Daniel FRANCIOA, 19 in 1815, painter from Arhaw, Poland

14 Oct 1813: Charles O'DONNELL, 21 in 1800, labourer from Acheny [?], Fermanagh

23 Oct 1813: George PARKS, 20 in 1800, tailor from St. Bridget's, Dublin

 8 Nov 1813: James COTTER, 24 in 1802, from Mayo

 9 Nov 1813: John DONALDSON, 19 in 1800, weaver from Anahill [Annahilt], Down

10 Nov 1813: James DOUGHERTY, 24 in 1800, labourer from Mullingar, Westmeath

 2 Dec 1813: William DOUGHERTY, 26 in 1800, tailor from Kilkerou...ehan [?]

12 Dec 1813: William PHILLIPS, 27 in 1807, cordwainer from St. Michael's, Limerick

22 Dec 1813: George NICHOLS, 22 in 1798, weaver from Clones, Monaghan

23 Jan 1814: Patrick McDERMOTT, 30 in 1804, hatter from Kilecuty [?], Roscommon

 3 Feb 1814: George CARR, 21 in 1803, slater from Hexham, Northumberland

23 Feb 1814: Cpl. Robert STAIKE, 28 in 1802, labourer from Partington, Yorkshire

11 Mar 1814: Patrick WARD, 20 in 180–, cordwainer from [St] Peter's, Louth
18 Mar 1814: Timothy NOONEY, 46 in 1802, labourer from Sand [?], Westmeath
 7 Apr 1814: John WETHERALD, 20 in 1802, weaver from Clonalty [?], Tipperary.
13 Apr 1814: Sgt. Bernard McCRINOR, 2o in 1800, weaver from Morafelt [Magherafelt], Antrim
14 Apr 1814: Samuel SPILSBURY, 23 in 1802, needle maker from Tickingham [Ticklenham],
        Worcestershire, England.
16 Apr 1814: Daniel CLEARY, 24 in 1812, nailor from Turloss [Thurles], Tipperary
27 Apr 1814: Alexander MUNRO, 40 in 1802, tobacconist from St.. James, Dublin
 5 May 1814: James ROBINSON, 26 in 1802, labourer from Copperstow [?], Berkshire
14 May 1814: Sgt. Tullins SLEAVIN, 28 in 1807, carpenter from Donegal Town
23 May 1814: Daniel B— [appears in alphabetical sequence Bi/Bo. Illegible on microfilm], labourer
        from Kingso–tone [King's Somborne], Hampshire
26 May 1814: John GRIFFIN,17 in 1803, labourer from Arford [Ardfert], Kerry
17 July 1814: William SMITH, 30 in 1804, bricklayer from St. Mary's, Surrey.
29 July 1814: Adam FARRELL, 21 in 1807, flaw dresser from Stranolland [Stranorlar], Donegal
 2 Aug 1814: James SHEERAN, 26 in 1807, weaver from Arteleguy [Artikellys?], Donegal
23 Sep 1814: Donald McDONALD, 40 in 1803, weaver from Urquhart, Ross-shire
24 Sep 1814: William McQUILLAN, 24 in 1807, weaver from Clough, Armagh [sic; Co. Down]
25 Oct 1814: John REED, 22 in 1800, labourer from Huntington, Devon
25 Oct 1814: Robert WHITE, 30 in 1802, labourer from St. Giles, Berkshire
 1 Nov 1814: Samuel LACKEY, 30 in 1802, weaver from Blenburn [?], Longford
 4 Nov 1814: James SAWYERS, 29 in 1813, weaver from High Church, Lanark, Scotland
 9 Nov 1814: George McCOLLOUGH, 20 in 1800, weaver from Drumswords [townland in the Parish
        of Killeevan], Monaghan
10 Nov 1814: William EVANS, 17 in 1813, labourer from Welsh Fitton, Shropshire
 7 Dec 1814: William PRIOR, 20 in 1804, labourer from Lead, Kent
22 Dec 1814: John KENNEDY, 19 in 1807, weaver from Coleraine, Antrim
 7 Jan 1815: George DOBSON, 20 in 1809, labourer from Mohill, Leitrim
20 Jan 1815: John McCABE, 36 in 1802, weaver from Loughan, Monaghan [surely in Cavan?]
 1 Feb 1815: John MULCAHY, 25 in 180–, labourer from Banehy [Barnane-ely], Tipperary
 6 Feb 1815: John STEPHENS, 30 in 1803, collier from Landale, Glamorganshire
13 Feb 1815: James MURPHY, 22 in 1800, tailor from Timboy [Tempo], Fermanagh
 3 Mar 1815: Richard WHITE, 20 in 1800, labourer from Rathgrave [Rathgarve], Westmeath
14 Mar 1815: John DAVIS, 18 in 1803, labourer from Rythan [?], Derbyshire
24 May 1815: Cpl. Samuel KILPATRICK, 20 in 1800, weaver from Tillisk [Tullylish], Down
        [Colour Sgt.Samuel William Kilpatrick married Bridget MOLONY. Issue.]
 1 June 1815: Joseph HUNTER, 24 in 1807, weaver from Donegal, Antrim [sic]

(Source: PRO, W.O. 25, Vol. 449 [NAC mfm B5472].)

(C) THE 81st   REGIMENT, 1821-1829

     The 81st (Loyal Lincoln Volunteers), whose colonel, Sir James Kempt (died 1854), a veteran
of the Battle of Waterloo, was lieutenant-governor of Nova Scotia ,1820 to 1828. Between July 1821
and October 1829, 123 men were taken off strength. Seventy died, thirty-six deserted and
seventeen were discharged, six of them with military pensions. Despite its name, 57% of the "other
ranks" in the regiment were Irish. None of the forty Englishmen came from Lincolnshire;

Warwick, Dorset, Gloucester, Lancashire and Hampshire account for the majority. There were eight Welshmen, three Scots, a German, a Gibraltarian and a Swiss. Unless otherwise stated, all these men were privates.

DIED (70 men)

The depot description books occasionally add snippets of information. Three men (Archer, Davenport and Hoskins) drowned at various times in the Saint John River. The summertime dates suggest that they may have been swimming. Sangster died suddenly at Annapolis in the barracks. Connolly, March and Parry's deaths support the view that in the 1820s a soldier's life "was not a happy one". McGill's father is mentioned, while Wilson seems to have had theoretical military training.

ARCHER, Thomas, 18 in 1813, labourer, Brails, Warwick, died at Woodstock, NB, 17 Sep 1828 [Cpl. Archer drowned in the Saint John River]

BIRD, James, 24 in 1820, labourer, St. James, Dublin, died at Halifax, 18 Apr 1822

BOOTH, Adam, 19 in 1804, weaver, Manchester, Lancashire, died at Halifax, 27 Aug 1822

CAVENAGH, Michael, 20 in 1809, labourer, Johnstown, Wexford, died at Halifax, 10 Oct 1825 [Michael Kavanah was buried 12 Oct 1825, age 36 (Catholic record).]

CLEARY, John, 15 in 1812, labourer, Cappashagel [Cappasallagh], Galway, died at Halifax, 24 Nov 1822 [Buried 25 Nov 1822, age 27 (Catholic record says he was of Ballinasloe).]

CONNOLLY, John, joined 1811, labourer, Plymouth, Devon, died at Fredericton, NB, 6 Jan 1829 [Source states that he "died through excessive drinking".]

CONNOR, Timothy, 28 in 1815, labourer, Killarney, Kerry, died at Halifax, 11 May 1822

COONEY, John, 17 in 1810, labourer, Clonmel, Tipperary, died at Saint John, NB, 1 Mar 1827

COVEY, Henry, 17 in 1821, weaver, Urney, Cavan, died at Halifax, 6 July 1822

DAVENPORT, John, 18 in 1813, labourer, Coventry, Warwick, drowned in Saint John River near Fredericton, NB, 28 July 1827.

DAVIS, Daniel, 19 in 1807, cordwainer, Tawyn, Merioneth, died at Halifax, 24 June 1824

DAVIS, Hugh, 23 in 1809, labourer, Uanfawd, Merioneth, died at Halifax, 7 Dec 1824

FARREN, Thomas, 18 in 1809, labourer, Templemow [Templemoyle]. Derry, labourer, died at Halifax, 31 July 1821

FENTON, John, 29 in 1812, slater & plasterer, Midleton, Cork, died at Halifax, 2 Dec 1822 [He died in the Barracks at Halifax and was buried, 3 Dec 1822, age 35 (Catholic record). His wife was Mary KIDNEY, also from County Cork.]

FLYN, Patrick, 19 in 1821, labourer, Clunbroney [Clonbroney], Longford, died at Halifax, 8 Jan 1822 [Buried 8 Jan 1822, age 20 (Catholic record).]

FORD, Michael, 22 in 1815, labourer, Kilcunly [Kilconla], Galway, died at Halifax, 18 June 1822 [Buried 20 June 1822, age 28 (Catholic record).]

FOX, John, 21 in 1807, bleacher, Clondalkin, Dublin, died at Halifax, 13 Nov 1823 [Buried, 14 Dec 1823, age 45 (Catholic record).]

GARRETT, Henry, 17 in 1815, tailor, "Donough", Offaly, died at Fredericton, NB, 26 Jan 1828.

GOSLAN, William, 18 in 1825, labourer, Ballymodan, Cork, died at Halifax, 27 Dec 1828

HALLAM, Frank, 15 in 1810, shoemaker, Darnell, Yorkshire, died at Saint John, NB, 23 Feb 1827

HANLON, John, 23 in 1819, labourer, Tydevnet [Tedavnet], Monaghan, died at Saint John, NB, 20 Nov 1827.

HOSKINS, Samuel, 21 in 1811, labourer, Beaminster, Dorset. drowned in the Saint John River near Fredericton, NB, 12 Aug 1829

HOULAGHAN, William, 25 in 1820, labourer, St. John's, Limerick, died at Halifax, 4 Nov 1827.

JACKSON, William, 23 in 1806, labourer, Winchcombe, Gloucester, died in Prince Edward Island, 11 May 1826

JONES, Joseph, 24 in 1806, mason, Carmarthen Town, Wales, died at Halifax, 20 Apr 1822

JOYCE, Edward, 27 in 1813, labourer, "Rathfole", Donegal, died at Halifax, 7 Aug 1821

JUDD, Richard, 19 in 1814, plasterer, St. Mary's, Warwick, died at Saint John, NB, 21 Feb 1828

KEIRNAN, James, 18 in 1819, labourer, Tempo, Fermanagh, died at Halifax, 22 May 1822 [Buried, 24 May 1822, age 22 (Catholic record).]

KELLY, Patrick, 25 in 1807, labourer, Dunshaughlin, Meath, died at Saint John, NB, 7 Dec 1826

LAWN, Edward, 17 in 1820, labourer, Ballyshannon, Donegal, died Saint John, NB, 27 Sep 1828

LLOYD, John, 19 in 1811, miller, Gwyddilwan, Merioneth, Wales, died at Fredericton, NB, 29 Nov 1826

LOCK, James, 20 in 1811, labourer, Piddleton, Dorset, died at Fredericton, NB, 25 Feb 1829

LOVETT, Thomas, 18 in 1821, weaver, O Droney [O'Dorney], Kerry, died at Halifax, 12 Feb 1822 [Thomas "Lonworth" from Inniskillen was buried 13 Feb 1822, age 21 (Catholic record).]

McGILL, Henry, 21 in 1808, baker, "Killibegs", Antrim, died at Halifax, 25 May 1825 [Buried 27 May 1825, age 38, son of Henry McGill, gardener to Lord O'Neill, a native of Change Castle, Antrim (Catholic record).]

MAISH, James, 20 in 1811, labourer, Beaminster, Dorset, died at Saint John, NB, 3 Mar 1828

MANNING, James, 19 in 1811, carpenter, Stockland, Dorset, died at Halifax, 30 Jan 1823

MARCH, John, 14 in 1811, labourer, Shoreham, Sussex, died at Halifax, 20 June 1826 ["shot himself at Halifax, while on guard duty."]

MILLER, William, 9 in 1803, labourer, St Warbus [St Werburgh's], Dublin, died at Fredericton, NB, 18 Mar 1828

MILLMAN, John, 6 in 1812, labourer, born on ship at Gibraltar, died at Fredericton, NB, 10 Nov 1826. He was a drummer

MORGAN, William, 25 in 1806, labourer, Llanteigsant [Llantrisent] ,Glamorgan, Wales, died at Halifax, 5 Jan 1823

OLIVE, Thomas, 29 in 1805, cotton weaver, St. Catherine's, Dublin, died at Halifax, 21 Apr 1825 [Buried 21 Apr 1825, age 50 (Catholic record).]

PARRY, Valentine, 12 in 1811, labourer, All Saints, Hereford, died at Saint John, NB, 3 Sep 1829 while being given 300 lashes.

PATTERSON, William, 30 in 1811, gardener, "Inverask", Midlothian, died Halifax, 7 June 1825

PHILLIPS, Daniel, tailor, 19 in 1809, Eglaswad [Eglwys], Carmarthen, Wales, died Fredericton, NB, 29 Dec 1826

POWER, Thomas, 19½ in 1821, labourer, Lady's Bridge, Cork, died at Saint John, NB, 27 July 1827

REDMOND, Patrick, 27 in 1815, blacksmith, "Tarvise", Wexford, died at Saint John, NB, 28 Nov 1826.

ROGERS, Cpl. William, 18 in 1801, labourer, Quinton, Gloucester, died at Windsor, NS, 16 Oct 1826 [His widow was buried 10 Jan 1828 at Halifax (Catholic record).]

SANGSTER, John, 19 in 1811, labourer, Fontmell Magna, Dorset, died suddenly in the barracks at Annapolis Royal, NS, 16 May 1825

SAXTON, James, 20 in 1818, labourer, Kilmore, Monaghan, "found Frozen to Death the morning of the 21st January 1828" at Fredericton, NB

SCARLET, Joseph, 18 in 1821, weaver, Urney, Cavan, died at Halifax, 4 July 1821 [earliest date]

SMITH, James, 19 in 1821, weaver, Ballymoren [Ballymodan], Cork, died Halifax, 30 July 1823

SMITH, William, 19 in 1811, gun barrel filer, Birmingham, England, died Halifax, 16 May 1826

SQUIBB, Richard, 24 in 1811, labourer, Chaldon [Chaldon Herning], Dorset, died at St Andrew's, NB, 14 Dec 1828

STACEY, Abraham, 19 in 1803, labourer, Liverpool, Lancs., died Windsor Rd., NS, 22 Aug 1826
STUART, Richard, 18 in 1805, Bromsgrove, Worcester, nailer, died at Halifax, 3 May 1824.
SWEET, Mathew, 20 in 1813, labourer, Merriot [Meriott], Somerset, died at Halifax, 25 Aug 1828
TAYLOR, Samuel, 18 in 1805, labourer, Leominster, Hereford, died Saint John, NB, 27 Dec 1826
THOMAS, Evan, 27 in 1806, labourer, "Llanwilog", Carmarthen, Wales, died at Halifax, 12 Jan 1825
TILLET, Benjamin, 23 in 1814, cooper, St. James, Bristol, Glos., died at Halifax, 12 Aug 1825
TONE, John, 14 in 1815, labourer, Edenderry, Offaly, died at Fredericton, NB, 15 June 1827
TOULMAN, William, 18 in 1813, weaver, Southampton, Hants, died Fredericton, NB, 17 Oct 1826
TRENEGH, George, 20 in 1812, weaver, Clontibret, Monaghan, died at Annapolis Royal, NS, 25
          Apr 1825
TWINCH, John, 14 in 1820, labourer, Galway Town, died at Halifax. 19 Mar 1824
VIRGOE, Cpl. Richard, 17 in 1804, labourer, St Owen's, Hereford, died at Halifax, 7 Mar 1825
WALSH, John, 19 in 1811, shoemaker, Kilmain[e], Mayo, died at Halifax, 29 Dec 1822
          [Buried 31 Dec 1822, age 32 (Catholic record states that he was from Castlebar, Mayo).]
WILSON, John, 14 in 1820, drummer, County Dublin, died at Halifax, 28 May 1824 [Source notes
          that he had attended the Hibernian Military School at Dublin]
WINLEDGE, Sgt.–, 20 in 1813, brass founder, Birmingham, Warwick, died at Saint John, NB, 19
          May 1827 [compare with Wooledge entry, infra]
WOODS, Stephen, 21 in 1807, labourer, R[e]ynagh, Offaly, died at Halifax, 22 Sep 182–.
WOODWARD, Joseph, 21 in 1804, labourer, Bars[t]on, Warwick, died in Prince Edward Island, 18
          Jan 1824
WOOLEDGE, Cpl. Joseph, 18 in 1813, brass founder, Birmingham, Warwick, died at Halifax, 27
          Dec 1825 [compare with Winledge entry, supra]

[Also noticed was the burial of Patrick CONNELL, Private, 81st Regiment, 20, from Dungarvan,
          Waterford, at Halifax, 31 July 1823 (Catholic record).]

"RAN" (36 men)

Most of these men were absent on their own. Three pairs of desertions occur: Dwyer and
Whelan, Hagarty and Thompson, Sullivan and Young, The unfortunate William Trimmell ran, only
to die in confinement in the Halifax Bridewell. The exact date of going AWOL is given for each.

BESTON, Patrick, 17½ in 1821, labourer, Clonmel, Tipperary, at Halifax 13 Apr 1824
BROCK, Cpl. John, 18 in 1813, shipwright, Bristol. Somerset, at Halifax, 14 Aug 1824
          [Returned to the Regiment on 19 August 1824.]
BURNS, Thomas, 19 in 1821, labourer, "Crag", Carlow, at Halifax, 20 Jan 1822
CONNOLLY, Patrick, 20 in 1819, labourer, Stamollan [Stamullin], Meath, at Halifax,17 June 1823.
CROWLEY, Daniel, 17 in 1821, labourer, Bandon, Cork, at Saint John, NB, 23 July 1827
DONEGAN, Daniel, 18 in 1825, labourer, "Baliesh", Cork, at Saint John, NB, 26 Aug 1829
DWYER, Michael, 19 in 1826, labourer, Annacarty, Tipperary, at Fredericton, NB, 31 May 1828
FOWLER, James, 18 in 1820, labourer, "Killada", Antrim, at Halifax, 21 July 1822
FOX, William, 27 in 1820, labourer, Granard, Longford, at Saint John, NB, 1 June 1822
HACKETT, William, 17½ in 1821, labourer, Coppowhite [Cappagh White], Tipperary, at
          Halifax, 3 Apr 1824
HAGARTY, James, 20 in 1823, hatter, Cavan[s], Fermanagh, at Saint John, NB, 22 Apr 1829
HARTLEY, Peter, 19 in 1813, shoemaker, Warrington, Lancs., at Saint John, NB, 10 Oct 1828

HEFFERNAN, John, 19 in 1813, shoemaker, Kilbride, Offaly, in Newfoundland, 10 Nov. 1824

HENRY, John, 17 in 1820, labourer, Rossory, Fermanagh, at Saint John, NB, 4 July 1827 [He had been AWOL briefly at Halifax, 1 - 2 Sep 1823.]

HUGHES, Michael, 22 in 1823, labourer, Naas, Kildare, at Halifax, 5 June 1825

KNIGHT, Richard, 16 in 1815, labourer, Southampton, Hants, at Halifax, 5 June 1825

McFADDEN, Michael, 22 in 1819, labourer, Kilskerry [Kilskeery], Tyrone, at Halifax, 29 June 1824

McGUIRE, John, 27 in 1821, labourer, Daunbar [Drumbar], Cavan, in Prince Edward Island, 24 Aug 1824.

McLAUGHLIN, Hugh, 18 in 1815, shoemaker, Shinrone, Offaly, at Saint John, NB, 17 July 1827

MASTERSON, Michael, 22 in 1821, labourer, Drummard, Longford, at Saint John, NB, 24 Oct 1828.

MEDLEY, Thomas, 15½ in 1809, carter, Birmingham, Warwick, at Halifax, 24 Dec. 1828

MONAGHAN, Edward, 17 in 1820, labourer, Lea, Leix, at Saint John, NB, 8 Sep 1828

MORRIS, Hugh, 18 in 1815, labourer, Rosenallis, Leix, at Saint John, NB, 16 Apr 1829 [Buried 23 June 1825, Hanna, 2, dau of Hugh & Hanna Morris, 81st Regt (Catholic record, Halifax)

NORRIS, William, 31 in 1814, shoemaker, Twyford, Hants, at Halifax, 9 Oct 1823 ["alias Thomas Pane."]

QUIN, Thomas, 17 in 1820, labourer, Clonmel, Tipperary, at Saint John, NB, 11 July 1827

ROGERS, William, 20 in 1820, labourer, Drumkereen [Drumkeeran], Leitrim, at Saint John, NB, 2 May 1827

SHIERAN, James, 20 in 1821, "Ballinagowen", at Saint John, NB, 6 Nov 1826 [The place is undoubtedly Ballynagowan, of which two are in Limerick and a third is in Armagh. People named Shearan lived in both counties.]

SULLIVAN, John, 17 in 1821, labourer, Castletown, Cork, at Annapolis Royal, NS, 28 Aug 1823

SULLIVAN, Timothy, 20 in 1820, labourer, Kenmare, Kerry, at Halifax, 25 May 1822

TAYLOR, Edward, 18 in 1806, sawyer, Newent, Glos., at Halifax, 6 Aug 1824

THOMPSON, John, 19 in 1805, labourer, Bird, Aberdeen, Fredericton, NB, 24 Nov 1826

THOMPSON, Joseph, 20 in 1826, ribbon weaver, Toleshill, Warwick, at Saint John, NB, 22 Apr 1829

TRIMMELL, William, 18 in 1820, labourer, Derravulleen [Derryvullan], Fermanagh, at Halifax, 17 Oct 1823 [Died in the Halifax Bridewell (jail).]

WALSH, Francis, 15 in 1821, labourer, Upper Shandon, Cork, at Halifax, 1 Aug 1822

WHELAN, Philip, 17 in 1820, labourer, Kyle, Leix, at Fredericton, NB, 31 May 1828

YOUNG, James, 18 in 1821, sawyer, Drumlain [Drumlion], Cavan, at Annapolis Royal, NS, 28 Aug 1823.

DISCHARGED (17 men)

BARRY, William, 16 in 1813, labourer, Bideford, Devon, discharged at Halifax, 25 Mar 1822

BIERY, Sgt. Peter, 32 in 1821, tailor, Berne, Switzerland, discharged at Fredericton, NB, 31 Dec 1828 [The surname Bieri is found in Canton Berne, especially in the Emmental and west of the Thunersee. He was awarded a pension, 25 June 1829. His wife, Mary Cecily LeCAINE died, Dartmouth, NS, 21 Mar 1837, age 35. He headed a household of 11 people at Halifax in 1838 (Census), and was a tailor in Halifax as late as 1843. His son Thomas Peter was married in 1854 at New York City.]

BONN, William, 33 in 1807, musician, Odenban, Düsseldorf, Germany, discharged at Saint John, NB, 24 Dec 1827. Noted that he served, 1804-1807 in the Chasseurs Britannique. His name was properly Wendilius Bonn, as appears from his pension award, 30 Jan 1828.

COLBOURNE, Sgt. William, 27 in 1803, gunsmith, Rilston, Staffordshire, discharged at Fredericton, NB, 24 Feb 1828. [Awarded a pension at Halifax, 21 May 1828]

COLEMAN, Hospital Sgt. Andrew, 24 in 1807, labourer, Kilcullen [Kilcollin, Parish Kilbride], Offaly, discharged at Fredericton, NB, 24 Sep 1829 [Awarded a pension at "St. Johns", 9 Dec 1829. Mary Ann, 13 months, dau of Andrew & Mary Coleman, 81st Regiment, was buried 12 Dec 1824 at Halifax (Catholic record).]

CONNYER, Sgt. Joseph, 23 in 1802, labourer, Glenn, Cavan, discharged at Fredericton, NB, 24 Nov 1825

DWYER, Michael, 21 in 1821, labourer, Cappagh, Tipperary, discharged at Halifax, 9 Aug 1828

FROMENT, William, 18 in 1826, carpenter, Waterbeach, Cambridge, discharged at Fredericton, NB, 1 Sep 1828 [His short length of service suggests that his health was poor]

GRAHAM, William, 22 in 1820, labourer, Ballyhane [Ballyhean], Mayo, discharged at Halifax, 24 June 1822 [His brief period of service suggests that his health was poor]

JACKSON, Charles, 18 in 1826, labourer, Westbury, Wiltshire, discharged at Fredericton, NB, 18 Oct 1829 [latest date in this record]

JOHNS, Sgt. William, 19 in 1804, labourer, St. Oswalds, Cheshire, discharged at Halifax, 8 Sep 1825 [Appointed Halifax Town Sgt. Married 10 Aug 1836 (St George's, Halifax) Maria Magdalena, dau of Rev. Ludwig FLOHR of Germany. He was an iron founder in Halifax]

LEWIS, Sgt. William, 22 in 1806, miner, Swansea, Glamorgan, Wales, discharged at Halifax, 24 May 1827 ["Matt^w Lewis awarded a pension at Halifax, 8 Aug 1827]

McCARTY, Michael, 15 in 1821, labourer, Killingly [Killeenleagh, Parish Ross], Cork, discharged at Fredericton, NB, 12 Nov 1828 ["Drummed out as a notorious bad Character"]

McMANUS, John, 17 in 1825, weaver, Killishandro [Killashandra], Cavan, discharged at Saint John, NB, 6 Sep 1829

MITCHELL, John, 22 in 1819, labourer, Gillan [Gallen], Offaly, discharged at Halifax, 25 Mar 1822

MOLINEAUX, Sgt. Samuel, 18 in 1799, nailer, Sterling, Edinburgh, Scotland, discharged at Halifax, 25 Apr 1824 [Awarded a pension in Nova Scotia, 16 June 1824, later lived at Kingston, Ontario, and died 5 Feb 1857 (Cf., Crowder, 50, 205).]

TAYLOR, James, 35 in 1806, weaver, Oldham, Lancs., discharged at Saint John,. NB, 24 Dec 1827 [Awarded a pension in Nova Scotia, 30 Jan 1828 (Cf., Crowder, 50).]

(Source: PAC, W.O. 25, Vols. 482, 484 [NAC mfm B5483 and B 5484].)

(D) THE 74TH REGIMENT, 1822-1828

Thirteen members of the 74th Regiment of Foot, a Highland unit, were taken off strength in the Atlantic region: nine at Halifax, Nova Scotia. two in New Brunswick, one at St. Andrews, New Brunswick, and one at St. John's, Newfoundland. Seven of these men were Scots, four were English, with two Ulster Irishmen. The ages show are those at the time of enlistment in the unit.

BRAMBLE, George, 17 3/4 in Feb 1823, labourer from Reighton, Yorkshire, deserted at Halifax, NS, on 21 May 1823.

DYER, Peter, 17 in 1825, labourer from Letterkenny, Sligo, Ireland, discharged at Halifax, NS, on 19 Aug 1828. [Letterkenny is in Donegal]

FALL, John, 20 in 1823, labourer from Oldborough, Yorkshire, discharged in New Brunswick on 27 Aug 1827 [Possibly Oldborough in Devonshire was intended.]

GALLAGHER, Patrick, 19 in 1820, labourer from Holywell, Fermanagh, Ireland, discharged at Halifax, NS, on 4 July 1827 [Holywell in Antrim perhaps]

GIBB, William, 17 in 1820, shoemaker from Kilmarnock, Ayrshire, Scotland, discharged at Halifax, NS, on 16 Aug 1828 [Private William Gibb married Mary BRODDERS at St. Paul's Anglican, Halifax, on 8 July 1826.

GILMORE, Joseph, 17 in 1820, labourer from Sowean, Ayrshire, Scotland, discharged at
     Halifax, NS, on 24 Mar 1828.
KEMP, William, 20 in 1816, flax dealer from Old Deer, Aberdeenshire, Scotland, deserted at St.
     John's, NL, on 24 Oct 1822. He rejoined the unit on 28 Jan 1823.
LIVESTON, Archibald., 17 in 1823, weaver from Kintyre, Ayrshire, Scotland, deserted at
     Halifax, NS, on 21 May 1823.
PLATT, Thomas, 14 in 1811, weaver from Warrington, Lancashire, died at Halifax on 2 Dec 1828.
     He was a drummer.
ROBERTSON, Henry, 17 in 1820, stocking weaver from West Church, Midlothian, Scotland,
     deserted in New Brunswick on 2 July 1823, but returned to the unit on 18 Nov 1823.
SUTHERLAND, David, 19 in 1816, flax dresser from Rogart, Sutherlandshire, Scotland, deserted
     at St. Andrew's, NB, on 10 July 1827, but rejoined on 24 July following.
THORP, Thomas, 17 in 1823, pipe maker from Hull, Yorkshire, deserted at Halifax, NS, on
     7 Aug 1828.
YOUNG, William, 18 in 1825, comb cutter from Cannongate, Edinburgh, Scotland, deserted at
     Halifax, NS, on 24 Oct 1826.

Overall, five discharged men and four of the deserters remained in the region, and one man
was buried at Halifax, NS. Bramble and Liveston deserted on the same day, within three months of
enlisting and probably within days of their arrival in North America. There is nothing in this record
to suggest that they were ever found.
(Source: PRO, W.O. 25, Vol. 470 [NAC mfm B5478].)

6 - DUBLIN TRADESMEN IN THE *CONCORD*, 1815/1817

In 1815, 77 Dublin tradesmen went to St John.'s, Newfoundland, in the *Concord*, John Stobo
master. Two years later, 44 of them were reported in a distressed state and were sent to Halifax,
Nova Scotia, in the *Kitty*, Duggan master, in July or August 1817. (Source: CO 194/160 *f* 175ff)

George ABRAHAM	Christopher DONOHOE	Michael LANERGAN
John BARNETT	James DOYLE	John McEVOY
James BERNE [BYRNE]	Mathew DUHY	Daniel McKIERNAN
Patrick BERNE [BYRNE]	John DUNN	Patrick MAHON
John BONHAM	Michael FARRELL	Michael MURPHY
John BRYAN	James FOGARTY	Thomas O'MERA
John BYRNE	Denis GARDAN	Mark PROCTOR
Lawrence BYRNE	Joseph GILLAM	James REDDY
John CALLAGHAN	Michael GILLAM	William ROONEY
and his wife	Terence HAIG	James SMITH
Maurice CARTHY	Peter HAYDEN	William SWORDS
Thomas COONAN	Joseph HEALY	John WALL
Richard CROAKER	Martin HEALY	John WALSH
and his wife Judith	John JACKSON	Patrick WALSH
Henry DONNELLY	George KEATING	

7 - IRISH-BORN INMATES OF THE HALIFAX BRIDEWELL, 1817-18

A bridewell was a jail in which relatively short sentences were served. This is a roster of those born in Ireland who appear in a document entitled "List of Persons committed to Halifax Bridewell, from Dec. 1, 1817, to Dec. 1st 1818 & & - James Winton, Keeper". Since this was a period of major immigration following the end of the Napoleonic War and since there exist no coherent records of passenger arrivals in Nova Scotia prior to Canadian confederation in 1867, this small roll of names supplies dates of arrival in the city of a number of people who were sentenced to short-term confinement, presumably for minor offences, given the often draconian punishments for crime in those days. I have not attempted to reconcile the conflicting arrival dates shown in this document.

Name of Inmate	Term	Details	Committed	Ship - added by TP
Thomas HUST	1 mo	Landed NL 10 May 1816; came to Halifax 1 July 1817	9 Dec 1817	
John WALSH	1 mo	Landed Halifax 18 July 1817	9 Dec 1817	*Brunswick*
Thomas SMITH	1 mo	Landed NL 1 June 1817, came to Halifax 9 Aug 1817	24 Dec 1817	*New Brunswick Packet*
John FOULER	14 d	Landed Halifax 1 June 1817	24 Dec 1817	*N.B. Packet*
Stephen HABERLAND	3 mos	Landed Halifax 10 Aug 1817	26 Dec 1817	*Lively*
Thomas LANDERGAN	1 mo	Landed NL, resided Windsor	23 Jan 1818	
Patrick RYAN	2 mos	Landed Pictou, came to Halifax 17 July 1817	7 Feb 1818	*Brunswick*
Michael CASEY	1 mo	Landed NL 10 May 1816, came to Halifax 18 Jan 1817	11 Feb 1818	*Consolation*
Richard GRANT	1 mo	To Halifax 16 June 1817	24 Feb 1818	
Mary MAGUIRE	1 mo	To Halifax with 8th Regiment, lived at Lawrencetown - years	24 Feb 1818	
Thomas SMITH (again)	3 mos	Living in Windsor, NS, came to Halifax 1 June 1817	17 Mar 1818	
Morice TINOLLY	3 mos	Landed Prince Edward Island, came to Halifax 1 Nov 1817	17 Mar 1818	*Angelique*
Richard GRANT (again)	1 mo	To Halifax 16 June 1817	30 Mar 1818	
John WALSH (again?)	1 mo	Came to Halifax 16 June 1817	30 Mar 1818	
Mary MAGUIRE (again)	3 mos	(As in former entry for her)	16 May 1818	
John MAHAR & wife	7 d	To NL in 1816, Halifax in 1817	23 May 1818	
Mary WILSON	1 mo	To Halifax with 15th. Foot Regt.	26 May 1818	
Mary JEFFERY	1 mo	To Halifax with 15th Foot Regt.	1 July 1818	
John O'BRIEN	1 mo	To Halifax 8 August 1817	13 July 1818	*Lively*

Name of Inmate	Term	Details	Committed	Ship - added by TP
James O'BRIEN and Thomas MEALY	1 mo	Seamen deserting vessel	13 July 1818	
Michael PARKER	1½ yr	Landed NL, to Halifax 1 July 1817	22 July 1818	
Mary STACK	6 mos	To Halifax with 8th Foot Regt.	29 Aug 1818	
John O'BRIEN (again)	3 mos	(As in former entry for him)	1 Sep 1818	*Lively*
David ROACH	4 mos	To NL in 1816, came to Halifax 8 August 1817	1 Sep 1818	
Henry ROE	1 yr	Landed Pictou 17 July 1816, came to Halifax 10 May 1817	20 Oct 1818	
Patrick McCLACKLIN	1 mo	To Halifax 8 Aug 1817	29 Oct 1818	*Lively*
Molly GILLAM	1 mo	To Halifax with 7th Foot Regt.	9 Nov 1818	
Mary JEFFERY (again)	1 mo	(As in former entry for her)	30 Nov 1818	

(Source: NSARM, RG 1, Vol. 411, document 87)

8 - IRISH IN NOVA SCOTIA CHURCH RECORDS, 1818 - 1852

A) ZION LUTHERAN CHURCH, LUNENBURG, N. S., 1818-1823

9 June 1818: Pierce, eldest son of Bartholw M'GRATH, Ireland, to
Sophia Elizabeth, dau of Georg CONRAD, Port Medway, NS

16 June 1818: Thomas, 5th. son of Roger MEAGHER, England, to
Anna Barbara [dau. of Peter] HIRTLE.

10 July 1821: Nicholas POWER, Waterford, to
Sarah JENKINS, widow of [Michael] PUBLICOVER

3 Dec 1823: Thomas, eldest son of Lorenz McGRAETH, Ireland, to
C. Elizabeth, dau of John McGREGOR, widow of Ludwig PINCHON.

B) ST.JOHN'S ANGLICAN, LUNENBURG, N.S., 1819-1845

BURIALS

By 15 Aug 1819: George WILSON, nailer, "Tennicell", Cork. George, born 10 June 1815, son of Jane and the late George WILSON, baptised this date.

13 Dec. 1823: Edmund HICKEY, Ireland, 62, master of Lunenburg Grammar School.

9 July 1825: Edward **CARNY**, Ireland, 31.

6 June 1826: Mrs. Mary **MULHAWL**, Ireland, 88, widow, late teacher of a small school.

8 Sep. 1827: John **AULL**, Newtown Hamilton, Armagh, Ireland, 26, mariner.

14 Nov. 1827: William **LYNCH**, Ireland, 21, servant of Dr. **BOLMAN**, Lunenburg.

11 Feb. 1828: Anne, Ireland, 40, wife of Nicholas **VENN**, farmer; died in childbed.

10 Nov. 1829: Helen **WISE**, Waterford, Ireland, 43, wife of — **CONNORS**, shoemaker. She was a Roman Catholic.

3 Jan. 1830: William **HORAN**, Co. Kildare, Ireland, 40, labourer, a Roman Catholic.

7 May 1831: Thomas **WELSH**, Ireland, 36.

19 Oct. 1832: Patrick **GRACE**, Kilkenny, Ireland, 35.

20 July 1833: Mrs. **MURPHY**, Ireland; lived at Indian Point, NS.

4 June 1836: Mrs. [Elizabeth **WATSON**, widow of Christian] **RUHLAND**, Ireland, 76

14 Oct. 1844: Dr. John **HARLEY**, [Dublin], Ireland, 68, surgeon at Lunenburg, NS. [The Halifax *Times* newspaper, 22 Oct. 1844, gives his age as 64, that he died on 11 October and had lived at Lunenburg "upwards or 40 years".]

MARRIAGES

16 Aug. 1827: Paul **WHITE,** County Wexford, Ireland, [labourer], bachelor, to Irene Elizabeth **MOONEY**, spinster

13 Jan. 1828: Martin **McCARTHY,** Waterford, Ireland, tailor, bachelor, to Lucy Catharine **SEELIG**, Lunenburg, spinster.

20 Apr.1828: Nicholas **VENN**, Ireland, [farmer], widower [of Anne], to Sophia Brown **COMINGO**, widow [of Martin] **AITKENS**

28 Dec. 1828: Richard **O'GORMAN**, Ireland, schoolmaster, bachelor, to Christiana **PUBLICOVER**, New Dublin, NS, spinster.

2 Feb. 1829: James **GALLAGHER,** Ireland, bachelor, to Margaret **HENRY**, Ireland, spinster, both in the service of Mr. James **MILLER**, Lunenburg.

3 Mar. 1829: Thomas **SHEY**, Ireland, tailor, bachelor, to Catharine **TEEL**, Lunenburg, spinster.

15 Feb. 1831: James **HAWKS**, Ireland, bachelor, to
Elizabeth, widow [of William] **HORAN**.

22 Nov. 1832: John **HICKEY**, Cashel, Tipperary, Ireland, [mariner], bachelor, to
Lucy **SEELIG**, Lunenburg, spinster.

11 Dec. 1832: Matthew **SHEEHAN**, Parish of Ballyhale, Kilkenny, bachelor, to
Caroline **MEISTERS**, Sherbrooke, NS, spinster.

12 Feb. 1833: James **LONG**, Waterford, Ireland, cooper, bachelor, to
Catharine Elizabeth **LOWE**, Fauxbourg, NS, widow.

C) ST. ANSELM'S CATHOLIC, CHEZZETCOOK, N. S. , 1821 - 1832

MARRIAGES

30 Jul 1822: Nicholas, son of Richard & Bridget (**CUL[LA]N**) **MURPHY**, Taylorstown, Wexford;
and Susana Elizabeth, a minor, dau of Anthony & Mary (**SMITH**) **KEYZAR**, Porter's Lake,
NS

27 Aug 1822 Charles, son of Patrick & Elizabeth (**CONNORS**) **TEARNEY**, Ballynordan, Wexford
and Rebecca, a minor, dau of Peter & Hannah (**FROST**) **BRENNAN**, Porter's Lake, NS

between 16 Feb & 14 Sep 1824: Robert, son of Patrick & Margaret (**RYAN**) **FORAN**, Waterford,
and Hannah, dau of Peter & Hannah (**FROST**) **BRENNAN** [Porter's Lake, NS]

BURIALS

21 May 1821 Michael **KEATING**, 64, Ireland

14 Jan 1831 Michael **DELOUGHRY**, 72, Ireland [Kilkenny], widower of Mary **SMITH**

30 Oct 1832 Gerald **MURPHY**, 84, Ireland [Cork], husband of Mary [**KEILY**]

D) OUR LADY OF MOUNT CARMEL CATHOLIC, PROSPECT, N. S., 1823 - 1830

7 Nov 1824: Patrick, son of Patrick & Honora (**WALSH**) **GOUGH**, Stradbally, Waterford;
Ruth, dau of Nathaniel & Ruth (**MILLARD**) **SMITH**, Liverpool, NS.

19 Jan 1825: James, son of John & Margaret (**MAHER**) **MIHAN**, Co. Carlow;
Mary, dau of William & Eleanor (**CROUCHER**) **MULLINS**, Prospect, NS.

3 June 1825: John, son of John & Margaret (**CASHIN**) **GAUL**, Co. Kilkenny;
Eleanor, dau of Richard & Eleanora (**EVANS**) **TOBIN**, Dalhousie Settlement, NS.

21 Oct 1825: Michael (shoemaker), son of John & Mary (**SAUL**) **LANIGAN**, Cashel, Tipperary;
Mary, dau of Cornelius & Bridget (**RILEY**) **LEE**, Dalhousie Settlement, NS.

24 Oct 1825: John (shoemaker), son of John & Honora (**MORISSY**) **MURPHY**, Tallow, Waterford
Elizabeth, dau of Alexander & Mary (**FILPOT**) **HORNER**, Dalhousie Settlement, NS.

22 Nov 1825: Thomas, son of John & Margaret (**MULLINS**) **BARRON**, Borris, Idrone, Carlow;
Honora **CONLIN**, widow of Thomas **DELOUGHRY**, Halifax, NS.

25 Nov 1825: Thomas, son of John & Mary (**FLEMING**) **RICE**, Passage, Waterford;
Catherine, dau of John & Ann (**RYAN**) **COULIN**, Lower Prospect, NS.

21 Oct 1827: Patrick, son of James & Catherine (**POWER**) **FLINN**, Bantry, Cork;
Sarah, dau of Charles & Rose (**McALISTER**) **GILMORE**, Co. Derry.

21 Oct 1827: William, son of Maurice & Joanna (**O'SULLIVAN**) **KEAN**, Listowel, Kerry;
Sophia, dau of Conrad & Abigail (**HATTIE**) **RYER**, Shelburne, NS.

4 Nov 1827: Patrick, son of Denis & Sarah (**DILLON**) **COGLY**, Old Ross, Wexford;
Mary, dau of Isham & Mary (**MAHN**) **BAGGS**, Ardmore, Waterford.

10 Oct 1828: James, son of John & Bridget (**MURPHY**) **FANNING**, Slieverue, Kilkenny;
Margaret, dau of Andrew & Margaret (**BEAN**) **ANDERSON**, Liverpool, NS.

18 Oct 1828: Patrick, son of Patrick & Mary (**SHORTALL**) **LEACY**, "Drumbarry", Carlow;
Mary, dau of John & Jane (**CAMERON**) **KEAN**, Co. Carlow.

19 Oct 1828: Michael, son of James & Mary (**CULLITON**) **HAYES,** Raybarry [Rathbarry], Cork;
Margaret, dau of Cornelius & Mary (**McCARTHY**) **DONOVAN**, Co. Cork.

20 Oct 1828: Denis, son of John & Mary (**CULLITON**) **HAYES**, Raybarry [Rathbarry], Cork
Margaret, dau of James & Eleanor (**COLLINS**) **DONOVAN**, of same place.

7 Nov 1828: Patrick, son of Patrick & Sally (**FLINN**) **TULLY**, [Poor Union of] Kells, Cavan;
Catherine, dau of James & Mary (**DUFFY**) **LYONS**, Cornwallis, NS.

15 Nov 1828: Morgan, son of Terence & Margaret (**HARDY**) **O'BRIEN**, Stradbally, Waterford;
Margaret, dau of Patrick & Rose (**O'NEIL**) **DONNELLY**, Cappagh, Waterford.

17 Nov 1828: Gregory, son of Michael & Mary (**DOYLE**) **BRIEN**, Greagh [Graige], Kilkenny;
Mary, dau of Edward & Catherine (**MACKEY**) **DORAN**, Windsor, NS.

17 Nov 1828: Michael, son of Michael & Mary (**MAXWELL**) **CLEARY**, Tammon [Teighmon],
Eliza, dau of Michael & Catherine (**MORRISEY**) **FOLLY**, Ring, also Co.Waterford.

2 Dec 1828: Edward **MORAN**, Clontibret Parish, Monaghan;
Mary, widow of James **McMORRIS**, Herring Cove, NS.

12 Jan 1829: Moses, son of Walter & Mary (**CULLITON**) **BROOKES**, Tullicor [Tullogher, Parish of Desertmore], Kilkenny;
Sarah, dau of Peter, Sr. & Sarah (**McLEAN**) **MARTIN**, Ketch Harbour, NS.

19 May 1829: Jeremiah, son of Timothy & Honora **SOLOVAN**, Tralee, Kerry;
Margaret, dau of John & Margaret (**GLEESON**) **CUNAGAN**, Fermoy, Cork.

E) ST. GREGORY'S CATHOLIC CHURCH, LIVERPOOL, N. S., 1832 - 1833

10 Dec 1832: Michael, son of John & Anne (**LARKIN**) **LEONARD**, Ballindoon Parish, Galway;
Anne, dau of George & Mary (**ROBINSON**) **SPINKS**, Shelburne, NS.

1 Jan 1833: Thomas, son of Richard & Margaret (**FLYN**) **MAHER,** Co. Kilkenny;
Barbara, dau of Peter & Barbara (**BURGONY**) **HARTLIN**, Lunenburg, NS.

10 Jan 1833: Timothy, son of Philip & Mary (**KEHOE**) **KENEDY**, [Co. Waterford], Ireland;
Jane, dau of Thomas & Sarah (**DANE**) **KELLY**.

4 May 1833: Pierce, son of John & Catherine (**KENNEDY**) **RYAN**, Ireland;
Mary, dau of Daniel & Ellen (**WHEELER**) **O'SULIVAN**.

24 May 1833: John, son of Cormick & Margaret (**CRAIG**) **CARTIN**, Belfast;
Martha, dau of Dr. Andrew & Anne (**BARSS**) **WEBSTER**, Liverpool, NS.

F) ST. PETER'S CATHOLIC CHURCH, DARTMOUTH, N. S., 1830 - 1852

MARRIAGES

16 Oct 1830: Capt. Michael **DARMODY**, Kilmacoo [Kilmacow][, Kilkenny;
Mary **MEAGHER**, widow of William **SHORTAL**, stonecutter.

30 Sep 1832: Patrick **MULLENS**, Waterford City;
Jane, dau of John & Ann (**RYAN**) **COOLIN**, Prospect, NS

22 Jul 1833: Thomas, son of Michael & Bridget (**BOYLE**) **CROAK**, Mullinahone, Tipperary;
Elizabeth, dau of James & Elinor (**CROOKS**) **SHORTELL**, Dartmouth, NS.

8 June 1842: Edward, son of Gregory & Elizabeth (**HARDWARD**) **DAY**, Dingle, Kerry; widower of Susan **DeBAY**.
Catherine, dau of James & Elizabeth (**TURPLE**) **WOULFE**, Ship Harbour, NS.

10 Apr 1844: Denis, son of Daniel & Catherine (**HURLEY**) **DONOVAN**, Drinagh, Cork;
Mary Ellen, dau of Patrick & Ellen (**PATTON**) **BRENNAN**, Preston, NS.

24 Oct 1844: Cornelius, son of Maurice & Mary (**MURRAY**) **BUTTOMER**, Co. Cork;
Elizabeth Ann, dau of Patrick & Margaret (**KENNEDY**) **DOWLING**, Nova Scotia.

15 June 1851: Thomas, son of Michael & Margaret (**KEATING**) **IRVIN**, Waterford City;
Mary Anne, dau of William & Ellen (**MADDOX**) **CASHIN**, Halifax, NS.

22 Feb 1852: Edward, son of Sebastian & Rebecca (**HATFIELD**) **RICHARD**\ Preston, NS;
Bridget, dau of Dominick & Anne (**LAHEY**) **FARRELL**, Waterford City.

BURIALS

3 Sep 1838: John **SKERRY**, Ballyhail, Kilkenny, age 74, [ferryman].

19 May1839: Denis **FENTON**, Cla[sh]more, Waterford, age 40.

29 July 1842: John **KENNEDY**, [Carrick-on-Suir, Tipperary], Ireland, 75; husband of Elizabeth **MUNGAVAN**.

28 July 1843: Joseph **MOORE**, Wexford, 55; lived in Dartmouth for 24 years.

9 - CAPE BRETON CENSUS OF 1818: THE IRISH

From 1784 until 1820 Cape Breton Island was a separate British colony. In 1820 it was re-annexed to Nova Scotia, of which Canadian province it forms four counties. The last census before the annexation was that of June 1818. Much of that enumeration survives and was published in1935 by the Public Archives of Nova Scotia as Appendix B in *Holland's Description of Cape Breton Island and other documents*. The census asked people to state their birthplace and that of their father. This enables us to find the Irish population of Cape Breton at that period.

Another question asked the head of each family how long he had been in Cape Breton, which enables us to see when immigration occurred. There were 94 Irish-born, of whom 55 had been less than 4 years (i.e., came post 1814) in Cape Breton, while 24 had resided there between 6 and 17 years (i.e., arrived 1801-1814, the war years). One man gave no date of arrival but since his son was born in Cape Breton about 1785 he is counted among the 16 who arrived in 1800 or earlier. Seniority goes to Pierce Kennedy from Waterford, Ireland, who arrived about 1771.

The census takers evinced variations in the way they asked questions. At Louisbourg he took place of birth to mean county in Ireland, rather than simply Ireland. At St. Andrews Channel the arrival date is given in years and months which should help people to find out in which ship an ancestor arrived in Cape Breton.

The information is presented in the order: name, age, time in Cape Breton, country of birth, country of father's birth, trade, Married/Single/Widowed, and number of children.

Ship Harbour, Gut of Canso (modern Port Hawkesbury area)

Thomas LANGLEY	65	14	Ireland [Belfast]	Ireland	Farmer	M	6
Thomas LANGLEY	30	14	Canada [Québec/Ontario]	Ireland	Fishing	M	5
John LANGLEY	21	14	Québec	Ireland	Fishing	M	1

North end of the Gut of Canso (modern Port Hastings area)

Martin BRIEN [Breen]	27	1½	Ireland		Ireland	Labourer	S	
John DOWLING	28	2	Ireland		Ireland	Labourer	S	
James WALSH	27	5	Nova Scotia [i.e .mainland]	Ireland	Labourer	W	2
Thomas FITZPATRICK	25	2½	Ireland		Ireland	Labourer	S	
John FERRAL	22	1	Ireland		Ireland	Schoolmaster	S	
Henry BRETON	23	2m	Nova Scotia		Ireland	Shoemaker	S	
Walter WALSH	24	1	Ireland		Ireland	Labourer	S	
Martin DORAN	24	1	Ireland		Ireland	Labourer	S	
David CASHMAN	24	1	Ireland		Ireland	Labourer	S	
Morris POWERS	26	1	Ireland		Ireland	Labourer	S	
John MARTIN	25	2½	Ireland		Ireland	Labourer	M	
Patrick MARTIN	27	2½	Ireland		Ireland	Labourer	S	
John DORAN	22	1½	Ireland		Ireland	Labourer	S	
John CASEY	32	1½	Ireland		Ireland	Labourer	S	

From Balhache's Point in Gut of Canso to Grand Judique

Thomas FOX	65	25	Ireland [Ulster]	Ireland	Farmer	M	4
Edward WALSH	55	20	Ireland	Ireland	Farmer	M	3
Thomas FOX	22	22	Cape Breton	Ireland	Farmer	S	
John FOX	20	20	Cape Breton	Ireland	Farmer	S	
Alexander FOX	17	17	Cape Breton	Ireland	Farmer	S	

Port Hood District

Daniel O'CONNOR	24	6	Ireland [Down]	Ireland	Port Hood	Farmer	S	
James MURPHY	30	2	Ireland [Wexford]	Ireland	Port Hood	Blacksmith	S	
Andrew DORAN	23	2	Ireland [Wexford]	Ireland	Port Hood	Farmer	S	
William MacKEEN	28	6	Nova Scotia	Ireland	Mabou	Merchant	M	3
James MacKEEN	34	6	Nova Scotia	Ireland	Mabou	Merchant	S	
William McDONALD	23	3	Ireland	Ireland	Port Hood	Fishing	S	
Michael GREEN	25	4	Ireland	Ireland	Port Hood	Shoemaker	S	
John BAIRDSLEY	33	4	Ireland	Ireland	Port Hood	Farmer	M	3
Laurence DORAN	26	9m	Ireland	Ireland	Port Hood	Farmer	S	
James FANNING	31	3	Ireland [Waterford]	Ireland	Mabou	Weaver	S	
John COSTLEY	26	3	Ireland [Kilkenny]	Ireland	Port Hood	Butcher	S	
Walter WHITTY	34	2	Ireland [Wexford]	Ireland	Port Hood	Farmer	M	1
John DURER [Dwyer]	22	1	Ireland	Ireland	Mabou	Farmer	S	
William BARREN	33	9m	Ireland	Ireland	Port Hood	Weaver	S	
William MINCHIN	22	2	Ireland	Ireland	Port Hood	Shoemaker	S	
Patrick DOWNEY	29	2	Ireland [Kilkenny]	Ireland	Port Hood	Tailor	M	5
James BULL	45	2	Ireland [Kilkenny]	Ireland	Port Hood	Miller	M	10
Robert BULL	21	1	Ireland [Kilkenny]	Ireland	Port Hood	Millwright	S	
Christopher BULL	19	2	Ireland [Kilkenny]	Ireland	Port Hood	Millwright	S	

Simon WALSH	21	3	Ireland	Ireland	Port Hood	Shoemaker	S
John MULLINS	31	10	Nova Scotia	Ireland	coal mines	Cooper	M 4
Peter MURPHY	26	4	Nova Scotia	Ireland	Mabou	Farmer	M 1
Michael SHANAHAN	25	3	Ireland	Ireland	Port Hood	Farmer	M 1
John FITZPATRICK	31	1	Ireland	Ireland	Port Hood	Joiner	S
Ebenezer LEDBETTER	30	4	Nova Scotia	Ireland	Mabou	Farmer	M 3
Dennis MURPHY	47	21	Ireland [Wexford]	Ireland	Port Hood	Farmer	M 6
Mathew MacGLAUGN	22	7	Ireland	Ireland	Gr.Judique	Schoolmaster	S
William MORTIMER	40	9	Ireland	Ireland	Mabou	Blacksmith	S \
Peter BREEN	62	19	Ireland	Ireland	Mabou	Farmer	M 7
Edward HAYES	55	30	Ireland [Wexford]	Ireland	Port Hood	Trader	M 1
William WRIGHT	32	7	Ireland	Ireland	Port Hood	Farmer	M
Michael HEALY	30	3	Ireland	Ireland	Mabou	Farmer	S
James SHEA	19	1	Ireland	Ireland	Port Hood	Farmer	S

Margaree and Broad Cove, 12 May 1818

James ROSS	61	35	Ireland	Scotland	Margaree	Farmer	M 2
Patrick POWER	28	7	Ireland	Ireland	Margaree	Farmer	M 1
James DUNN	26	1½	Ireland[Tipperary]	Ireland	Margaree	Farmer	M 1
Joseph ROSS	19	19	Cape Breton	Ireland	Margaree	Farmer	S
Daniel GRIFFIN	30	3	Ireland	Ireland	Margaree	Farmer	M 1
Thomas POWER	30	2	Ireland	Ireland	Broad Cove	Farmer	M 1
Joseph RYAN	21	21	Cape Breton	Ireland	Broad Cove	Farmer	S
Michael BURNS	27	1½	Ireland	Ireland	Broad Cove	Farmer	M
Bazil RYAN	22	22	Ireland	Ireland	Broad Cove	Farmer	S
Moris FITHZCHAUD	59	14	Ireland [Cork]	Ireland	Broad Cove	Farmer	M 12
William FITHD[7]	24	14	Nova Scotia	Ireland	Broad Cove	Farmer	S
Miles MacDONALD[8]	27	11	Ireland [Wexford]	Ireland	Broad Cove	Farmer	M 4
John DUGGAN	27	½	Ireland	Ireland	Broad Cove	Farmer	S
Edward FLING[9]	27	1	Ireland	Ireland	Broad Cove	Farmer	S
Patrick COWDY [10]	27	3	Ireland	Ireland	Margaree	Tailor	M 1
Cyriaque ROACH	34	32	Nova Scotia	Ireland	Cheticamp	Farmer	M 8

South End of the Gut of Canso

Larance FORISTEL	60	18	Ireland	Ireland	- - - -	S
John LAFFIN	70	11	Ireland	Ireland	Fishing	S

---

[7] Morris and William FITZGERALD were father and son

[8] Miles MacDANIEL.

[9] Edward FLINN

[10] Patrick COADY

Michael DUDIE[11]	60	12	Ireland	Ireland	Fishing	M	2
John OBRINE	49	6	Ireland	Ireland	Cooper	M	2
James STUDART	69	19	America	Ireland	Cooper	M	8
Thomas STABTON	60	17	Ireland	Ireland	Fishing	M	4

Lower Settlement of River Inhabitants

Michael WATT[S]	30	2	Ireland	Ireland	- - - -	S	
Thomas HOPTEN	20	20	Cape Breton	Ireland	- - - -	S	
John HOPTEN	58	20	Ireland	Ireland	Farmer	M	10
James JOHNES	63	16	Ireland	Ireland	Fishing	M	
Thomas CHRIL[12]	57	8	Ireland	Ireland	Fishing	M	4
John McNORMAN, Sr.	61	11	Ireland	Ireland	Fishing	M	7
James McNORMAN	23	11	Nova Scotia	Ireland	- - - -	S	
John McNORMAN, Jr.	20	11	Nova Scotia	Ireland	- - - -	S	
James McDONALD	40	2	Ireland	Ireland	Fishing	S	
John BENSON	24	2	Ireland	Ireland	- - - -	S	

Louisbourg Harbour and Vicinity

Michael SLATTEREY	65	28	Co. Limerick	Ireland	- - - -	M	6
James SLATTEREY[13]	35	35	Cape Breton	Ireland	- - - -	M	3
John SLATTEREY	26	26	Cape Breton	Ireland	- - - -	S	
Josehp[sic] SLATTEREY	20	20	Cape Breton	Ireland	- - - -	S	
George SLATTEREY[14]	17	17	Cape Breton	Ireland	- - - -	S	
Nick SPRICE	55	26	Co. Waterford	Ireland	- - - -	M	7
Timothy DOYL[E]	30	22	Co. Waterford	Ireland	- - - -	M	3
Edward KELLY	47	18	Co. Wexford	Ireland	- - - -	S	
Patrick FITZGERALD	60	15	Co. Kerry	Ireland	- - - -	M	1
Pierce KENNEDY	72	47	Co. Waterford	Ireland	- - - -	M	
Pierce KENNEDY	37	37	Cape Breton	Ireland	- - - -	S	
Denny KENNEDY	30	30	Cape Breton	Ireland	Carpenter	S	
William KENNEDY	28	28	Cape Breton	Ireland	- - - -	S	
James YONGUE[Young]	63	18	Ire [Kilkenny]	[Ireland]	- - - -	-	

Baddeck Division, 20 June 1818

Patrick DAYLEY	50	16	Ireland	Ireland	Baddeck	- - - -	S
Patrick OBRIAN	24	6m	Ireland	Ireland	Baddeck	- - - -	S

---

[11] This and the following names are properly Doody, O'Brien, Stoddard and Stapleton.

[12] Chril is Carroll.

[13] James Slattery was a blacksmith and Joseph a merchant at Gabarus.

[14] George was a son of Michael SLATTERY (*supra*).

Name	Age		Born	From	Location	Occupation	Status	Children
John McGOWEN	27	27	Cape Breton	Ireland	Baddeck - - - -		S	
John ROSS	22	22	Cape Breton	Ireland	St.P.Channel - - - -		S	
Henry CONNORS	18	18	Cape Breton	Ireland	Baddeck - - - -		S	
Philip BROWN	23	1	Ireland [Wexford]	Ireland	Wagamatcook[15] - - - -		S	
James BROWN	25	1	Ireland [Kerry]	Ireland	Wagamatcook - - - -		S	
William ROSS	50	28	Ireland	N.Britain[16]	St.P.Ch.[17]	Carpenter	M	13

Boularderie, 1 June 1818

Name	Age		Born	From	Occupation	Status	Children
William MELVIN	63	--	Ireland	Ireland	Farmer	M	2[18]
John MELVIN	33	-	Nova Scotia	Ireland	Labourer	S	
George MELVIN	18	[18]	Cape Breton	Ireland	Labourer	S	
James ROBERTSON	19	[19]	Cape Breton	Ireland	Servant	S	

District of St. Andrews - all farmers

Name	Age		Born	From	Location	Status	Children
Thomas HAYES	45	12	Ireland	Ireland	Red Island	M	5
John GALLAGHER	60	12yr5m	Ireland[Tipperary]	Ireland	St. Andrews Channel	M	4
John CASH	30	14m	Ireland	Ireland	St. Andrews Channel	S	
Richard BARNES	31	3yr6m	Ireland	Ireland	St. Andrews Channel	M	3
John MURPHY	40	6yr5m	Ireland	Ireland	St. Andrews Channel	S	
Stephen BOYLAN	26	6yr6m	Ireland	Ireland	St. Andrews Channel	S	
Philip CODY	34	5m	Ireland	Ireland	St. Andrews Channel	S	
James STAFFORD	35	18m	Ireland	Ireland	St. Andrews Channel	M	1
Andrew FITZHARRIS	30	2yr6m	Ireland	Ireland	St. Andrews Channel	S	
John HAYES[19]	22	3yr3m	Ireland	Ireland	St. Andrews Channel	M	
James BARNES	40	13m	Ireland	Ireland	St. Andrews Channel	S	
John McILLOP [20]	23	10m	Ireland	Ireland	St. Andrews Channel	S	
Edward CUMAFORD	46	2	Ireland	Ireland	St. Andrews Channel	M	3
Phillip CUMAFORD	36	4[21]	Ireland	Ireland	St. Andrews Channel	M	3

---

[15]"Waganatcook", a Mi'Kmaq Indian word, is now written Whycocomagh.

[16] "N. Britain" meant North Britain, a term then occasionally used for Scotland.

[17] "St. P. Ch." is St. Patrick's Channel on Lake Bras d'Or.

[18]The two children were "under age". Two sons who were of age are listed after their father *supra*.

[19]Son of Thomas Hayes. John arrived in Cape Breton in 1814.

[20]Spelled more recently as McKillop, a branch of the Clan Donald found in Co. Antrim.

[21]He was actually more like 6 years in Cape Breton by 1818.

10 - IRISH PEOPLE IN THE CAPE BRETON LAND PAPERS, 1794 TO 1839

From 1784 until 1820 the island of Cape Breton formed a British colony distinct from Nova Scotia, from which it had been separated following the Loyalist influx at the end of the American Revolutionary War. The island was reunited with Nova Scotia in 1820 for a variety of fiscal and administrative reasons, not least of these being the inability of the Island government to properly attend to the needs of the multitudes of immigrants from the British Isles that came to this region after the end of the Napoleonic Wars in 1815.

Intending settlers, and probably some who meant to push on later, sought grants of land within the colony. Customarily, such a person submitted a petition to the appropriate colonial officials at Sydney, asking to be considered for a land grant or at any rate for a licence to occupy land pending an outright grant. Most petitioners indicated their place of birth, helping us to discover the Irish people among the more than thirty-three hundred arrivals who filed a petition for land. Most mentioned their age and number of dependents, as the extent of a grant could depend on the size of the family. Many stated the length of time that they had resided in Cape Breton which is particularly valuable information for a colony which seems not to have preserved any record of immigrant arrivals.

The relevant documentation now resides at Nova Scotia Archives and Records Management in Record Group 20, series "B" (NSARM, RG 20 "B": Cape Breton Land Papers). At the end of each of the selected entries below the reader will note a number in parentheses ( ). These numbers correspond to the entry number in a typed summary of these documents at NSARM in Halifax, Nova Scotia. Since the purpose here is primarily the identification of Irish immigration into the Atlantic Canada region, from which thousands formed a diaspora across North America, a reader should treat this listing as a finding aid rather than as a transcription of the entire record. A little more than ten percent of the entries (357 here) relate to Irish-born people. The vast majority of the newcomers to Cape Breton in that era were Highland Scots, many of whom figure in the three volumes by Donald Whyte, *A Dictionary of Scottish Emigrants to Canada before Confederation*. Some information about these and other Irish people may be read in A. A. MacKenzie's *The Irish in Cape Breton*.

In an effort to manage spelling variants created by the vagaries of nineteenth-century clerks, the information is grouped beside a modern spelling of the surname in the left-hand column. The entries are arranged alphabetically first, then chronologically. It will be apparent that many of the same people occur more than once, e.g., Peter Heron and Peter Ahearn are the same person. The entries are cross-referenced to the 1818 Census of Cape Breton which appears elsewhere in this book. A very few entries match names in the surviving fragment of the 1811 Census. The references appear at their proper places. When identification of a person in the list with a householder in the 1838 Nova Scotia Census can confidently be made, I have inserted the fact.

(A)HEARN   1821 Peter Heron, 28, born in Ireland [Waterford], 18 months in Cape Breton; married with seven children, the eldest 12 years old. (2630, 2651)

               1825 Peter Ahearn; married with a large family; has tavern in Sydney. (3009) [1838 Census: Peter A Hern, tavernkeeper, Sydney]

ATKINSON   1816 John Atkinson, born in Ireland, late lieutenant in the 99th. Regiment; in 1815 received 200 acres on Boularderie Island, and in 1816 an adjacent 300 acres (1250a)

BARRON   1812   James Barron, born in Ireland; 5 years in Cape Breton (776)

            1820   James Barron, born in Ireland; 2 years in Cape Breton (2294)

            1819   Martin Barron, 26, born in Ireland, 3 years in Cape Breton; single;
                    note: "Lis Duggan" [Lisduggan, County Waterford] (2069)

            1821   Martin Barron, 27, born in Ireland; 4 years in Cape Breton; single (2577)

            1815   Richard Barron, 26, born in Ireland; 5 years here; married; one child (1089)

BIRMINGHAM 1803 Richard Burmingham, born in Ireland; at Point Edward since 1788 (65)

BOYLAN   1812   Stephen Boilan, 24, native of Ireland; 4 years in Cape Breton (778) [Census
                    1818: Stephen Boylan, 26, farmer, St. Andrew's Channel; single; 6 yrs. 6 m.
                    in Cape Breton; 1838 Census: Stephen Boylaen, farmer, Richmond County].

BREEN   1818   Martin Been [sic], 27, native of Ireland' 2 years in Cape Breton; single(1848)
                    [1818 Census: labourer, Gut of Canso; 1838 Census: Martin & Peggy Breen,
                    farmer, Richmond County].

            1818   Peter Breen, native of Ireland; to Cape Breton in 1798; married with seven
                    children (1854) [1818 Census: farmer, 62, 19 years in Cape Breton, Mabou].

BRIEN   1831   Katharine, 50, native of Ireland, widow of Matthew Brian. She had one son
                    aged 16. (3294)

            1822   Matthew Brien, 28, native of Ireland; married with one child (2815)

BROWN   1816   David Brown, 22, native of Ireland; 7 years in Cape Breton; married with
                    two children (1266a)

            1817   James Brown, native of Ireland, "Kerry"; came out in 1817; single (1856)
                    [1818 Census: farmer, 25, Wagamatkook, single; 1838 Census: James
                    Brown, turner, Margaree].

            1821   James Brown, native of Ireland; 4 years in Cape Breton (2587)

            1817   Philip Brown, 21, native of Ireland, 2 years in Cape Breton (1857)
                    [1818 Census: farmer, 23, Wagamatkook, single; 1838 Census: Philip Brown,
                    farmer, Margaree; native of Silverspring, Mayglass Parish, Co. Wexford].

            1822   William Brown, 28, native of Ireland; single (2816)

BROWNER 1820   John Browner, 33, native of Ireland, 1 year in Cape Breton; single; note
                    "Ooligan'[Templeludigan], Co. Wexford (2306) [Lived at Bridgeport; 1838
                    Census: John Browner, farmer, Lingan area].

BUCKLEY   1803   Paul Buckley, Irish-born; at Catalone Lake (64) [1838 Census, at
                    Catalone].

BULL   1820   Christopher Bull, 21, Ireland [Kilkenny], 3 years in Cape Breton; father in
                    Cape Breton (2307) [son of James Bull, infra; 1818 Census: farmer, 19, at
                    Port Hood, next to Robert Bull, 21, single, farmer, his brother].

            1818   James Bull, from Kilkenny; came out in 1816; married with ten children
                    (1858) [1818 Census: miller, 45, Port Hood].

            1821   James Bull, 48, native of Ireland; 4 years in Cape Breton; married with ten
                    children (2589) [1818 Census: Port Hood; 1838 Census: James and Robert
                    Bull, farmers at Port Hood].

BURCHEL 1822   George Burchel, 22, native fo Ireland [Co. Cork]; married man (2817)

BURKE   1818   Patrick Burke, 30, native of Ireland; came to Cape Breton from Newfound-
                    land; married with three children; note: "Mockhill" [either Mothel in Co.
                    Waterford, or Mothell, Co. Kilkenny, intended] (1859)

            1827   John Burke, 57, native of Ireland; married with three children (3180)
                    [Married in the Catholic Church, Halifax, 30 July 1821, Mary, dau. of John
                    & Mary (KENNEDY) Burke of Mainadieu, Cape Breton, and Michael, son
                    of Michael & Mary (KENNEDY) SLATTERY, Louisbourg, Cape Breton

BURKE   1806   Michael BURKE, 150 acres at Catalone (224)

               1821   Sarah, wife of Michael Burke, is old and infirm   (2592)

               1820   William Burke, 80, native of Ireland; lived for 40 years in Prince Edward
                        Island, where he served 17 years as a non-commissioned officer in the St.
                        John Volunteers, or Prince Edward Island Fencibles (2309)

BUTLER   1820   James Butler, 24, native of Ireland; came to Cape Breton, November 1819
                        and was single; note: "Coolfinn" [in Kilmeadan Parish Waterford] (2310)

               1820   Martin Butler, 35, native of Ireland, 3 months in Cape Breton; single; note:
                        "Ballyragget" [a town in Co. Kilkenny] (2311)

BYRNE   1826   Timothy Byrne, 34, native of Ireland; married with three children (3091)
                        [1838 Census: Timothy Byrne, carpenter, and wife, at Arichat].

CAHILL   1819   John Cahill, 30, native of Ireland; one year in Cape Breton; married (2088)

CALLANAN 1813   Patrick Callanan, native of Ireland, 24 years in Cape Breton (901)

CAMERON 1819   Duncan Cameron, 21, native of Ireland; 8 years in Cape Breton (2090)

               1820   Duncan Cameron, 21, native of Ireland; single man   (2314)

CAMPBELL 1823   John Campbell, 24, native of Ireland; married with one child   (2911)

CARLIN   1817   James Carlin, native of Ireland [Ulster]; 11 years in Cape Breton; married,
                        eight children (1599) [1838 Census: James Carlin, farmer, Syrney River].

CARROLL   1828   Jane, widow of John Carroll, merchant at Halifax, NS (3250)

               1815   John Carroll, native and resident of Halifax; 280 acres at Mabou (1111)

               1821   John Carroll, 32, native of Ireland, 9 years in Cape Breton; married
                        with one child (2599)

               1827   Patrick Carroll, 30, native of Ireland; single man (3182) [1838 Census:
                        Patrick Carroll, labourer, and wife, Richmond County].

               1803   Thomas Carrol, grant of 90 acres, east shore of Sydney River (66) [1818
                        Census state that he was born in Ireland].

               1812   Thomas Carrol, native of Dungarvan, Co. waterford; 5 years in Cape
                        Breton; married with six children   (790)

               1819   Thomas Carroll, 25, native of Ireland, cast away 16 months before while en
                        route to Halifax from Newfoundland. Note: "Kilkenny"   (2099)

CASEY   1821   Ann Casey on behalf of her infant granddaughters who were born in Cape
                        Breton, namely Catherine, 10, and Ann, 7, daughters of Matthew TOBIN
                        and his wife, a daughter of Ann Casey (2600)

               1812   Martin Casey, 30, native of Ireland, 20 years at Halifax; no family (791)

               1829   Mary Casey, daughter of Mary CONNORS who died in December 1827;
                        her only brother was Andrew CONNORS. Mary Casey has five childrem.
                        Her husband is ill "in head"   (3264)

               1817   Michael Cassey, 28, native of Cape Breton   (1600)

               1818   Michael Cassey, 29, native of Cape Breton; married with one child (1875)

CASH   1826   Edward Cash, 33, native of Ireland; married (3097) [1838 Census: Edward
                        Cash, farmer, Richmond County]

CASHEN   1817   Thomas Cushin, 35, native of Carlow, Ireland; married to the widow
                        DOYLE (1610a) [widow of Maurice Doyle, New Victoria, died 1816;
                        1838 Census: Thomas Cashin, farmer, Cape Breton County].

               1822   Thomas Cashen, age 30 to 40, Irish-born; married with 7 children (2819)

CAVANAGH 1821   Thomas Cavanagh, 45; here 22 years; married with six children (2601)

CLEARY   1819   Thomas Clary, native of Ireland

COADY   1812   John Coady, born in Ireland in 1790; emigrated to Newfoundland in 1808,
                        and to Cape Breton in 1810; granted 25 acres at Cheticamp

COADY	1819	John Cody, 25, native of Wexford, Ireland, 4 years in Cape Breton; married (2105) [1838 Census: John Cowdy, farmer, Margaree].
	1821	John Cody, 30, native of Ireland; married with three children (2633)
	1813	Nicholas Cody, 26, native of Wexford, Ireland; 5 years in Cape Breton; married with one child (908)
	1816	Patrick Cody, native of Ireland, 2 years in Cape Breton, Southwest Margaree (1287) [1818 Census: Patrick Cowdy, tailor, 27, married with a child, here 3 years; 1838 Census: Patrick Cowdy, farmer, Margaree].
	1821	Patrick Coady, native of Ireland, 5 years in Cape Breton; married with two children (2607)
	1824	Patrick Cody, 30, native of Ireland, married with five children (2975)
	1821	Philip Coady, native of Ireland, single (2608) [1818 Census: Philip Cody, St. Andrew's Channel, 34, single, farmer, here 5 months.
COCKLIN	1821	Daniel Cocklin, 21, native of Ireland (2609)
	1827	Daniel Cochlin, 40, native of Ireland, married man (3196)
COLLINS	1822	Daniel Collins, 25, native of Ireland, single man (2820)
COMFORT	1817	Edward Cumerford, native of Ireland, married with three children (1610) [1818 Census: Edward Cumaford, 46, farmer, St. Andrew's Channel, married, three children, 2 years in Cape Breton].
	1812	Philip Comford, 27, native of Ireland, married with one child (795) [1818 Census: Philip Cumaford, 36, farmer, St. Andrew's Channel, married, three children, 4 years in Cape Breton; 1838 Census: Philip Comeford, farmer, Richmond County].
CONELLY	1821	William Conelly, 40, native of Ireland, 19 years in Cape Breton, single man; had served 3 years in the Surrey Rangers (2610)
CONNORS	1818	Bartholomew Conner, 30, native of Ireland, 18 months in Cape Breton; single man [native of Co. Kilkenny; name also rendered O'Connor; 1838 Census: Bartholomew & Mary Connor, farmer, Cape Breton Co.] (1881)
	1821	John Connor, 24, native of Ireland, single man; shipwrecked in Cape Breton three years before (2611)
	1823	John Connors, 28, native of Ireland, single man (2914)
	1808	Mary Connors, widow with five children, had 200 acres at Lingan, near her brother, Thomas ROACH, a farmer at Lingan (358)
CONWAY	1817	Daniel Conway, 39, native of Ireland, 2 years in Cape Breton, single (1603)
COSTLY	1816	John Costly, 26, native of Kilkenny, single, to Newfoundland in 1814, and to Cape Breton in August 1815 (1286) [1818 Census: butcher, 26, Port Hood]
COUSINS	1839	James Cousins, 35, native of Ireland [probably Wexford]; married daughter of the late Peter BIRETTE of L'Ardoise [1838 Census: James Cousins, fisherman, near St. Peter's; latest date in these extracts].
CROAKE	1819	Richard Croake, 28, native of Kilkenny, married with one child; moved to Newfoundland, then in June 1818 to Cape Breton, and to the USA in the fall of 1818; land formerly (1817) of Michael WALL. Note: "Mt Juliet" [townland in the Parish of Jerpointchurch, Kilkenny] (2107)
CROWLEY	1819	Patrick Crowley, 23, native of Ireland, 6 months in Cape Breton. Note: "Bally Charsney" [Ballytarsna, Kilkenny] (2106)
CUMMINS	1822	John Cumming, 23, native of Ireland, married (2823)

CUMMINS   1809   William Cummins, native of Wexford; married with three children; 5 years in Cape Breton; refused land at Enginish [Ingonish]   (471)

CUNNINGHAM 1824 James Cunningham, 42, native of Ireland, widower with three children (2976)

                    1821   Patrick Cunningham, 28, native of Ireland, married with one child (2615)

CUSACK   1818   Patrick Cusack, 45, native of Ireland, widower with five children; one year in Cape Breton. Note: "Ashgrove" [townland in Co. Cork] (1885)

                    1821   Patrick Cusack, 23, native of Ireland, single man, 3 years in Cape Breton (2619)

DALTON   1821   Michael Dalton, 38, native of Ireland, married with two children, has just arrived in Cape Breton [1838 Census: Michael Dalton, Gut of Canso] (2620)

DALY   1819   Edward Daly, 22, native of Ireland, single man. Note: "Balinvair" [Ballinvir townland, Templemichael Parish, Tipperary] (2111)

            1802   William Daly, 500 acres at Cow Bay, Cape Breton   (32)

            1803   William Dayley, 127 acres, west side of Sydney Harbour [1838 Census: William Daly, farmer, Northwest Arm, Sydney]

DAY   1817   Luke Day, 27, native of Ireland, married with three children; 8 years in Cape Breton (1611)

DEE   1816   John Dee, 24, native of Ireland, single man (1292) [1838 Census: John Dee, farmer, Cape North]

DELAHUNT 1823   Richard Delahunt, 33, native of Ireland, married with four children (2916)

DELANEY   1821   Martin Delaney, 23, native of Ireland, 2 years in Cape Breton, and has a wife and two children in Newfoundland (2622)

DEVEREAUX 1824   Patrick Devereaux, blacksmith, 36, native of Ireland [probably Wexford], married with five children (2977)

DILLON   1803   Edward Dillon, 16 years in Cape Breton, married with six children living at Mainadieu; has 400 acres at Mira Bay (71) [His wife was Ann MARTELL]

DOLLARD   1821   Michael Dollard, 39, native of Ireland, married with four children (2625)

            1820   Rev. William Dollard, native of Ireland, a missionary in Cape Breton (2341) [Born 29 Nov 1789 at Ballytarina, Kilkenny, ordained in 1817, spent five years based in Arichat, Cape Breton. He was later Bishop of Fredericton in New Brunswick, where he died 29 Aug 1851.]

DOODY   1822   George Doody, 23, native of Ireland, married (2825)

DORAN   1819   Andrew Doran, 25, native of Ireland, single man, 3 years in Cape Breton, where he had an uncle and a cousin. Note: "Ferns" [in Wexford] (2115) [1818 Census: farmer, age 23, at Port Hood]

DOWLING   1826   Alexander Dowlan, 23, born in Cape Breton, married, three children, was. sole heir of the late Patrick Dowlan [from Down] who was granted land in 1806 and 1809 (3184) [1838 Census: Alexander Doulen, Gut of Canso]

            1818   John Dowling, 29, native of Kilkenny, single man, 5 years in Cape Breton (1894) [1818 Census: labourer, Gut of Canso, 2 years here; 1838 Census: John Doulen, Gut of Canso]

DOWNEY   1817   James Downey, 51, native of Ireland, married with eight children, four in Cape Breton. Note: "Balina Mara" [Ballinamara, Kilkenny] (1612)

            1816   Patrick Downey, native of Kilkenny, went to Newfoundland in 1809, and now at Port Hood, Cape Breton (1293) [In 1818 Census; next entry]

            1820   Patrick Downey, 32, native of Ireland [Kilkenny], married with five children, 4 years in Cape Breton (2342) [1818 Census: tailor, 29, Port Hood]

DOYLE	1812	Daniel Doyle, 30, native of Ireland, came to Cape Breton in 1810 (805)
	1820	James Doyle, native of Ireland, 3 years in Cape Breton (2343)
	1825	James Doyle, 32, native of Ireland, married (3093)
	1827	James Doyle, 47, native of Ireland, married with three children (3185)
	1822	John Doyle, 26, native of Ireland, single man (2827)
	1823	John Doyle, 23, native of Ireland, single man (2918, 2919)
	1814	Michael Doyle, native of Ireland, 7 years in Cape Breton (1128)
	1808	Morgan Doyle, 5 years at Dundas Island, Nigenish Bay (363) [Wexford]
DRISCOLL	1820	Darby Driscoll, 29, native of Ireland, [Cork], married, 4 years here (2344)
DUGGAN	1816	Christopher Duggan, 42, native of Ireland, 7 years in Cape Breton, married with ten children (1295)
	1823	Daniel Dugan, 23, native of Nova Scotia, single man (2920)
	1818	John Dugan, native of Ireland, 5 months in Cape Breton. Note: "Wingal" [Windgap, Kilkenny] (1895) [1818 Census: farmer at Broad Cove, 27, in Cape Breton ½ year]
	1814	Patrick Dougan, born in Antrim, and moved with his parents to Cork; to Newfoundland in 1809, and in 1811 to Cape Breton, at Mabou (1127)
DUNN	1817	James Dun, native of Ireland (1615) [1818 Census: farmer at Margaree, 26, married with 1 child, 1½ years in Cape Breton; 1838 Census: James Dunn, farmer, Margaree] [Tipperary]
	1817	Michael Dunn, 22, carpenter, native of Ireland, single man (1616)
DUNPHY	1819	John Dunphy, 25, native of Ireland, single, recently came out to Halifax. Note: "Mary Park" [? in Co. Kilkenny] (2117)
	1826	John Dunfy, 29, native of Ireland, married with a child (3103)
	1819	Martin Dunphy, 35, native of Kilkenny, married with a child. He moved to Cape Breton from Newfoundland in July 1818. His uncle, Sylvester Dunphy at Low Point, Cape Breton. Note: "Bally Kan" [Ballycallan Parish] (2118) [Martin Dunphy died 31 Mar 1845, at Lake Kilkenny, Cape Breton, age 62]
	1825	Patrick Dunfy, 31, native of Ireland, single man, recently arrived (3019) [1838 Census: Patrick Dunphy, fisherman, Cape North]
	1823	Roderick Dunfy, native of Ireland, single man (2921) [1838 Census: Roderick Dunphy, farmer, Inverness County]
DWYER	1819	Anthony Dwyre, 29, native of Ireland, single man, 2 years in Cape Breton. Note: "Killcash" [Kilcash Parish, Tipperary] (2119) [Kavanagh's servant]
EAGAN	1805	Mathew Eagan (178)
EDWARDS	1808	John Edwards, native of Oswestry, Shropshire, England, married with four children; served twelve years in the 66th. Regiment of Foot, 6 years in Cape Breton, land at Petit Nez, St. Peter's Bay (364)
	1814	John Edwards, 43, native of England, 11 years in Cape Breton, had four children, three of them in Cape Breton (991)
	1815	John Edwards, born in England, married with four children; served in the Army for *thirteen* years (1130) [1838 Census: John & Catherine Edwards, farmer, Arichat]
	1821	John Edwards, 50, tailor, native of England (2629) [1811 Census: Tailor & constable at Arichat, 2 boys, 1 girl]
ELWARD	1819	James Elward, 37, native of Ireland, married with a child; 15 years in Newfoundland, then to Cape Breton (2120)
ENGLISH	1821	John English, 27, married with a child (2630)

FANNING   1816   James Fanning, 30, native of Waterford, went to Newfoundland in 1814, and
                   to Cape Breton in 1815, single man (1297) [1818 Census: weaver, 31,
                   at Mabou, single; 1838 Census: James Fanning, farmer, Port Hood]
           1821   John Fanning, 25, native of Ireland, married with a child, 4 years in Cape
                   Breton (2632) [1838 Census: John Fanning, butcher, Cape Breton County]
FITZGERALD 1810 James Fitzgerald, native of Ireland, married with five children, was 26
           years in Belle Isle and Labrador, and came to Cape Breton in Sep 1809,
                   and has four other sons coming to join him; 200 acres next to SLATTERY
                   [at Louisbourg] (570)
           1819   James Fitzgerald, 54, native of Ireland, married with eleven children, of
                   whom six were in Cape Breton; 10 years in Cape Breton (2124)
           1822   James Fitzgerald, age 50 to 60, native of Ireland, married with twelve
                   children, was a farmer & fisherman (2830)
           1827   James Fitzgerald, 19, native of Cape Breton, married (3186)
           1805   Maurice Fitzgerald, married with seven children, 500 acres at Margaree
                   (179) [1818 Census says he was born in Ireland, and in Cape Breton 14
                   years; 1838 Census: Maurice Fitzgerald, farmer, Margaree]
           1810   Morris Fitzgerald, native of Ireland, married with ten children, and has
                   lived seven years at Margaree (571)
           1816   Maurice Fitzgerald, native of Co. Cork, had served on HMS *Magnificent 74*
                   [i.e., of 74 guns rating] during the first   American War. He was paid off
                   at Portsmouth Dock on his return there from the West Indies Station; in
                   mainland Nova Scotia from 1784 until 1804 and then to Cape Breton.
                   He had twelve children (1298) [1818 Census: farmer at Broad Cove, age 59,
                   had lived 14 years in Cape Breton]
           1815   Patrick Fitzgerald, native of Ireland, served seven years in the Navy (1132)
                   [1818 Census: Patrick Fitzgerald, 60, from Co. Kerry, 15 years in Cape
                   Breton, married with a child, living at Louisbourg]
           1816   William, 22, son of Maurice Fitzgerald (1299) [1818 Census: farmer, 24,
                   Broad Cove, single]
FITZPATRICK 1816 Darby Fitzpatrick, 28, native of Ireland, went to Newfoundland in 1814,
                   and thence to the Gut of Canso, Cape Breton, in May 1816 (1301)
           1817   Thomas Fitzpatrick, 27, native of Ireland, single man one year in Cape
                   Breton (1618) [1818 Census: labourer, Gut of Canso, age 25]]
           1827   William Fitzpatrick, 50, native of Ireland, widower with two children, with
                   his son Garrett Fitzpatrick, age 23, native of Ireland, single man (3187)
                   [William died 26 Feb 1852, age 79, at Sydney; native of Cork]
FLAHAVEN 1819   John Flahaven, 31, native of Ireland, married with five children, 11 years
                   in Cape Breton (2125)
FLANNIGAN 1825 Patrick Flannigan, 30, native of Ireland, single man (3021) [1838 Census:
                   Patrick Flanigan, widower, farmer, Arichat]
FLINN   1818   Edward Fling, native of Ireland, 7 years in Cape Breton. Note:'Knockahead'
                   [possibly Knockea, New Ross, Wexford] (1901) [1818 Census: Edward Fling,
                   27, farmer at Broad Cove, single, here *one year*]
           1821   Edward Flinn, 30, native of Ireland, married with two children. [A note in
                   1822 says that his family was in Ireland] (2633)
FLOOD   1819   Mary, parted from her husband (married 1818) Michael Flood. Her father
                   was Michael SHANAHAN, and her brother was Peter SHANAHAN (2126)

FLOOD   1818   Michael Flood, 24, native of Ireland, single, 4 years in Cape Breton (1902)
                   [1838 Census: Michael Flood, cooper, Richmond County]
FORAN   1820   John Foran, 23, native of Ireland, single man, recently arrived (2348)
FORD   1815   John Ford, 29, native of Cóbh, Cork, emigrated to Pictou, NS. He was
                   captured in 1812 by an American privateer and landed at Lingan where he
                   married the widow of John HALL; 220 acres at Lingan Harbour (1133)
FORTUNE   1821   Walter Fortune, 26, native of Ireland, married with a 6-year-old child; 3
                   years in Cape Breton (2635) [1838 Census: Fortune was a farmer, Margaree]
           1827   Walter Fortune, 28, native of Ireland, married (3185) [Wexford]
FOWLEY   1819   David Fowley, 29, native of Ireland, for 14 months was on the Isle of
                   Jersey and since 1816 in Cape Breton, served 7 years in the Kerry Militia
                   (2129) [at Rocky Bay, near Arichat]
FREEMAN   1817   Charles Freeman, 60, native of Ireland, single, 12 years in Cape Breton;
                   213 acres at Plumb Island (1625)
FURLONG   1821   Thomas Furlong, native of Ireland [Wexford], single, 4 years here (2639)
GALLAGHER 1812 John Gallagher, 40, native of Tipperary, raised in Nova Scotia, and moved
                   to Cape Breton eight years ago (810) [1818 Census: farmer, 60, married, five
                   children, St. Andrew's Channel, 12 years 5 months in Cape Breton]
GRENON   1803   Joseph Grenon, Arichat, over 10 years in Cape Breton (80)
           1807   Joseph Grenon, next to Daniel KAVANAGH at Arichat (300)
                   [1811 Census: Mariner at Arichat, with 2 boys, 5 girls]
HALEY   1820   Michael Haley, 30, native of Ireland, single, 5 years in Cape Breton (2365)
                   [1818 Census: Michael Healy, 30, farmer at Mabou, 3 years here]
HAMMOND 1815   John Hammond, native of Monaghan, had 84 acres, entered His Majesty's
                   Service during the American Revolution, and was discharged at Manchester,
                   NS, but moved to Cape Breton in 1795 (1152)
           1820   John Hammond, 60, native of Ireland, married, 25 years here (2366)
                   [Probably from the Parish of Currin, in Monaghan]
           1822   John Hammond, native of Ireland, served in the 40th. Regiment during the
                   American Revolution, then to Manchester, NS, and to Cape Breton (2837)
                   [1838 Census: Widow Hammond, farmer, Port Hood]
HANKARD   1821   Michael Hankard, 23, native of Ireland, married with a child (2646) [Cork]
HANRAHAN 1821   Lawrence Hanrahan, 27, native of Ireland, single, 4 years here (2647)
           1821   Michael Hanrahan, brother of the preceding, 21, single (2648)
HARRINGTON 1825 Michael Harrington, 30, native of Ireland, married (3030)
           1818   William Harrington, 27, native of Kilkenny, married with a child, 5 years
                   in Cape Breton (1929)
HAYES   1810   Edward Hayes, native of Ireland [Wexford], lived 20 years at Port Hood;
                   brother was Miles DONOHOE (582)
           1820   Edward Hayes, native of Ireland, 32 years at Port Hood (2369) [1818
                   Census: trader at Port Hood, 55, 30 years in Cape Breton, married, 1 child]
           1821   Edward Hayes, 59, native of Ireland, married with a child; with James
                   WHITEHEAD, Halifax, trader, in 1785 to Cape Breton in 1796 (2649)
           1826   James Hayes, 27, native of Ireland, married with two children, 2 years in
                   Sydney (3112) [1838 Census: James Hays, smith, Lingan]
           1815   John, single, son of Thomas Hayes, farmer at Bras d'Or Lake, just arrived
                   in Cape Breton from Ireland (1153) [1818 Census: John Hayes, 22, farmer
                   at St. Andrew's Channel, married, 3 years 6 months in Cape Breton]

HAYES   1810   Thomas Hayes, 34, native of Parish of Ferns, Wexford, 3½ years in Cape
                    Breton, had wife and three children still in Ireland (583) [1818 Census:
                    Thomas Hayes, 45, farmer at Red Islands, married with 5 children, here
                    for 12 years]
HAYNEY   1821   James Hayney, 26, native of Ireland, married with a stepchild (2650)
                    [1838 Census: James Heaney, fisherman, Arichat]
HEALEN   1818   Maurice Healen, 26, native of Ireland, single, 3 years in Cape Breton
                    (1930) Maurice Healan, native of Cork, died at Low Point, 11 Oct 1850, age
                    59]
HEFFERNAN 1816 Dennis Heffernan, 22, native of Nova Scotia, 2 years in Cape Breton (1316)
            1816   James Heffernan, native of Halifax, 2 years in Cape Breton. Note: "Pat
                    DUGGAN, his servant, drowned, 17 March 1816" (1316a) [James, 23, and
                    the preceding man, were sons of Patrick and Margaret Heffernan of
                    Halifax. Patrick (1755-1816) was a baker and trader and a native of
                    Ireland.]
            1825   William Heffernan, 40, native of Ireland, to Newfoundland in 1824 and to
                    Cape Breton in Oct 1824 (3031) [1838 Census: William Heffrin, farmer,
                    near Judique]
HENRY   1813   John Henry, native of Co. Down, married but had no children, 27 years in
                    Cape Breton (921)
HICKEY   1817   Richard Hickey, 30, native of Kilkenny, single man (1643)
HIGGINS   1820   John Higgins, native of Ireland,, emigrated to the United States and then,
                    as a Loyalist, came in 1784 to St. Peter's, Cape Breton (2370)
            1820   John Higgins, 31, native of Nova Scotia, 4 months in Cape Breton (2371)
HOGAN   1809   Timothy Hogan, native of Limerick, went to Newfoundland and in 1796
                    removed to Cape Breton (488) [schoolmaster in 1800]
HOULAHAN 1803   Darby Hoolahan, 300 acres on the north side of the Mira River (83)
            1821   John Houlahan, 24, native of Ireland, single man (2653)
HOWLETT   1820   Timothy Howlett.4, native of Ireland, single man. Note: "Red Acre"
                    [Redacres townland, Parish of Killahy, Kilkenny] (2373)
HOWLEY   1822   James Howly, 32, native of Ireland, married with six children (3189)
            1815   John Howley, 23, native of Ireland [Kilkenny], single man (1317)
JACKSON   1814   Samuel Jackson, native of Carrickfergus, Antrim, married with nine
                    children, 27 years in Cape Breton (1004)
            1820   Samuel Jackson, 59, native of Ireland, married with eleven children, 35
                    years in Cape Breton (2379) [1838 Census: Samuel Jackson, fisherman,
                    Ingonish]
JOYCE   1804   John Joyce (146a)
KAVANAGH 1815   Catherine, native of Scotland, widow of William Kavanagh, had four
                    children (1323)
            1811   Daniel Kavanagh, native of Ireland, married with two children, 12 years in
                    Cape Breton (694) [at Lennox Passage]
            1806   Daniel Kavanagh, at Arichat (239a)
            1815   Daniel Kavanagh, 34, native of Ireland, married with three children, 14
                    years in Cape Breton, had 100 acres, was a lieutenant in the Militia (1159)
                    [1838 Census: Daniel & Jane Kavenagh, farmer, Richmond County]
            1817   Edward Kavanagh (1651) [1838 Census: Edward Kavenagh, farmer]
            1818   Edward Kavanagh, had grant in 1816 (1940)

KAVANAGH 1821   Edward Kavanagh, 27, native of Ireland, single man, 8 years in Cape
                Breton (2666) [at Rocky Bay, near Arichat]

         1803   Lawrence Kavanagh settled at Rocky Bay, between Arichat and
                Descousse, in 1802, and had shop and cattle by Sep 1803 (86) [native of
                Waterford]

         1805   Lawrence Kavanagh, 350 acres near St. Peter's and 9 near Arichat (189)

         1808   Lawrence Kavanagh, married, four children; 300 acres, Rocky Bay (383)
                [1811 Census: Yeoman, etc., near Arichat, 1 boy, 4 girls]

         1815   Lawrence Kavanagh, Jr., 24, native of Cape Breton, 500 acres (1160)
                [1838 Census: Lawrence Kavenagh, MLA, St Peter's]

         1819   Lawrence Kavanagh was at St. Peter's since 1784 (2154, 2155, 2157)

         1819   Lawrence Kavanagh, 28, native of Ireland, single man, 3 months in Cape
                Breton. Note: "Bally Murphy" [Ballymurphy, Carlow] (2156)

         1820   Lawrence Kavanagh (2383)

         1806   Thomas Kavanagh at Baddeck (239)

         1826   Thomas Kavanagh, 22, native of Cape Breton, single man with two
                unmarried sisters (3116)

KEATING 1816   David Keating, 28, native of Ireland, has no family (1324)

         1827   John Keating, 50, native of Ireland, married with five children, one year in
                Cape Breton (3194)

KEEGAN   1816   James Keegan, 25, native of Cape Breton (1325)

         1811   Sarah, widow of Luke Keegan, and their son James Keegan (696)
                [Sarah JONES, widow Keegan, lived at Mainadieu, Cape Breton]

         1823   Owen Keegan, 59, native of Ireland, married with ten children (2930)
                [Keegan lived at Sydney. His wife was Elizabeth GRANDY.]

KELLY   1826   Martin Kelly, 40, native of Ireland, married with four children (3117)
                [at Rocky Bay, near Arichat]

         1818   Thomas Kelly, 31, native of Ireland, married with three children (1941)

KENNEDY 1805   Michael Kennedy, married with three children; son-in-law of Charles
                MARTEL (190) [His wife was Mary Martell]

KENNY   1821   Edward Kenny, 28, native of Ireland, married with a child, 4 years in
                Cape Breton (2665) [at Rocky Bay, near Arichat]

         1826   Edward Kenny, 33, native of Ireland,, married with four children (3118)
                [1838 Census: Edward & Margaret Kenny, farmer, Arichat]

KENT   1821   Michael Kent, 34, native of Ireland, married, 2 years in Cape Breton (2666)
                [at Rocky Bay, near Arichat]

KERRY   1809   Michael Kerry, 60, native of Ireland, no family, 10 years in Cape Breton,
                and 22 years in the Army (492)

KING   1820   Patrick King, 76, native of Ireland, married with nine children, 12 years in
                Cape Breton (2386)

LACY   1820   William Lacy, 29, native of Ireland, single man, 2 years in Cape Breton.
                Note: "Barney O'Balle" [? Ballynabola, Kilscanlan Parish, Wexford] (2387)
                [1838 Census: William Leacy, farmer, Inverness County]

LAMBERT 1818   James Lambert, 30, native of Ireland,, single man, one year in Cape
                Breton. Note: "Cavan" (1943)

LANDERS 1827   John Landers, 30, native of Ireland, married with a child (3196)

McDANIEL 1818   Miles McDaniel, native of Ireland,, came to Cape Breton as a trader in
                1807. Note: "Kimmolin Ford" [Kilmoleran, Waterford] (1955, 1956)

McDANIEL   1819   Miles McDaniel, native of Ireland. Notes: "Balina Kilty" [? Ballynakill, Co. Waterford]. Census: Miles MacDonald, 27, merchant at Broad Cove, married with four children, 11 years in Cape Breton]

McDONNELL 1802   Daniel McDonnell, River Inhabitants (44)

McGRATH   1827   Luke Magrah, 30, native of Ireland, married with one child (3231) [1838 Census: Luke & Mary Magrath, Lingan]

McGUIRE   1801   Edward McGuire, Gut of Canso (19b)

McKEAGNEY 1831 Rev. Henry McKeagney, 36, native of Co. Tyrone, and his brother (3301) [Born at Clogher 15 June 1796, died at Sydney, NS, 4 June 1856; 1838 Census: Catholic priest at Sydney]

MADDEN   1812   Edward Madden, 27, native of Ireland, 5 years in Cape Breton (864)

MALONEY   1821   Hugh Meloney, 50, native of [Co. Waterford], Ireland, had eight children, eldest son was John Meloney (2762)

          1829   Hugh Meloney mentions his late daughter, the wife of David POWER, and their daughters, Rosamond and Rachel POWER (3276)

          1817   Michael Maloney, 30, native of Ireland, single man, 7 years in Cape Breton (1768)

MARTIN   1816   John Martin, 25, native of Ireland, emigrated to Newfoundland in 1813, and to Cape Breton in 1815, single man (1435) [1818 Census: labourer, Gut of Canso; married]

MATTICKS 1819   Mathew Matticks, 29, native of Ireland, married with two children, was 5 years in Newfoundland, one year in Cape Breton. Note: "Wexford" (2250)

MEAGHER   1825   Donald Meagher, 26, native of Ireland, married man (3075) [Killaloe, Kilkenny; 1838 Census: Donald Meagher, farmer, Port Hood]

          1827   Michael Maher, 38, native of Ireland, single man (3232)

MERRICK   1822   Nicholas Merrick, 40, native of Ireland, single man (2887)

MOORE   1821   Patrick Moore, 21, native of Ireland, single man (2764)

          1822   Patrick Moore, 28, native of Ireland, single man (2888)

          1823   Patrick Moore, 29, native of Ireland, married man (2914) [1838 Census: Patrick Moore, fisherman, Cape North]

MORGAN   1826   James Morgan, 27, native of Ireland, single man (3159)

          1827   John Morgan, 30, native of Ireland, married with three children (3234)

          1827   Margaret, 52, native of Ireland, widow of — Morgan. She had six children, but only the youngest, Lawrence Morgan, 24, lives with her (3235)

MORRISSEY 1821   Lawrence Morrisie, 30, native of Ireland, single man, 2 months here (2766)

MORTIMER 1820   William Mortimer, blacksmith, 46, native of Ireland, single man, he moved from mainland Nova Scotia to Mabou, Cape Breton, in 1807 [1818 Census: blacksmith, 40, 9 years in Cape Breton]

MULLINS   1817   Daniel Mullins, native of Ireland, married man (1787)

          1825   Michael Mullins, native of Ireland, married with nine children (3078) [1838 Census: Michael Mullins, farmer, Sydney; another of name was a pilot]

MURPHY   1806   Adam Murphy, Margaree (258)

          1801   Dennis Murphy, 300 acres at Port Hood (19i) [1818 Census: farmer, 47, born in Ireland, 21 years in Cape Breton, living at Port Hood; see infra]

          1819   Dennis Murphy, native of Wexford, emigrated to Halifax in 1791, to Port Hood in 1795, married with six children (2255) [brother of James, infra]

          1812   Francis Murphy, born in Monaghan Town, Ireland, came to Cape Breton in 1785, had 318 acres at Grand Grove, St. Peter's Bay, served as magistrate and captain of Militia (867)

MURPHY   1815   James Murphy, native of Co. Wexford, married with two children, 11 years in Cape Breton, had 200 acres at Port Hood, had served as a private under Captain WATTS (1250) [brother of Dennis Murphy, *supra*; 1818 Census: blacksmith, age 30, at Port Hood]

1826   James Murphy, 25, native of Ireland, married with a child (3121)

1817   John Murphy, 40, native of Ireland,, single man (1788) [1818 Census: John Murphy, 40, farmer, St. Andrew's Channel, single, 6 years 5 months here]

1817   John Murphy, 28, native of Kilkenny, married with four children (1789)

1817   John Murphy the 2nd., 28, native of Ireland, married, four children (1790)

1818   John Murphy, 28, native of Ireland, married with two children, 6 years in Cape Breton (2029)

1821   Michael Murphy, 23, native of Ireland, single man, came to Cape Breton in November 1820 (2769)

1820   William Murphy, 27, native of Ireland, married with one child, 6 years in Cape Breton (2524)

NEAL   1826   Lawrence Neal, native of Ireland, married with three children (3161)

1827   Lawrence Neale, native of Ireland, married with three children (3237)

NEMOW   1791   Denis Nemow, 27, native of Kerry, 3 years in Cape Breton (1791)

O'BRIAN   1812   John O'Bryan, native of Ireland, came to Nova Scotia 15 years ago, and was an apprentice cooper at Halifax, 120 acres at Gut of Canso (868) [1818 Census: John Obrine, 49, cooper, married, 2 children, 6 years in Cape Breton; 1838 Census: John & Rebecca O'Brien, cooper, Richmond Co.]

O'BRIEN   1819   Patrick O'Brien, 30, native of Ireland, single man, 4 years in Cape Breton. Note: "Glyn Mahon" [?Clonmahon, Meath?] (2258)

O'CONNOR 1815   Daniel O'Connor, native of Co. Down, came out, 1811, to Pictou in a lum- ber ship, was shipwrecked on Scatari Island, and came to Port Hood (1253)

1816   Daniel O'Connor, 22, native of Ireland, single man (1441) [1818 Census: farmer at Port Hood.4, single]

1820   Daniel O'Connor, 27, native of Ireland, single man, 8 years here. (2528)

1831   Daniel O'Connor, 33, native of Ireland (3302)

ODEL   1826   John Odel, 60, native of Ireland, had seven children, including sons Thomas Odel, 26, and John Odel, Jr., 22, both born in Newfoundland (3163)

O'NEIL   1818   Dennis O'Neal, 34, native of Ireland, married with five children (2032)

1825   John O'Neil, 35, native of Ireland, (3080)

1803   Patrick O'Neil, married with two children, served through the American War, lives at Cap le Round, near St. Peter's Bay (107) [1838 Census: Patrick & Joanna O'Neil, carpenter, Richmond County]

1815   Patrick O'Neil, 53, native of Limerick, married, ten children (3 minors) several times wounded during 23 years in the Army, 14 years in the 44th. Regt. and 9 years under General Fanning in Prince Edward's Regt. (1255)

PEEPLES   1809   James Peeples, 22, native of northern Ireland, emigrated to Nova Scotia in 1805. In 1806 he and his brother Timothy Peeples settled on the south side of the Gut of Canso (527)

1812   Timothy Peeples and his brother James Peeples, natives of northern Ireland (871)

PENDERGAST 1816 Michael Pendergass, native of Ireland, 25 years in His Majesty's Service (1445)

1823   Patrick Pendergast, 25, native of Ireland, single man (2958)

PHELAN   1812   Edward Phealon, native of Ireland, 5 years in Cape Breton (872) [1838
                    Census: Edward Phealon & wife, smith, Arichat]
            1817   John Phelan, 25, native of Ireland, single man, came to Cape Breton in
                    November 1816 (1798) [1838 Census: John Phelen, farmer, Cow Bay]
            1802   Patrick Phealon, Cow Bay, was son-in-law of John L'ANGO (50)
            1810   Patrick Phalon, Cow Bay, married to the daughter of John Le ANGO and
                    has four children, the eldest age 10 (632)
            1815   William Phelan, native of Newfoundland, married with one child, 12 years
                    in Cape Breton (1257)
POOLEY   1816   William Pooley, native of Dublin, single man, taught school in Sydney for
                    the past thirteen months (1448)
            1817   William Pooley, 21, native of Ireland,, single man, school teacher, 2 years
                    in Cape Breton (1802)
            1820   William Pooley, 23, native of Ireland, schoolmaster, 5 years here (2535)
POOR   1811   Patrick Poore, native of Waterford, 8 months at Margaree (762)
            1821   Thomas Poor, 31, native of Ireland, married with two children (2778) [1818
                    Census: Thomas Power, 30, carpenter at Margaree, married with a child, 2
                    years in Cape Breton; 1838 Census: Thomas Power, carpenter, Port Hood]
POWER   1823   David Power, 24, native of Ireland, married with one child (3000)
            1827   Edward Power, native of Ireland, married with four children. Had been
                    shipwrecked at Grand River en route from Newfoundland to Prince
                    Edward Island (3241) [1838 Census: Edward Power, farmer, St. Peter's]
            1821   James Power, 34, native of Ireland, married with one child (2779)
            1812   Nicholas Power, 40, native of Co. Waterford, had six children, 12 years in
                    Nova Scotia (874)
            1812   Patrick Power, 21, native of Tipperary, 5 years in Cape Breton (875)
                    [1818 Census: farmer at Margaree, 28, 7 years here, married, 1 child]
            1818   Patrick Power, 50, married with five children, 25 years in Cape Breton
                    Note: St. Patrick's Farm" (2036)
PURCELL   1816   Philip Purcell, 52, native of Ireland, married with five children (1451)
                    [Native of Co. Tipperary]
QUINN   1801   John Quinn, Southeast Branch, Mabou Harbour (19a)
            1818   Michael Quin, 24, native of Ireland, 6 months in Cape Breton. Note:
                    "Carnock" [Carnagh, Wexford] (2037)
ROACH   1820   James Roach, 32, native of Ireland,, married with one child, 2 years in Cape
                    Breton. Note: "Castle Hyde" [Castlehyde, Cork] (2540)
            1824   Matthew Roach, 21, and Michael Roach, 19, natives of Cape Breton (3001)
                    [1838 Census: Matthew Roach, farmer, Lingan]
            1812   Patrick Roach, 25, native of Detmore [apparently Ardmore], Waterford, 20
                    acres at Margaree, 5 years in Cape Breton (957)
            1802   Thomas Roach, Lingan, formerly private in the Nova Scotia Regiment (52)
            1804   Thomas Roach, three lots at Lingan (164) [1838 Census: Thomas Roach,
                    blacksmith, Northwest Arm]
            1810   Thomas Roach, 41, native of Tipperary, married with five children, served 9
                    years in the Army, and has lived in Cape Breton for 8 years (637)
ROCHFORT 1821   Patrick Rochfort, 32, millwright, native of Ireland, single man (2787)
ROCKETT   1823   Peter Rocket, 21, native of Ireland, single man, 15 months here (2959)
                    [1838 Census: Peter Rocket, farmer, Sydney]

ROCKETT 1822   Richard Rockett, 23, native of Ireland, single man (2900)
                    [1838 Census: Richard Rocket, farmer, Sydney]

ROSS   1812   William Ross, native of Ireland, married with nine children, 20 years in
                    Cape Breton (878) [1818 Census: carpenter, 50, St. Patrick Channel, had
                    thirteen children, 28 years in Cape Breton]

       1815   William Ross, 46, native of Ireland, married with eleven children, 24 years
                    in Cape Breton, lieutenant of Militia (1260) [In 1818 Census: *supra*]

RYAN   1805   Joseph Ryan, 460 acres, Northwest Margaree River (215)

       1814   Joseph Ryan, 450 acres near Margaree (1079) [1818 Census: 21, single,
                    born in Cape Breton to Irish parents]

       1812   Martin Ryan, native of Co. Waterford, 5 years in Newfoundland and Cape
                    Breton (960) [1838 Census: Martin Ryan, farmer, Sydney]

       1821   Michael Ryan, 27, native of Ireland, single man, one year here (2788)

       1824   Patrick Ryan, 25, native of Ireland, single man (3003) [1838 Census:
                    Patrick Ryan, farmer, single man, Lingan]

       1826   Patrick Ryan, 35, native of Ireland, married with four children (3169)
                    [1838 Census: Patrick & Mary Ryan, farmer, Ball's Brook]

SHANNAHAN 1819 Peter Shannahan, 24, native of Ireland, one year in Cape Breton, brother-
                    in-law of Michael FLOOD. Note: "Ochen a Nochen" [? appears to refer to
                    Rosbercon, in Kilkenny] (2272) [Shannahan was a cooper by trade]

SHARKEY 1821   Peter Sharkey, 41, native of Ireland, single man, 9 years here (2792)

SHEA   1823   Patrick Shea, 27, native of Ireland, married man (2960)

       1824   Patrick Shea, 26, native of Ireland, married with a child (3003)

SHEEHAN 1819   Michael Sheehan, 36, native of Ireland, married with three children,
                    3 years in Cape Breton. Note: "Ross" [New or Old Ross, Wexford] (2273)

       1821   Michael Sheehan, 37, native of Ireland, married with three children (2779)

SLATTERY 1816 John Slattery, 24, of Louisbourg, son of Michael Slattery (1457) [1818
                    Census: John Slaterey, single man, 26, native of Cape Breton]

       1794   Michael Slattery licenced to occupy 300 acres at Louisbourg Harbour; by
                    attached indenture, dated 1826, he gives this land to his son George (9)
                    [1818 Census: George Slaterey, single man, 17, native of Cape Breton]

       1810   Michael Slattery, 50, native of Limerick, married with eight children,
                    has lived 17 years at Louisbourg (638) [1818 Census gives his age as 65,
                    and says that he had lived in Cape Breton for 28 years]

       1816   Michael Slattery, Jr., 22, of Louisbourg, son of Michael Slattery (1458)
                    [1818 Census: Michael Slaterey, 23, single, born in Cape Breton; Michael,
                    son of Michael & Mary (MULLOWNEY) Slattery, married 30 July 1821 in the,
                    Catholic church at Halifax, NS, Mary, dau of John & Mary (KENNEDY)
                    BURKE, Mainadieu, Cape Breton]

       1817   Michael Slattery, married with nine "small children", had been 25 years at
                    Louisbourg (1814)

       1831   Patrick Slattery, native of Ireland, had brickworks in Sydney (3303) [had
                    applied for a lot in 1826]

SMITH   1817   John Smith, 19, native of Dublin, one year in Cape Breton (1815)

STAFFORD 1803 William Stafford, 37 acres on the eastern shore of Maloney's Creek (114)

STRANG   1824   Thomas Strang, 26, native of Ireland, single man (3008) [?Tipperary?]
                    [1838 Census: Thomas Strang, farmer, Lingan]

SULLIVAN 1823   John Sullivan (2963)
                    Patrick Sullivan (2963)

SULLIVAN   1818   William Sullivan, 59, native of Ireland, 3 years in Cape Breton where he married the widow of Henry ADAMS who had been here 20 years. Note: "Clonmel" [in Tipperary] (2047, 2048)

SWEENEY   1823   Michael Sweeney, 35, native of Ireland, married man (2963a)

SYNNET   1817   John Synnet, native of Ireland [Co. Wexford], 8 years in Cape Breton (1818)

THOMPSON 1826   Mathew Thompson, native of Ireland, married, 7 years here (3171)

TOBIN   1822   John Tobin, 22, native of Ireland, single man (2905)

TOOLE   1820   William Toole, 41, native of Ireland, married with seven children, was 3 years in the Army, 17 years in Cape Breton

TRENAMAN 1825   Joseph Trinnaman, 28, native of Ireland, married, 5½ years here (3085)

TYRELL   1822   John Tyrell, 26, native of Ireland, married with three children, and Michael Tyrell, 36, single man (2904) [1838 Census: John Tyrell, carpenter, and wife, Arichat]

WALL   1816   Michael Wall, 29, native of Ireland, single man (1464) [1818 Census: Michael *Watt*, 30, farmer, River Inhabitants, here 2 years]

WALSH   1814   Edward Walsh, 40, native of Ireland, married with five children, 15 years here (1084) [18*11* Census: Farmer, Plaster of Paris Cove, 3 boys, 3 girls]

                 1819   George Walsh, 31, native of Ireland, married, 9 years in Cape Breton (2285)

                 1813   Rodger Walsh, native of Tipperary, with two sons, a former soldier who had been in Cape Breton 10 years, a lot a Port Hood (964)

WELCH   1821   David Welsh, 25, native of Ireland, married man, 2 years here (2803) [1838 Census: David Walsh, farmer, Port Hood]

                 1816   James Welch, 28, native of Ireland, single man (1466)

                 1826   Peter Welch, 30, native of Ireland, married with two children (3172) [1838 Census: Peter & Catherine Walsh, Lingan]

                 1826   Simon Welsh, 28, shoemaker, native of Ireland, married with two children (3121) [1818 Census: Simon Walsh, 21, shoemaker at Port Hood, single]

WHELAN   1817   Edward Whelan, 30, native of Ireland, married with two children (1825)

WHITE   1815   John White, 22, native of Ireland, 5 years in Cape Breton (1244a)

                 1816   John White, 24, native of Ireland, single man (1467)

                 1818   Michael White, 26, native of Ireland, married, here 18 months (2059) [1838 Census: Michael & Bridget White, farmer, Inverness County]

WHITEHEAD 1820   Abigail, widow of James Whitehead, 30 years in Cape Breton. She had three sons by first husband HAWLEY and two by her second Whitehead (2564)

                 1815   James Whitehead, native of Kilkenny, coaster and trader, came to Nova Scotia, 1785, and to Cape Breton in 1789 (1245a) [?Powerstown, Kilkenny]

WHITTY   1816   James Whitty, 26, native of Co. Waterford, single man, emigrated in 1809 to Newfoundland and in 1815 to Cape Breton (1468)

                 1821   James Whitty, 33, native of Ireland, single man (2577) [again in 1822]

                 1820   Thomas Whitty, 24, native of Ireland, single man, 4 months here (2565) [1838 Census: Thomas Whitty, farmer, Port Hood]

                 1818   Walter Whitty, 34, native of Ireland, married with five children, 2 years in Cape Breton, at "Chestecorps" [Juste-au-Corps, a former name for Inverness County, NS], having previously been in Newfoundland. He has a brother in Cape Breton (2063) [1818 Census: farmer at Port Hood, with *one child*; 1838 Census: Walter Whitty, farmer, Port Hood] [James, Thomas and Walter Whitty were brothers from Waterford]

WOOD   1812   William Wood, native of Limerick, married with eight children, 28 years in Cape Breton (967)

WRIGHT   1815   William Wright, native of Co. Cavan, went to New York in 1805, but in 1807 was barred from the USA as a British subject, under the Non Intercourse Act, and then came to Cape Breton(1249) [1818 Census: farmer, 32, 7 years in Cape Breton, married, Port Hood]

YOUNG   1811   James Young, native of Graces Parish, Barony of Crany [Crannagh], Co. Kilkenny, went to Newfoundland in 1779, thence [about 1792] to Halifax, NS, where he married (775) [1818 Census gives his age as 63 and says that he had been 18 years in Cape Breton; located at Louisbourg]

           1818   James Young, 60, native of Ireland, married with one child, 17 to 18 years in Cape Breton (2064)

11 - *CUMBERLAND*: A PARTIALLY RECONSTITUTED PASSENGER LIST, 1827

There survive no lists of Irish passengers arriving in Nova Scotia in the period between 1815 and 1845. Occasionally there is enough information in contemporary records to permit us to identify at least some of those who were aboard specific ships. In the present instance this enables identification of about one-sixth of those travelling in an immigrant vessel in 1827 from Waterford, Ireland, to Halifax, Nova Scotia.

The Halifax newspaper, the *Novascotian*, of 5 July 1827 reported the arrival in the preceding week of the *Cumberland*, 43 days out of Waterford, carrying about 350 passengers. This would mean that the vessel arrived between 28 June and 4 July, and had sailed between 16 and 22 May. The Catholic registers of that summer narrow the dates further, as Pierce Clear was "born on the *Cumberland* on its way from Waterford" and baptised in Halifax on 1 July, age 6 weeks, giving a birth date of 19/20 May, placing the voyage between 16/18 May and 28/30 June. This can be narrowed further by noting that John Buggy was buried in Halifax, but had died at sea on 28 June, presumably within sight of port. The voyage was made from 16/7 May and 28/9 June 1827. Probable or certain passengers in the *Cumberland* were the following:

1. William EGAN
2. Bridget HICKEY, his wife
3. Elizabeth, their daughter, buried 2 July 1827 age 18 mos.
   This couple had two children baptised in 1830 and 1832, then appear to have left Halifax.

4. John BUGGY, died at sea 28 June 1827
5. Mary CRAWLEY, his wife
6. John, their son, buried 2 July 1827, age 1 day; born after their arrival.
7. Mary, their daughter, buried 10 July 1827, age 2 years.
   Mary CRAWLEY, Leix, remarried, 11 Jan. 1831, Thomas WALSH from Co. Cork.

8. John BRIAN
9. Ann BYRNE, his wife
10.Charles, their son, buried 3 July 1827, age 13 years.
   As they then vanish from local records, they must have moved on quite soon afterwards.

11. John LOWREY
12. Catherine MYERS, his wife
13. Michael, their son, buried 8 July 1827, age 8 years.
14-16. Honora, Mary, and Julia, their daughters.
  Honora was then 12 years old, and married 29 Oct 1833, Philip PURCELL of Co. Tipperary.
  The marriage record states that Honora was also of that county.

17. Francis WHELAN, buried 9 July 1827, age 35, native of Kilkenny City

18. James DOWLING, "passenger in the *Cumberland*"
19. Eleanor MULHALL, his wife, buried 9 July 1827, age 40, native of St. John Parish,   Kilkenny
20. Eleanor, their daughter, buried 9 July 1827, age 2½ years
21. Peter, their son, buried 9 July 1827, age 7 days, born after their arrival, baptised 4 July 1827.
22-23. Ann, and Bridget, their daughters

24. Denis GORMAN, blacksmith
25. Catherine PARKER, his wife, buried 11 July 1827, age 25, from Inistioge, Co. Kilkenny

26. John MEANEY, buried 12 July 1827, age 40, from Brownstown, Co. Kilkenny
27. Richard, his son, buried 12 July 1827, age 13, from Brownstown, Co. Kilkenny

28. Thomas KERWIN, tailor, buried 12 July 1827, age 40, of County Waterford

29. John LOUGHNAN, buried 12 July 1827, age 34, of County Carlow

30. Nicholas KENNY, buried 20 July 1827, of County Kilkenny. Died in the fever hospital.
31. Catherine BRENNAN, his wife, buried 12 July 1827, age 45, of County Kilkenny

32. Thomas REED
33. Margaret NARY, his wife
34. Eliza, their daughter, buried 13 July 1827, age 10 months
  Since they then vanish from the local record, they must have moved along soon afterwards.

35. Patrick WALSH, buried 14 July 1827, age 58, from Cashel, Co. Tipperary "left 7 children"
36. Mary MOLONY, his wife
37-39. Margaret, Mary, and Catherine, their daughters
40. Patrick, their son
41,42,43 three children whose names are not found

44. Thomas FOYLE
45. Judith SALLY, his wife, buried 14 July 1827, age 50, of the Parish of Castlecomer, Kilkenny

46. Thomas DOWLING, buried 15 July 1827, age 57, of Thomastown, Co. Kilkenny
47. Margaret McCARTHY, his wife
48. Mary, their daughter
49. Patrick, their son, buried 28 July 1827, age 27, of County Kilkenny

50. Henry HAMMON, blacksmith, buried 15 July 1827, age 60, of Gowran, Co. Kilkenny

51. Margaret HICKEY, buried 16 July 1827, age 30, of Cashel, Co. Tipperary

52. John CARROLL, cooper, buried 17 July 1827, age 23, from New Ross, Co. Wexford

53. William KEATING, buried 23 July 1827, age 50, of the Parish of Mothell, Co. Kilkenny; died in the fever hospital.

54. John BUGGY, buried 12 August 1827, age 64, at the Poor Asylum
55. Mary CANFILL, his wife, buried 25 July 1827, age 63, of Castlecomer, Co. Kilkenny
While no relationship with John BUGGY (#4) is indicated, their relative ages and their being on board the same vessel is suggestive of a connexion between them.

56. William CLEAR
57. Margaret DELANEY, his wife
58. Pierce, their son, baptised 1 July 1827, age 6 weeks, "born on the *Cumberland* on the way from Waterford".

12 - APPRECIATIVE PASSENGERS, 1828-1846

In the absence of passenger lists, immigration historians and genealogical researchers in Atlantic Canada depend on a variety of sources to remedy the lack, at least in part. From time to time a few passengers published a newspaper notice of appreciation of a ship's captain and we learn the identity of some of those who had sailed in a particular vessel between specific ports and arrived about a certain date. A selection of six such notices follows.

The brig *Huskisson*, Capt. Davys, from Ballyshannon, Ireland, to Saint John, New Brunswick. Notice of appreciation signed by Owen and Richard **CASSIDY**, John **GALLAGHER**, John **INGRAM**, Hugh **McIVER** and James **O'NEIL**. - *New Brunswick Courier*, 28 June 1828.

The brig *Zephyr*, Capt. John Hughes, from Donegal, Ireland, to Saint John, New Brunswick. Notice signed on behalf of the passengers by John **BROGAN**, James **COLVIN**, Pat. **DUNBEVIE**, Andrew **HIGARTY**, Ben. **JOHNSON**, Andrew **LOVE**, Frs **MILLER**, James **MULLEN**, Robt. **PATERSON**, and James **ROGLE**. - *New Brunswick Courier*, 21 May 1836.

The barque *Atlantic*, Capt. Morton, from Dundee, Scotland, thanked for his efforts during the wreck of the vessel at Pouch Cove, near St. John's, Newfoundland. All but one boy had been saved. Charles and Margaret **ALEXANDER**, Elizabeth **DICH**, John **DUFF**, Benjamin **HOGG** and his wife, Jemima Hay **JAMESON**, Don. **M'GREGOR** and his wife, Peter **MacFARLANE**, Jessie **M'KEILLER**, Alexander **M'KENZIE**, Henry **MATTHEWSON**, Elizabeth **REWANS**, James **ROBERTSON** and Thomas **RUTHERFORD** signed on behalf of the passengers. Isabella **CHAPMAN** made her mark. -*The Newfoundlander*, 14 May 1840.

The barque *Royal William*, Capt. Michael Driscoll, from Cork, Ireland, to Saint John, NB. The notice was signed on 28 May 1841 while the vessel rode off Partridge Island in Saint John Harbour, having arrived the day before. Signatories were George H. **BALDWIN**, Patrick **BRYAN**, William **BUTLER**, John **CARDEN**, Daniel **DUNN**, Robert **EDGAR**, James **FITZGERALD**, Henry **FOWLER**, Patrick **KEEFER**, John **KEOHAN**, Richard **PENNEY**, and John **RYAN**. - Saint John *New Brunswick Courier*, 5 June 1841.

The brig *George*, Capt. Richard Power, mate Edmund Power, from Cork, Ireland, to Saint John, NB, arrived in port on 21 June 1841. Passengers put a notice in the *New Brunswick Courier* of 10 July 1841: John **AIGAN**, Patrick **COMONS**, Daniel **COURTENAY**, David **GRADY**, Michael **GRIFFIN**, John **MAHON**, Michael **O'DONNELL**, and Michael **SULLIVAN**.

The ship *Chieftain*, Capt. Henry Duffy, mate McKenzie, from Galway, Ireland, to Saint John, NB, lost her mainmast six days out, and safely reacher Saint John after a passage of 47 days, with passengers mainly from Galway and Clare. Six men signed a notice published in the *Morning News* of Saint John, 10 August 1846, namely, James **DAVIN**, Bryan **DUGGAN**, John **SELLORS**, Thos. **SMYTH**, Thos. **THORNTON**, and Pat. **WALSH**.

13 - PERSONS SOUGHT ADVERTISEMENTS, *1831-1841*

The *Boston Pilot* began on 2 January 1836 as the successor of newspapers that had been known variously as the *Jesuit Sentinel and Catholic Sentinel* (Sept. 1829 to Oct. 1831), *The Catholic Intelligencer* (Oct. 1831 to Dec. 1832), and *The Jesuit, or Catholic Sentinel* (4 Jan.1833 to 26 Dec. 1835). Thereafter it was known by its familiar title, *The Boston Pilot*. Among the notices seeking lost relatives in those earlier papers thirteen concerned people who were or had been in Atlantic Canada. Thirty-seven more such notices appeared in *The Pilot* to Dec. 1841. A single instance noted in a Nova Scotia newspaper is included here.

The Boston Pilot, 10 Apr 1841: Michael **BYRNS**, of the Parish of Whitechurch, Cork, carpenter, went to Prince Edward Island on 20 May 1820. He was in New York City 18 months ago, but was said to be on his way to New Orleans. Sought by his son, Dennis **BYRNS**, c/o Henry **CAMPBELL**, carriage maker, Charlotte St., Saint John, NB

The Boston Pilot, 21 Aug 1841: Peter **BYRNE** of Thomastown Parish, Kilkenny, went to St. John's, NL, in 1821, and was in Portland, ME, 3 years since. Sought by his brother, Martin **BYRNE**, c/o Mr. **CARROLL**, Quincy, MA..

The Boston Pilot, 13 Aug 1836: Jeremiah **COGHLAN**, Co. Cork, was at St. Andrews, NB, two years ago. Sought by his brother, Cornelius **COGHLAN**, c/o James **BARRY**, 99 Broad Street, Boston.

The Boston Pilot, 28 July 1838: Mary **CRADDOCK**, alias **FORD**, Hetford [Headford], Galway, landed at Saint John, New Brunswick, 6 or 7 years ago; now said to be near Boston. Her husband, John **FORD**, 123 Broad Street, Boston, seeks her. [Saint John records indicate that she arrived with her husband and two of his siblings in the ship *Sea Horse* which left Galway on 29 April 1834.

The Jesuit, or Catholic Sentinel, 21 Feb 1835: James **CUNNINGHAM**, Parish of Killenaud [Killenaule], Tipperary, emigrated in April 1831, and was last reported to be at Barns Island, NL He is sought by his brother Richard **CUNNINGHAM**, Burlington, VT.

The Boston Pilot, 17 Nov 1838: James and Eugene **DAILY**, Tralee, Kerry, went to America five years since. They were last at Halifax, NS, and were about to go to Canada. Sought by their cousins, Timothy and Michael **O'CONNOR**, 6 Graphic Court, Boston.

The Boston Pilot, 18 Sep 1841: Thomas **DOOLEY** of Ballymack [Parish of Burnchurch], Kilkenny, was last known to be at Lowell, MA. Sought by his brother Patrick **DOOLEY**, c/o James **MALCOLM**, Halifax, Nova Scotia.

The Boston Pilot, 20 Apr 1839: Gerald **DOUGHERTY** of Ireland, went to Prince Edward Island in 1832, then in 1833 to Boston. In August 1835 he was working on the railroad at Bangor, ME. He is sought by his brother John **DOUGHERTY**, Charlestown, MA.

The Boston Pilot, 26 Jan 1839: Michael **DUGGAN** of Ower [Parish of Killursa or that of Killannin], Galway, went to St. John's, NL, 2 or 3 years ago. His brother William **DUGGAN** of Waltham, MA, seeks news of him.

The Jesuit, or Catholic Sentinel, 9 Mar 1833: Francis **DUNOHER**, alias **DONEHES**, Parish of Ardagh, Longford, arrived at Saint John, NB, with his sister Mrs. **M'CAULY** in August 1831. He went to the USA in April 1832. Mrs. **McCAULY**, c/o William **GLEASON**, East Cambridge, MA, seeks news of him.

The Novascotian, 1 Mar 1832: Patrick **DWYER**, tailor, City of Waterford, sailed from there to St. John's, NL, in 1821, and is now at Manchester, Sydney [now Guysborough] County, NS. His son, Henry L. **DWYER**, Albion MInes, near Pictou, NS, wishes to hear of him.

The Boston Pilot, 3 Sep 1841: Thomas **FAGAN**, Coleraine, Derry, tanner, left for Saint John, NB, 26 June 1840, and arrived there about 1 September 1840, and in December left to go to the USA. Sought by the Postmaster at Saint John, NB.

The Boston Pilot, 23 Nov 1839: Martin **FANNING** left Nova Scotia in 1836. He is asked to write to this newspaper regarding a legacy.

The Jesuit, or Catholic Sentinel, 5 Apr 1834: James and Peter **FITZPATRICK**, Co. Cavan, are sought by their aged mother in Cavan. James left Belfast 14 years before, and 7 years ago was in Saint John, NB. Peter left Dublin 10 years ago and has not been heard from since.

The Boston Pilot, 18 May 1839: Julia **FLAHERTY** of Boston is informed of the arrival of her sister-in-law from Saint John, NB. She is now at 156 Hanover Street, Boston.

The Boston Pilot, 24 July 1841: Thomas **FLEMMING** of Glanaglogh [Aghabulloge Parish], Cork was in Vernon Ginnings [Jennings], Indiana, 4 years since. Sought by his brother, Michael **FLEMMING**, c/o Francis **GALLAGHER**, cooper, Saint John, New Brunswick.

The Jesuit, or Catholic Sentinel 7 Mar 1835: Margaret **FLYNN**, Co. Waterford, niece of Rev. Edmund **FLYNN**, PP, Dunhill, Co. Waterford, has not been heard of since she sailed from Waterford to Halifax, NS, in spring 1831. Sought by her brother and sisters at Albany, NY. [Margaret, dau of Maurice & Mary (**AHERON**) **FLINN** of Co. Waterford, married 5 Oct 1833 at St. Mary's Catholic Cathedral, Halifax, Philip **MERLIN** of Nova Scotia.]

The Boston Pilot, 15 Aug 1840: William **GILLY** of Ballymurphy [Parish of Castlelyons], Cork, sailed in the *Mary* from Cork in spring 1834 to go to the British provinces. His brother Michael **GILLY** of Augusta, ME., seeks news of him.

The Boston Pilot, 2 Nov 1839: Thomas **HARE**, shoemaker from the Parish of Adare, Limerick, was in Boston in December 1838. He left on 29 March 1840 in the brig *Emily* to go to Québec. He is sought by Colour Sgt. John **FITZGERALD**, 36th. Regt., Fredericton, NB.

The Boston Pilot, 22 Aug 1840: Daniel **HARRINGTON** of Cork left home 4 years ago and was last heard from at Lowell, MA. His sisters, Mary and Eleanor **HARRINGTON** are at Halifax, Nova Scotia, and wish to hear from him.

The Boston Pilot, 2 Oct 1841: Patrick **HARRINGTON** of Castletown Berehaven, Cork, landed last summer at Saint John, New Brunswick, and is sought by his brother, Timothy **HARRINGTON**, Pittsford, Ballard County, VT.

The Boston Pilot, 2 Oct 1841: Miss Howard **KELLEHER** or **KELLARD** of Killorglin, Kerry,   i Saint John, New Brunswick, last summer. News of her is sought by her brother, James **KELLEHER** or **KELLARD**, East Rutland, VT.

The Boston Pilot, 4 Dec 1841: Jeremiah **KELLY**, Templemartin Parish, Cork, went to Newfoundland or the USA in 1837. Sought by his sister Mary **KELLY**, Newton, Union Falls, MA.

The Boston Pilot, 6 Nov 1841: Owen **KELLY** of County Mayo, was in Pictou, Nova Scotia, last July, then went to the United States. His whereabouts are sought by his wife, Ann **KELLY**, then at Charlestown, MA.

The Boston Pilot, 3 July 1841: Peter **KILLALAGH** of Dysart Parish, Roscommon, went to Saint John, NB, 8 years ago in May, then went to Digby, Nova Scotia. Sought by his brother Patrick **KILLALAGH**, c/o Patrick **NEILAN**, 671 Washington St., Boston. [Peter **KILLALY**, age 25, labourer, was a passenger in the *Sea Horse* which left Galway on 29 Apr 1834. Celia **KILLALEY**, age 17, was also a passenger in that ship.]

The Boston Pilot, 26 Jan 1839: Jeffrey and Thomas **LEIHEY** of County Waterford went to Newfoundland 4 years ago, and were recently in Boston en route to Worcester, MA. Johanna **LEIHEY** of Providence, RI, seeks them.

The Boston Pilot, 3 July 1841: James **McCREBLE** of Holy Cross Parish, Cork, sailed 7 years since in the brig *Laugheil,* and was last heard of at Boston. He is sought by his son John **McCREBLE**, c/o Samuel H. **PATTON**, Portland, New Brunswick.

The Catholic Intelligencer, 31 Aug 1832: Nancy and Catherine **M'DEVITT** of Donegal left Saint John, NB, about 10 weeks ago to go to Eastport, ME. News of them is sought by their sister Elizabeth **M'DEVITT** c/o P. **HARKINS**, 11 Cross St., Boston

The Boston Pilot, 18 July 1840: Patrick **McDONOUGH** of County Clare was last at St. Andrews. New Brunswick, and is supposed to be somewhere in the Canadian provinces [Ontario or Québec]. Sought by his brother Michael **McDONOUGH**, c/o Thomas **CUSACK**, Boston. [Patrick **McDONOUGH**, age 30, carpenter, arrived at Saint John, NB, in the *Elizabeth*, which cleared Galway on 20 April 1833, and arrived at Saint John on 24 June 1833.]

The Catholic Intelligencer, 3 Feb 1832: Thomas, son of Terrence and Susan (**O'BRIEN**) **McLAUGHLIN** of the Parish of Dromore, Tyrone, emigrated to Saint John, NB, about 14 years ago, and visited Maryland and Pennsylvania. There has been no word of him for 8 years. Sought by his sister Mary **POTTS**, Charlestown, MA.

The Boston Pilot, 10 July 1841: Mary **McPARTLAND** of the Townland of Grey Ellen [Greyhillan], Loughgilly Parish, Armagh, left Warren Point en route to Saint John, NB, on 1 May 1840. She is sought by her siblings, John and Betty **McPARTLAND**, Sandwich Glass Factory, MA.

The Jesuit, or Catholic Sentinel, 15 July 1833: Margaret and Winifred, daughters of Peter and Winifred (**CLANCY**) **McTIERNAN** of the Parish of Killargy [Killarga], Leitrim, left on 12 July 1827 to go to Saint John, NB. They are sought by their sister Bridget **McTIERNAN**, 121 Franklin St., New York City.

The Boston Pilot, 9 May 1840: Thomas **MANNING**, Kilcullen, Kildare, left Dublin on 13 May 1839 to go to Saint John, NB, with John **DOYLE**. Manning then went on to Eastport, ME. Sought by John **DOYLE**, 99 Merrimack Street, Boston.

The Jesuit, or Catholic Sentinel, 20 June 1835: Catherine **MOONEY**, Co. Monaghan, went to Halifax, NS, in 1828. Her brother in Boston seeks news of her.

The Boston Pilot, 3 July 1841: Timothy **MOREY** of Carbonear, NL, was last reported in New York City. News of him is requested by Michael **BRENNAN**, 7 Southac St., Boston.

The Boston Pilot, 5 Oct 1839: James **MORGAN** of Boyle, Roscommon, went from Sligo to Saint John, NB, and was last known to be in Eastport, ME. He is sought by his father William **MORGAN** of Boyle. [James Morgan, farmer, age 20, appears on the passenger list of the brig *Preston* which cleared Sligo on 28 June 1834 and arrived at Saint John, NB, on 13 August 1834.]

The Jesuit, or Catholic Sentinel, 1 Mar 1834: John **MULLAN** was last seen on 6 August 1828 at St. John's, NL, by his brother Patrick **MULLAN**, who seeks news of him.

The Boston Pilot, 10 Dec 1836: Patrick **MULLINS**, Parish of Bandon, Cork, emigrated with Daniel **SULLIVAN** in spring 1835 to St. Andrews, NB. Believed to be in Maine. Sought by Daniel **SULLIVAN**, Walpole, MA.

The Jesuit, or Catholic Sentinel, 18 July 1835: Owen **MULOY**, Killalar [Killala], Mayo, lived ten years in NL, then went to Montréal or Québec. Sought by his brother William **MULOY** of Boston.

The Boston Pilot, 19 June 1841: Ellen **MURPHY**, Parish of Innishannon, Cork, went to British North America 18 years ago. She was in Upper Canada [Ontario] 3 years ago. Her sister Mary **MURPHY**, 106 Sea St., Boston, wishes to hear of her. [What looks like a correction of this notice appeared in *The Boston Pilot* of 17 July 1841. The seeker of news is then Ellen **MURPHY**, and the sister sought is Margaret **MURPHY**.]

The Boston Pilot, 7 Aug 1841: Nicholas **MYLON**, Athlone, Kiltoom Parish, Roscommon, emigrated with Daniel **KENNADY** of the same place. They landed 10 years since at Saint John, NB. He was last in New York state. Sought by his brother Patrick **MYLON**, c/o Thomas **DUFFY**, Roxbury, MA.

The Jesuit, or Catholic Sentinel, 25 July 1835: John **O'DONNELL**, Buttevant, Cork, was in Halifax and Nova Scotia from 1822. In August 1834 he was at Boston. Sought by his brothers William and Maurice **O'DONNELL**, Providence, RI.

The Catholic Intelligencer, 15 June 1832: Owen **PROUTY**, Drummerhave near Roslea [Drumharriff near Rosslea], Fermanagh, went to Saint John, NB, in June 1831, and on to New York City that autumn. Sought by his sister Margaret **PROUTY** and by Robert **KENNEDY**, Sister St., Boston.

The Catholic Intelligencer, 29 June 1832: John **QUINN**, carpenter from Laghigh [Laghil, Parish of Glencolumbkille], Donegal, went to Saint John, NB, in 1819, then to Boston. He was last heard of in Dedham, MA. Sought by Hugh **QUINN**, 644 Washington St., Boston.

The Boston Pilot,, 28 May 1836: Patrick **REGAN**, Adair [Adare], Limerick, is believed to have come out to Saint John, NB, last spring, and then to have proceeded to the USA. Sought by his brother John **REGAN**, c/o *The Pilot*.

The Boston Pilot, 12 Nov 1836: Margaret **RODDEN** of the Parish of Lakepatrick near Strahan [Leckpatrick near Strabane], Tyrone, was last reported at St. Andrews NB. Sought by her brother John **RODDEN**, 14 Distillhouse Square, Boston.

The Boston Pilot, 13 Aug 1836: Lawrence **RYAN** of Killoskehane, Parish of Drom, Tipperary, went to Miramichi, NB, 10 years ago, and lived 6 years at Richebucto, NB. He was last employed at River Phillip, Cumberland Co., NS. Sought by his brother, Michael **RYAN**, Taunton, MA.

The Boston Pilot, 20 June 1840: Edward **SAUNDERS** of Castletown Berehaven, Cork, emigrated in spring 1833, lived for a time at Fall River, MA., then went to Halifax, Nova Scotia. Sought by his wife at Fall River, MA.

The Boston Pilot, 2 Feb 1839: Charles **SHEA** of the Parish of Kilgibbin [Kilgobban], near Tralee, Kerry, went to America 7 years ago and landed at Halifax, Nova Scotia, then went on to Boston. Sought by his son, James **SHEA**, of Salem, MA.

The Boston Pilot, 23 Oct 1841: Hugh and Philip **SULLIVAN** of County Longford were said to be in Boston. They are sought by their brother, John **SULLIVAN**, who sailed with them to Miramichi, New Brunswick. Write c/o Thomas **RYAN**, Wharf and Broad St., Boston.

The Boston Pilot, 30 Jan. 1841: Stafford **WILLIAMS**, seaman, then aged about 32, tall, slender, with blue eyes and light hair, left Halifax, Nova Scotia, towards the end of 1836 to go to New York. Sought by **CASSERLEY** & Sons, 108 Nassau St., New York City.

14 -COUNTY DERRY TO NEWFOUNDLAND, 1834/1835

In Volume 6 of the *Ordnance Survey Memoirs of Ireland,* for the Parish of Ballyscullion West, County Londonderry, twelve persons are indicated as having emigrated to St. John's, Newfoundland, in 1834. They are named, with their ages and religion.

Samuel **McCAHY**, 50, his wife Jane, 48, and their children: Ann, 25, Margaret, 20, John, 18, Eleanor, 16, Charles, 14, Jane, 12, and Sarah, 6, all Presbyterians.
Samuel **ADAMS**, 25, also Presbyterian
Daniel **SCULLION**, 20, a Roman Catholic.
Jane **MULLAN**, 20, of Oldtown Deer Park, Co. Londonderry, Church of Ireland.

In 1835, six further emigrants are mentioned" Izabela **BRADLEY**, 32, James BRADLEY, 12, and James BRADLEY, 3-, from Leitrim, Catholic. Francis **DIXON**, 40, William DIXON, 30, and John DIXON, 28, Presbyterians, from Ballymacombsmore Townland in Ballyscullion Parish.

15 - CHARITABLE IRISH SOCIETY OF HALIFAX, NOVA SCOTIA, MEMBERSHIP 1834-1837

The Charitable Irish Society of Halifax was formed on 17 January 1786 when "a number of respectable Inhabitants" who were "natives of the Kingdom of Ireland" met at the Golden Ball Tavern. They were motivated by "an affectionate and compassionate concern for any of the Irish Nation, who Shall be reduced by Sickness, Old age, Shipwreck or other misfortune..." They agreed "to associate themselves for the relief of such of their poor and indigent Countrymen and their Descendants as may hereafter be found worthy of their countenance and protection." The Society still exists in 2007, the senior Irish organization in Atlantic Canada.

Based on the membership rolls in the minute books of the Society, this article lists the membership at and about the 50th anniversary of the founding of the Society, at a time when Irish immigration into the community was at a high level. Each member is listed, together with the year in which he joined the Society. The remarks within quotation marks are found in the original. All other observations are those added by the compiler. - TMP

Name of the Member	Joined	Observations
ACHISON, F. W.	1829	"Left for St. Andrews" in 1834
AHERN, William	1836	"Dead 1849" - Blacksmith from Co. Cork
AKINS, Thomas	1834	Author of a History of Halifax
ALBRO, Samuel	1817	"Died Oct 1842'
ALLISON, Hon. Joseph	1817	"Died Oct 1839"
ARCHIBALD. Judge Samuel	1820	"Died Jan 1846"
BALLARD, William	1832	"Left for the US, July 1836"

BARRETT, James	1835	"Won't pay" in 1839
BARRON, Peter	1825	"Died"; bur. 28 Aug. 1834, age 45; native of Co. Wexford
BARRON, William	1832	"Died Aug 1844" - Trader from Co. Kilkenny
BARRY, John L[awrence]	1828	"In the country" - 1838
BATES, William	1828	Truckman from Clonmel, Tipperary
BAUER, Thomas A[ndrew]	1835	Died Sep 1871, native of Halifax
BEAMISH, Thomas Ott	1826	"Will not pay" - 1838, native of Halifax
BENNETT, Michael	1789	Grocer from Ardfinan, Tipperary, died May 1847
BIEREY, Peter	1835	Tailor from Switzerland
BOHANNAN, Michael	1835	Mason from Ireland, died July 1849
BROWN, John	1828	
BROWNER, Joseph	1837	"Away to the country"
BUCKLEY, Daniel	1835	"Died 8 Nov 1839" - Shopkeeper from Co. Cork
BUCKLEY, William	1832	"No use to continue him"- 1837, from Co. Cork
BULGER, Richard	1819	"Not residing here now"
BURNS, Bernard	1831	"Erased" - 1845
BUTLER, James	1836	Died Aug 1862, cooper from Co. Kilkenny
CAHILL, John	1831	"Withdrew" - 1845, from Co. Kilkenny
CARROLL, Thomas	1829	"Resides in St. Andrews"
CARTEN, John	1836	"Withdrew 17 Feb 1845", from Co. Derry
CARTEN, Samuel	1829	"Withdrew 17 Feb 1845", from Co. Derry
CASEY, John	1823	"Erased" - 1834, from Cork City, died Jan 1850
CASSIDY, Thomas	1825	Painter from Co. Wicklow, died Mar 1844
CHAPPLAIN, William	1824	
CHARLES, James	1832	Shoemaker from Co. Meath; died Oct 1837, age 44.
CHRISTY, Robert	1835	"Left for New York"
CLARKE, John H.	1829	"Died 1833"
COBLENTZ, Michael	1828	
COCHRAN, James	1835	Merchant from Co. Longford, died Mar 1877
COCHRAN, Loran D.	1836	
COLWELL, Thomas	1837	"In the country" - 1838
COMPTON, John	1826	[perhaps re-joined in 1837?]
COMPTON, John	1837	"In the country" - 1838
CONNORS, James	1836	
CONROY, William	1810	"Does not intend to pay dues" - 1840, died 1868
COSTELLO, Patrick	1835	"Costen", from Co. Tipperary, died Apr 1875
COUPLES, Joseph	1832	"Died 1835" - Died Sep 1835 at Annapolis, NS
COWEN, Samuel	1832	
CRAWLEY, Daniel	1831	"Refused to pay" - 1838, tailor from Co. Cork
CREAMER, Daniel	1827	Merchant from Co. Cork, died Jan 1862
CREAMER, Michael	1812	"Died Apr 1840"; ship's carpenter from Co. Cork
CROKE, James Thomas	1836	"Died 11 July 1840"; tailor from Co. Tipperary
CRONAN, Daniel	1835	"Mistake. He has not yet paid.", died Sep 1892
CROSIER, John	1835	"Readmitted when returned from New Brunswick." "Left again for N. B., from thence to Canada"-1837
CROSSKILLE, James	1836	"Withdrew Oct 1840"
CUMMINS, Andrew	1825	"Not residing here at present" - 1834; mason from Carlow
CUMMINS, John E.	1825	"Resides in New York" - 1834. "Readmitted, 17 Feb 1838"; merchant from Co. Carlow, died Feb 1864.

CUNNINGHAM, James	1836	"Withdrawn on night of 17 May 1837"
CUNNINGHAM, Roger	1832	"Withdrawn on night of 17 May 1837", merchant from Donaghmoyne, Monaghan; died Jan 1886.
CURRAN, Murtaugh	1835	"Died 1835"; Murtagh Cornyn buried 1 June 1835, age 64 at Halifax; native of Co. Leitrim.
CURRY, Jacob	1834	Previously resided in Scotland
DARCY, John	1831	"Left the country" - 1834
DEAN, Joseph	1828	"Left for New Brunswick" - 1836
DeCOURCEY, Garrett	1831	"Left the country." - 1834
DILLON, William	1825	Mason from Co. Waterford, died May 1845.
DIXON, Robert	1819	"Died 1834"
DIXON, Thomas	1819	"No use to continue him" - 1836. "Lives Pictou" - 1845.
DONOHOE, James	1835	Stationer from Co. Kildare, died Nov 1886.
DONOVAN, Henry G	1829	"Left for New York" - 1834
DONOVAN, Simon	1826	"Left for Chicago, in June 1836", readmitted July 1840. "Living at Arichat, N.S." - 1843
DOOLEY, James S	1833	"Died 1834"
DOYLE, Lawrence, Esq.	1797	"Died 1834/35"; native of Co. Carlow, died June 1835.
DOYLE, Lawrence O'C[onnor]	1828	"To U.S." - 1854; died Sept 1864 at New York.
DOYLE, Michael	1832	Died Jan 1859, clerk from Co. Sligo
DOYLE, Morgan	1835	"Proposed without permission", from Co. Wexford
DRUMMOND, Patrick	1837	"Refused to pay" - 1838
EGAN, Michael	1834	Grocer from Co. Tipperary, died May 1847
EUSTACE, John	1833	"Died 1836" - bur. 18 Dec 1836, age 29
EUSTACE, Roland	1836	Carpenter from Co. Kilkenny, died Sep 1885
FALVEY, Cornelius	1830	"Left for the States" - 1834; native of Lissavane, Kerry
FALVEY, Dennis	1836	"Left for New York"; brother of preceding
FALVEY, Edward	1832	"Died of cholera"; bur. 9 Sep 1834; brother of preceding
FIELDING, Thomas	1836	"Non-payment" - 1843, from Co. Carlow, died 1847
FILLIS, George J	1836	"Withdrawn Oct 1840"
FINN, Thomas	1789	"Died Oct 1842"; age 95, had lived 60 years at Halifax
FITZGERRALD, James	1835	"Erased at own request" - 1845
FLETCHER, David	1811	"Died" 19 June 1836, age 58; a merchant
FLETCHER, Capt. William	1836	"Died" 9 June 1836, age 42; of schooner *Industry*
FLYNN, Michael	1832	"Arrears" - 1832
FLYNN, William	1832	"Grocer, died 1845"; from Moathill, Waterford
FLYNN, William	1832	"Non-payment" - 1848
FOLEY, John	1834	
FOLEY, Morrice	1835	"Will not join" - 1835
FURLONG, Peter	1831	"Retired Feb 1856"; merchant, died Aug 1856
GEARY, Rev. Denis	1829	"Withdrew 17 May 1845; leaving Halifax"; from Co. Waterford, died Nov 1862.
GEORGE, Sir Rupert, Baronet	1819	"Left for England 1 June 1841"
GORMAN, Patrick	1829	"Erased at his own request"-17 Feb 1846, labourer from Callan, Co. Kilkenny, died Mar 1875.
HACKETT, Bartholomew	1820	"Left the country" - 1833
HARE, David, Esq.	1820	"Died 13 Jan 1857"
HARE, Richard F.	1823	"Withdrawn, 17 Feb 1841"
HARNEY, John	1835	"Left for Chicago, July 1836"

HEAD, Dr. Samuel	1791	"Died of the fever, 15 Nov 1837"
HENNESEY, John	1835	"Died May 1843"
HICKEY, John	1834	From Co. Tipperary
HILL, Charles P.	1819	"at present residing at Dartmouth, cannot pay, Nov Nov.1839"
HILL, Robert	1835	"Daniel O'Brien who proposed. left here and he is not likely to attend."
HOWE, Joseph	1832	Died 1873, native of Halifax; editor and politician
HOWE, Lieut.	1819	"Left for Bermuda - a long time..." - 1834
HUTCHINSON, Archibald	1834	Died Jan 1834 at Sackville, NS, native of Ireland
INGLIS, Richard	1819	"Left for Canada" - 1837
JAMES, Thomas C.	1835	"Withdrew 17 July 1845"
JENNINGS, Andrew B.	1833	"No use to continue him." - 1836, died Jan 1844
KEHOE, Luke	1829	"Left the country" - 1836, died July 1849 at New York
KELLY, Capt. Daniel	1802	"Died" - bur. 30 Oct 1837, age 66
KENNY, Bernard H.	1837	Trader from Co. Wexford, died Jan 1848
KENNY, Edward	1828	Died May 1891, from Kilmoyly, Co. Kerry, knighted
KENNY, Thomas	1828	"Died August 1868", brother of the preceding
KENT, Patrick	1837	"Died 15 July 1841", native of Co. Wexford
KERRENS, Nicholas	1827	"Cannot pay" - 1838
KIELLEY, John	1831	"Lost on a voyage from Newfoundland" - 1836
LANE, Edward	1835	"H.M.C[ustoms]" "Won't pay" - Nov 1839
LAUGHLIN, Peter	1833	"Will not attend", merchant from Co. Tyrone, died 1857
LAURENCE, Samuel	1837	"Died" Dec 1839, native of England[!]
LAWSON, George P.	1831	"Erased" - 1845, merchant, died 1868
LEWIS, William	1831	"Died of cholera" - Sep 1834
LONERGAN, Thomas	1831	"Gone to Prospect long since" - 1841
LONG, Robert	1836	"Liverpool"
LOUGHLIN, James	1836	"Died 13 Feb 1868", shopkeeper from Co. Kilkenny
LOUGHNAN, Rev. John	1828	Native of Co. Cork, died Nov 1878 in Cape Breton Island
McCARTHY, John	1834	"Left for New York" - 1834
McCARTHY, Thomas	1833	"Left for the States" - 1834
McCLEVERTY, Alexander	1835	"Left the Town"
McCRIERY, Edward	1836	"Gone to England" - 1838
McEVOY, Nicholas	1834	"Died"; bur. 14 May 1835, age 31, native of Ireland
McGRATH, Edward	1833	"Unable to pay" - 1844
McGRATH, James	1828	"Erased" - 1848
McGRATH, Patrick	1831	"Left the country" - 1834
McGRATH, Capt. Thomas	1835	"Died on his passage from the West Indies"; he died on 1 Sep 1837, age 40, on board the *Heroine* en route from St. Kitts [*Nova Scotia Royal Gazette*, 20 Sep 1837]
McKENNA, Michael	1832	"Erased" - 1843
MADDEN, J[ohn] W.	1831	"Died 23 Dec 1835"
MAHER, John	1833	Died Jan 1862, a baker from Co. Kilkenny
MAHER, John, Jr.	1830	
MAHER, William	1831	
MAHONEY, Michael	1832	"Withdrew" - 17 Feb 1845
MAHONY, Patrick	1826	"Erased at own request" - 1845

MAXWELL, James	1833	"In U. S. Asylum" - 1845
MOORE, Joseph	1828	Died 26 July 1843, Dartmouth, age 54; from Wexford
MORAN, Thomas	1833	"Left, dues unpaid" - 1836
MORRIS, John Spry	1828	"Refused to pay dues" - 1834; Surveyor-General, NS.
MORRISY, Capt. Michael	1836	
MORISCY, Peter	1823	"Died 6 Aug 1868, aged 80 years", from Co. Kilkenny
MORRISCEY, Timothy	1832	"Left for the States" - 1836
MURDOCH, Beamish	1823	Historian, died Lunenburg, NS, in 1876; born in Halifax
MURPHY, Andrew	1835	Died June 1867, native of Castlelough, Co. Kerry
MURPHY, Anthony	1837	"Gone away 10 Aug 1839"; native of Co. KIlkenny
MURPHY, Denis	1833	"Left" - 1836
MURPHY. John	1835	"Died 21 June 1867"
MURPHY, Michael	1835	"Died 24 July 1856", grocer from Co. Kilkenny
MURPHY, William	1831	"Gone to Cape Breton" - 1834
MURPHY, William, Jr.	1836	"To U. S." - 1852 "Died California" - 1854
NEVILLE, James	1835	Shopkeeper from Co. Cork, died Nov 1865
NOONAN, Denis	1836	"Left the country" - 1837
NOONAN, John H[yacinth]	1820	"Died 14 Jan 1839"
NUGENT, John	1835	"Erased - 1845, from Co. Longford, died Nov 1855
O'BRIEN, Daniel	1831	"Left for the States" - 1834
O'BRIEN, David	1825	"Refused to pay dues" - 1834
O'BRIEN, Mathew	1829	"Died Oct 1839", a cooper
O'BRIEN, Roderick	1835	"Died" - March 1837; bur. 1 Apr 1837, age 21.
O'CONNOR, James	1836	
O'CONNOR, John	1836	
O'CONNOR, Timothy	1824	"Withdrew " - 17 Nov 1845; a cooper at Halifax
O'FINN, John	1835	"Left for the States" - 1836
O'MEARA, Thomas	1828	"Left for New York" - 1834
O'MEARA, William	1832	"Withdrew" - 17 Nov 1845, from Co. Carlow, d. 1847
O'NEILL, Cornelius	1818	
O'SHAUGHNESSY, Michael	1825	"Marked off" - 1836, from Co. Cork, died Dec 1863
O'SULLIVAN, Cornelius	1833	"Died 7 Jan 1850", wood measurer, from Co. Cork
PHELAN, Robert	1809	"No use to continue him" - 1836, from Waterford
POWER, Jeffrey	1828	"Is said to be in the States" - 1836; died 7 June 1838 at Emmetsburg, Illinois [*Acadian Recorder*, 21 July 1838]
POWER, John	1831	"Left the country" - 1834
POWER, Patrick	1835	"Antigonish - 1835; died Feb 1881, from Waterford
POWER, Peter	1835	"Prospect" - 1835, "Struck" - 1838
QUINAN, Joseph W.	1833	Gauger from Québec, died May 1861
RAY, Martin	1837	"Erased" - 1844
RIELY, John	1833	"Useless to bring name forward" - 1834
RING, Thomas	1834	merchant from Ballyragget, Kilkenny, died Mar 1862
ROACH, John	1831	"Erased for arrears" - 1844
ROALS, Joseph	1831	"Left the country" - 1834
RUSSELL, George N.	1818	"Left Nov 1838"
RUTLEDGE, Edward	1828	"Left Halifax" - 1834, died 30 Dec 1837 at Sydney, NS, age 41 [*Acadian Recorder*, 3 Feb 1838]
SCHRAGE, John	1830	From Rahrbach, Westphalia, died Apr 1864, a grocer

SHORTIS, Edward	1832	"Left the country" - 1832/33
SHULTZ, William	1834	"Marked off" - 1836, died Sep 1840, born Halifax
SKERRY, William	1824	"Died Oct 1853", from Ballyhail, Co. Kilkenny
SLAYTER, John, Esq.	1821	"Died" Dec 1848, native of Halifax
STARR, Hon. John Leander	1831	"Withdrew" - 19 Feb 1842
STAYNER, William F.	1837	"Died" Oct 1837, native of Halifax
STUART, John	1835	"Out" - Feb 1845, died Nov 1859, born Ireland
SULLIVAN, Patrick	1836	
SUTTON, Thomas	1832	"Away" - 1839/40, died Apr 1869, born Newfoundland
SWAINE, Patrick	1836	"Withdrew Feb 1845", died June 1855, born Co. Carlow
SYNNOTT, James	1831	"Erased" - 1845, canal contractor at Dartmouth, NS
TAYLOR, Donald	1832	"Marked off" - 1836
THOMSON, George	1831	"Won't pay" - 1838
TILLMAN, Charles	1834	"Died" Aug 1836, organist, native of Halifax
TOBIN, George, Esq.	1835	merchant, died Aug 1861, son of Hon. Michael Tobin
TOBIN, Hon. James	1797	"Died 3 Nov 1838", father of Michael Tobin, Jr.
TOBIN, James C.	1831	"Dead" - May 1850, native of Roscrea, Co. Tipperary
TOBIN, John P.	1831	"Left for Chicago" - 1834
TOBIN, Hon. Michael	1810	"Died April 1843", brother of Hon. James Tobin
TOBIN, Michael, Jr.	1832	Died Dec 1883, son of Hon. James Tobin
TOBIN, Thomas	1819	"With country" - 1838
TOBIN, Thomas S., Esq.	1835	Died Feb 1883, son of Hon. Michael Tobin
TOBIN, William	1834	"Marked off" - 1836
TYNAN, Michael	1832	"Left the country" - 1832/33; born Portlaw, Waterford
UNIACKE, James Boyle	1826	"Hon. J.B. Uniacke died 26 Mar 1858"
UNIACKE, Judge Richard John	1819	"Died 21 Feb 1834"; brother of the preceding.
WALL, James	1826	Died June 1859, native of Athy, Kildare
WALLACE, Dr. Alexander	1820	"Withdrawn" - 1836, died Aug 1845 at Musquodoboit Harbour, NS
WALLACE, James	1834	"Refused to attend meetings since 1851", died Oct 1885, a customs officer born in Co. Wexford
WALSH, Edward	1831	"Not paid" - 1834
WALSH, Martin	1817	"Cannot pay" - 1838, died Aug 1848, born Co. Kilkenny
WALSH, Michael	1826	"Not likely to attend in future" - 1834, died Aug 1835 at Pictou, NS
WALSH, Patrick, Esq.	1835	"merchant", died Sep 1869, native of Newfoundland
WALSH, Thomas	1832	
WALSH, William	1831	"Guysboro", "Retired 17 Aug 1854"
WARREN, Edward	1832	"Erased" - 1845, died Apr 1855, born Co. Tipperary

16 - IRISH REPEALERS IN THE MARITIMES, 1843/45

The Act of Union was a watershed in Irish political history. Many people then and most historians since considered it a mistake. If the Act had been implemented to include full Catholic emancipation, or had undeniable benefits been seen to flow from the Union, all might have been well. Instead, promises were dishonoured, the King was bound by his coronation oath to uphold the Protestant religion, and Ireland felt betrayed. The end of the Napoleonic wars brought economic depression and political repression to a country which was rapidly becoming overpopulated. Irish opposition to the Union was organized within the Loyal National Repeal Association, led by Daniel O'Connell, M. P. The LNRA was not a revolutionary secret society, but an open agitation for constitutional change, in particular for the restoration of an Irish Parliament.

Predictably in an era of Irish emigration, the cause was carried abroad, first to Boston, where *Friends of Ireland* collected a *rent* of 12¢ a month to be transmitted to Dublin. A similar group in New Orléans collected funds and published the *Emigrant's Register.*[22] Repeal organizations soon appeared in New York, Philadelphia and Albany. The excitement was not confined to the United States. Montréal and Halifax were the earliest Repeal centres in British America. A Catholic newspaper in Halifax, *The Register*, regularly reported Repeal progress in the region.

A) HALIFAX, 1843

The LNRA counted 355 members at Halifax by 18 May 1843. A further 295 joined by the end of 1843. Membership transcended gender, ethnicity and religion. Nine were women, at a time when we are told that women were not politically involved. Eight Scots, three Englishmen and a Frenchman were members, suggesting that not only ethnicity motivated support for Repeal. Likewise, five in the published lists are noted as being Protestant; records indicate that there were three times as many (e.g.,Clay, E.J. Gleeson, Mills, Rugg, in the first of the following lists). This confirms that Repeal was more than a Catholic issue.

The Repeal membership of 650 included 48 whose Irish origin is unspecified, and twelve of other nationalities. Thirty-four were apparently Nova Scotians, eight native to Newfoundland, and one born in Québec, indicating 547 as Irish-born. Thirteen of these cannot be given a county of origin, further reducing the base number to 534. Munster (Tipperary 99, Cork 82, Waterford 75, Kerry 30, others 12) accounts for 298 (56%); Leinster (Kilkenny 102, Wexford 44, Carlow 18, Longford 17, others 23) for 204 (38%); Ulster for 23 (4.3%), and Connacht a mere 9 (1.7%). These proportions reflect closely those of the origins of the Halifax Irish population.

The full socio-economic spectrum is represented, but Repeal membership tended towards the higher end of the occupational scale: 6.3% were professional and major businessmen; 15.5% were small businessmen and white-collar workers; 37.3% were artisans and farmers; and just 40.9% were semi-skilled and unskilled workers. Political literacy and the greater tendency of more established individuals towards organized activity were factors in producing this outcome. Repeal membership in Halifax was four-fifths Irish-born, mainly Catholic, proportionate by county of origin to the Halifax Irish population, and represented a rather more socially and economically advanced cross-section of the Irish in that time and place.

---

[22] William Forbes Adams, *Ireland and Irish Emigration to the New World from 1815 to the Famine* (New York: Russell & Russell, 1967), pp. 385-386. Earl F. Niehaus, *The Irish in New Orleans 1800-1860* (Baton Rouge: Louisiana State University Press, 1965), p. 149.

OFFICERS OF THE LOYAL NATIONAL REPEAL ASSOCIATION, HALIFAX BRANCH, 1843

President: Lawrence O'Connor Doyle   Vice Presidents: Peter Furlong and James Wallace
Treasurer: Thomas Ring   Secretary: James C. Tobin

Repeal Wardens

Ward One - William Dillon, John McDonough, Valentine Molloy, Michael Power
Ward Two - William Doyle, James Donohoe, Thomas Hobin, Patrick Power, John Walsh,
    Mathew Young
Ward Three - James Cochran, William Condon, James Loughlan, Michael Monaghan, Mathias
    Mooney, Thomas Mooney, John Nugent
Ward Four - Dennis Carroll, William Donovan, Roger Cunningham, Michael Malony, Dennis
    Murphy, Bernard O'Neill
Ward Five - Patrick Deegan, Thomas Donovan, Roland Eustace, William Keenan, William
Skerry, Patrick Swayne
Ward Six - William Donovan, Michael Eagen, John Etchingham, Timothy Linahan, Jeremiah
    Murphy

These men are marked by an asterisk (*) in the following lists of LNRA members.

REPEAL MEMBERSHIP IN HALIFAX

Membership on 18 May 1843, reported in *The* [Halifax] *Register*, 23 May 1843:

ANDERSON, Richard [Carrick-on-Suir, Tipperary, shoemaker]
AUSTIN, William, Killarney, Kerry
BANON, Christopher, Longford
BARBER, Edmund P. [cooper; born Halifax; father from Manchester, England!]
BARRETT, James [Kilkenny Town, shopkeeper]
BARRON, William [Inistioge, Kilkenny, shopkeeper]
BARRY, Patrick, Ballymaudy [Ballymodan], Cork [labourer]
BARRY, William, Waterford [labourer]
BATES, William [Tipperary, truckman]
BENNETT, Arthur, Davidstown, Wexford [carpenter]
BENNETT, James, Davidstown, Wexford [shopkeeper]
BENNETT, Michael [Ardfinan, Tipperary, storekeeper]
BENNETT, Timothy, Davidstown, Wexford
BERGIN, Patrick, Thomastown, Kilkenny
BLAKE, Peter [Galway]
BOHANNAN, Michael, Kellubrun [Kiltubbrid], Leitrim [mason]
BOLEN, James [Wexford, truckman]
BOND, James, Dublin
BOWES, Timothy [Kilkenny, tailor]
BRAY, Patrick [Ireland]
BROWN, John, Ventry, Kerry [truckman]
BROWN, Thomas [Tipperary, huxter]
BUCKLEY, John [Mallow, Cork, shopkeeper]
BUCKLEY, Thomas [Tipperary]
BUCKLEY, William, Cartwoell [Carrigtwohill], Cork [tavern keeper]

BULGER, Michael, [Coolback],Wexford [cooper]
BURTON, John, Meath [labourer]
BUTLER, Thomas, Main-a-Dieu, Tipperary
BYRNE, Michael, Thomastown, Kilkenny [shopkeeper]
BYRNES, Bernard [Ireland], tailor
BYRNES, James, Mooncoin, Kilkenny [carpenter]
CAHILL, John, Thurles, Tipperary [shopkeeper]
CAHILL, John, Tullerone [Tullaroan], Kilkenny [labourer]
CALDWELL, William, a Protestant [Longford, blacksmith]
CALLAHAN, James, Ventry, Kerry [labourer]
CALLAHAN, John, Parish Arglish [Aglish], Cork [tailor]
CALLAHAN, Thomas [Kerry, grocer]
CALLNAN, Jeremiah [St. Finbar's, Cork, shopkeeper]
*CARROLL, Dennis [Middleton, Cork, shoemaker]
CARROLL, Patrick, T. Ovine [Templeorum], Kilkenny [labourer]
CASEY, John, Cork City [boardinghouse keeper]
CASEY, Thomas, Dungarvan, Waterford [butcher]
CASHMAN, Michael, Dungarvan, Waterford [gardener]
CLAY, Richard, Cheltenham, Gloucestershire [England; tavern keeper]
CLEARY, John, Sancroft [Suncroft, Parish of Carn], Kildare
*COCHRAN, James [Granard, Longford; merchant; later a Legislative Councillor in NS]
COCHRAN, Michael
COCHRAN, Patrick, Ballyhale, Kilkenny [gardener]
COFFEE, Michael [Ireland]
COLBERT, William, Crook[e], Waterford [labourer]
COLEMAN, Redmond [Waterford]
COLTER, Edmund
COMPTON, Philip [newspaper editor, born in Halifax]
CONDON, John, Ballymaday [Ballymodan], Cork
CONDON, John, Tipperary [labourer]
CONDON, Michael, Waterford [labourer]
CONDON, Patrick, Thurles, Tipperary [labourer]
*CONDON, William [shopkeeper; born Halifax]
CONROY, James, Kilkenny
CONROY, John [Ireland, carpenter]
CONWAY, Jeremiah [Golden, Tipperary, shopkeeper]
COSTIGAN, Patrick, Gowran, Kilkenny [shopkeeper]
COSTIN, Patrick [near Dungarvan, Waterford, shopkeeper]
COTTER, William, Garmorice [Garrymore], Cork [shopkeeper]
COUGHLIN, John, Carrigston [Carrick-on-Suir], Tipperary [tavern keeper]
CRONAN, Daniel [Cork, merchant]
CROTTY, John, [Affane], Waterford [cooper]
CUDDIHEY, James, Gortmar [Inishloughnaght, Gortmore], Tipperary [tavern keeper]
CULLEN, James, Crough [Croagh], Limerick [grain measurer]
CUNNINGHAM, James [grocer]
*CUNNINGHAM, Rodger [Donaghmoyne, Monaghan, shopkeeper]
CUNNINGHAM, Thomas, Glasgow, Scotland [clerk; son of Rodger]
CURRIN, Dennis, Parish Lispole, Kerry [labourer]
CURRIN, Patrick, Parish Lispole, Kerry [labourer]

DALY, Edward, Parish Adamstown, Wexford [confectioner]
*DEEGAN, Patrick [Leix, tavernkeeper]
DELANEY, Patrick [Grange, Kilkenny, shopkeeper]
DILLON, John, Portlaw, Waterford [mason]
DILLON, John, Mullinahone, Waterford [labourer]
DILLON, Michael, Parish Mullinahone, Tipperary [labourer]
DILLON, Robert
*DILLON, William [Coloughmore, Waterford, mason]
DOLLARD, Garrett, Thomastown, Kilkenny [truckman]
*DONOHOE, James [Kildare, stationer]
DONOHOE, Jeremiah, Parish Lestry [Kilbonane, Listry], Kerry
DONOHOE, Thomas [Kildare, coal measurer]
DONOVAN, Denis, Killarney, Kerry
DONOVAN, Michael [blockmaker; native of Halifax]
*DONOVAN, Thomas, Aglish, Waterford [labourer]
*DONOVAN, William, Sleverough [Slieveardagh], Tipperary [brewer]
DOWN, Cornelius, Klands [Killashandra?], Cavan
DOWNEY, Morris, Leinster [shopkeeper in Dartmouth, NS]
DOYLE, Lawrence O'Connor [barrister; born Halifax; Member of NS Assembly]
DOYLE, Michael [Kilrush, Wexford, labourer]
DOYLE, Morgan, Clonmoling [Clonmelsh], Carlow [merchant]
DOYLE, Thomas, Ballyhuskard, Wexford
DUFFIE, John [Louth, trader]
DUFFIELD, John [Tintern, Wexford, shoemaker]
DUGGAN, John, Duguan [Dungarvan?], Waterford
DUNN, James [Ballyanne, Wexford, tavern keeper]
DUNN, John, Wetemford [Urlingford?], Kilkenny
DUNN, John, Callan, Kilkenny
DUNN, Thomas, Dungarvan, Waterford
DUNPHY, John, [Listerlin], Kilkenny [truckman]
DUNPHY, Michael [Listerlin, Kilkenny, trader]
DUVAL, Peter [Granville, France]
*ETCHINGHAM, John, McMorris [Macmurroughs], Wexford
*EUSTACE, Roland [Kilkenny, carpenter]
FARRELL, Edward [Longford]
FARRELL, William, Middleton, Cork [master mariner]
FEARN, Thomas, Kilbroney, Cork
FENTON, John [Cork, butcher]
FINAN, Michael, Portadown [sic; Portlaw], Waterford [mason]
FITZGERALD, John [Cork]
FITZGERALD, Michael, Dingle, Kerry
FITZPATRICK, Winnifred [Kilkenny]
FITZPATRICK, William, Mullenoclough [Mullenkeagh], Tipperary [labourer]
FLANNERY, Michael, Mullinahone, Tipperary
FLANNERY, Thomas [Thurles, Tipperary]
FLAVIN, Patrick [Waterford, truckman]
FLAVIN, Thomas. Cavion [Callan], Kilkenny
FLEMING, James, Kilkenny [tavern keeper]
FLINN, William, Cashel, Tipperary [tavern keeper]

FOGARTY, James [Carlow, trader]
FOLEY, Jeremiah
FOLEY, Robert, [Bray], Dublin [blacksmith]
FOX, Michael [Longford, tavern keeper]
FULLER, Hyacinth H. [merchant; native of Arichat, NS]
FURLONG, James [Wexford]
FURLONG, Peter [Wexford, merchant]
GAHAN, John, Cashel, Tipperary
GALL, Edward [Newfoundland, cooper]
GAMMON, Joseph [of Nova Scotia]
GARVEY, Thomas, Keel, Kerry [tailor]
GAUL, Pierce, Kilkenny
GEARE, Thomas, Middleton, Cork [shoemaker]
GIBBS, Patrick, Coola [Coolaghmore], Kilkenny
GILCHRIST, John [Longford]
GILFOYLE, John, Kilkenny [truckman]
GILFOYLE, Thomas, Castlecue [Castlecomer], Kilkenny [truckman]
GLEESON, E. J.
GLEESON, Robert, a Protestant, Newry, Down
GORMAN, Patrick, [Callan], Kilkenny [shoemaker]
GRAFTON, John, Enniscorthy, Wexford
GRANT, Thomas [Tipperary, labourer]
GRIFFIN, James, Kilmacow, Kilkenny [cooper]
GRIFFIN, Thomas, Mooncoin, Kilkenny
HARRINGTON, Patrick, Thomastown, Kilkenny
HARTY, Maurice [Waterford, shipwright
HEADEN, Patrick [Wexford, blacksmith]
HENESY, Thomas, Parish Arthfin [Ardfinan], Tipperary [truckman]
HIGGINS, David
HIGGINS, John
HIGGINS, Michael [Derry, shopkeeper]
HOBAN, Robert, Mooncoin, Kilkenny [cooper]
*HOBIN, Thomas, Mooncoin, Kilkenny [hay dealer]
HOGAN, James [Kilkenny, grocer]
HOGAN, John, Cashel, Tipperary [merchant]
HOWLEY, John, Kilkenny
HOWLEY, Thomas, Mooncoin, Kilkenny
HUNTER, Andrew, Cavan [recte Cork, victualler]
INGLIS, John M [Limerick, shopkeeper]
JORDAN, Daniel, Killyobond [New Ross], Wexford
JOYCE, Bartholomew, Kilveith [Killeagh], Cork [mason]
KAVANAGH, William [Carrick-on-Suir, Tipperary, blacksmith]
KEARNS, Nicholas, Kilkenny
KEATING, John, Dublin [tavern keeper]
KEATING, Michael, Kilbriggan [Kilbeggan], Wes tmeath [farmer]
KEEFE, William
KEEHAN, Patrick, Ballybrack, Waterfo rd
*KEENAN, William, Fermanagh
KEHOE, James, [Old] Leighlin, Carlow [carpenter]

KEHOE, William, [Old] Leighlin, Carlow
KELLY, James [labourer]
KELLY, Mathew, [Kildare, cabman]
KELLY, Michael, Gowran, Kilkenny [labourer]
KELLY, Patrick, Suttons, Waterford [labourer]
KELLY, William [Ireland, labourer]
KENNEDY, Rev. James [Waterford; PP of Windsor, later at Ketch Harbour & Prospect]
KENNEDY, James, Garfray [Garfinny], Kerry [labourer]
KENNEDY, William [Kilkenny, tavern keeper]
KENNEDY, William, Kilmacow, Kilkenny [labourer]
KENNEFICK, Michael, Lady's Bridge, Cork City [labourer]
KENNY, Edward [Kilmoyly, Kerry, merchant; later Sir Edward Kenny, Canadian Senator]
KERBY, David [huxter]
KERBY, Edward, Carlow
KERBY, Thomas, Waterford City [tailor]
KIDNEY, Timothy [Cóbh, Cork, tailor]
KINEALY, John, Mooncoin, Kilkenny [labourer]
KING, Thomas, Esq., "also a member of the Dublin body"
KINSELLA, Edward, Gowran, Kilkenny
LANE, John, Knockfoyce [?], Cork [labourer]
LAUGHLIN, Peter, Monaghan [shopkeeper]
LAWLOR, John, Michel [Myshall], Carlow [mason]
LAWRENCE, John
*LINEHAN, Timothy, False [Tralee], Kerry [tailor]
LONDERGAN, Thomas [Clonmel, Tipperary, shopkeeper]
LONE[R]GAN, James, Glashin [Glasha, Kilronan], Waterford [labourer]
*LOUGHLAN, James [Kilkenny, shopkeeper]
LOUGHREA, John, Ostray [Ardstraw], Tyrone
LUNN, John [born in Halifax; tavern keeper]
LYNCH, Patrick, Ferns, Wexford [labourer]
LYONS, Patrick [Cork, labourer
McCANN, Thomas [Offaly, grain measurer]
McCARTHY, Charles, St. Patrick's, Waterford [labourer]
McCARTHY. Moses [Wexford]
McCARTHY, Pierce, Killarney, Kerry
McCARTHY, Timothy, Cóbh, Cork [labourer]
McCORMICK, Michael [Caher, Tipperary, tavern keeper]
McDERMOT, Bartholomew, Newtown Forbes, Longford; moved to the USA
McDONNELL, Thomas [Cork, mason]
McDONOUGH, John, Donegal
McDUFF, Michael, Cork City [brewer]
McGEE, Bernard, Sr. [Monaghan]
McGEE, Bernard, Jr. [Monaghan, trader]
McGEE, Patrick, Ballymena, Armagh [recte Antrim, doctor]
McGEE, Thomas, Ballymena, Armagh [recte Antrim, tailor]
McGOWING, Patrick [Kerry, labourer]
McHENNERY, Henry, Drangan, Tipperary [farmer]
McHENRY, Patrick, Lady's Well, Kilkenny [labourer]
McKAY, Alexander, Scotland

McKENNA, Michael [Myshall, Carlow, labourer]
McNAMARA, James, Carrick-on-Suir, Tipperary
MABERLINE [HABERLIN], Patrick, Kilmolan [Kilcolumb], Kilkenny
MAHER, John [Clonbrogan, Tipperary, trader]
MAHONY, Patrick [Ireland, tavern keeper]
MALONE, James, Tulloughen [Tullagher], Kilkenny [labourer]
*MALONY, Michael [Cork]
MARTIN, Thomas, Davidstown, Wexford
MEAGHER, Catherine [widow of Michael, Tipperary]
MEAGHER, James [Kilkenny, baker]
MEAGHER, John, Derry City [carpenter]
MEAGHER, John, [Fethard], Tipperary [tavern keeper]
MEAGHER, John, Pilltown, Kilkenny [baker]
MEAGHER, John [Ireland, brewer]
MEAGHER, Martin, Waterford City [cooper]
MEAGHER, Thomas [Ireland, labourer]
MELADY, James [Westmeath]
MILEY, Lawrence, Dunhill, Waterford
MILLS, William, Scotland [constable]
*MOLLOY, Valentine, [Whitechurch], Wexford, [truckman]
MONAHAN, James, [Newtown Forbes], Longford [mason]
*MONAGHAN, Michael, Newtown Forbes, Longford [mason]
MONAGHAN, Patrick [labourer]
MONAHAN, Thomas [Carlow, farmer]
MOONEY, James [Dungarvan, Waterford, butcher]
*MOONEY, Mathias, Dungarvan, Waterford [shopkeeper]
*MOONEY, Thomas, Dungarvan, Waterford [shopkeeper]
MOORE, James, Dingle, Kerry
MORAN, James, [Old] Leighlin, Carlow [labourer]
MORIARTY, Patrick, Ventry, Kerry [clerk]
MORRISCY, Peter [Wexford, brewer]
MULCAHY, John [Leix]
MULROONEY, John, [Old] Leighlin, Carlow [shopkeeper]
MURPHY, Andrew [Castlelough, Kerry, postal employee]
MURPHY, Arthur, [Kilmagney, near Ross], Wexford [mason]
MURPHY, Edmund, Ballybacon, Tipperary
MURPHY, Edward, Cork [storekeeper]
MURPHY, Jeremiah, [Cork , labourer]; moved to the USA
MURPHY, John, [Middleton], Cork [victualler]
MURPHY, John, Wexford [farmer]
MURPHY, Martin, Ballyhuskard, Wexford [labourer]
MURPHY, Patrick, Gowran, Kilkenny [seaman]
MURPHY, Pierce [Ninemilehouse, Tipperary, shoemaker]
MURPHY, Thomas, Hook, Wexford [labourer]
MURPHY, William [Cork , victualler]; moved to the USA
MURRAY, Thomas [Waterford, blacksmith]
NELAN, James [Kilmurry], Clare [labourer]
NELAN, Michael [Kilmurry], Clare [labourer]
NEVILLE, William, Youghal, Cork

NEWMAN, John, Castlemartin [Castlemartyr], Cork [shoemaker]
NORRIS, William, Ballyhale, Kilkenny [labourer]
*NUGENT, John, [Meath, tavern keeper]
NUGENT, Michael [Ireland]
O'BRIEN, Denis, Ballyhague [Ballyheige], Kerry [gardener]
O'BRIEN, Denis, Kilmacol [Kilmakill, Parish of Moyne], Tipperary [labourer]
O'BRIEN, John
O'BRIEN, Rev. R[ichard B[aptist] [First Principal of St. Mary's College]
O'CONNELL, Daniel, Kerry [labourer]
O'CONNELL, John, [Mallow], Cork [coal measurer]
O'CONNOR, Patrick, Ballylongford, Kerry [labourer]
O'CONNOR, Timothy [St. John's, Newfoundland, cooper]
O'DONNELL, John [Cork, labourer]
O'MEARA, Michael [Templeorum, Kilkenny, ship master]
*O'NEILL, Bernard [Lurgan, Armagh, merchant]
O'ROURKE, James, Hubustown [Herbertstown], Limerick [labourer]
O'SHAUGHNESSY, Crattaloa [Cratloe], Clare [labourer]
O'TOOLE, Cornelius, Kare [Caher], Tipperary [labourer]
PARRETT, Patrick [Rosegarland, Wexford]
PENDERGAST, Patrick, Kilkenny
PHELAN, Thomas, Pope's Harbour, NS [Placentia, Nfld]
POWER, Edward, Kilkenny [recte Tipperary, cooper]
POWER, James [Kilkenny]
POWER, John, Wexford [truckman]
POWER, John, 2nd, Waterford [City, baker]
*POWER, Michael, Dunhill, Waterford [truckman]
*POWER, Patrick [Kilmacthomas, Waterford , merchant, later MP for Halifax]
PRANDY, Thomas [Wexford, storekeeper]
PRINGLE, John [of Halifax]
QUARRY, John, Munster
QUIN, John, Thurles, Tipperary [labourer]
QUINAN, Joseph W. [Québec, saddler]
QUINN, John [Tipperary, shopkeeper]
QUINN, Patrick [Kilmacthomas, Waterford, shopkeeper]
REA, Martin, Waterford [brewer]
REID, Lawrence, Donnogher [Kells], Kilkenny [shoemaker]
*RING, Thomas [Ballyragget, Kilkenny, merchant]
RONAN, Maurice, Ballysarder [Ballysalla, Parish of Corcomohaide], Limerick
RUGG, David, Keatness [Bower, Caithness], Scotland [brewer]
RYAN, Michael [St. Lawrence, Nfld]
RYAN, Pierce, Graigamauna [Graiguenamana], Kilkenny [tailor]
SCULLY, John, Mullinahone, Tipperary
SHANNAHAN, Simon, Kilrush, Clare
SHANAHAN, William, [Tipperary, shoemaker]
SHEA, Patrick, Rogarmery [?], Waterford [labourer]
SKERRY, John [native of Halifax, cooper]
*SKERRY, William [Ballyhale, Kilkenny, merchant]
SULLIVAN, John, Beacheavne [Bearhaven], Cork [pensioner]
SULLIVAN, Patrick [Cork, labourer]

SULLIVAN, Philip [Cork, carpenter]
SULLIVAN, Timothy, Murrough [Murragh], Cork [labourer]
SULLIVAN, William
SUTLIFFE, Mary Ann
*SWAYNE, Patrick [Carlow, shoemaker]
*TOBIN, James C. [Roscrea, Tipperary, merchant]
TOBIN, John, Tipperary [labourer]
TOBIN, Patrick [Mullinahone, Tipperary, tavern keeper]
TOBIN, Thomas S. [merchant; native of Halifax, son of Hon. Michael Tobin, MLC]
TOOHILL, John, Caher, Tipperary [mason]
TOOHILL, Michael, Caher, Tipperary [labourer]
TOOMELLY, Patrick, Gora [Gowran], Kilkenny
TUCKER, Timothy, Drumly [Drumcliff], Sligo [mason]
*WALLACE, James [St. James Parish, Wexford, shopkeeper]
WALLACE, Thomas, Henckinshin [Inchinabacky], Cork [shoemaker]
WALSH, Edward, Mooncoin, Kilkenny [labourer]
WALSH, Frances [widow of Capt. George Walsh of Halifax]
WALSH, James, Mooncoin, Kilkenny [truckman]
WALSH, John, Enniscorthy, Wexford [truckman]
*WALSH, John, Mooncoin, Kilkenny [shipwright]
WALSH, John P, [Waterford City, ship carpenter]
WALSH, Patrick, Clarmery [Clonamery], Kilkenny [labourer]
WALSH, Patrick, Cashtertown [Cushenstown], Kilkenny
WALSH, Richard [Kilkenny, carpenter]
WALSH, Thomas, Waterford City [butcher]
WALSH, William, Kilkenny [shopkeeper]
WASHINGTON, Martin [Poorstown, Kilkenny, labourer]
WHELAN, Edward [Tipperary, shoemaker]
WHELAN, Edward, Sligo [labourer]
WHELAN, Fenton [Laois]
WHELAN, John, Gowran, Kilkenny [labourer]
WHELAN, William
WHITE, John, Johnstown, Wexford [labourer]
WHITE, Paul, Kilturk, Wexford [news vendor]
YOUNG, John, Kilkenny, living at Sydney, NS [seaman]
*YOUNG, Mathew [Wicklow, blacksmith]

On 13 June 1843, *The Register*, added 15 names to the list of members following a Repeal meeting held on the evening of 5 June:

BARRON, John, Inistiogue, Kilkenny
CALDWELL, Thomas, Longford, "Protestant" [blacksmith]
CARNEY [KEARNEY], James, Cavan [shopkeeper]
COOGAN, James, Kilkenny
*DOYLE, William, [Adamstown], Wexford [shoemaker]
ENGLISH, Robert, Longford [schoolmaster]
GRIFFIN, Henry, [Cork]
LOUGHLIN, John, Clonegal, Carlow
MAHONEY, W[illiam] Lismore, Waterford [labourer]

MORAN, Patrick [native of Halifax, builder]
MULLOWNEY, James, Cork
*MURPHY, Dennis, [Middleton], Cork [victualler]
MURPHY, Michael, Carlow [labourer]
O'GORMAN, R[ichard], [Dromin, Limerick]
WALSH, Michael, Kilkenny [farmer]

At a meeting on 4 August, the Halifax Branch, LNRA, added a further 100 names, as reported in *The Register*, 8 August 1843:

BAGNAL, John, at Miramichi
BARRY, John, [Cóbh], Cork [tavern keeper]
BOYLE, Andrew, Waterford [tinsmith]
BRENNAN, John, [Thomastown], Kilkenny [cooper]
BRETON, John
BUCK, John, Waterford
BUCK, William, Tipperary
BUCKLEY, David, [Ardnageehy], Cork [shopkeeper]
BUCKLEY, Thomas D. [Tipperary, clerk]
BULGER, Paul, Wexford
BUTLER, Edward, Tipperary [sparmaker]
BUTLER, Michael, Tipperary
CAIN, Cornelius, Waterford
CAFFREY, Jerry [Tipperary, teacher]
CAREY, Edward, Tipperary [cooper]
CARLEY, Thomas, Waterford
CHAMBERLAIN, John M [of Halifax; Protestant]
CONELLY, Mathias, [Mora], Tipperary [gunsmith]
CONNELL, John, Tipperary [labourer]
CONNELLY, Arthur, Tipperary
CONNER, John, Longford [labourer]
CONNORS, John, Tipperary [coachman]
CONNORS, William, Waterford, living at Pictou, NS
CORMAC, John, Longford
CUMMINS, Widow [Bridget, Wexford]
DELEHANTY, Andrew [Kilkenny]
DILLON, David, [Mullinahone],Tipperary [labourer]
DILLON, Thomas [Tipperary, labourer]
DONNOLLY, James, [Moore], Roscommon [truckman]
DONOHOE, Patrick, Kildare [labourer]
DONOVAN, Morgan, Kerry
DOOLY, James [Kilkenny]
DURNEY, John [Ireland]
FAHIE, James, [Kilgobnet],Waterford [farmer]
FARRELL, Mrs. [Elizabeth, widow of John], Westmeath
FERGUSON, Austen [Mayo, labourer]
FITZGIBBON, Michael, Cork
FLANNIGAN, Michael, Waterford
FLINN, Maurice, Waterford [labourer]

FOARD, John [Cork]
FOGARTY, John, [Grange],Tipperary [labourer]
FOGARTY, Malachy
FOLEY, John [labourer]
GALLAGHER, Patrick, Tipperary
GRADY, Timothy, Tipperary [truckman]
GRAHAM, Patrick
HAYS, Peter
HOLDEN, Philip [Templeorum, Kilkenny, truckman]
HOLLAND, William, Armagh [measurer]
HOWLEY, Michael, [Mooncoin], Kilkenny [truckman]
HUNT, Patrick, Cork
JORDAN, William, Kilkenny
KELLY, Daniel, Cork
KELLY, Edward [Clonmel, Tipperary]
KELLY, Gregory [Kilkenny, truckman]
KENNEDY, John, living at Dartmouth, NS [Carrick-on-Suir, Tipperary, innkeeper]
LANNIGAN, John [Kilkenny]
LARRACY, John, [Thomastown], Kilkenny [shopkeeper]
LARRACY, William, Kilkenny [labourer]
LENNEHIE [?], Daniel
LYONS, Jerry, Cork
McCARTY, Patrick [Cork, truckman]
McCARTY, Roderick, Tipperary [shopkeeper]
McDERMOT, Michael, Roscommon [labourer]
McKENNA, Patrick [Kerry]
McLEAN, Michael, [Myshall, Carlow, truckman]
MADRYAN [?], George
MAHONY, Thomas [Innishannon, Cork]
MAY, Patrick, Longford [farmer]
MEAGHER, Edward, [Callan], Kilkenny [farmer]
*MURPHY, Jerry, [Oyster Haven], Cork [blacksmith]
MURPHY, John, Sr. [Middleton], Cork [victualler]
NEWMAN, William F. [native of Halifax, tinsmith]
O'CONNOR, Edward, Waterford
O'FLAHERTY, Richard B., Limerick [clerk]
O'NEIL, John [Tipperary]
OWEN, Michael, Kilkenny [recte Carlow, via St. John's, NL]
POWER, David, Esq., living at Havre Boucher, NS
POWER, Edmund K. [of Halifax]
POWER, Edward [Tipperary, cooper]
POWER, James, Kilkenny
POWER, John, Waterford [labourer]
POWER, Moses, Waterford
POWER, Nicholas, Kilkenny [labourer]
POWER, Patrick, Waterford [farmer]
POWER, Richard, Waterford [farmer]
QUIRK, Edward [Waterford]
QUIRK, James, [Waterford City, cooper]

QUIRK, Patrick, Waterford
RUBY, John, Longford [farmer]
RYAN, John [truckman]
SCULLY, William [Tipperary]
STANTON, William, Cork [servant]
STOKES, Patrick, Tipperary [truckman]
SULLIVAN, James, Wicklow [labourer]
SWEENEY, Dennis, Donegal
WALLACE, Richard, [Mallow], Cork [truckman]
WALSH, John, Waterford [City, ship carpenter]
WALSH, Thomas, Waterford [City, butcher]
WHEBS [WEBB], Thomas, Cork [servant]

A large accession to the membership occurred at a Repeal meeting held on 8 September, reported in *The Register* of 12 September 1843. Three clergymen figured in the proceedings: a future Archbishop of Halifax, Thomas Louis CONNOLLY, OSF; the Principal of St. Mary's College, Richard Baptist O'BRIEN; and James KENNEDY, described as the PP at Prospect and Ketch Harbour. Ninety-two laymen became members or associate members that evening:

AHEARN, Andrew [Wexford, blacksmith]
BARRY, David [Lislee, Cork, coal measurer]
BARRY, Patrick, Kilkenny [mason]
BOWEN, Maurice, Cork
BROWNRIGG, William B., Carlow
BUTLER, Edward, Waterford
BUTLER, James, Tipperary
CADIGAN, Timothy, Cork [truckman]
CANTIVIL [CANTWELL], John, Newfoundland [sailor]
CASEY, Michael, [Caher], Tipperary [painter]
CAVANAGH, Lawrence, Kerry
CURREN, Thomas, Kerry [labourer]
DAILY, Richard, Wexford
DONOVAN, Cornelius [Bantry, Cork, truckman]
DOYLE, John, Wexford [labourer]
DOYLE, Lawrence, Wexford [labourer]
DOYLE, Richard, [Enniscorthy], Wexford [pedlar]
DRISCOLL, Daniel, Cork [labourer]
DRISCOLL, Martin, Tipperary [labourer]
DROLIN, Dennis, Kilkenny
DUGGAN, Joseph, Tipperary
DUNDASS, Thomas, "formerly master of the Orange Lodge, Enniskillen" [Fermanagh]
FINDLAY, Peter [Waterford]
FINLAN, John, [St. Mullin's], Carlow
FINN, William [Cork, labourer]
GALLAGHER, Thomas, of Halifax
GEARY, John, Tipperary
GOGGEN, Henry [*recte* Kenny], Longford
GRAHAM, James, of Nova Scotia
HALPIN, Thomas, Tipperary

HAYES, Michael [Carrick-on-Suir, Tipperary]
HEFFERNAN, Andrew, Tipperary [carpenter]
HEFFERNAN, Patrick, [native of Halifax, carpenter]
HENNESY, John, Cork
HIBBETS, Patrick, Kilkenny [truckman]
HINGSTON, William, England
KELLY, Hugh, Tipperary
KELLY, Terrence, [Dromore], Tyrone [tailor]
KENEFICK, Thomas [Cork]
KENNY, John, Waterford
LEMARSNY [LEMASNEY]. Edward [Newfoundland, fisherman]
LENDRYAR [?], Daniel, Tipperary
LONG, Robert, living at Liverpool, NS
McCARTY, Charles, Cork [labourer]
McDERMOTT, James [Longford]
McDONNELL, Jones
McGRATH, John, [native of Halifax, labourer]
McGUN, John, Kilkenny
McGUN, John, Newfoundland
McKENNA, Patrick, Monaghan
McLEAN, Daniel, living at Liverpool, NS [shopkeeper]
McNALLY, Patrick
McNAUGHTON, Daniel
MALONY, Daniel, living in Hants Co., NS [Kilkenny]
MANNING, Thomas, Newfoundland [native of Kilkenny, coachman]
MEAGHER, Michael, Tipperary [labourer]
MEAGHER, Thomas, Newfoundland
MORIARTY, T[homas, Kerry]
MORRISY, Timothy [Leix, blacksmith]
MURPHY, John, Lanark [butcher]
MURPHY, Patrick [seaman]
NEVILLE, Thomas [Shanakill, Cork]
NORTON, Edward, Westmeath
O'BRIEN, Daniel [Cork, labourer]
O'BRIEN, Timothy [Cork, labourer
O'BRINE, Michael, [Kilmacthomas], Waterford
O'CONNELL, James [Mullinahone, Tipperary]
O'DONNELL, James [Gammonsfield], Tipperary
PENDER, Thomas [Ireland, labourer]
PITTS, William, Yorkshire [England, master mariner]
PUNCH, John, [Middleton], Cork, [victualler]
QUINN, Arthur, Tyrone [trader]
READY, John, Sligo [tailor]
REGAN, James, Newfoundland [labourer]
RONAN, Patrick, Waterford
RYAN, John, Tipperary [truckman]
SCULLY, Dennis, Cork
SPENCE, Thomas [Waterford, sailor]
SULLIVAN, Daniel, Cork [builder]

SULLIVAN, Dennis, living at Milton, N.S. [Castletown Bearhaven, Cork]
SULLIVAN, Michael, Kerry
SULLIVAN, Patrick, Kilkenny
SUMMERS, Martin, Wexford
TRACEY, John, Kilkenny [labourer]
TROY, John, Waterford [labourer]
WALSH, Patrick, Kilkenny [labourer]
WALSH, Peter [Kilkenny, shopkeeper]
WALSH, Stephen, of Nova Scotia
WASHINGTON, John, [Poorstown], Kilkenny, [labourer], moved to the USA
WHELAN, Mathew, Cork [recte Tipperary]
WHELAN, Richard
WHITE, Martin, Limerick

The LNRA acquired further adherents at its meeting in Halifax on 6 October. Fifty-eight men and one woman joined, as reported in The Register, 10 October 1843:

BIRGIN [BERRIGAN], Edward, Kilkenny
BURKE, John, of Nova Scotia
BUTLER, Joseph, Kilkenny [labourer]
CASHEN, John [Kilkenny, schoolmaster]
COLLINS, Patrick, Carlow
CONNELLY, Lawrence [Kilkenny, mason]
CONWAY, John, Carlow [truckman]
COX, John S. [Cork, tailor]
CUMMINGS, Thomas, Waterford
CUNNINGHAM, Thomas, Waterford
DALY, Catherine
DOYLE, William, Waterford
DWYER, Jerry, Tipperary [labourer]
*EGAN, Michael [Templeachally, Tipperary, shopkeeper]
FARRELL, Thomas, Kilkenny
FITZGERALD, Richard, Waterford [labourer]
GAFFNEY, Samuel, Leitrim
GAHAN, Arthur, of Nova Scotia
GIBBEN, John, Tipperary [servant]
GOWIN, James, Tipperary [labourer]
HAMS, James, of Nova Scotia
HANNABERRY, James, Waterford [City]
HANY [HEANEY], Edward, Tipperary, [labourer]
HAYDEN, John [Kilkenny, truckman]
HEFFER[NA]N, Lawrence [Clonmel], Tipperary
HOWLEY, James, Wexford
JAIDE, William, Waterford
KEARNS, Michael, Cork
KENNEDY, William, Tipperary
KENNY, Bernard, Wexford [trader]
KIERNAN, Dr. [Bryan], Dungannon, [Tyrone, surgeon]
LAHEY, Patrick, Tipperary [truckman]

LANIGAN, Patrick, Kilkenny [mason]
LARKIN, William
LEMASTHEY [LEMASNEY], William, Cork. [trader]
LYNCH, William, Cork
McKENNA, Thomas, Tipperary
McPHERSON, Alexander, Scotland
McSWEENEY, Walter, Cork
MALCOLM, James, Kerry [labourer]
MEAGHER, Philip, Tipperary [labourer]
MEAGHER, Wilson, Tipperary
MEHIN, Michael, Tipperary [labourer]
MORRISAY, Henry, living at Ragged Is., NS, "Protestant" [Cork, labourer]
NEVILLE, James [Cork, shopkeeper]
O'BRIEN, Henry, living at Ship Harbour, NS, [farmer]
O'BRIEN, Patrick, living at Ship Harbour, NS, [farmer]
O'KIEF, Michael, living at Windsor, NS
O'NEILL, Thomas, [Tintern], Wexford, [cooper]
POWER, John, Waterford
POWER, John, Waterford, [labourer]
QUIRK, Timothy, Tipperary, [labourer]
RYAN, Martin, [Callan, Kilkenny, labourer]
TOWELL, Patrick, [Caher], Tipperary
WESTON, Patrick, Waterford
WHELAN, James, Nova Scotia, [shopkeeper]
WHELAN, Lawrence, Waterford [*recte* Kilkenny, labourer]
WHITE, Michael, Newfoundland
WHITE, Morris

The last group of new members to join the Halifax Branch of the LNRA that year were the twenty-seven men and two women reported in *The Register* of 12 December 1843:

BARRY, James, living at Chester, NS [labourer]
BRENNS, Patrick, Esq., living at Arichat, NS
BYRNE, Rev. Lawrence
CASEY, William [Dungarvan, Waterford, livery stable keeper]
ESSON, John, [Aberdeen], Scotland [grocer; he was MLA for Halifax 1851-1863]
FITZGERALD, Owen, Kerry [*recte* Cork]
GRACE, Thomas [Tipperary, labourer]
GRANT, Peter [Keith, Banffshire], Scotland [carpenter]
HILL, Leonard, living at Prospect, NS
JORDAN, Daniel
KENNY, Bryan
KENNY, Thomas, Esq. [Kilmoyly, Kerry, merchant; brother of Sir Edward Kenny, MLC]
LAHY, William [Lismore, Waterford, shopkeeper]
LOOLY [LOOBY], Patrick
McDEAD [McDADE], Edward [Donegal, labourer]
McDADE, James [Ireland, labourer]
McGRATH, James, Waterford
McKEAGNEY, Rev. Patrick [Tyrone]

McLENNAN, Benjamin
MALONE, Patrick, Longford [shopkeeper]
MALONY, Margaret
MALONY, Mary
MULCAHY, James, Waterford [tailor]
MURPHY, Martin, [Inistioge], Kilkenny [labourer]
MURPHY, P[atrick, tavernkeeper].
NOWLAN, Martin, Dublin
O'SULLIVAN, D.
READY, Patrick, Kilkenny
RONAN, Patrick [Youghal, Cork]

B) IRISH REPEALERS IN PRINCE EDWARD ISLAND, 1843/44

The Register, 15 August 1843, reported a Repeal meeting at Tenmile House, St. Peter's Road, PEI, on 11 July. Seventeen names are given, all but four of whom (*) turn up on later lists.

AFFLECK, Joseph, Repeal Warden for St. Peter's Road [now Corraville, PEI]
CARMICHAEL, Archibald *
DONNELLY, James
DUGGAN, Anthony, Mill Cove, Secretary
DUGGAN, James, Repeal Warden for Mill Cove
FITZPATRICK, William, Charlottetown, Repeal Chairman
McCARRON, John, Repeal Warden for Frenchfort [Co. Monaghan]*
MacDONALD, John, Jr., Alisary, Repeal Warden for Portage * [Allisary, PEI]
McPHEE, Andrew, Repeal Warden for Black River
McQUADE, Francis, Repeal Warden for St. Peter's Road
MOONEY, Harry, Sr., age 74
MOONEY, Robert, Repeal Warden for Mill Cove [Donagh, Monaghan]
MOYNAGH, John
O'CONNOR, James, Repeal Warden for Sandhills [in Prince County, PEI]
O'KANE, Thomas, President of St. Andrew's College *
SLATTERY, John [Kerry]
WALSH, Richard

The Register, Halifax, NS, 26 September 1843, recorded Repeal meetings at Monaghan and Fort Augustus, PEI, on 15 August, chaired by John SLATTERY, Charlottetown (*supra*), with Francis KELLY, agent to Rev. John MacDONALD, as Secretary. Repeal Wardens were:
Patrick HUGHES, [Tehallan, Monaghan]; Francis KELLY, Head Warden;
James KELLY, [Inistiogue, Kilkenny]; Peter McCLEARY, James 'Sandy' MacDONALD of Glenfinnan; John Morgan O'CONNOR, James WHITE.

John SLATTERY chaired a meeting of Repealers, mainly from Lot 19, at Barretts Cross Roads [now Kensington], PEI, on 21 August. Six Repeal Wardens were named for locations in Prince County, PEI:

DEAGAN, Michael, Tryon
KEHOE, Martin, Bedeque Road
MULLIGAN, Felix, Southwest
O'CONNOR, James, Wilmot Creek, Bedeque
PERKINS, James, Southwest
WOODS, John W., Miscouche

The Register, Halifax, NS, 24 October 1843, listed those who had attended a few days earlier what turned out to be the largest Repeal meeting held in PEI, with 220 new names listed:

ALLAN, Miss Bridgit, NL
BARRON, Pierce
BEGAN, Patrick, Monaghan
BLAKE, John, Thurles, Tipperary
BOWERS, John, Carrick-on-Suir, Tipperary
BOYLE, John, Castlecomer, Kilkenny
BRADY, Rev. Mr. [James, PP St. Andrew's, PEI]
BRENNAN, Edmond and Peter, Newtownbarry, Wexford
BRENNAN, Martin, Adamstown, Wexford
BROWN, James, Miss Margaret and Thomas, Mullinahone, Tipperary
BROYDERICK, Thomas, Freshford, Kilkenny
BROYDERICK, William, Youghal, Cork
BURKE, Thomas, NL
BURNES, James, Louth
BUTLER, John, New Ross, Wexford
CAHILL, John, Castletown, Tipperary
CARRIGAN, John, Mullinahone, Tipperary
CARROLL, John, Thurles, Tipperary
CARROLL, Joseph
CARROLL, Thomas, Kilkenny
CARTER, John, Gowran, Kilkenny
CASSEDY, Terrence, Ballybay, Monaghan
CHURLTON [perhaps CHARLTON], Thomas
CODY, James, Inistioge, Kilkenny
CODY, Tobias, Kilkenny
COLFORD, Martin, Scullaboge [Parish Newbawn], Wexford
COGHLAN, Patrick
COLLINGS, William, Youghal, Cork
COLLINS, Mrs. Thomas, New Ross, Wexford
CONDON, Patrick, Fermanagh
CONDON, Thomas, Mitchellstown, Cork, and his son Edward O'Mahon CONDON
CONNORS, James, Halifax, Nova Scotia
CORE [*recte* CORLEY], Patrick, Tedavnet, Monaghan
CORLEY, Patrick, Tedavnet, Monaghan
CORMACK, Richard, Tipperary
COSTELLO, John, Windgap, Kilkenny
COSTIN, John, Waterford
DALTON, John, Armagh
DEIGHAN. James, Monaghan
DELANEY, Michael, Kilkenny
DEWAR, James, Scotland
DOBBIN, James, Tynan, Armagh
DOBBIN, John, Monaghan
DONAHY, Daniel, Doneraile, Cork
DOOLING, Dennis, Crumlam [?], Kilkenny
DOWN, John and Michael, Dungarvan, Waterford

DOYLE, Hugh, New York
DOYLE, James
DOYLE, James, Adamstown, Wexford
DOYLE, Michael, Monaghan
DOYLE, P.B., Wexford
DOYLE, P.F., New Ross, Wexford, and his eldest son
DUFFY, James, Geashill, Offaly
DUFFY, James, Aghareagh [Parish Aghabog], Monaghan
DUFFY, William
DUNN, Robert, Inhabitant [?], Sligo
EGAN, John, Cork
EGAN, Martin, Tipperary
FEURE, William, Loguettetown [Licketstown, Parish Portnascully], Kilkenny
FINEGAN, Patrick, Armagh
FITZPATRICK, William, Riverchapel, Ardamine, Wexford
FLANNIGAN, John, Fermanagh
FLINN, James, Rosslea, [Parish Clones], Fermanagh
FLOOD, Martin, Kiltealy [Parish Templeshanbo], Wexford
FLOOD, Peter, Stonepark [Parish Clonmore], Co. Wexford
FOGARTY, Patrick, Waterford
FORISTALL, Michael [Waterford]
FORISTALL, Patrick, Compile [Camphire, Lismore], Waterford
FOWLER, Richard, Youghal, Cork
GAFFNEY, Patrick, Oulart [Parish Meelnagh], Wexford
GAINSFORD, John, England
GILLIGAN, Patrick, Athlone, and his son James
GRINSON, Andrew, New Ross, Wexford
GRUMBY [Grumley], Barnabas, Tynan, Armagh
GRUMLEY, James Sr., Dugary [Doogary, Tynan], Armagh
GRUMLEY, James Jr., Armagh
HARNEY, Michael
HARRINGTON, James
HAYES, Miss Bridget
HEANEY, Martin, Nine Mile House [Ninemilehouse], Tipperary
HOWLEN, Widow, Waterford, and her son George
HUGHES, Francis, Armagh
HUGHES, Patrick, Aghnasedagh [Parish Monaghan], Monaghan
KAVANAGH, John, Aghabog, Monaghan
KAVANAGH, Michael, Kilkenny
KAVANAGH, Terrence, Aghnamullen, Monaghan
KEATING, John, Adamstown, Wexford
KEIKHAM [KICKHAM], Edward and John, Fethard, Tipperary
KELLY, John, Inistioge, Kilkenny, and his son Henry
KELLY, John, Ramlish [Drumlish, Killoe], Longford
KELLY, Lawrence
KELLY, Patrick, Carrick-on-Suir, Tipperary
KELLY, Thomas
KENNEDY, Philip, Carrick-on-Suir, Tipperary
KEOGHAN, William

KING, James, Portlaw, Waterford
LACHEURRE [LeLACHEUR], John E., Esq., Isle of Guernsey
LACY, William, Wexford
LAHEY, John, Waterford
LAMBERT, Martin, Hewstown [Hayestown, Parish Rathaspick?], Wexford
LAPPIN, Peter [Armagh?]
LITTLE, John, Esq. [Charlottetown, PEI]
LITTLE, Philip, Esq. [Charlottetown, PEI]
LYNCH, Thomas, New Ross, Wexford
LYONS, Michael, Freshford, Kilkenny
McCAHY, Michael [Monaghan?]
McCARDILL [McCARDLE], John [Monaghan]
McCARRON, Barnabas, Knockaturly [Monaghan Parish], Monaghan
McCARRON, James, Monaghan
McCARRON, James, Puilford [?], Monaghan
McCARTHY, Miss Catherine
McCARTHY, Denis, Cappamore [Parish Tuogh], Limerick
McCOURT, Constantine, Monaghan
McDONNELL, Miss Mary, Tehallen [Tehallan], Monaghan
McELROY, Peter, Tedavnet, Monaghan
McEWEN, John, Armagh
McGINNIS, Donagh, Monaghan
McGOODWIN, Felix [Monaghan]
McINTYRE, Donald, Bell Isle, Scotland
McKAY, Michael, Monaghan
McKENNA, Bernard [Monaghan]
McKENNA, Miss Bridget, Donagh, Monaghan
McKENNA, Hugh and James, brothers, Monaghan
McKENNA, Patrick, Monaghan
McKENNA, Patrick, Monaghan
McKENNA, Peter, Donagh, Monaghan
McKENNA, Mrs. Anne, Monaghan
McKENZIE, John, Scotland
McKIERNEY, William, Kilmore, Monaghan
McLEARY, Parish Erskine, Renfrewshire, Scotland
McMURRY, Arthur, Glaslough [Parish Donagh], Monaghan
McNABE, Miss Margaret, Armagh
McNAUGHTON [alias McNORTON], Francis, Ballybay, Monaghan
McNEIL, Hector
McPHERSON, Angus, Nova Scotia
McPHILIPS, Owen
McQUADE, John, Donagh, Monaghan
MIRRIGAN [MERRIGAN], Maurice, Waterford
MOYNAGH, John, Monaghan
MULLIGAN, Owen, Monaghan
MULLIN, Edward
MURPHY, Dennis, Cork
MURPHY, Francis, Aghabog, Monaghan
MURPHY, John, Wexford

MURPHY, Matthew and William, Clonard, Wexford
MURPHY, Patrick, Ballymurphy [Ballymurragh?], Wexford
NEALE, Edward and James, Ballincurra [Parish Rathkieran]. Kilkenny
NOLAN, Capt. Edward, New Ross, Wexford
NOLAN, Thomas North, New Ross, Wexford
O'BRIEN, Hon. Lawrence, MLC [Legislative Council], Newfoundland. [Clashmore, Waterford]
O'NEIL, Arthur, Monaghan
O'NEIL, James
PHELAN, John, Horetown, Wexford
PHELAN, Martin and Walter, Carrickbeg, Waterford
PIGEON, John
POWER, Pierce, Dunkitt, Kilkenny
POWER, William, Stradbally, Waterford
PRICE, Richard, Callan, Kilkenny
QUINN, Miss Anastatia, Ballygriffin, Kilkenny
READE, James, Thomastown, Kilkenny, and his son John
REDDIN, Denis, Leix, and his son James
REYNOLDS, Rev. Malachi, PP Charlottetown, Rumlish [Drumlish, Killoe], Longford
RIELLY, Widow, Tipperary
ROACH, Moses, Carlow
ROONEY, Patrick, Monaghan
RONAYNE, Maurice, Middleton, Cork
RYAN, Martin, Borris, Carlow
RYAN, Patrick, Waterford
RYAN, Richard, Cashel, Tipperary
SHEEHAN, John, Kilkenny
SHEEHAN, Thomas, Tedavnet, Monaghan
SHREENAN, John, Puilford [?], Monaghan
SLATTERY, George and James, sons of the late Robert, Tralee. Kerry
SLATTERY. John, St. Andrew's College, nephew of the late Robert Slattery [Tralee]
SLUCK [sic] Nicholas, Kilkenny
TATE, Andrew, New Ross, Wexford
TIERNEY, Mr., Carlow
TIERNEY, James, Tedavnet, Monaghan
TOBIN, Philip and Thomas, Curraghduff, [Parish Ballybrazil],Wexford
TOOLE, William, Dublin
TOOLE, Patrick Sr and Patrick Jr., Kilmacthomas, Waterford
TOOLE, James, Woodbrook, [Parish Killann]. Wexford
TOOLE, Garret, New Ross, Wexford
TOY, Patrick, Carrickbeg, [Parish Kilmoleran],Waterford
TREANOR, Patrick, Tehallan, Monaghan
TREANOR, Patrick, Donagh, Monaghan
TREANOR, Peter, Monaghan
TROY, Thomas, Carlow
WADE, John, Kilkenny
WALSH, Edward, Kilvellane, Tipperary
WALSH, James and John, Newfoundland
WALSH, James, Nenagh, Tipperary
WALSH, John, Wexford

WALSH, Richard, Mountneill, [Parish Aglish], Kilkenny
WALSH, Richard, carpenter, Clonmel, Tipperary
WISE, James, Waterford
WYNN, William, Puilford [?], Monaghan, and his sons James and John
WYNN, Patrick, Puilford [?], Monaghan
WYNN, Thomas, Monaghan

The Register, Halifax, NS, 6 November 1843, published five lists of PEI Repealers. Several of those of the first list have been mentioned above, and are indicated (*). Thirty-eight attended the meeting at Ten-Mile House, St. Peter's Road.:

AFFLECK, Joseph, Dumfries-shire, Scotland *
BRADLEY, Daniel, and wife, Donagh, Donegal
BYRNES, John, Monasterevin, Kildare
CAMPION, John, Gowran, Kilkenny
CLARKIN, John, Monaghan Town
COYLE, Philip, Drumsnat, Monaghan
DONNELLY, James, Mullybrannon, Tyrone *
DOUGAN [DUGGAN], Anthony, Donagh, Monaghan *
DOUGAN [DUGGAN], James, Donagh, Monaghan *
DOUGAN [DUGGAN], Thomas, Donagh, Monaghan
FITZPATRICK, Arthur, Charlottetown, PEI
FITZPATRICK, James, Portarlington, Leix
FITZPATRICK, Mrs. J[ames], Donagh, Monaghan
HUGHES, James, Tehallen [Tehallan], Monaghan
McCARRON, John, Donagh, Monaghan *
McDONALD, James *
McKENNA, Bernard, Donagh, Monaghan
McMANUS, Owen, Kilmore, Monaghan
McPHEDEY, John, Donagh, Monaghan
McPHEE, Andrew [Rockcorry, Monaghan] *
McPHEE, Peter, Rockcorry, Monaghan
PHEE [McPHEE], John, Rockcorry, Monaghan
McQUAID, Francis, Carnahoe [Carnowen, Parish Killeevan], Monaghan *
McQUAID, James and John, Carnahoe [Carnowen, Parish Killeevan], Monaghan
McWEID, John, Donagh, Monaghan
MOONEY, Henry, Jr., and Patrick, County Monaghan
MOONEY, John, and Robert, Donagh, Monaghan
MOONEY, Mrs. L., Donagh, Monaghan
MOONEY, Robert, Donagh, Monaghan *
MORNEY [MOONEY], Henry, Donagh, Monaghan * [as Harry Mooney]
MOYNAGH, James, Donagh, Monaghan
MOYNAGH, John, Donagh, Monaghan *
O'CONNORS, James, Graiguenamanagh, Kilkenny *
TREANOR, Michael, Scotstown, Monaghan

Seven were listed for New London Settlement, PEI:
CORRICK, Matthew, The Rower, Kilkenny
DEAGAN, John, Willan [Wilton?], Offaly

FINLAY, Alexander, Banffshire, Scotland
McLAUGHLIN, James, Sr., and Jr., Donegal Town
MORRISON, Neil, Scotland
MORRISON, Patrick, Tehallen [Tehallan], Monaghan

Six were recorded for Tryon Settlement, PEI:
BEGAN, Philip, Annaghbeg [Parish Donagh], Monaghan
BRENNAN, John, Geashill, Offaly
DEEGAN, Michael, Rathdowney, Leix*
DOYLE, James, Bannow, Wexford
KIERVAN, Patrick, Newbawn, Wexford
McKAY, James, Newbawn, Wexford

Eighteen appear on the list of Repealers at Grant River Settlement, PEI:
BARRY, John, Waterford City
CAMPBELL, Joseph
FORAN, Mark, St. James Parish, Wexford
FUNEHAN [FUNCHION], James, Callan, Kilkenny
GILLIS, John
KENT, John, and Nicholas, Old Ross, Wexford
McDONALD, Donald, Sr., and Donald, Jr.
McDONALD, Roderick
McDOUGALD, John
McENALLY, John, Carlow
McLENNAN, Alexander, Angus, and Donald, Jr.
O'CONNELL, James, Waterford City
PERRY, Paul
WELSH, Mathew, Wexford

The largest autumn gathering, eighty-one strong, took place at Bedeque, PEI:

BARRETT, James, Leix
BARRETT, Mrs. Thomas, Carlow
BRENNAN, John, and Martin, Wexford
BURKE, John, Wexford
CAMPBELL, John
CONNERS, James, Kerry
CONNICK, John, Sr., Kildare or Wexford [sic]
CONNORS, Daniel, Kerry
CONNRICK, James, and Margaret, Wexford
CORMICK, Mrs. Moses
CROACKIN, Bernard, Monaghan
CULLATON, John, Wexford
CURRAN, Maurice, Waterford
DEEGAN, Michael, Leix
DEEGAN, William [Leix]
DELANEY, Edward, Callan, Kilkenny
DELANEY, Mrs. Edward, Kilkenny
DELANEY, John, Leix

DELANEY, Simon, Kilkenny
DEMPSEY, Garrett, Wexford
DONOGHUE, Miss Julia, Portarlington, Leix
DRISCOLL, Timothy, Drumbeg, Cork
DUGGAN, John, Leix
DUNN, Anne, Leix
DUNN, John, Kilmacthomas, Waterford
DUNPHY, Thomas, Kilkenny
FERRIS, Daniel, Cork
HENNESY, John, Youghal, Cork
HICKEY, Peter, Sr., Leix
HICKEY, Thomas, and William
KAVANAGH, John Terence, Monaghan
KEED, Ephraim, Nova Scotia
KELLY, Patrick, Tyrone
LACEY, Michael, Wexford
LARRISSY, John, Kilkenny
McGILL, Arthur, Antrim
McINTYRE, John, and Roderick
McKENNA, John, Monaghan
McKINNON, Alexander
McLELLAN, Alexander, Angus, Angus, Donald, and John
McMILLAN, James
McMULLEN, Donald
McNEIL, Hugh, and Malcolm
MAHER, Dennis, Edmond, and Thomas, Mullinahone, Tipperary
MEAGHER, Michael, Tipperary
MORRISON, Niel *
MORRISON, Mrs., Tralee, Kerry
MULLALY, Lawrence, Kilkenny
MULLIGAN, Luttrell, Monaghan
MULLIN, Michael, and Peter, Monaghan
MURPHY, Patrick, and Patrick, Monaghan
O'BRIEN, James, Clashmore, Waterford
O'SHEA, Mathew, Tipperary
PERKINS, John
POWER, James, John, Patrick, and Mrs., Waterford
SHEHAN, Margaret, Michael, and Norah, Midleton, Cork
SHEHAN, Patrick, Cork
TIPH, Hugh [also entered as Hugh ZEPT], Sussex, England
TRAYNOR, James, Monaghan
TREANOR, Miles, Monaghan
WALSH, Thomas, Ballinaskill, Leix
WHELAN, John, Monaghan
WHELAN, William, Drumsnat, Monaghan

The Palladium, Charlottetown, PEI, continued the coverage for Prince Edward Island, in its issue of 28 December 1843, when it published a list of thirty-five Repeal subscribers at St. Peter's Bay:

BUTLER, John, Newfoundland
CODY, Richard, Mullinavat [Tipperary]
CONDON, Thomas, Wilbarry, Limerick [Kilbarry, Cork?]
COOK, Mrs. E[dward], Inverness-Shire, Scotland
DONOVAN, Thomas, Kilma[c]thomas, Waterford
GLEESON, Thomas, Thurles, Tipperary
HENNESSY, Thomas, Ballybricken, Waterford
HICKEY, Patrick, Gowran, Kilkenny
HILLGROVE, Patrick, Youghal, Cork
HORAN, Daniel, Borrisokean [Borrisokane], Tipperary
KAIRNS, Peter, Kilmore, Monaghan
KEEFE, Patrick, Caher, Tipperary
KEHOE, Simon, Pollparty [Pollpeasty, Parish Killegney], Wexford
KENNEDY, John, Cappoquin, Waterford
McAULAY, Angus, Inverness-Shire, Scotland
McAULAY, Archibald, and Laughlin, PEI
McDONALD, Donald, Inverness-Shire, Scotland
McINNS [McINNIS], James, PEI
McISSACK, Dougald, Inverness-Shire, Scotland
McKAY, James, Knockbyrne [Knockbaun?], Wexford
MULLALLY, Michael, Mullinahone, Kilkenny [recte Tipperary]
MULLOWNEY, Thomas, Mullinavat, Kilkenny
MURPHY, Thomas, Ballyhale, Kilkenny
PHELAN, John, Treshford [Freshford], Kilkenny
REDMOND, Patrick, Taghmon, Wexford
ROACH, James, Thomastown, Kilkenny
RYAN, John, Shankill, Kilkenny
SCULLY, Michael, Sr., Kilderin [Kiledermine], Tipperary
SHEA, Edmond, Cullan [Kilcullen], Kilkenny
SWEENEY, John, and Patrick, Anacarthy [Shanballyduff], Tipperary
THOMAS, Michael, Saltonells [Saltmills, Parish Tintern], Wexford
WALSH, John, Kilmacow, Kilkenny
WYSE, Michael, Thurles, Tipperary

The Palladium, Charlottetown, PEI, 20 January 1844, named thirty-five subscribers to Repeal who attended a meeting at Mr. Egan's home in Charlottetown on 15 January:

BAMBRICK, Patrick, James, Mary, and Patrick, Blanchvillea Park [Blanchvillespark, Parish
        Gowran],Kilkenny
BARRETT, Thomas, Lawrence, and Patrick Ryan, Red House [Redhouse, in either Parish
        Killaloe, Kilkenny, or Parish St. Mary's, Wexford]
CAMPIAN, Alexander, Elizabeth, and John, Gowran, Kilkenny
CONNOLLY, Edward, and James, Windgap, Waterford
EGAN, David, John, Michael, and Richard, Tooks Mill, Wexford [Parish Tuckmill, Wicklow]
FEEHAN, Edward, Ballypatrick, Tipperary
GANE, Thomas, Wexford
GRIFFIN, Patrick, Ullard, Kilkenny
LONG, John, Jr., St. Andrew's, PEI
McDONALD, Angus, Savage Harbour, PEI

McDONALD, Roderick, St. Peter's, PEI
McGRATH, Thomas, Jr.
McKINNON, Donald, Hillsborough Head, PEI
PHELAN, Catherine, Dennis, James, and Michael, Treshford [Freshford], Kilkenny
RAGSIDER [ROSSITER], Patrick,. Dittlestown [Littletown, Parish Tomhaggard], Wexford
RICE, James, Clontiburet [Clontibret], Monaghan
RICE, David, Shankell [Shankill], Kilkenny
SAPPAN [LAPPIN], Peter, Parish Monaghan
SINNOT, Peter, Roachestown [Rochestown], Wexford
WALSH, Julian, and Thomas, Nenagh, Tipperary

The Palladium, Charlottetown, PEI, 7 March 1844, named eighteen Repeal subscribers in the East Point District, Prince Edward Island:

CAMPBELL, Dougald, Surveyor's Inlet, PEI
CAVANAGH, Patrick, New Ross, Wexford
COGHLAN, Jeremiah, Bantry, Cork
COLLINS, Daniel, Miss Ann, and William, Kenturk [Kanturk], Cork
DOYLE, James, Souris, PEI
FINN, Felix, Wexford
IRWIN, Thomas, Sligo
McLELLAND, John, Little Harbour, PEI
MacMAHON, Thomas, Killdysart [Kildysart], Clare
MacPHARLAN, James, Souris, PEI
MORRIS, Thomas, Grange, Tipperary
MORRISSEY, James, Cashel, Tipperary
O'BRIEN, Michael, Tenterem [Tintern], Wexford
O'BRIEN, Thomas, Ardpatrick, Kilkenny [*sic*; Limerick?]
SHEA, Edmond, Callan, Kilkenny
STONE, Thomas, Kilmurry, Kilkenny

The Palladium, Charlottetown, PEI, 7 March 1844.supplied a list of twenty-nine Repeal subscribers in the eastern end of Prince Edward Island, who met at Georgetown:

BROUGHTON, Robert, Br[o]adford [Parish Kilseily], Clare
BURKE, John, Thomas, and Thomas, Jr.
BYRNE, Martin, Kilkenny
CANTWELL, Michael, Newmarket, Kilkenny
CANTWELL, Thomas, Nova Scotia
CARROLL, James, Island [Parish Kilfintinan & Parish Killilagh], Clare
DALTON, James, and Peter, Ballyduff [Parish Graiguenamanagh & Inistioge], Kilkenny
DOHANEY, Patrick, Cullin, Kilkenny
HACKETT, Lawrence, Kilkenny
HACKETT, Stephen, Nova Scotia
HOWLETT, John B., Ballyduff [Parish Graiguenamanagh & Parish Inistioge], Kilkenny
KEARNEY, John, Kilkenny
KEATING, James, Ballycullen [Ballycallan], Kilkenny
McANALTY, Thomas, Ederney Bridge, Fermanagh
McAVOY, James, PEI

McAVOY, Thomas, Cullen, Kilkenny
McDONALD, Donald, Cape Breton, Nova Scotia
McKEW, John, Kilimur [Parish Killimor & Tinanascragh], Galway
MAHER, Henry, Coolank [?], Kilkenny
NOLAN, Patrick, Dublin
PENDERGAST, Edward, PEI
PENDERGAST, Thomas, Graigue [Parish Coolmore], Kilkenny
POWER, Joseph, Carlow
RYAN, William, and William, Jr., Limerick City
SWEENEY, John, Waterford City

The Palladium, Charlottetown, PEI, 7 March 1844, carried an account of a Repeal meeting at St. Peter's, Prince Edward Island, on 15 January 1844. Fifty-four people were named, eight of them repeated from the 28 December 1843 edition (*):

AYLWARD, James, and Peter, Callen [Callan], Kilkenny
BARRY, Edward, Lady's Bridge [Parish Ightermurragh], Cork
BARRY, Peter, Slurra [Slieverue?], Kilkenny
CAREY, Edward, Ballydagon [Ballindaggan, Parish Templeshanbo], Wexford
CLEAR, James, Michael, and Mrs., Goren [Gowran], Kilkenny
CODY, Richard, Mullinvat, Tipperary *
CONNELL, Murty, Monaghan
COOKE, Edward, Gurtnahoe [Gortnahoe, Parish Buolick], Tipperary
CORMACK, Richard, Holy Cross, Tipperary
CULLEN, Richard, Killan[n], Wexford
FINEGAN, Hugh, Tulecorbet [Tullycorbet Parish], Monaghan
GILLIS, Donald, "Native Scotchman"
HAFFY, William, Matris [Magheross Parish], Monaghan
HENNESY, Patrick, Gowren [Gowran], Kilkenny
HICKEY, Daniel, Gowren [Gowran], Kilkenny
HICKEY, Patrick, Gowren [Gowran], Kilkenny *
HOGAN, Dennis, Tipperary
HOGAN, Patrick, Ballycullan [Ballycullin, Parish Kilvemnon], Tipperary
KEHOE, Simon, Pollparty [Pollpeasty, Parish Killagney], Wexford *
KELLY, Patrick, Killahy [Parish Killashea], Longford
KELLY, Thomas, Kellbarrowmadian, Wexford [Parish Kilbarrymeaden, Waterford]
McAULAY, James, "native Scotchman"
McDONALD, Donald, Jr., "native Scotchman"
McDONALD, --------, "native Scotchman"
McDONALD, Ronald, Long Island, Scotland
McISAAC, Donald, "native Scotchman"
McMILLAN, Donald, Highlands of Scotland
McRAY, James, Wexford
MULLALLY, Michael, Mullinahone, Tipperary *
NOONAN, Thomas, Waterford City
O'DONNELL, Cornelius, Killanale [Parish Killenaule], Tipperary
O'HENLEY, Donald, "native Scotchman"
PENNY, William, Somersetshire, England
PHELAN, Honour, and Mary, Treshford [Freshford], Kilkenny

PHELAN, John, Treshford [Freshford], Kilkenny *
QUIGLEY, John, Chappo [Parish Chapel], Wexford
REDMOND, Ann, Taghmon, Wexford
REDMOND, Patrick, Taghmon, Wexford *
RYAN, Mathew, Turtnahoe [Gortnahoe], Tipperary
SKULLY, John, and Michael, Jr., Killederman [Kiledermine], Tipperary
SKULLY, Michael, Sr., Killederman [Kiledermine], Tipperary *
STANTEN, Dennis, Slearae [Parish Slieverue], Kilkenny
STAPLETON, William, Mine [Moyne], Tipperary
TOBIN, Patrick, Grange, Tipperary
TOBIN, Patrick, Windgap, Kilkenny
WALSH, John, Kilmacow, Kilkenny *
WALSH, John, Talerone [Parish Tullaroan], Kilkenny
WALSH, Thomas, Ballylooby, Tipperary
WILSON, Angus, Long Island, Scotland

The Palladium, Charlottetown, PEI, 3 October 1844, adds a final nine names of Island
Repealers:
   HANRAHAN, Thomas, Quaistoge [Inistiogue], Kilkenny
   KEATING, John, Adamstown, Wexford
   MacINNIS, James, Donagh, Monaghan
   MULLIGAN, Owen, Clontibut [Parish Clontibret], Monaghan
   MULLOWNEY, David, Clonmel, Tipperary
   PRICE, Richard, [Callan, Kilkenny]
   SLATTERY, Patrick, Pilltown, Kilkenny
   THOMSON, Charles, Pictou, Nova Scotia
   WEBSTER, Capt. Horatio, Charlottetown, PEI

My appreciation to Christine Gorman, Amherst, NS, for drawing the notices in *The Palladium* to
my attention.

ORIGINS OF PRINCE EDWARD ISLAND REPEALERS

The different immigration patterns from Ireland, even to the adjacent provinces of Nova
Scotia (Halifax), and Prince Edward Island, more generally comprehended within the published
lists, are noticeable in the membership lists of the Repeal Association.

We know the place of origin of 499 of the 567 different individuals: 20 Scots, 3 English, 7
Nova Scotian, 6 Newfoundland, 17 from Prince Edward Island, and one each from New York and
Guernsey. It is probable that many, even most, of the 68 whose native place is not given were born
in Prince Edward Island. Of 445 born in Ireland, Leinster contributed 191 (Kilkenny 89, Wexford
67, Leix 13, Carlow 7, Wicklow 4, Longford and Offaly 3 each, Dublin and Kildare 2 apiece, Louth
one), or 43% of the total. Munster supplied 127, or 28.5% (Tipperary 54, Waterford 37, Cork 23,
Kerry 6, Limerick 4, Clare 3), followed by Ulster, 122, or 27.5% (Monaghan 101, Armagh 10,
Fermanagh and Donegal 4 each, Tyrone 2, and Antrim one). Connacht produced a mere 5, or 1%
(Roscommon and Sligo 2 apiece, and Galway 1).

While the proportion of Irish from Leinster was nearly 40% in both locations, it was only the greater share from Wexford that maintained the balance. The major difference in place of origin between the Irish of Halifax and those of Prince Edward Island was the presence among the latter of a substantial immigration from the northern county of Monaghan, 23% of the total. Ulster's nine counties accounted for barely 4% of the Halifax Irish. Three Munster counties - Tipperary, Cork and Waterford - supplied nearly half the Halifax Irish Catholics, but a quarter of Prince Edward Island's Irish Repealers. The proportions of Irish Repealers in Halifax in 1843 do not differ much from those reported in my book, *Irish Halifax: The Immigrant Generation, 1815-1859* (Halifax: Saint Mary's University, 1981), p. 12, which are based on 7,440 Irish-born persons recorded between 1825 and 1903. None of the seven Irish counties absent from the PEI Repeal lists (Cavan, Derry, Down, Leitrim, Mayo, Meath and Westmeath) accounted for even one percent of the Halifax Irish community of that period.

C) REPEALERS IN SYDNEY, CAPE BRETON, NOVA SCOTIA, 1843/44

The Register, Halifax, NS, 10 October 1843 reported that twenty-eight people attended a Repeal meeting in Sydney, Cape Breton Island, that month, chaired by Rev. [James D.] DRUMMOND:

L[awrence] BARRY; Edward BOWN, Esq.; J[ames] COX, [Dungarvan, Waterford]; Michael FLAVEN; James LEAHY; John O'KEEFE; & James WOOD.
The Baddeck Committee: Joseph CAMPBELL & Jeremiah O'SULLIVAN
The Bridgeport Committee: William CADDIGAN & John SHEHAN
At Cow Bay: John CASS
At East Bay: James SLATTERY
The Little Bras d'Or Committee: Thomas MEHAN & Thomas WHALEN
The Low Point Committee: L[awrence] BARRON, B[artholomew] CONNER & John MURPHY
The Mainadieu Committee: William BUTLER, Esq., & Owen DUNPHY
The North Bar Committee: P[atrick] LONERGAN & David ORMOND
The Sydney Committee: John DUNPHY, R. HUNTINGTON & James McKEAGNEY, Esq.
The Sydney Mines Committee: Thomas CALDWELL & Robert HAMILTON.

The *Cape Breton Free Press*, Sydney, NS, 24 May 1844, mentioned nineteen names (eight repeated from the previous list, but with added information about several of them) active as Repealers in Sydney as of 15 January 1844. Those who formed the committee at that date are indicated by an asterisk (*):

Peter A'HEARN, Waterford *
Lawrence BARRY, Kilkenny
Edward BOWN, Esq.
Dennis BRACKEN, Leix *
William BRYAN, Waterford
Jeremiah H. CORCORAN, Galway
Rev. James DRUMMOND, PP, Mohill, Leitrim
Garret FITZPATRICK, [Cork] *
Robert HAMILTON, Waterford
James LEDDY, Limerick *

Patrick LONNERGAN, Tipperary
William MacNAMARA, Limerick
Thomas MEEHAN, Limerick City
David ORMOND, Waterford
Thomas ROACH, Wexford
Thomas WALSH, Kilkenny
James WHELAN, Kilkenny
John YOUNG, Kilkenny
James McKEAGNEY, M.L.A.
[assemblyman; Clogher, Tyrone; brother of Rev. Henry McKeagney]

D) REPEALERS IN BATHURST, NEW BRUNSWICK, 1843*

The Register, Halifax, Nova Scotia, 5 September 1843, named the officers elected at a Repeal meeting at Bathurst on 3 August: P[atrick] COUGHLAN, Chairman; Christopher McMANUS, Secretary; Joseph REID, and John RONALDS [Reynolds].

The [Halifax] *Register,* 3 October 1843, named the 114 Repealers at Bathurst, New Brunswick, as of 16 September 1843. John RONALDS, Esq., was Chairman.

* Other records indicate that the Bathurst Repealers lived all over New Brunswick. For instance, Baldwin resided in Saint John; Boyle at Pennfield, Charlotte County; Michael Brown at Westfield, Kings County; Conway at St. David, Charlotte County; and Devereaux at Durham, Restigouche County, New Brunswick.

BALDWIN, Thomas [Cork]
BANNAN, Patrick
BARRON, Rev. Andrew
BASSET, John S., Kilkenny
BOYLE, Hugh, Donegal
BROWN, John, and Michael [Donegal]
BURKE, John, Waterford
CALANAN, John
CAREW, Walter
CLIFFORD, Timothy
COLLINS, Matthew, Cork
CONNELL, Francis
CONWAY, Edward [Tyrone]
COOMBS, James
COUGHLIN, Cornelius, and Daniel [Cork]
COWHIG, James [Cork]
CRONAN, David
CULLEN, Edward, Kilkenny
CULLEN, John
CURRAN, Arthur, Kerry
CURRY, John
DALEY, John, Sr.
DARBY, Andrew
DEMPSEY, Maurice [Wexford]
DEMSEY, John, John, John, and Patrick
DEVEREAUX, Paul [Wexford]
DOYLE, James, Michael, P., and Patrick
DOYLE, Patrick, and Mrs. Patrick, Kilkenny
DOYLE, Richard, and Richard
DRISCOLL, John, Sr. [Cork], and John, Jr.
DUNPHY, Michael [Kilkenny]
EGAN, Cornelius, Dominick, and Mrs.
EGAN, Thomas
FAHY, William

FITZPATRICK, James
FLANNERY, John
FOLEY, Daniel [Kerry]
FOLEY, Jeremiah, and Patrick
GALLAGHER, John
GILLIGAN, Barnaby
HAGARTY, Patrick
HALL, Mrs.
HAYES, James, and Patrick, Kerry
HAYES, Thomas [Kerry]
HAYES, Widow [Kerry]
HICKSON, Robert P.
HOWARD, Patrick, Clare
KENNY, John
KIRBY, John, Cork
KNIGHT, John, Sr., Cork
LAWLER, Mrs. John
LAWLER, Mary, Leix
LOFTEY, Thomas
LOVITT, George, Kerry
McCARTHY, Michael, Cork
McCULLOUGH, James, Tyrone
McGOWAN, Thomas, Mayo
McISAAC, John
McKAY, Daniel
McKENNA, John
McMANUS, Christopher
MADDY, Thomas
MALO, Rev. Louis Stanislaus
MEEHIN, Charles, and John
MEEHIN, Hugh, Tyrone
MOLOUGHNEW [Molyneux], Patrick
MULLINS, James [Derry]
MULLINS, Philip

MURPHY, Cornelius, Dennis, & Jeremiah
MYERS, Daniel
O'BRIEN, John
O'LEARY, Jeremiah [Cork]
O'NEALE, Jeremiah, and Michael
POWER, John, and William
POWER, Patrick, and Patrick, Cork
QUINNAN, Edward
RONALDS [Reynolds], James
SALTER, James
SHEEHAN, Maurice

SISK, Patrick [Cork]
SPAIR, Daniel
SULLIVAN, Benjamin, and John
SWEENEY, Edward, Cork City
TOBIN, Patrick, Tipperary
ULTIHAN, John, and Mrs. John
UPTON, James
WALSH, William, and William
WHELTON, William, Jr.
WHITE, Henry

E) REPEAL EXECUTIVE, DARTMOUTH, NOVA SCOTIA, 1845

The Register, 23 December 1845, named the four men who formed the committee of the Repeal Association in that town, across the harbour from Halifax, namely:

James SINNOTT, chairman   [Wexford]
M[ichael]. DUNN, warden   [Wexford]
Dominick FARRELL, warden [Waterford City]
R[ichard] B. O'FLAHERTY, warden [Croom, Limerick]

17 - FORTUNES OF SEA TRAVEL FROM IRELAND

PASSENGERS IN THE *GOOD INTENT,* ST. JOHN'S, NL, 1816

The *Newfoundland Royal Gazette*, 31 March 1818, carried a notice listing 42 Irish passengers who sailed from Waterford, Ireland, to St. John's, Newfoundland in spring 1816. They were advised to pay their fares or proceedings for recovery would commence. They had sailed in the *Good Intent*, Thomas **Fox**, Master. These passengers most probably came from the counties inland from Waterford City: Kilkenny, Tipperary, Wexford and Waterford.

ASPER, Bridget
BROPHY, Mary
CHRISTOPHER, William
DUNN, Thomas
FLOOD, Richard
HALL, Nicholas
HEARN, W. A.
KELLY, John
KYLY, David
MARTIN, Thomas
POWER, John
RYAN, Patrick
TOBIN, Patrick
WELLS, Catherine

BIRMINGHAM, Michael
BURKE, William
CLANCEY, John
FINNAGAN, Ellen
GRECHY, John
HARRIS, James
HIGGINS, Francis
KENNEDY, John
LYNAGH, Daniel
M'GRATH, Roger
POWER, Michael
SCOTT, Thomas
TURNEY, John
WHELAN, Thomas

BOLAND, Thomas
CAIN, Andrew
DOYLE, Edward
FLANNIGAN, Edward
HALL, Bridget
HAYES, John
KEEFE, John
KYLEY, Patrick
MAHER, John
PHELAN, Mary
REDMOND, Joseph
SHALLOW, Betsy
WALSH, Edward
WRIGHT, John

SHIPWRECK IN NOVA SCOTIA: THE *ALEXANDER BUCHANAN*, 1818

In Spring 1818 the brig *Alexander Buchanan*, Thomas **Clements**, Master, cleared the port of Londonderry, Ireland, en route to Saint John, New Brunswick. It carried about 200 passengers when it went aground on Cape Sable Island, Nova Scotia, on 14 June and was "totally lost, and with her, the whole of the Passengers effects." [*Acadian Recorder*, Halifax newspaper, 27 June 1818] The passengers were saved, though many were destitute due to the loss of their possessions.

On 11 February 1819 the Overseers of the Poor at Yarmouth, Nova Scotia, whither the rescued people had been taken, reported having had eleven passengers on their hands. Eight of them had been on board the wrecked vessel: Christopher, Mary and Elizabeth **BROWNLEIGH**; Robert and Jane **RUTLEDGE**; John and Jane **ARMSTRONG**; and William **IRVINE**. They were "all sick of Typhus Fever whereof Irvine died.".

Three other seafarers were reported at the same time. Jacob **NEWBURY** was a Swede travelling from the West Indies and had been sent on to the Poor House in Halifax, NS. Two men from Ireland had sailed out of Newfoundland: Patrick **DWYER** survived, but James **SULLIVAN** died. The survivors, other than Dwyer, left Yarmouth, apparently for Saint John, New Brunswick.

(Source: NSARM: RG 5, Series "P", Vol . 80, doc. # 19)

A HAPPY LANDING: THE *EAGLE* AT HALIFAX, 1843

The Halifax *Morning Herald*, 29 May 1843, announced the safe arrival in port on 26 May of the brig *Eagle*, **Edwards**, master, just 19 days out of Waterford, Ireland with 88 passengers, 30 of them children, and two-thirds of the total being female. The passengers were described as "a fine robust, healthy looking set of people" On 30 May twelve male passengers signed and had published in the *Novascotian*, 5 June 1843, a "Complimentary Address to Captain Samuel **Edwards** of the Brig *Eagle*" Signatories were:

John **ADDIS**	Edward **BUTLER**	John **CARUE** [Carew]
John **CONNORS**	David **DAYDELANY**	Mathew **DOYLE**
James **HEAYDN**	Rody **HEFFERNAN**	James **HENECY**
James **KEATING**	Thomas **MURPHY**	Patrick **TOBIN**

(Source: *Morning Herald*, 29 May 1843, and *Novascotian*, 5 June 1843)

STRANDED IN CAPE BRETON: THE *SIR GEORGE PREVOST*, 1844

On 9 April 1844 the barque *Sir George Prevost*, William **Savage** master, cleared Newry, Ireland, en route to Québec. On 31 May the vessel struck rocks and became stranded at Cape Hinchinbroke, on Cape Breton Island, Nova Scotia. Four days later the passengers were rescued by the local Lloyd's agent John **Janvrin** who took the passengers to Arichat, NS. He sent them on their way in the schooner *Mary Ann*, Zephrin **Bourdages** master, to Gaspé, from where they could obtain passage to their destination. In his claim to the government, Janvrin mentioned the names of fifteen passengers:

John **CAVEL**, a boy
Lucindy **COLLINS**
Catherine **CONNERY**
Patrick **DOREN** and wife
Thomas & Mary **DOREN**
John **FARNIGEN**

Hugh & Mary Ann **HANNAWAY**
Thomas **KELLY**
Catherine **MICHAELMARRY** [McElmurray]
John **O'NIEL**
Michael **RUNNELS** [Reynolds]
Nancy **TIMMONS**

(Source: NSARM, MG 100, Vol. 279, item 1,)

DID THE *FANNY* GO ON TO NEW YORK IN 1852?

On or before 13 November 1851 a group of emigrants contracted with Evans & Sons of Galway to be transported in the brig *Fanny* to New York. William **Rudolf**, a Halifax merchant, owned the vessel, and John **Rudolf** (a relative) was master. Meeting with rough weather, the captain put in at Lunenburg, NS, on 25 January 1852, and on 6 February made an overnight sail to Halifax. A week later the Irish passengers petitioned the Nova Scotia government for rations, and to oblige the shipowner to fulfill his contract to take them to New York. Sixty-two adults are named, and there were twelve unnamed children. The adults were

Patt **BARRET**, Patt **BARRETT**, Honora **BEATY**, Francis **BREW**, Honour **CLANCEY**, Thomas **CONNELL**; Dudley, Kate and Mary **CONNEELLY**; John **DAILY**, Margaret **DEE**, Sibley **DELANEY**, Honora and Thymothy [*sic*] **DONLON**; Thomas **DUDLEY**, Honora **DUFFY**, Judy **GALY**. Kate **GIBENS**, Catherine **GLYNN**, Kate **HALEY**, Patt **HAVERTY**, Bridget, Martin, Mary and Michael **JOYCE**; Salley **JOISE**, Bridget **KEANE**, Ann **KEARN**; Catherine, Patt and Thomas **LALLY**; Mary and Michael **LEE**; John **LINAHAN**, Thomas **LOUGHLIN**, Catherine **LYNCH**, Mary **LYONS**, John **McMAHON**; Bridget and Connor **MALBRIE**; Patt **MELLET**, Mary **MOLONEY**; Honora, John and Thomas **MORONEY**; Patt **NEE**, Patt and Margaret **O'BRIEN**; Catherine **O'DONNELL**, Mary **O'DUIRE**, William **O'MALEY**, Law **O'MALLEY**. Thomas **O'MALLY**, Bridget **O'MEALY** [4 versions of O'Malley in one record!]; Sally **O'NEIL**, James **PHILLIPS**, John **SULIVAN**; Bridget, Catherine, Patt and Sibena **WALSH**, Bridget **WELSHE**, and 12 children.

(Source: NSARM, MG 100, Vol. 167, item 14)

18 - MILITARY ATTRITION IN BRITISH AMERICA

A) THE 101ST REGIMENT, 1807 - 1809

Part of the 101st (Duke of York's Irish) Regiment served in New Brunswick and Nova Scotia as garrison during the height of the Napoleonic Wars. The high proportion of men from Connacht (Galway, Mayo, Roscommon, etc) or adjacent areas (Tipperary, Clare and Limerick) indicates that recruiters for this unit had been busy in western Ireland during 1806.

Between 23 October 1807 and 24 October 1809 the unit lost fifty-six men. Twenty-seven died, twenty-five deserted ("ran") and four were honourably discharged from the Regiment. The proximity of the American border helps to explain why the desertions took place almost entirely from Saint John and St. Andrews, New Brunswick, rather than in Nova Scotia. Descendants of the successful escapees would more likely be found in the United States than in eastern Canada.

BALDWIN, Sgt. Henry   21/1805   Terey Glass [Terryglass], Tipperary, woolcomber,
                                              AWOL ,Saint John, 17 Oct 1808

BANAHAN, Cpl. Patrick   24/1806   Killereran [Killererin], Galway, weaver,
                                              AWOL, Saint John, 24 June 1808

BARNEVILLE, John   24/1806   Killereran [Killererin], Galway, weaver,
                                              AWOL, Saint John, 1 Dec 1808

BARRETT, John   17/1806   Oughavall, Mayo, labourer, AWOL, Saint John, 8 May 1808

BIRD, Robert   18/1806   "Toheran, Clare" [Togher, Clare *barony, County* Galway]
                                              died at Windsor, NS, 9 July 1809.

BRAY, Cpl. Henry   22/1806   Crosmaline [Crossmolina], Mayo, labourer,
                                              AWOL, Saint John, 7 Sep 1808

BURKE, Arthur   18/1805   Ardaught [Ardagh], Mayo, weaver,
                                              AWOL, Saint John, 8 May 1808

BURKE, Miles   18/180-   . . . ., died at Halifax, NS, 18 May 1808

CANOW, Frederick   34/1807   Grandsee [Gransee], Berlin, Prussia, musician,
                                              AWOL, Saint John, 24 Aug 1808

CARROLL, John   19/1806   Kilmoumay [Kilmoremoy], Mayo, brogue maker,
                                              discharged at Halifax, 24 Dec 1808

CARROLL, Michael   23/1808   Limerick City, labourer. AWOL, Saint John, 4 Sep 1808

CAWLEY, Roger   18/1806   Killbeghagh [Kilbeagh], Mayo, labourer,
                                              AWOL, Saint John, 24 June 1808

COLGAN, Lacky   27/1805   St. Mary's, Westmeath, wheelwright,
                                              died at Annapolis, NS, 15 July 1809

CONNIFFE, Edward   17/1806   Athlone, Roscommon, sleator [slayter],
                                              died at Saint John, NB, 23 July 1808

CONNOR, Edward   33/1805   Tuam, Galway, tailor, AWOL, Saint John, 17 June 1808

COOPER, Luke   19/1807   St. Peter's, Roscommon, labourer,
                                              died at Saint John, NB, 24 Aug 1808

CORRIGAN, Hugh   20/1806   Tynan, Armagh, weaver, died at Halifax, 23 Oct 1807

CUNNIAN, Patrick   23/1805   "Mongholy, Mayo" [?], labourer,
                                              died at Halifax,. NS, 24 Dec 1808

DARCY, Sgt. Patrick   24/1806   Cros[s]molina, Mayo, mason,
                                              AWOL, Saint John, 7 Sep 1808

DUFFEY, Cpl. Patrick   26/1806   Templeboy, Mayo [*recte* Sligo], labourer,
                                              AWOL, Saint John, 5 June 1808

FAULKNER, Patrick   17/1806   Anna[gh], Cavan, labourer,
                                              AWOL, St. Andrews, NB, 24 Aug 1808

FECHERTY[1], Brian   26/1806   Aughrim, Roscommon, labourer,
                                              died at Halifax, NS, 8 Apr 1808

FLEMING, John   19/1806   Cloonbannion [Cloonbanniv], Galway, labourer,
                                              drowned at Halifax, 23 Oct 1807

FOSTER[2], Sgt. Miles   25/1806   Tomore, - -, weaver, drowned, Bay of Fundy, 19 Oct 1808

---

[1] Fecherty is likely Fenerty, although Fogarty is also a possible interpretation of the name.

[2] Tomore may refer either to Toomore, Mayo, or Toomour, Sligo. The former is the more likely, inasmuch as Foster enlisted at Castlebar, Mayo.

GIBBONS, Miles   28/1806   Borishoole [Burrishoole], Mayo, weaver,
                                   AWOL, Saint John, 17 June 1808

GIVERAN, John   23/1806   Toughmoreconnell Galway [Taghmaconnell, Roscommon],
                                   labourer, drowned, Windsor, NS, 9 July 1809

GORDON, Edward   20/1807   Kiltombe [Kiltoum], Roscommon, labourer,
                                   died at Saint John, NB, 16 July 1808

GRADY, Francis   29/1805   Kilmurry, Kerry, labourer, AWOL, Saint John, 7 Sep 1808

GREAGHAN, Patrick   24/1806   Kil[l]nvoy, Roscommon, labourer,
                                   died at Halifax, NS, 17 Nov 1807

HOCKAN, Cpl. James   29/1806   Killcondriff [Kilconduff], Mayo, labourer, accidentally
                                   shot at Saint John, NB, 19 Oct 1808

JACOB, Michael   18/1805   St. Andrew's, Dublin City, servant,
                                   discharged at Saint John, 1 Aug 1808

JOYCE, Patrick   19/1805   Ballinrobe, Mayo, labourer,
                                   discharged at Saint John in 1808

KELLY, Joseph   16/1806   Segort, Kildare [Saggart, Dublin], labourer,
                                   drowned at Halifax, 23 Oct 1807

KELLY, Michael   19/1806   Killmurray [Kilmurry], Clare, clerk,
                                   AWOL, Halifax, NS, 14 Apr 1808

KELLY, Patrick   34/1806   Cashel, Longford, labourer,
                                   AWOL, Saint John, 17 June 1808

KEOGH, Michael   18/1806   Toughmoconnell [Taghmaconnell], Roscommon, labourer,
                                   died at Halifax, NS, 20 Mar 1808

KILDAY, Patrick   30/1806   Castlebar, Mayo, labourer, AWOL, Saint John, 24 Aug
                                   1808

KINNEVAN, John   20/1806   Knock, Mayo, tailor, AWOL, Saint John, 24 June 1808

LANGAN, James   20/1806   Anna[gh]down, Galway, labourer, "Drowned in the Well in
                                   the North Barracks", Halifax, 15 Oct 1807

LAWLER, William   19/1806   Gort, Galway, labourer, "Suffocated when Drunk", at
                                   Halifax, NS, 14 Apr 1808

LENNAN, James   22/1806   Kil[l]evy, Armagh, weaver, AWOL, Saint John, 17 Oct 1807

McCALE[3], Michael   22/1806   Turlough, Mayo, blacksmith, died at Saint John, NB, 7 July
                                   1808

McDANIELL, George   15/1805   Pallis [Pallas], Limerick, weaver, AWOL, Saint John, 17 June
                                   1808

McEVOY, Patrick   18/1805   A[g]haboe, Leix, labourer, AWOL, Saint John, 17 Oct 1808.[4]

McGINNIS, Bernard   20/1806   Drumlummea [Drumlumman], Cavan, labourer, "Drowned
                                   in the Garrison Well", Halifax, 7 Jan 1808

McKEALE, Richard   28/1806   Turlough, Mayo, labourer, AWOL, Saint John, 17 June
                                   1808

MONAHAN, Michael   20/1807   Galway Town, labourer, died at Halifax, NS, 8 Apr 1808

MULKERAN, Patrick   20/1806   Gort, Galway, labourer, died at Halifax, NS, 19 Apr 1808

O'DONNELL, Waters   25/1806   Muckully [Muckalee], Kilkenny, labourer, died at
                                   Annapolis, NS, 24 Oct 1809 [latest date]

---

[3] This is the common Mayo surname McHale, taken down "by ear".

[4] Notation: "Given in charge of Civil Power."

ORMSBY, James	15/1806	Back, Mayo [*recte* Galway], labourer, committed suicide at Halifax, NS, 4 Apr 1808
RAMSDEN, John	25/1809	Liverpool, Lancashire, cloth draper, AWOL, Saint John, 2 Sep 1809
RIVETT, Benjamin	23/1806	St. Brides [St. Bridget's], Dublin City, painter, died at Halifax, NS, 1 Dec 1807
TOBIN, Timothy	26/1806	St. Mary's, Limerick, tailor, discharged at Saint John, NB, 22 July 1808
TONE, Charles	21/1806	Moistown [Moystown, Parish of Tisaran], Offaly, labourer, died at Saint John, NB, 19 July 1809
WARD, Edward	17/1806	John's Gate, Limerick, weaver, AWOL, Saint John, 17 June 1808
WRIGHT, Mark	15/1806	Scrab[b]y, Cavan, weaver, "Shot by an Inhabitant" at Halifax, NS, 26 Mar 1809.

(Source: W.O. 25, Vol. 554 [NAC mfm. B5510].)

B) THE 74ᵀᴴ REGIMENT, 1818 - 1826

The 74th Regiment of Foot had originally been recruited in the Scottish Highlands. A cursory glance at the places of birth of the men whose names follow reveals that the Army had thrown the net more widely as the lengthy Napoleonic Wars had ground on. One hundred and forty-seven men left the strength of this unit in Atlantic Canada between June 1818 and July 1826 and, of these, just forty-six had birthplaces in Scotland, as compared to seventy-one in Ireland and thirty in England.

Among the soldiers' occupations and trades in civilian life we notice, in descending order: labourer (69), weaver (37), shoemaker (11), tailor (5), carpenter (4), servant (3), baker and mason (2 each). Single representatives occur for trades such as brogue maker, coach maker, cooper, cropper, cutler, edge-tool maker, flax dresser, hosier, last maker, miner, roper, spinner and turner. One man declared no occupation.

Of the 147 men listed, 60 were discharged, 49 "ran" (deserted), 37 died, and one man was transferred to the Newfoundland Garrison Company. One man drowned in Prince Edward Island. Of the remainder, 100 left strength in New Brunswick, 25 in Nova Scotia, and 21 in Newfoundland. In many cases the veterans did not remain in their place of discharge. The successful deserters put considerable distance between themselves and the Army, especially when, as in the case of those going AWOL in New Brunswick, the border of the United States beckoned nearby.

IRISH-BORN (71 men)

ADAMS, Francis	21/1809	Glenavy, Antrim, weaver, AWOL, Saint John, 24 July 1822
BAIRD, John	25/1816	Tydavenet [Tedavnet], Monaghan, labourer, discharged at Fredericton, NB, 24 Mar 1823
BLACK, John	14/1813	Kamane [Carnmoney?], Antrim, labourer, AWOL, Saint John, NB, 15 June 1822
BOYD, James	18/1815	Ballybay, Monaghan, weaver, discharged at Saint John, NB, 20 July 1818
BOYLE, Christopher	14/1810	Roscommon, Roscommon, labourer, AWOL, Saint John, NB, 23 Oct 1822

BRADLEY, Patrick   21/1809   Mapasquin [Macosquin], Derry, weaver, AWOL, Saint
                                 John, NB, 25 June 1821

BROWN, James   17/1813   Drumholen [Drumhome?], Donegal, labourer, AWOL,
                                 Saint John, NB, 30 June 1821

BURNS, Peter   23/1816   Downpatrick, Down, labourer, discharged at Saint John,
                                 NB, 19 Oct 1821

CAHILL, Thomas   26/1816   Loughill [Laughil], Longford, weaver, died at Halifax,
                                 22 Jan1826

CRAWFORD, Henry   20/1809   St. Andrew's, Dublin, cutler, discharged at Fredericton,
                                 NB, 11 Nov 1818

CUMMINS, James   24/1817   Stickallen [Stackallan], Meath, labourer, discharged at St.
                                 Andrews, NB, 26 Apr 1819

CURRY, Thomas   18/1815   Desertcrete [Desertcreat], Tyrone, tailor, died at Saint
                                 John, NB, 14 May 1819

DAILEY, Daniel   26/1808   Loughall, Armagh, labourer, died at Halifax, NS, 25 June
                                 1818; the earliest date in this record.

DANIEL, Thomas   20/1816   Dungarvan, Waterford, servant, AWOL, Saint John, NB,
                                 31 May 1822

DOLAN, Patrick   21/1811   Kilcloony, Galway, labourer, died at St. John's [NL or NB?
                                 Ambiguous placename], 13 Jan 1821

DOUGHERTY, Charles 25/1809   Carrickmacross, Monaghan, shoemaker, died at
                                 Fredericton, NB, 25 Apr 1820

DOWD, William   22/1809   Armagh Town, shoemaker, died in NL, 22 July 1818
DUFFY, William   15/1815   Amatress [Ematris], Monaghan, labourer, deserted at
                                 Saint John, NB, 13 June 1821

DWYER, James   17/1816   Rathkeale, Limerick, tailor, AWOL, Saint John, NB,
                                 6 July 1821

GIBSON, Alexander   25/1816   Donoughmore, Tyrone, weaver, AWOL, Saint John, NB,
                                 15 July 1821

GIBSON, Andrew   19/1817   Killinchy, Down, tailor, AWOL, Saint John, NB, 1 Aug 1821
GOGGINS, William   23/1816   Kildimo, Limerick, shoemaker, discharged at Fredericton,
                                 NB, 24 May 1820

GOWDIE, John   27/1816   Belfast, Antrim, weaver, AWOL, Saint John, NB, 28 Oct
                                 1819

HART, John   15/1810   Moylough, Galway, labourer, died at Halifax, 23 July 1825
HART, William   19/1810   Ballymacward, Galway, labourer, AWOL, Saint John, NB,
                                 2 Oct 1825

HEFFERNAN, William 31/1813   Callan, Kilkenny, brogue maker, AWOL, Saint John, NB,
                                 11 Oct 1822

HICKEY, Thomas   19/1815   Stonehall, Limerick, labourer, AWOL, NL, 4 Nov 1821
HICKEY, Pvte.William[5] 22/1810 Kildeemo [Kildimo], Limerick, carpenter, died at Halifax,
                                 NS, 22 Nov 1824

HYNES, Patrick   18/1815   Mountrath, Leix, labourer, AWOL, Saint John, NB,
                                 25 June 1821

---

[5] Buried 25 Nov 1824, age 36 (Catholic record, Halifax).

IRWIN, William[6]   25/1816   Augharlee [Aghaloo], Tyrone, labourer, 1 Oct 1821.

KELLY, Michael   17/1816   Tuam, Galway, servant, AWOL, Fredericton, NB,
                                               25 July 1818

KENNY, Martin   20/1815   Rahoon, Galway, labourer, AWOL, St. Andrews, NB,
                                               7 July 1820

KERR, John   19/1810   Mulla[gh]brack, Armagh, weaver, died at Saint John, NB,
                                               1 Mar 1821

KYLE, John   23/1813   Ballykelly, Derry, mason, discharged at Fredericton, NB,
                                               24 Dec 1820

LALLY, Michael   16/1810   Kiltormour [Kiltormer], Galway, labourer, died at
                                               Halifax, NS, 12 July 1818

LEARY, James   18/1808   Dungarvan, Waterford, weaver, discharged at
                                               Fredericton, NB, 10 June 1819

LINDSAY, John   16/1815   Enniskeen, Cavan, weaver, AWOL, Saint John, NB,
                                               2 Sep 1821

LITTLE, Cpl. George[7]   27/1808   Armagh Town, weaver, discharged at Halifax, 24 Oct 1819

LOVE, John   26/1817   Donoughmore [Donaghmore], Down, labourer, AWOL,
                                               Fredericton, NB, 25 July 1818

McBREARTY, Michael   19/1816   Oreny [Urney], Tyrone, weaver, AWOL, St. Andrews, NB,
                                               1 July 1820

McCULLOCH, Andrew   19/1806   Inth [?], Monaghan, carpenter, died in Newfoundland,
                                               19 Apr 1820

McGUIGGAN, Hugh   20/1809   Desartlin [Desertlyn], Derry, labourer, discharged at
                                               Fredericton, NB, 10 June 1819

Mc[C]RAE, Andrew   21/1809   Drumholm [Drumhome], Donegal, labourer, discharged at
                                               Fredericton, NB, 10 June 1819

MAKINS, Hugh   15/1813   St. Mary's, Athlone, Westmeath, labourer, discharged at
                                               Saint John, NB, 24 June 1822

MALLONE, James   18/1816   Conshane [?], Cavan, labourer, AWOL, NL, 26 July 1823
                                               Returned to Regiment, 8 Oct 1823

MAYNES, John   20/1816   Ballinasaggart [Ballynasaggart], Tyrone, labourer, died at
                                               Halifax, NS, 30 Dec 1824

MELVIN, John   22/1815   Loughadian [Aghaderg Parish], Down, labourer, AWOL,
                                               Fredericton, NB, 19 June 1822

MULLOY, James   24/1815   Loughrea, Galway, servant, discharged at Fredericton, NB,
                                               10 June 1819

MURPHY, Patrick   18/1815   Coomb [Coombe, Merchant's Quay Ward], Dublin, last
                                               maker, AWOL, Saint John, NB, 15 July 1821

O'BRIEN, Daniel   24/1814   St. Nicholas, Galway, labourer, died at Halifax, NS,
                                               3 Oct 1825

O'BRIEN, Patrick   17/1816   Gammonsfield, Tipperary, labourer, AWOL, St. John's.
                                               [Nfld or NB? Ambiguous], 5 June 1820

---

[6]"Drummed out of the Regt as a disgrace to the Service", in New Brunswick.

[7] Little was granted 100 acres (lot 8 South) at Wellington Settlement, NS, 2 Dec 1822, and was awarded a Chelsea pension, 25 Nov 1825. He died at Hammonds Plains, near Halifax, NS, 26 Dec 1858, age 77. (*Cf.*, NSARM, RG 20, Series "A": John Mara, 1822).

O'CONNOR, Dennis	18/1816	Rathkeale, Limerick, labourer, AWOL, St. Andrews, NB, 29 Aug 1820
O'NEIL, John	20/1815	Loughgale [Loughgall], Armagh, weaver, AWOL, St. Andrews, NB, 20 Oct 1820
O'NEILL, John	18/1816	Augharloo [Aghaloo], Tyrone, weaver, AWOL, St. Andrews, NB, 20 Oct 1820
O'NEILL, William	14½/1813	Lun[e]y, Derry, labourer, AWOL, NL, 18 Oct 1819
OPREY, Hugh	25/1816	Loughan Island [Loughinisland], Down, labourer, died at Fredericton, NB, 2 Mar 1822
PHOENIX, John	22/1809	Shankill, Armagh, weaver, discharged at Fredericton, NB, 23 July 1822
PIERCE, Robert	20/1815	Askeaton, Limerick, labourer, discharged at Fredericton, NB, 10 June 1819
REILLY, John	21/1809	Killevy [Killanny], Louth, cooper, discharged at Fredericton, NB, 10 June 1819
ROCK, John	14/1812	Carnesear [Cornaseer], Roscommon, labourer, AWOL, Saint John, NB, 17 Oct 1821
ROGERSON, John	25/1812	Cabbragh, Galway [no place so-named in Galway; Sligo or Mayo possibly], labourer, died at Fredericton, NB, 19 Sep 1818
ROGERSON, Michael	21/1811	Aharough [Ahascragh], Galway, tailor, died in NL, 23 Apr 1819
ROONEY, Stephen	26/1814	Athenry, Galway, labourer, died in NL, 17 June 1822
ROSE, Andrew	16/1816	Nantenan [Nantinan], Limerick, labourer, discharged at Saint John, NB, 24 June 1822
RYAN, Charles	20/1815	Queensboro [Queensfort ?], Galway, carpenter, AWOL, Saint John, NB, 6 July 1821
SCULLY, Patrick	12/1809	Cabinteely, Dublin, labourer, died at Fredericton, NB, 18 Apr 1821
SHAUGHNESSY, Wm.	20/1815	Headford, Galway, shoemaker, discharged at Fredericton, NB, 11 June 1819
SMITH, John	18/1809	Derrynews [Derrynoose], Armagh, weaver, died in NL, 5 May 1822
TREACEY, Denis	19/1815	Birr, Offaly, labourer, AWOL, Saint John, NB, 6 July 1821
WALSH, James	17/1815	Ballinanty [Ballynanty, Tullabracky Parish], Limerick, labourer, AWOL, NL, 1 June 1819
WHITE, Stephen	23/1810	Kilclooney [Kilcloony], Galway, labourer, discharged at Fredericton, NB, 24 Sep 1820

SCOTS-BORN (46 men)

ARNOTT, George	37/1812	Dalkeith, Edinburgh, shoemaker, discharged in Fredericton, NB, 27 Apr 1819
AULD, John	- -/18 - -	Irvine, Ayrshire, weaver, AWOL, Fredericton, 25 May 1822.
BROWN, Hugh	15/1814	New Mills [Newmilns], Ayrshire, weaver, died in Newfoundland, 20 Aug 1818
BRUNTON, James	18/1813	Jedburgh, Roxburgh, hozier, AWOL, NL, 31 May 1821
COOPER, George	26/1816	Kneeler [Kinnellar], Aberdeen, weaver, died at Halifax, NS, 17 Jan 1825

COOPER, William	15/1813	Stirling, Stirlingshire, labourer, died in NL, 16 Oct 1822
CRAIG, James	19/1816	E[a]ssie, Forfar, labourer, AWOL, Saint John, NB, 15 July 1821
DICKSON, Charles	22/1813	Kelso, Roxburgh, shoemaker, died at Halifax, 1 Feb 1825
DOWE, William	15/1812	St. Cuthbert's, Edinburgh, tailor, died, NL, 29 Mar 1819
DUNCAN, Andrew[8]	25/1807	Falkland, Fifeshire, weaver, discharged at Halifax, NS, 24 Aug 1825.
FINLAYSON, John	18/1808	Lochalsh, Ross-shire, labourer, died at Sydney, NS, 29 Aug 1820
GORDON, Sgt. Hugh[9]	22/1807	Heatherton, Ross-shire, labourer, discharged at Halifax, NS, 24 Oct 1819
GOWAN, Robert	13/1811	Watten, Cathness, labourer, discharged at Fredericton, NB, 24 Jan 1819
HOWIE, James	20/1807	Irvine, Ayrshire, weaver, discharged at Saint John, NB, 6 Mar 1819
HUTCHINSON, Ewen	34/1811	Lochmalin [Lochmaben], Dumfries, labourer, discharged at Saint John, NB, 24 Feb 1820
KERR, David	16/1813	Montrose, Forfar, carpenter, AWOL, Saint John, NB, 16 Oct 1819
LAUGHLIN, Edward	17/1816	Kilmarnock, Ayrshire, weaver, AWOL, St. Andrews, NB, 20 Oct 1820
LOCKART, Thomas	17/1815	Kilmarnock, Ayrshire, weaver, drowned in Prince Edward Island, 13 Jan 1820
McCONNELL, John	19/1817	Stranraer, Wigtown, labourer, AWOL, NL, 13 May 1820
McKAY, John	13/1810	Halkirk, Caithness, labourer, discharged at Fredericton, NB, 24 June 1822
McKERCEY, Robert	19/1817	Auchtermuchty, Fife, weaver, discharged at Halifax, NS, 24 July 1824
McLEOD, Donald	17/1808	Kilrush [?], Caithness, labourer, discharged at Saint John, NB, 30 Sep 1821
McLEOD, James	14/1808	Tongue, Sutherland, labourer, discharged at Fredericton, NB, 10 June 1819
McNABB, John	15½/1808	Glasgow, weaver, died at Fredericton, NB, 24 Aug 1818
McPHERSON, John	19/1816	Aberdeen Town, shoemaker, died at Fredericton, NB, 1 Aug 1818
McPHERSON, Hugh[10]	18/1808	Laggan, Inverness, labourer, discharged at Halifax, NS, 24 Oct 1819

---

[8] Duncan was awarded a military pension in Nova Scotia, 13 Apr 1824, and later moved to Prince Edward Island, dying at Charlottetown Royalty in 1861. He married Agnes SHIRLEY and had two sons and several daughters.

[9] He was granted 200 acres (Lot 6) at Wellington Settlement, 2 Dec 1822, and awarded a military pension, 9 May 1823 (Cf., NSARM, RG 20, Series "A": John Mara, 1822).

[10] Sgt. McPherson was granted 200 acres (Lot 7) at Wellington Settlement, 2 Dec 1822, and was awarded a military pension in Nova Scotia, 16 Aug 1825 (Cf., NSARM, RG 20, Series "A": John Mara, 1822).

McQUEEN, Terence	18/1813	Glasgow, labourer, AWOL, Saint John, NB, 11 Feb 1821
McREADY, James	15/1814	Glasgow, Lanark, weaver, died at Halifax, 13 Apr 1824
MALCOM, James[11]	16/1810	Dunnett, Caithness, labourer, discharged at Halifax, NS, 24 Oct 1819
MATHER, David	21/1812	Marykirk, Kincardine, weaver, discharged at Saint John, NB, 26 July 1823
MATHISON, Colin	14/1808	Loch Elsh [Lochalsh], Ross-shire, labourer, discharged at Saint John, NB, 10 Dec 1819
MITCHEL, Alexander	18/1813	Glamis, Forfar, weaver, discharged at Saint John, NB, 22 June 1820
ORR, James	28/1816	Ayr, Ayrshire, weaver, discharged at Saint John, NB, 10 Sep 1819
ROXBURGH, John	18/1816	Kilmarnock, Ayrshire, weaver, died at Saint John, NB, 6 Apr 1823
SINCLAIR, James	22/1800	Cannongate, Edinburgh, weaver, died at Halifax, NS, 19 Nov 1824
SMITH, Alexander	17/1812	St. Cuthbert's, Edinburgh, coach maker, discharged at Saint John, NB, 24 Jan 1821
SMITH, Hugh	13/1808	Troy [Tore?], Inverness-shire, labourer, discharged at Saint John, NB, 24 June 1820
STEWART, Peter	16/1816	Dumfries, Dumfrieshire, labourer, AWOL, Saint John, NB, 8 Oct 1819
STEWART, Samuel	15/1812	West Kirk, Edinburgh, baker, discharged, NL, 24 Dec '22
SUTHERLAND, James[12]	14/1810	Leathern [Latheron], Caithness, weaver, discharged at Saint John, NB, 1 Dec 1821
TAITE, Alexander	17/1813	Enwith, Galloway [Anwoth, Kirdudbrightshire], labourer, discharged at St. Andrews, NB, 11 Aug 1819
THOMSON, James	16/1813	Lasweade [Lasswade], Midlothian, shoemaker, AWOL, Saint John, NB, 12 Nov 1822
THOMSON, Thomas	20/1816	Kelton, Galloway, shoemaker, AWOL, Fredericton, NB, 21 July 1818; returned 26 July 1818
WEBSTER, David	17/1817	Edinburgh, labourer, AWOL, Saint John, NB, 1 Sep 1820
WILLIAMSON, Henry	15/1807	St. Nicholas, Aberdeen, labourer, discharged at Saint John, NB, 2 Apr 1819
WILSON, William	23/1819	Middleby [Middlebie], Dumfries, labourer, AWOL, Saint John, NB, 19 Oct 1818.

ENGLISH-BORN (30 men)

ATKINSON, Thomas	24/1816	Weatherel [Wetheral], Cumberland, no trade stated, AWOL, Fredericton, NB, 8 May 1823
BLACK, John	21/1813	Malmesbury, Wiltshire, mason, discharged at Saint John, NB, 24 Dec 1821

---

[11] Pvte. Malco[l]m was granted 100 acres (Lot 8 North) at Wellington Settlement, 2 Dec 1822 (*Cf.*, NSARM, RG 20, Series "A": John Mara, 1822).

[12] Sutherland was AWOL at Fort Cumberland, NB, 22 to 30 Nov 1820, but returned.

BOOTH, George	21/1816	Frickleton [Freckleton], Lancashire, roper, AWOL, St. Andrews, NB, 20 Oct 1820
BOULTER, Thomas	21/1816	Thrushington [Thrussington], Leicester, shoemaker, discharged at Fredericton, NB, 7 June 1823
BOYLE, John	16/1808	Catham, Rutland [*recte* Kent?], labourer, discharged at Fredericton, NB, 10 June 1819
CROOKS, James	18/1816	Blackburn, Lancashire, weaver, died at Fredericton, NB, 13 May 1820
DEVERDOCK, Peter	15/1812	Carlisle, Cumberland, labourer, discharged at Saint John, NB, 24 Dec 1822
EASTWOOD, Joseph	14/1811	Halifax, Yorkshire, spinner, discharged at Fredericton, NB, 10 June 1819
FOSTER, Henry	15/1813	Chester, labourer, discharged at Halifax, NS, 29 Mar 1825
FOSTER, John	20/1812	Hawkhurst, Kent, labourer, died in NL, 14 Feb 1823
GARNETT, Joseph	18/1813	Bradford, Yorkshire, turner, AWOL, Saint John, NB, 6 July 1821
HAMPSHIRE, Joseph	17/1813	Leeds, Yorkshire, flax dresser, died, Halifax, 17 July 1823
HETHRINGTON, Wm.	21/1813	Alston, Cumberland, miner, discharged at St. Andrews, NB, 24 Oct 1820
HILTON, Jonathan	20/1813	Sculcots [Sculcoates], Yorkshire, weaver, died in NL, 20 July 1821
HOLLAND, John[13]	18/1813	Pontefract, Yorkshire, labourer, discharged at Fredericton, NB, 14 June 1819
JOHNSTON, Benjamin	14/1811	Warrington, Lancashire, labourer, died at Halifax, NS, 23 July 1826; latest date in this record.
LAWTON, Henry	13/1811	Leigh, Lancashire, weaver, AWOL, Saint John, NB, 1 Aug 1821
MOULDER, Joseph	25/1813	Chilton, Bucks, labourer, discharged at Fredericton, NB, 2 Apr 1820
MOUNTAIN, James	25/1813	Fenton, Yorkshire, cropper, discharged at Saint John, NB, 24 Dec 1820
PATTISON, Joseph	13/1810	Nesson [Neston], Cheshire, weaver, AWOL, St. Andrews, NB, 13 June 1820
PERKINS, John	23/1813	Droxford, Hants, labourer, discharged at Fredericton, NB, 26 June 1819
PHILLIPS, Isaac	16/1813	Birmingham, edge-tool maker, died Halifax, 12 Nov 1825.
RABBIE, Richard	23/1813	Stainfleet [Stainforth?], Yorkshire, labourer, discharged at Saint John, NB, 24 Dec 1820
ROBINSON, William	19/1813	Hythe, Kent, weaver, discharged at Fredericton, NB, 24 Dec 1820
ROBSON, John	15/1813	Farlem [Farlam], Cumberland, labourer, died in NL, 3 Dec 1819

---

[13] Holland, his wife and a child lived on lot 39 South, Dalhousie Settlement, on 16 Oct 1820 (W. A. Calnek, *History of the County of Annapolis,* 263).

TAYLOR, John	18/1811	Upholland, Lancashire, labourer, transferred to the NL Garrison Company, 25 May 1826.
THOMSON, Thomas	25/1813	Rawden [Rawdon], Yorkshire, weaver, discharged in Cape Breton, 24 Dec 1820
WALL, George	31/1813	Ombresby [Ombersley], Worcester, baker, discharged in Fredericton, NB, 10 June 1819
WALSH, John[14]	19/1812	Wighel [?], Hereford, labourer, discharged at Halifax, NS, 24 Oct 1819
WILLEY, James	20/1813	Leeds, Yorkshire, shoemaker, died at Halifax, NS, 5 Apr 1825

(Source: W.O. 25, Vols. 482, 484 [NAC mfm. B5477, 5478].)

C) THE 52nd REGIMENT, 1823 - 1830

The 52nd Regiment of Foot, or Oxfordshire Light Infantry, was based in the Maritimes from 1823 until 1831, so that its depot description books extracted here cover almost the entire period. One hundred and six men left the strength of this unit during the seven years between 18 June 1823 and 11 September 1830. One took his discharge in Dublin, Ireland, and seven left at unspecified locations. Forty-six members of the Oxfordshires were English, though only two of them were born in the county for which the unit was named. There were five Welshmen, two Scots, and - the reason for which all of them have been listed here - fifty-three were Irishmen.

Among the soldier's occupations and trades in civilian life we notice, in descending order: labourer (74), cordwainer (5), tailor and weaver (4 each), boatman, butcher and nailer (2 each). Single representatives account for the remainder: baker, blacksmith, brazier, carpenter, caster, coach maker, dyer, fustian cutter, gardener, hawker, locksmith, mason, and sword cutler.

Of the 106 men listed below, 57 died, 32 "ran" (deserted), 10 were discharged. Seven men's departure is not stated, though all figure in civilian records at Halifax. Apart from those and the man discharged in Dublin, we have a balance of 98, of whom 61 were delisted in Nova Scotia (57 at Halifax, 3 at Annapolis, and one in Cape Breton), and 37 in New Brunswick (Saint John 17, Fredericton 12, St. Andrews 5, Miramichi 3). Desertion, or going AWOL, was mostly a solitary affair, but in five instances a man "ran" with a companion from the same unit. Climate played a role, as well, all but five of the desertions occurred in the warmer months between mid-April and mid-October. In the five exceptional cases, the men left from posts near enough to the United States border that they could hope to find safety before winter closed in. No one deserted from mid-December until mid-April, quite a comment on a Maritime winter!

---

[14] Pvte. Walsh was granted 100 acres (Lot 9 North) at Wellington Settlement, 2 Dec 1822 (NSARM, RG 20, Series "A": John Mara, 1822). He and his wife Susanna COSTELLO had a dau., Susanna, baptised 29 June 1822, buried 14 Sep 1823 (Halifax Catholic records).

IRISH-BORN (53 men)

BARKER, John	14/1823	Moneymore, Derry, gardener, discharged at Halifax, NS, 12 Jan 1830 "for being an incorrigible Vagabond".
BATTERSBY, Nicholas	20/1822	St. James, Dublin, labourer, AWOL, St. Andrews, NB, 28 Apr 1825
BRISNAHEN, John	24/1819	Herbertstown, Armagh, labourer, died at St. Andrews, 24 May 1824
BROWNE, Charles	15½/1822	Cashel, Tipperary, labourer, died Halifax, 11 Jan 1827
BRYAN, Michael	20/1821	Croom, Limerick, labourer, died Halifax, 8 Sep 1828
BUTLER, James[15]	18/1822	Annacarty, Tipperary, labourer, died Halifax, 5 Apr 1829
CAHILL, Cornelius	19/1822	Fethard, Tipperary, tailor, AWOL, Fredericton, 1 June 1824
CAVANAGH, James	20/1809	Iniskeen [Enniskeen], Cavan, baker, died at Annapolis, NS, 2 Sep 1829
CLINTON, Joseph[16]	21/1816	Termangan [Termonamongan], Tyrone, labourer, died at Halifax, NS, 1 Oct 1825
COFFILL, Farrell[17]	19/1809	Kilcloney [Kilcloony], Galway, nailer [nothing more]
COFFWELL, Patrick[18]	22/1809	Kilcloney [Kilcloony], Galway, labourer [nothing more]
COLCLOUGH, Samuel[19]	18/1821	Ennis, Clare, labourer, AWOL, Halifax, 28 May 1829
COLLINGS, Dennis[20]	15/1810	Tullough [Tullagh], Cork, labourer, died at Saint John, NB 18 July 1825
COLLINGS, Dennis	16/1810	Abershady [Aberstrowry], Cork, labourer, died at Halifax, NS, 11 Aug 1830

---

[15] Buried 8 Apr 1829, Pvte. James Butler, age 25, from Golden, Tipperary. Golden is the Catholic parish several miles south of Annacarty.

[16] Clinton was promoted to Corporal 12 Sep 1821, and to Sgt. on 6 June 1822.

[17] Farrell, baptised 24 Sep 1826, age 7 days, son of Farrell & Mary (Coles) Coffill; and Andrew, baptised 17 Jan 1832, son of Farrell & Mary (Cole) CAULFIELD (Halifax Catholic records). He was awarded a military pension in Nova Scotia, 14 Dec 1831.

[18] Michael, baptised 11 June 1827, buried 18 June 1827, age 3 yrs., son of Pvte. Patrick & Bridget (Murry) CAWLFIELD; and Anne, baptised 29 Nov 1829, dau. of Patrick & Bridget (Murry) Cawlfield (Halifax Catholic records). From 25 Aug 1815 to 30 Jan 1819 Patrick had been a corporal. He was awarded a military pension in Nova Scotia, 14 Dec 1831.

[19] Colclough deserted at the same time as John Farley (infra). Married 10 July 1828 were Samuel, son of John & Mary Colclough, and Marian, dau. of Pierce & Elizabeth (Dunn) Power (Halifax Catholic records).

[20] He was wounded severely in his right thigh, 15 Jan 1812 [Battle of Ciudad Rodrigo]

CONNOLLY, Michael 29/1823   Rathkeale, Limerick, tailor, discharged at Halifax, NS,
                               31 Oct 1825

CONNOR, Martin   18/1806   Stradbally, Leix, labourer, died at Halifax, NS,
                                 15 Aug 1828; corporal in 1810-1811

CORBIT, Cpl. Thomas[21]   17½/1822   Clon[o]ulty, Tipperary, tailor, died at Halifax, 21 Dec 1829

FARLEY, John[22]   17½/1821   Clonmel, Tipperary, labourer, AWOL, Halifax, NS,
                                 28 May 1829

GILLIVAN, John[23]   20/1804   Mullingar, Westmeath, labourer, died Halifax, 20 Aug 1825

GREEN, Robert   ../1825   Geashill, Offaly, labourer, AWOL, Halifax, 2 Nov 1827

HICKEY, Sgt. Patrick   17/1822   Clonmel, Tipperary, labourer, AWOL, Halifax, NS,
                                       25 Aug 1830; Sgt. from 1828

HIGGERTY, Thomas   24/1812   Tullought [Tullagh], Cork, cordwainer, died at Halifax,
                                   NS, 22 July 1828

HUGHES, John   26/1819   All Saints, Limerick, labourer, died at Saint John, NB,
                               9 Feb 1825

HUNT, John   18/1816   Tebohim [Tibohine], Roscommon, labourer, died at
                             Halifax, NS, 5 Dec 1827

KEEGAN, Patrick   20/1822   Killan[n]y, Louth, cordwainer, AWOL, Halifax, NS,
                                  12 Oct 1829

KELLY, John[24]   20/1816   Bally Brechon [Ballybroghan], Roscommon, labourer
                                  [nothing more]

LAMB, John   22/1822   Cloongess [Clongash], Longford, labourer, died in Cape
                             Breton, NS, 18 Oct 1828

LAWLESS, Patrick   18/1815   Augdown [perhaps Annaghdown?], Galway, carpenter,
                                   AWOL, 28 May 1824

LAYDEN, Patrick   20/1810   Kilmackapenny [Kilmactranny], Sligo, labourer, died at
                                  Saint John, NB, 23 Sep 1824

McCARDLE, John[25]   19/1810   Killoney [Killeany], Galway, labourer [nothing more]

---

[21] Buried 22 Dec 1829, Pvte. Thomas CORBET, age 25 (Halifax Catholic records).

[22] Farley deserted with Colclough (*supra*). Farley had been promoted Sgt., 1 Jan 1824.

[23] Gillivan was promoted from Cpl. in 1805, and Sgt. in 1806. He was AWOL at Canterbury, England, from 11 to 28 Nov 1815. Sgt. again from 28 Nov1815 to 1819.

[24] Kelly made Cpl., 4 Oct 1822, and Sgt., 25 June 1825. Buried 11 Sep 1826, William, 16 mos., son of Sgt. John & Anne (Reed) Kelly. The boy died en route from Saint John, NB, to Halifax. Buried 8 Oct 1827, Catherine, 5 mos., dau of Sgt. John & Anne (O'Donnell) Kelly (Halifax Catholic records). No explanation for the different maiden name of the wife was given, though possibly he married her as a widow and one entry called her by her former married name.

[25] McCardle was a Sgt. from 1813; Quarter-Master Sgt., 1 Jan 1824 Buried 6 Mar 1827, Matilda, 3 mos, 8 days, dau of QM Sgt. John & Mary (Malone) McCARDELL (Halifax RC record)

McGREW, John	22/1808	Kilgavan [Kilgefin], Roscommon, tailor, died at Fredericton, NB, 13 June 1824
McLANE, James[26]	23½/1812	Inniscorthy [St. Mary's, Enniscorthy], Wexford, nailer, discharged at Dublin, Ireland, 18 June 1823
MACHRY, Patrick	19/1822	Clonargood, Carlow, labourer, AWOL, Saint John, NB, 24 Aug 1824
MADINE, John	17/1822	Downpatrick, Down, butcher, AWOL, Saint John, NB, 9 May 1824
MAHER, Simon[27]	18/1816	Grogan, Leix, labourer, AWOL, Fredericton, 18 June 1824.
MALONEY, Patrick[28]	17/1811	Kilalerton [Killallaghten], Galway, labourer, died at Halifax, NS, 3 Dec 1826
MEARES, John	22/1822	Shaghill [Shankill], Roscommon, labourer, discharged at Halifax, NS, 8 Dec 1829
MOONEY, Michael	18/1822	Thurles, Tipperary, labourer, AWOL, Saint John, NB, 16 Nov 1824
MURNAN, Patrick	19/1822	Lat[t]in, Tipperary, labourer, AWOL, Saint John, NB, 14 May 1825
MURPHY, Patrick	20/1812	Tockmacconnel [Taghmaconnell], Roscommon, labourer, died at Fredericton, NB, 4 Aug 1824
O'GRADY, Dominick	23/1822	Kilfree, Sligo, labourer, AWOL, Saint John, 15 Nov 1824
O'NEILL, John[29]	20/1827	S[e]agoe, Armagh, weaver, AWOL, Halifax, 19 May 1830
O'REILY, Patrick	17/1822	Thurles, Tipperary, labourer, drowned at Fredericton, NB, 12 July 1826
POWER, John[30]	20/1825	Killenaule, Tipperary, mason, died at Halifax, NS, 30 Nov 1825
PROUDE, Thomas[31]	19/1822	Dundrum, Tipperary, labourer, AWOL, Halifax, NS, 9 July 1828

---

[26] McLane was wounded in Nov 1813 [Battle of the Nivelle] and was discharged due to rheumatism and ill health. This is the earliest date in this record. The unit had reached New Brunswick by late August, McLane apparently having been discharged just prior to embarkation.

[27] He deserted at the same time as John Taylor (*infra*).

[28] Buried 4 Dec 1826, Pvte, Patrick MALOWNEY, age 32, of Roscommon Town (Halifax Catholic records). The military record, having been made when the man was there to answer for himself, is more likely to be correct.

[29] O'Neill went AWOL at the same time as Edward Davey(*infra*).

[30] Buried 21 Sep 1826, Elizabeth, 12 mos., dau of Pvte. John & Anastasia (Dillon) Power (Halifax Catholic records).

[31] Proude went AWOL at the same time as John Sullivan (*infra*).

QUINLAN, Patrick[32]   18/1816   St. John's, Sligo, labourer [nothing more]

QUISHON, James[33]   18/1823   St. Mary's, Clonmel, Tipperary, labourer, died at
                                      Halifax, NS, 26 Dec 1828

RIELLY, Patrick   18/1824   Legin, Longford, labourer, died at Halifax, NS,
                                      30 Apr 1829

SHEEHAN, Michael   20/1822   Ballybricken, Waterford, labourer, AWOL, Saint John,
                                      NB, 17 Apr 1825, while on furlough

SIMMONS, John[34]   18/1822   Derat[c]reat, Tyrone, labourer, AWOL, St. Andrews, NB,
                                      13 Dec 1825

SULLIVAN, Cpl. John[35]   16/1823   Madalagan [Modelligo], Waterford, labourer, AWOL,
                                      Halifax, NS, 9 July 1828

TOBIN, John   17/1822   St. Mary's [Clonmel], Tipperary, cordwainer, died at
                                      Annapolis, NS, 18 Jan 1829

WOODS, Patrick   21/1823   Mullinahone, Tipperary, weaver, died at Fredericton, NB,
                                      22 May 1826

WELSH-BORN (5 men)

BOWENS, Isaac   20/1818   Jefferston [Jeffreyston], Pembroke, labourer, AWOL,
                                      Fredericton, NB, 30 May 1825

EVANS, John   24/1819   Gillsfield, Montgomery, labourer, AWOL, Saint John, NB,
                                      22 Aug 1823

OWENS, Hugh   24/1812   Beaumaris, Anglesey, labourer, died at Halifax, NS,
                                      9 Aug 1827

ROBERTS, John   26/1812   Workinsagh, Anglesey, cordwainer, died at Halifax, NS,
                                      3 Apr 1827

WILLIAMS, David   18/1809   Bangor, Caernarvon, labourer, died at Halifax, NS,
                                      3 Sep 1830

SCOTS-BORN (2 men)

KELLY, William   26½/1811   Gatehouse, Galloway, hawker, died at Saint John, NB,
                                      27 Dec 1824

SHAW, James   18/1820   Duddingston, Midlothian, labourer, died at Halifax, NS,
                                      30 Aug 1826

---

[32] Buried 17 Aug 1827, Alicia, 3 yrs. 8 mos. 18 days, dau of Sgt. Patrick & Mary (Dane) Quinlan; buried 25 May 1828, Mary Ann, 10 mos., dau of same (Halifax Catholic record).

[33] Quishon is an error for Cushen. James Cushen, age 25, from Clonmel, was buried 28 Dec 1828 (Halifax Catholic records).

[34] Simmons went AWOL at the same time as Sampson Rushton (*infra*).

[35] Sullivan went AWOL at the same time as Thomas Proude (*supra*). Sullivan made Corporal in 1826.

ENGLISH-BORN (46 men)

ADAMS, William	19/1828	Alfriston, Essex, labourer, died at Halifax, NS, 15 Nov 1829
ALDRIDGE, Thomas	22/1814	St. Laurence Walthen [Waltham St. Lawrence], Berks., labourer, died at Fredericton, NB, 9 Sep 1823
AMER, Richard	15/1813	Pursey [Pewsey], Wilts., labourer, died at Halifax, NS, 11 Mar 1827
BALDWIN, Samuel	18/1820	Willington, Derby, boatman, died at Halifax, 14 Aug 1827
BARNES, Martin	20/1820	Spilsby, Lincs., labourer, discharged at Halifax, NS, 24 Feb 1828
BONE, John[36]	18/1814	Ropley, Hants, blacksmith [nothing more]
BOWYER, David	16/1813	Wednesbury, Staffs., caster, died at Halifax, 18 July 1830
BOYE, Joseph	17/1804	Wantage, Berks., labourer, died at Miramichi, NB, 20 May 1826
BUSBY, William[37]	16/1826	Broadwell, Warwick, labourer, AWOL, Halifax, NS, 24 July 1829
CLISBY, William	27/1809	Grays [?], Oxon., labourer, died at Fredericton, 16 May 1824
CROSS, William	17/1813	Bawkham [?], Devon, labourer, died at Halifax, 7 Oct 1827
DAVEY, Edward[38]	17/1826	Rodmill [Rodmell], Sussex, labourer, AWOL, Halifax, NS, 19 May 1830
DAWSON, James	18/1812	Openshoe [Openshaw], Lancs., cotton dyer, died at Halifax, NS, 7 July 1827
DEAN, James	19/1812	Tourvey [Turvey], Bedford, labourer, died at Saint John, NB, 5 Sep 1823
DELICATE, William[39]	20/1810	As[h]ton under Lyme, Lancs., weaver, discharged at Halifax, NS, 8 Apr 1829, to become Town Sgt. of Halifax.
EDGINTON, William	17/1826	Woodstock, Oxon., labourer, discharged at Halifax, NS, 8 Dec 1829
GARSIDE, James	21/1812	Rochdale, Lancs., weaver, died at Halifax, NS, 13 Dec 1829
GRIFFITHS, Robert	30/1812	Aston, Warwick, sword cutler, died at Saint John, NB, 24 Jan 1825
HARRIS, Henry	14/1818	Cheriton, Kent, labourer, AWOL, Halifax, NS, 23 Aug 1829
HARVEY, John	19/1826	Cheltenham, Glos., labourer, died at Halifax, 14 Sep 1829
HATCHARD, Richard	29/1815	Stackpole, Kent, labourer, died at Annapolis, 17 May 1824
HAWES, Sgt. James	23/1813	Oakley, Bucks., labourer, died at Halifax, 23 Feb 1828

---

[36] Buried 12 Sep 1828, Marian, 4 mos., dau of John & Elizabeth (Bennett) Bone (Halifax Catholic records). Married 28 July 1827 Pvte. John Bane, and Elizabeth Bennett (St. Paul's Anglican, Halifax).

[37] Married 24 Mar 1829, Pvte. William Busby, and Susannah Cross (St. Paul's Anglican, Halifax).

[38] Davey went AWOL at the same time as John O'Neill (*supra*).

[39] Delicate made Corporal, 25 Jan 1812, and Sgt., 25 Oct 1815.

HOLLAND, George   17/1822   Sto[w]e, Staffs., coach maker, discharged at Halifax, NS,
                                22 Mar 1828

HYDE, William   23/1820   Cunsbury [Queensbury], York, labourer, discharged at
                                Halifax, NS, 24 Feb 1828

JOHNSON, Abram[40]   15/1808   Ware, Hants, labourer; regimental bugler [nothing more]

KEELING, Joseph   18/1819   Barton, Staffs., labourer, AWOL, Fredericton, 18 Nov 1825

LETCHER, Joseph   20/1813   Broadwater, Sussex, labourer, died at Halifax, NS,
                                11 Sep 1830 [latest date in this record].

LIDGET, John   18/1821   Normanby, Lincs., labourer, AWOL, Fredericton, NB,
                                22 May 1826

LOMAS, James[41]   28/1809   Manchester, fustian cutter, died at Halifax, NS, 26 Sep 1827

LOWANDS, Thomas   21/1813   Nantwich, Cheshire, cordwainer, died at Halifax, 28 May 1827

MILLER, Charles   20½/1814   East Grinstead, Sussex, labourer, died at Halifax, NS,
                                26 Feb 1830

MINNIS, Andrew   17/1822   St. Michael's, Staffs., labourer, AWOL, Halifax, NS,
                                22 July 1828

NORTON, William   17/1814   East Peckham, Kent, labourer, died at Halifax, 27 May 1830

OAKES, James   21/1813   Ramsey, Hants, labourer, died at Miramichi, NB,
                                24 Jan 1826

PARKER, Benjamin[42] 26/1815   Harwich, Essex, brazier, AWOL, Halifax, NS, 3 July 1828

PARRINGTON, Thomas 20/1813   Upham, Hants, labourer, drowned at Saint John, NB,
                                18 Apr 1824

PHEASANT, Edward   16/1812   Shenstone, Staffs., labourer, discharged at Halifax, NS,
                                24 Jan 1827

RAWTHAN, John   20/1813   Wharton, Northampton, boatman, died at Saint John, NB,
                                6 June 1824

RICHARDSON, Henry 16/1823   Rudgley [Rugely], Staffs., butcher, died at Saint John, NB,
                                2 Sep 1823

RUSHTON, Sampson[43]18/1823   Newbury [Newborough], Staffs., labourer, AWOL, St.
                                Andrews, NB, 13 Dec 1825

SIMMONDS, James   14/1810   Hinton, Warwick,[44] labourer, died at Halifax, NS,
                                3 Mar 1830

---

[40] Buried 10 Oct 1826, Rosilla, 27, wife of Pvte. Bugler Abram JONSSON; buried 30 Dec 1826, Frances, 18 mos., dau of Abraham & Rosanna (Currie) JOHNSON (Halifax Catholic records).

[41] Lomas had been a Sgt., 1807-1809, but a Cpl. in 1815-1817.

[42] Parker had previously been AWOL, 24 July to 1 August 1824.

[43] Rushton deserted at the same time as John Simmons (*supra*).

[44] There were several Hintons in England, but none of them was in Warwickshire.

TAYLOR, John[45]   19/1815   Piton [Potton], Beds., labourer, AWOL, Fredericton, NB,
                                                    18 June 1824

THOMASON, Thomas 21/1812   Wolverhampton, Staffs., stock lockmaker, died at Miramichi,
                                                    NB, 27 Mar 1826

TIBBETT, James[46]   16/1816   Fenstanton, Hunts., labourer, AWOL, Halifax, NS,
                                                    26 June 1828

WALL, William   21/1813   Brockhurst, Hants [*recte* Essex], labourer, AWOL, Saint
                                                    John, NB, 16 July 1826

WASSELL, John   21/1813   Bishop's Waltham, Hants, labourer, died at Halifax, NS,
                                                    19 July 1830

(Source: W.O. 25, Vol. 411 [NAC mfm. B5458].)

19 - TOWNSHIP BOOK, LIVERPOOL, N. S.: IRISH MARRIED, 1779 - 1833

New England Planters formed several settlements in Nova Scotia between 1759 and 1775. One of the more important on the Atlantic seaboard was Liverpool, capital of Queens County. During the first century of Liverpool's existence a town clerk continued the New England practice of recording births, deaths and marriages. The full record may be consulted at the Nova Scotia Archives and Records Management in Halifax (MG 4, Volume 180). Nine weddings of Irish people have been noticed, all but one from the period between 1779 and 1802.

22 Oct 1779: Robert, son of Robert & Elizabeth DICKSON, Markethill, Armagh[47], to Persis, dau of Thomas & Amey PEIRCE; widow of George GIFFIN, Liverpool

4 May 1781: Michael McGOWEN, Ireland[48], to Mary, dau of Samuel & Mary DOLIVER; widow of Angus CHISHOLM, NS

19 Jan 1785: Patrick, son of Patrick & Eloner DORAN, Waterford[49] to Desire, dau of William & Elizabeth CAHOON; widow of Samuel MACK

[45] Taylor deserted at the same time as Simon Maher (*supra*).

[46] Tibbett had previously been AWOL at Fredericton, NB, from July to September 1826.

[47] Robert Dickson was a sergeant in the King's Orange Rangers, a Loyalist unit during the American Revolution. A man of this name received a land grant at Digby, NS, in 1784.

[48] His wife was the widow of Angus Chisholm, a native of Scotland, who drowned at Port Medway, NS, 12 Apr 1779. McGowen was the cook in a privateering vessel in 1799/1800.

[49] Doran was born 6 Nov 1757 and died 17 Nov 1818. He was a ship master and Justice of the Peace, resident near Port Medway, NS. His wife's first husband, Samuel Mack, died 10 Oct 1783, at Mill Village, NS, age 46.

9 Sep 1787: Edward **SMITH**, surgeon, late of Ireland [50], to
    Maria **POTTER**, of NS.

13 Oct 1795: Patrick, son of James & Margaret **KNOWLAND**, Old Ross, Wexford, to Rhoda
    FITZPATRICK, widow; dau of Thomas & Susanna **PATTERSON**.

13 Oct 1796: Patrick, son of Morris & Catherine **CONNEL**, Lismore, Waterford, to
    Mary, dau of John & Elizabeth **PEACH**, of NS.

2 Nov 1802: Henry, son of John & Alice **NEILL**, Kilkenny, to
    Mary, dau of James & Rebeckah **PARKE**, Lunenburg County, NS

5 Dec 1802: John, son of Matthew & Elizabeth **POWER**, Waterford, to Susannah,
    dau of Benajah & Susannah **COLLINS**; widow of James **TAYLOR** [51]

21 May 1833: John, son of Cormac & Margaret **CARTEN**, Newtown Limavady, Derry, to Martha
    Elisabeth, dau of Andrew & Ann **WEBSTER**, of NS.

20 - TRANSFERS FROM THE IRISH BRIGADE TO THE ROYAL NOVA SCOTIA REGIMENT, 1798

During the lengthy wars with France during and after the French Revolution, the British Army underwent several changes. Developments included the transfer of men from the Sixth Regiment of the Irish Brigade into other units. One such change is noted in **W.O. 12/10818.** Seven non-comms. were sent to the Royal Nova Scotia Regiment on 2 June 1798, with a further draft of three non-comms. and twenty-four men on 24 June 1798.

2 June 1798: Sgts. Thomas DENNISON[52], John MILES[53], Lawrence POWER, and Robert
            STAPLETON, Cpls. Michael BURKE, John COUNLY, and James MURTOUGH.
28 June 1798: Sgts. Daniel McHENRY and James McVEIGH[54]; and Cpl. Michael KEARNEY.

----

[50] Smith had served in Tarleton's Legion against the American Revolution, and had a land grant at Port Mouton, NS, in 1784.

[51] James A. Taylor, who died 15 Jan 1801, age 30, was a Member of the NS Assembly.

[52] Sgt. Thomas Dennison had a warrant to survey a land grant of 200 acres at "Miray [Mira] River", Cape Breton, in 1807.

[53] Sgt. John Miles married 5 November 1822 at St. Paul's Church, Halifax, Mary MASSIE, widow. Her previous marriage to Sgt. Alexander MASSEY, on 7 August 1817 at St. Paul's Church, refers to her as Mary REILLY, widow, so she was married at least thrice.

[54] James McVeigh, or McVEA, married 14 November 1807 at St. Matthew's Presbyterian Church, Halifax, Sarah BALCOM. Three children of this couple were baptised at that church: Duncan, 13 June 1809; Mary Ann, 17 October 1811; and Sarah, 28 November 1814.

Pvtes. James APPLEBY, John BUTLER, Terence CLARKE, Richard COSTELLO, Patrick CURRAN, Patrick DWYER 1st, Kerns FARRELL, Patrick FLINN, Dennis FOWLER, Patrick GILLENY, Philip HINSEY (HENNESSY), Saunders JERVIS [55], Richard McCABE, John McEVATT (or M'EVITT), Timothy MAHONY, John MANNING, John MONTGOMERY, James MULANIX, William QUINN, and Thomas SMITH (or SMYTH). Drummers Michael DWYER, Richard FULLUM, Joseph REILLY, and Campbell SHERIDAN.

Andrew CREAGH, who eventually rose to Colonel, married 20 December 1804 at St. Paul's, Mary (1786-1835), daughter of Irish born Dr. Michael HEAD. Col. Creagh died 4 February 1845. He commanded the 81st. Regiment of Foot at Halifax from 1822 to 1826. His only daughter, Jean Elizabeth, married on 6 August 1831 Major G. V. Creagh, and died at Boulogne, France, on 26 June 1834.

21 - IRISH IMMIGRANT WEDDINGS AT ST. PETER'S CATHOLIC CHURCH, HALIFAX, NS, 1809 - 1820

Marriage records of Irish immigrants at this church for the years 1800 to 1845 were published from 1974 to 1977 in Terrence M. Punch, "Some Irish Immigrant Weddings in Nova Scotia," which appeared in six instalments in *The Irish Ancestor*, volumes 6 - 9. Eight further weddings have been found in these registers since the publication of those articles.

28 July 1809: Richard, son of Patrick & Mary (SHORTLE) **WALSH**, Co. Kilkenny; to
          Dorothy, dau.of John & Elizabeth (MAZIN) **FLIEGER**, Dasing, High Germany.[56]

29 July 1810: John, son of Walter & Mary (QUIN) **PAREL**, Co. Wexford; to
          Anne, dau. of William & Mary (McGRELLY) **GRANDY**, Sydney, Cape Breton.

21 Aug 1810: William, son of Bryan & Eloner (FARRELL) **CONRAHY**, Co. Cork; to
          Mary, dau. of James & Elizabeth (COWIE) **BOWEN**, Jeddore, NS.[57]

14 Nov 1810: Alexander, son of John & Jane (BURKE) **MANSFIELD**, Waterford; to
          Margaret, dau. of John & Mary (FLEET) **KING**, Lunenburg, NS.

---

[55] Pvte. Saunders Jarvis sought a land grant in October 1812. His petition states that he was born in England in 1774, had enlisted in the Irish Brigade and came with them to Nova Scotia, and settled there upon reduction of the brigade. He had a wife and child, and was recommended for 250 acres at Musquodoboit, Nova Scotia.

[56] Dasing is a small town just east of Augsburg, in Bavaria. Danzig is also a possibility.

[57] Both the groom and the witness, Martin Conrahy, signed "Conroy".

28 Aug 1817: Robert **BENNETT**, Kilmurray, Co. Wicklow; to
       Mary DOUL [**DOYLE**], Rossbarracum [Rosbercon], Kilkenny.

24 Sep 1819: Daniel **DREW**, Ireland [Co. Cork]; to Mary **BURNS** from Ireland.

6 Nov 1819: James **FREEMAN**, Kildare [Parish of St. Michael, Athy]; to
       Mary, dau. of John & Mary (WISDOM) **MARR**, Halifax, NS.[58]

6 May 1820: Lawrence, son of John & Mary (CASEY) **GRIFFIN**, Co. Tipperary; to
       Mary, dau. of John & Jennet (BEVERAGE) **COOKE**, Fifeshire, Scotland.

22 - IRISH PEOPLE MARRIED IN NEWFOUNDLAND, 1793-1828

Early Catholic registers provide the Irish origins of 174 couples. Wexford, Waterford, Kilkenny and Tipperary were the major sources of these settlers in the Avalon Peninsula and eastern Newfoundland. Here I have departed from my practice of supplying additions and corrections within square brackets [ ]. The reason for doing so is that the spellings of personal names and the geographical descriptions are so defective that it would nearly double the length of the compilation to include the original versions with their corrections. Only where I do not understand the intent of the originals will the reader find [?] after a word.

1793
  2 Apr.: Garret NEAGLE (Carrick, Waterford)/ Mary MICHELLE (St John's, NL)
  7 Apr.: Edmond HEALEY (Kilmacow, Kilkenny)/ Mary SEXTON (St John's, NL)
  9 Apr.: Richard QUAYS [KEYS] (Thomastown, Kilkenny)/ Mary NEILL (Carrick-on-Suir)
 13 Apr.: John HAUGHTON (Thomastown, Kilkenny)/ Mary RYAN (St John's, NL)
 11 Oct.: Thomas PENDERGAST (Suttons, Wexford)/ Mary KEEF (Toad's Cove, NL)
  5 Nov.: Patrick FLANNERY (Stradbally, Waterford)/ Bridget CULLETON (Suttons, Wexford)
  5 Nov.: Thomas MADDEN (Ballyneill, Kilmurry, Tipperary)/ Mary PHELAN (St John's, NL)
 11 Nov.: Edmund SLATTERY (Clonmel, Tipp.)/Anastasia DEVERIX alias WALSH (Waterford)
 11 Nov.: Sylvester TEE (Ross, Wexford)/ Margaret DINN (Toad's Cove, NL)
 17 Nov.: Michael POWER (Tintern, Wexford)/ Mary BRIEN (St John's, NL)
 23 Nov.: Maurice TOBIN (Cappoquin, Waterford)/ Margaret WALSH (St John's, NL)
1797
  3 Jan.: Patrick WALSH (Diocese of Cashel)/ Margaret MURPHY (Co. Waterford)
 17 Jan.: John BUTLER (Cashel, Tipperary)/ Sarah WILLIAMS (Crumarden) [?]
  9 Oct.: George DOHERTY (Suttons, Wexford)/ Catherine CONNORS (St. John's, NL)
  9 Oct.: Patrick WALSH (Mooncoin, Kilkenny)/ . . . . KENNA (Petty Harbour, NL)
 16 Oct.: Simon CLEARY (Nash, Owenduff, Wexford)/ Sarah MURREN (Quidi Vidi, NL)
 29 Oct.: William MOREY (Passage, Waterford)/ Hanora MUDGE, Port de Grave, NL

---

[58] Mary Marr became a Roman Catholic on the day of the marriage. She had been baptised on 8 June 1800 at St. Paul's Anglican Church in Halifax. Her father was Captain Marr.

3 Nov.: John BROWN (Tintern Wexford)/ Catherine MURPHY (St. John's, NL)

3 Nov.: Lawrence MURPHY (Wexford Town)/ Ann PIKE (St. John's, NL)

13 Nov.: Thomas O'DONNELL (Fethard, Tipperary)/ Mary BARRETT (St. John's, NL)

20 Nov.: Dennis KEEFE (Thomastown, Kilkenny)/ Mary MORISEY (St. John's, NL)

26 Nov.: Michael McNAMARA (Waterford City)/ Mary FORRISTAL (Harbour Grace, NL)

27 Nov.: William MOCKLER (Cashel, Tipperary)/ Mary 'Dolly' BRIEN (Bay Bulls, NL)

1 Dec.: Patrick POWER (Kilrossanty, Waterford)/ Mary SHANAHAN (St. John's, NL)

27 Dec.: John KERWICK (Moycarky, Tipperary)/ Joanna POWER (St. John's, NL)

27 Dec.: James MURPHY (Co. Wicklow)/ Bridget CONWAY (Bay Bulls, NL)

1798

22 Jan.: Andrew KEHOE (Suttons, Wexford)/ Anna BRIEN (St. John's, NL)

12 Feb.: Michael FARREL (Thomastown, Tipperary)/ Mary CAREY (Kilanallison[?], Tipperary)

13 Feb.: Thomas DOYLE (Enniscorthy, Wexford/ Elizabeth BRIEN (St. John's, NL)

15 Feb.: James POWER (Waterford)/ Margaret HAMHILL (St. John's, NL)

17 Feb.: Cornelius QUIRK (Kilcash, Tipperary)/ Margaret DENORY (St. John's, NL)

18 Feb.: John MURRAY (Ross, Wexford)/ Ellen MADDOCK (St. John's, NL)

20 Mar.: James TYLER (Fennor, Islandikane, Waterford)/ Mary BRIEN alias CAMPBELL (St J.)

8 Apr.: Michael MURPHY (Co. Wexford)/ Mary PENDERGAST (St. John's, NL)

20 June: Hugh DORAN (Thomastown, Kilkenny)/ Isabella MURPHY (St. John's, NL)

6 Aug.: Michael CUTHBERT (Knockboy, Co. Waterford)/ Elizabeth LANE (Fermeuse)

20 Nov.: Francis HENESY (Taghmon, Wexford)/ Honora WITHFORTH (Shandon, Cork City)

2- Nov.: Lawrence MURPHY (Wexford)/ Ann PIKE (St. John's, NL)

17 Dec.: Owen KELLY (Ballybrack, Waterford)/ Esther CASEY (Conception Bay, NL)

31 Dec.: William CLANCY (Kilcash, Tipperary)/ Martha KEATING (Harbour Main, NL)

1799

3 Jan.: William KENNEDY (Waterford City)/ Bridget SHEA (St. John's, NL)

5 Feb.: Stephen MADDOCK (Carrick-on-Suir)/ Mary MARSHALL (St. John's, NL)

9 Oct.: John GIBBS (Faha, Waterford)/ Judith JORDAN (Brigus, NL)

29 Dec.: Thomas DOWER (Carrick-on-Suir)/ Elizabeth CONNELLY (Ferryland)

1800

24 Nov.: Paul MACABOY (Ross, Wexford)/ Mary MIDDLETON (Bay Bulls, NL)

1801

3 Feb.: Robert DOOLING (Ross, Wexford)/ Mary MACKEY (Brigus, NL)

1802

29 Nov.: William RICHARDS (Ross, Wexford)/ Mary MACKEY (Brigus, NL)

1803

10 Aug.: Thomas SULLIVAN (Clonmel, Tipperary)/ Catherine AYLWARD (Keels, NL)

1804

10 May: Michael RYAN (Carrick-on-Suir)/ Anne McCARTHY alias RYAN (Waterford City)

18 Oct.: John MURRAY (Middleton, Cork)/ Mary PETERSON (Ferryland)

1805

1 Jan.: Patrick DELANEY (Inistioge, Kilkenny)/ Elizabeth KENNEDY (Harbour Main, NL)

22 Oct.: Martin NEAL (Faha, Waterford)/ Anne CAREW (Witless Bay, NL)

23 Oct.: Martin DELANEY (Balliv[ar]ogue, Wexford)/ Margaret DUNN, Witless Bay, NL)

23 Oct.: James KEATON (Co. Carlow)/ Margaret GLAVIN (Ferryland)

2 Nov.: Patrick ROACH (Moyacomb, Carlow)/ Honora DUNN (Witless Bay, NL)
1806
15 Jan.: Patrick MURPHY (Graigue, Kilkenny)/ Mary CASEY (Witless Bay, NL)
17 Feb.: Thomas LYNCH (Castletown, Limerick)/ Mary JENKINS (Fermeuse NL)
18 Feb.: Michael DWYER (St. Patrick's, Kilkenny City)/ Mary RONAN (Harbour Main, NL)
27 May: James LEAHY (Waterford)/ Jane HYDE (Bay Bulls, NL)
12 Nov.: James MURPHY (St. Mullin's, Carlow)/ Margaret POWER (Witless Bay, NL)
1807
6 Feb.: Philip NORRIS (Witless Bay, NL)/ Catherine SLATTERY (Clogheen, Waterford)
10 Mar.: James WALSH (Pollpeasty, Killegney, Wexford)/ Mary LEARY (Harbour Main, NL)
22 Aug.: Daniel NEALE (Tramore, Waterford)/ Elizabeth NORRIS (Witless Bay, NL)
1808
4 Feb.: David VAILE (Ardmore, Waterford)/ Peasey MONAHAN (Bay Bulls, NL)
27 May: James NEAL (St. Patrick's, Kilkenny City)/ Catherine CONNORS (Harbour Main)
12 Aug.: Owen CONNOR (Suttons, Wesford)/ Mary REDDY (St. John's, formerly of Fermeuse)
10 Nov.: Stephen YARD (Witless Bay, NL)/ Anne MALONE (Glenmore, Kilkenny)
20 Nov.: Edmund PHELAN (Balinnaning [?], Waterford)/ Eleanor JORDIN (Brigus, NL)
12 Dec.: Patrick POWER (Ballyhale, Kilkenny)/ Mary KINLEGHAN (Bay Bulls, NL)
22 Dec.: James MORRIS (Tintern, Wexford)/ Mary MULCAHY (Bay Bulls, NL)
28 Dec.: John PHELAN (Ferryland)/ Mary MEYLER (Ponss Casthead [?], Wexford)
28 Dec.: Thomas MURPHY (Old Ross, Wexford)/ Anne MURPHY alias AUDLIN (Ferryland)
1809
9 Jan.: Martin BOURKE (Bay Bulls, NL)/ Mary BARRY (Barthes Parish [?], Kilkenny)
18 Apr.: Michael MULLALY (Mullinahone, Tipperary)/ Annie STEVENS (Bell Island, NL)
9 Aug.: Richard BUTLER (Mullinavat, Kilkenny)/ Phillis GORDON (Witless Bay, NL)
6 Oct.: William LONDREGAN (Gammansfield, Tipperary)/ Mary CAREY (Witless Bay, NL)
1810
1 Oct.: William WALL (Rosbercon, Kilkenny)/ Nancy GORDON (Witless Bay, NL)
15 Oct.: Phillip SCOTT (Tintern, Wexford)/ Sarah MULCAHY (Bay Bulls, NL)
22 Nov.: William RYAN (Suttons, Wexford)/ Margaret DEVISE (Bell Island, NL)
1811
31 Jan.: James CODY (Carrick-on-Suir)/ Elizabeth WILLIAMS (Bay Bulls, NL)
10 Feb.: Michael FARRELL (Clonenagh, Leix)/ Joanna DELAHUNTY (Brigus, NL)
22 Apr.: Walter DOWER (Killea, Waterford)/ Elizabeth KAVANAGH alias STOKES (Bay Bulls)
20 May: Garret BYRN (Kilmacow, Kilkenny)/ Mary NEWLAN (Bay Bulls, NL)
22 Oct.: Thomas BUTLER (Knocktopher, Kilkenny)/ Dorah GLIN (Bay Bulls, NL)
6 Dec.: Laurence BYRNE (St. Mullins, Carlow)/ Elizabeth DELANEY alias KENNEDY,
[Harbour Main]
1812
7 Feb.: Laurence KELLY (Co. Kilkenny)/ Esther NEWLAN (Bay Bulls, NL)
17 May: George FRISBY (Co. Kilkenny)/ Bridget MULLOWNEY alias NORRIS (Witless Bay)
12 Oct.: John GREEN (Witless Bay, NL)/ Mary NORTH (Old Ross, Wexford)
3 Dec.: William DINIAN (Hay Cove, NL)/ Bridget LAWLOR `(Newbawn, Wexford)
19 Dec.: John LONERGAN (Co. Kilkenny)/ Fanny DRISCOLL (Toad's Cove, NL)

<u>1813</u>

21 Jan.: William DUGGAN (Co. Wexford)/ Catherine ELWARD (Ferryland)

19 May: Matthew MEANY (Old Leighlin, Carlow)/ Mary RYAN (Ferryland)

 4 July: James KAVANAGH (Co. Wexford)/ Agnes . . . . . (Bell Island, NL)

 4 Nov.: Joseph RIGHTHEAD [?], (Bay Bulls, NL)/ Bridget NEAL (Carrick-on-Suir)

30 Nov.: Bartholomew DUNPHY (Kilmichael, Wexford)/ Mary JORDAN (Brigus, NL)

30 Nov.: John CAREW (Witless Bay, NL)/ Margaret CARROLL (Barony of Kells, Kilkenny)

 4 Dec.: Thomas POWER (Witless Bay, NL)/ Mary WALSH (Owning, Kilkenny)

 9 Dec.: Philip HAYES (Kilmallock, Wexford)/ Bridget BRENNAN (Cape Broyle)

22 Dec.: William SCOTT (Tintern, Wexford)/ Bridget WILLIAMS (Bay Bulls, NL)

<u>1814</u>

17 Nov.: Richard LACY (Co. Waterford)/ Bridget CONDON (Ferryland)

<u>1815</u>   (Waterford)

 3 Jan.: John ROACH (Tallow, Waterford)/ Joanna HAWKINS alias CURRAN (Clashmore,

 7 Feb.: John SULLIVAN (Killarney, Kerry)/ Elizabeth CAHIL alias KEYS (Caplin Cove, NL)

<u>1816</u>

 – Feb.: Michael CODY (Bay Bulls, NL)/ Bridget CLARKE (Waterford City)

23 May: John QUINLAN (Brigus, NL)/ Mary HERON (Dungarvan, Waterford)

23 May: Richard ROCHE (Ferryland)/ Bridget FARREL (Co. Waterford)

21 Nov.: James CODY (Co. Kilkenny)/ Joanna ELLIS (Ferryland, NL)

25 Nov.: John TOWNSEND (Callan, Kilkenny)/ Mary ELWARD (Cape Broyle, NL)

 3 Dec.: James WALSH (Co. Cork)/ Catherine BRETTY (Trinity, NL)

<u>1817</u>

15 Jan.: John FURLONG (Rosegarland, Ballylannan, Wexford)/ Mary MULONY (Bay Bulls, NL)

12 Feb.: John BEGLY (Lismore, Waterford)/ Elleanor CAHIL (Witless Bay, NL)

17 Aug.: John BRYAN (Fogo, NL)/ Mary CARROLL (Co. Kilkenny)

30 Aug.: James FRAYARD (Dartmerley [?], Devonshire)/ Annie CORCORAN (Co. Kilkenny)

 6 Sep.: Michael WALLACE (Co. Waterford)/ Anne BRYAN (Tilting, NL)

30 Dec.: John MURPHY (Waterford City)/ Mary BURK (Witless Bay, NL)

<u>1818</u>

18 July: Maurice Robert GAMBOL (Co. Waterford)/ Joanna BRYAN (Fogo, NL)

 9 Aug.: Michael GREEN (Carrick-on-Suir)/ Mary BOURKE (Tilting, NL)

27 Sep.: Patrick BURK (Ross, Wexford)/ Kitty BRYAN (Bay Bulls, NL)

<u>1819</u>

19 Apr.: Patrick MURPHY (Glenmore, Kilkenny)/ Margaret TIMMONS (St. Mullin's, Carlow)

20 Apr.: Thomas McGRATH (Co. Waterford)/ Catherine WALSH (King's Cove, NL)

17 June: James POWER (Co. Waterford)/ Joanna McGRATH (Tilting, NL)

27 Sep/25 Oct.: Michael DOOLEY (Co. Waterford)/ Mary SULLIVAN (Clonmel, Tipperary)

 6 Nov.: James LONG (Monkstown, Cork)/ Mary BLAKE (Ferryland, NL)

<u>1820</u>

17 May: Patrick GRADY (Callan, Kilkenny)/ Mary BRENNEN (Cape Broyle, NL)

20 Aug.: Thomas HAYS (Carrick-on-Suir)/ Eleanor BRYAN (Tilting, NL)

21 Oct.: James KEOGH (Tintern, Wexford)/ Catherine MOKELER (Bay Bulls, NL)

 1 Nov.: Thomas ROSS (St. Iberius, Wexford City)/ Nancy YARD (Witless Bay, NL)

 3 Nov.: John BUTLER (Co. Waterford)/ Elizabeth GLYN (Bay Bulls, NL)

3 Nov.: Patrick DEEGAN (Thomastown, Kilkenny)/ Mary WALSH (Bay Bulls, NL)

3 Nov.: Patrick DOYLE (Enniscorthy, Wexford)/ Bridget BRAWDERS (Toad's Cove, NL)

14 Dec.: Denis MURPHY (Co. Cork)/ Honora KELLY (Plate Cove, NL)

21 Dec.: John SMITH (Cappoquin, Waterford)/ Catherine JORDAN (Ferryland, NL)

1821

24 Mar.: Maurice KELLY (Tramore, Waterford)/ Mary DRISCOL (Toad's Cove, NL)

7 Nov.: Edmund ROWNAN (Tramore, Waterford)/ Ellen POWER (Toad's Cove, NL)

8 Dec.: John WALSH (Fermeuse NL)/ Judith MAHER (Kilcash, Tipperary)

1822

11 Oct.: John NEVIL (Ramsgrange, Wexford)/ Catherine CALLIHAN alias CAHIL (St John's)

6 Nov.: Patrick DOYLE (Gowran, Kilkenny)/ Mary JORDAN (Bay Bulls, NL)

8 Nov.: Thomas MURPHY (Co. Carlow)/ Ann PHILIPS (Bonavista, NL)

18 Nov.: John SMYTH (Co. Cork)/ Mary KELLY (Plate Cove, NL)

22 Nov.: George CAREW (Bay Bulls, NL)/ Mary BARRY alias HYNES (Rosbercon, Kilkenny)

1823

3 Jan.: Thomas CULLIN (Tintern, Wexford)/ Judy McGRATH (Carrick-on-Suir)

5 Jan.: Walter BOLAN (Dunhill, Waterford)/ Catherine JORDIN (Brigus, NL)

20 Jan.: John FURLONG (Newbawn, Wexford)/ Mary POWER (Toad's Cove, NL)

23 May: Patrick ROACH (Abbeyside, Waterford)/ Mary CURREN alias FOLEY (Clonea, Water.)

17 Aug.: Richard WALSH (Co. Waterford)/ Betsy DROHAN (Tilting, NL)

21 Aug.: Richard TATE (Fethard, Wexford)/ Ellen REARDON (Tilting, NL)

7 Oct.: Michael WALSH (Adamstown, Wexford)/ Eleanor MACKEY (Catalina, NL)

9 Dec.: Michael MOLLOY (Co. Wexford)/ Mary McGEE (Ferryland, NL)

1824

15 Nov.: John COMERFORD (Carrick-on-Suir)/ Elizabeth MASON alias HICKS (Harbour Main)

1825

17 Apr.: Patrick DOOLIN (Callan, Kilkenny)/ Ellen WALSH (Witless Bay, NL)

23 Apr.: Michael HANRAHAN (Ferryland, NL)/ Honora BOYD (Co. Waterford)

10 Oct.: Thomas CONNERS (Co. Tipperary)/ Mary CAREY (Witless Bay, NL)

16 Oct.: Stephen DILLON (Mulrankin, Wexford)/ Mary KEENAN (Toad's Cove, NL)

8 Nov.: James PEARL (Bannow, Wexford)/ Ellen BROTHERS (Fermeuse NL)

11 Nov.: John MULLALY (Co. Kilkenny)/ Mary REDIGAN (Co. Kilkenny)

16 Nov.: Thomas MACKEY (Co. Wexford)/ Sarah JORDAN (Bay Bulls, NL)

22 Nov.: John BALDWIN (Kilbarry, Waterford)/ Eliza JORDAN (Bay Bulls, NL)

24 Nov.: Walter POWER (Dunmore, Killea, Waterford)/ Bridget DOYLE (Renews, NL)

26 Nov.: Michael KIELY (Co. Tipperary)/ Maria WILLIAMS (Bay Bulls, NL)

1826

5 Feb.: John BRIEN (Co. Waterford)/ Ellen BUCKLEY (Brigus, NL)

5 June: William CONWAY (Killahy, Kilkenny)/ Mary O'NEIL (Fermeuse NL)

12 Nov.: John REILY (Co. Wexford)/ Margaret ELLIS (Ferryland, NL)

28 Nov.: Lawrence CORISH (Co. Kilkenny)/ Mary CALLORAN (Fermeuse)

1827

12 Jan.: Michael HARRINGTON (Bantry, Cork)/ Margaret HEALY (Witless Bay, NL)

8 Feb.: Edward CONDON (Ireland)/ Ann SANDERS (Aquaforte, NL)

26 Feb.: Patrick WALSH (Co. Wexford)/ Mary RAYE (King's Cove, NL)

10 Mar.: Patrick REDMOND/ Mary DOYLE (couple from Ireland, probably Co. Wexford)
 9 June: James DWYER (Kells, Kilkenny)/ Anne ROOSTE (Renews, NL)
26 Aug.: William GORMAN (Co. Kilkenny)/ Bridget RYAN (Bonavista, NL)
27 Sep.: Thomas KELLY (Co. Wexford)/ Catherine GRIFFEN (Co. Kilkenny)
13 Nov.: Thomas BRYAN (Ferryland, NL)/ Mary CRANE (New Ross, Wexford)
15 Nov.: Michael RYAN (Carrick-on-Suir)/ Ellen DRISCOL (Toad's Cove, NL)
1828
 9 Jan.: Richard ASPELL (Adamstown, Wexford)/ Bridget MACKEY (Brigus, NL)
15 Nov.: Thomas KIRWAN (Tramore, Waterford)/ Jane POWER (Renews, NL)
22 Nov.: Martin HUNT (Suttons, Wexford)/ Catherine GARDNER (Renews, NL)

23 - EIGHT IRISH HEADSTONES IN NEWFOUNDLAND

At Bay de Verde: Timothy **DINEE[N]** of Lismore [Co. Waterford], Ireland,
                who died 30 May 1832, age 60, after living here 40 years.

                Edmund **MOORE** of Kilmacanney [Kilmaganny, Co. Kilkenny],
                who died 12 Jan. 1884, age 84.

At Ferryland: James **BARRON** of Co. Tipperary, who died 27 Feb. 1899, age 84.

                Edward **KEOUGH** of Co. Wexford, who died 17 Dec. 1876, age 80,
                after living here for 60 years. Erected by son Andrew.

                Valentine **KEEFE** of Co. Tipperary, who died 5 July 1872, age 80.
                Erected by son Thomas.

At Renews: John **SHEEHAN** of Thomastown, Co. Kilkenny, who died 21 Feb.
                1861, age 84.

                John **DEEGAN** of Thomastown, Co. Kilkenny, died 18 Jan. 1854,
                age 72. Erected by Edward **Sheehan** to his father and uncle.

At St. Mary's Bay: John **WALSH** of Kilmacthomas, Co. Waterford, who died
                4 Jan. 1872, age 85.

24 - IRISH CONVICTS, 1788-89

A) Irish Convicts Abandoned,1788

        On 18 October 1788,126 convicts were loaded onto the snow *Providence* at Dublin, Ireland,
to be transported to North America as punishment for their crimes. The term of transportation
ranged from 7 years to life. One account claims that these convicts were destined for Québec, that
the ship encountered ice conditions in the Gulf of St. Lawrence and decided to turn back. Another
source says the original destination was Nova Scotia. Whatever the story, Captain Debonham
decided to land his cargo on the sparsely inhabited eastern coast of Cape Breton Island. Forty-six

convicts had died, suggesting poor accommodation or mistreatment, rather than contagion, had played the principal part.

The *Freeman's Journal*, Dublin, 2 October 1788, stated that "A great number of felons have been brought to Newgate within these few days past, to be transported to British America, for the taking away of whom the Right Hon. Lord Mayor has engaged the snow *Providence*, of North Yarmouth, Captain Debonham, burden 200 tons, on board which ship two hundred of these unhappy people are to be embarked about the 13th to be landed at the first port she can make in Nova Scotia. The fate of unfortunate convicts on former occasions . . . is too great a reflection on the humanity of the nation and so disgraceful an infringement of the Laws of the Nation as to need repetition."

On 11 December 1788, Francis Dickson, chief pilot for Main-a-Dieu, observed a ship come to anchor between the mainland and Scatarie Island, just off the bar of Main-a-Dieu harbour. Charles Martell, Justice of the Peace, was cutting firewood about 3 miles south of the village, and saw the ship anchor and launch a small boat. Several people were quickly loaded into the boat and rowed to shore. The boat made several trips, bringing more people each time but landing them at several places on the shore.

The seamen used their pistols and cutlasses to drive the passengers out of the boat into the surf , forcing them to scramble through the icy waves and over the rocks to reach the snow-covered shore. One man died when he was dashed against the rocks. The rest - men, women, and boys - reached the shore in great distress. They lacked proper clothing and some had naked legs and feet. Many of them had festering sores caused by the irons shackling them while in the *Providence*. The ship sailed off, abandoning them to their fate.

Martell collected forty of these people and took them to the village of Main-a-Dieu. The villagers took these people into their homes where they were fed and could warm themselves by the fires. The men of the village returned to the landing site and rescued another thirty people or so and brought them to the village. Six who could not walk because they had no shoes were left at the landing site. By the time a boat was sent for them, all had died of exposure. John Kirkpatrick, was beaten and robbed by two other prisoners and left for dead.

Since the village lacked provisions to look after so many extra people for the winter, it was decided to send them to Sydney as soon as possible. On 15 December Luke Keegan took all the women, and those men who were sick or crippled to Sydney in his shallop the *Shilaley*. Frances Dickson became temporary master of the ship. He took along constables and peace officers to maintain order and security. On arrival at Sydney he anchored near the military dock, so as to prevent any of the passengers from landing. Twenty prisoners were left at Main-a-Dieu because the ship could not carry them all.

The arrival of the *Shilaley* with her human cargo caused consternation in Sydney, especially among the Colonial officials and the military. The Lt. Governor, William Macarmick, would not let the convicts come ashore but did direct the merchant, Richard Stout, to feed them while the council considered the situation. A survey of the stores held by the local merchants indicated that they did not have sufficient on hand to feed and clothe the convicts for the winter. It was too late in the year to order in extra rations.

They decided that the convicts should be sent on to Halifax which was much larger than Sydney. Governor Parr might have the resources to sustain the convicts for the winter. H.M. Brig *Relief* then about to sail from Sydney for Halifax could take at least some of them and that other vessels could be hired to transport the remainder.

When these measures were deemed impracticable, the council reconsidered the matter on 19 December. Macarmick then decided that the people should be brought ashore and accommodated as best they could, using the jail and other buildings. Many of the convicts were suffering from the effects of frost bite and a hospital was established to care for these and those who were ill, under the direction of William Robertson, surgeon of the 42nd Regiment then stationed in Sydney. Fifteen or sixteen were cared for in this way, though three died and several others were crippled for life.

Costs associated with the convicts came to £787 by 29 Sept. 1789. This report gives the number of convicts as being 76, but it is not clear if that is the number who were put off from the ship, or the number that survived to reach Sydney.

By October 1789 Macarmick reported that all of the convicts were gone except for two being held on a charge of murder. It is thought that many of the others made their way eventually to the United States but some may have remained in Cape Breton working as servants or becoming squatters.

This voyage of the *Providence* was the last official instance of convicts being transported from the British Isles to North America. While the practice of sentencing people to transportation continued for many years, all the subsequent transports went to Australia. Such undesirable outcomes as the following turned public opinion against further transportation of convicts to North America:
- The brig *Nancy* in 1784 ran short of food and offloaded 46 prisoners on the island of Ferro in the Canaries. The convicts were rounded up by Spanish soldiers and executed.
- In 1785, 176 prisoners were sold as indentured servants in Maryland
- In 1786,190 convicts were sold in Richmond, Virginia, as indentured servants
- In June 1787, the *Dispatch* of Yarmouth, Captain Nappers, attempted to land 183 convicts at Shelburne, NS. When the local residents refused to allow the landing, Nappers dumped them on shore in an uninhabited portion of the Bay of Machias, Maine, whence the survivors made their way to various towns in the U.S.
- A 1787 shipment of 100 convicts from Dublin was landed on a deserted island in the Bahamas where 51 died. The survivors had resorted to cannibalism before they were rescued.

The outcry caused by the news of the *Providence* incident was enough to convince the British government to end shipments to North America and on 27 July 1789 a directive was issued that all future convict transports were to go to New South Wales. However, there was a further landing of convicts in the summer of 1789 at Bay Bulls, Newfoundland, from the ship *Duke of Leinster*, apparently from a ship bound for Australia that had a severe outbreak of fever on board.

List of the known convicts from the Providence:

BUTLER, Judith, 7 years for vagrancy
CORRIGAN, Richard, theft of a watch
DOYLE, Patrick, buried at Sydney, Cape Breton, 2 Jan 1789
HART, John, 7 years for stealing 4 pounds of brass
HUTCHISON, Michael, 7 years for cow and sheep stealing
JONES, Elizabeth, 7 years for stealing 3 silver spoons
KIRKPATRICK, John, transported for life for sheep stealing; beaten, robbed, left to die
LYNCH, Ann, 7 years for vagrancy
MacDONALD, Joseph, murdered John Kirkpatrick (above)
O'DONNELL, ..., seems to have settled at Main-a-Dieu
PENDERGAST, Lawrence, 7 years for robbery; murdered John Kirkpatrick (above)

REDDY, Michael, age 14, 7 years for theft of a silver spoon
REILLY, Rose, 7 years for vagrancy
WALSH, Henry and John, theft of a ladder with intent
WOODHAUSEN, ..., buried at Sydney, 23 Dec 1788.

Joseph MacDonald and Laurence Pendergast, found guilty of murdering John Kirkpatrick on 11 Dec, 1788, were sentenced to be hanged 14 Mar 1789, but Governor Macarmick ordered a stay of execution due to uncertainty as to whether Kirkpatrick died from the beating or from exposure on that first night ashore. They escaped jail in Apr 1790 and were recaptured and pardoned in Dec 1790.

Sources:

Burke, Charles A.,"Irish Convicts Abandoned on Cape Breton's Shore", *Cape Breton Magazine*, No. 72 (June 1997).
Campbell, John, "Irish Convicts Dumped On Cape Breton", *Cape Breton Post*, April 11,1998.
"The Day The Convicts Landed", *The Cape Breton Genealogical Society*, Vol. 11 No. 30 June 1998.
The *Freeman's Journal*, Dublin, 2 October 1788 (www.irishnewspaperarcives.com).
Jackson, Elva E., "The Day The Convicts Landed", *Weekly Cape Bretoner*, 13 Oct 1956.
NSARM, RG 11, Vols. 319, 332, 334 (Records of Cape Breton as a Separate Colony).

B) Irish Convicts at Newfoundland, 1789

The original list (CO 194.38) has sixty-five names, but we know that seven were executed and therefore were never in Newfoundland. Fifty-eight were landed as labour at Petty Harbour and Bay Bulls, but Governor Milbanke sent many and perhaps all of them to England. Whether any of these men settled in Newfoundland is not known. The vessel was *The Duke of Leinster*. All these people were being transported. Three (marked by *) had been sentenced to death, but had their sentence commuted to transportation for life. One man, Gibbons, was to be flogged before being transported. O'Neil was transported for seven years, rather than for life.

NAMES	AGE	BIRTHPLACE	OFFENCE
*BROSNAHAN, Con.	23	Tralee, Kerry	Robbery & murder
BRYNE, John	22	Saggart, Dublin	Stealing a coat
BURLEIGH, John	19	Garlstown, Meath	Theft
*BUTLER, William	27	Limerick City	Robbery & murder
CAREY, Darby	54	Callan, Kilkenny	Swindling
CARPENTER,Nicholas	23	Crumlin, Dublin	
CASHELL, James	23	Limerick City	
CONNERY, Tim.	16	Dublin	
COYLE, John	21	Dublin City	Vagrant
DELANEY, Michael	22	Ballymore Eustace, Kildare	Theft
DUNCAN, Thomas	13	Kilcock, Meath	
ELLIS, Samuel	18	Tullow, Wicklow	Vagrant
FARRELL, John	14	Dublin City	Accomplice to house robbery
FINN, James	19	Edenahaugh[?]	
*FISHER, Robert	25	Dublin City	Robbery & murder
FLYNN, Michael	21	Cork City	Theft
FOLEY, John	19	Dublin City	Picking pockets

FRANKLIN, William	23	Dublin	Theft
GAINFORD, John	18	Dublin	Theft
GIBBONS, William	22	Dublin City	Attempted housebreak
GRANT, James	19	Dublin City	
HALFPENNY, James	23	Drogheda, Louth	Stealing lead
HART, Patrick	14	Dublin City	Picking pockets
HEALEY, Patrick	19	Dublin City	Theft
HOGG, David	16	Edenaclogh, Fermanagh	
HURLEY, John	22	Parteen, Clare	Theft
KELLY, John	30	Athlone	Theft
KELLY, Thomas	30	Rathcoole, Dublin	Stealing 2 saddles
KELLY, Martin	20	Oldcourt, Wicklow	Stealing wood
KEOUGH, John	22	Dublin ity	Famous Cart stealer
LACEY, Francis	41	Castledermot, Kildare	Sheep stealing
LAWLOR, John	16	Dublin City	Picking pockets
LEE, Patrick	24	Drogheda, Louth	
LEONARD, Patrick	40	Kinnegad, Westmeath	Swindling
MAHONEY, John	44	Mitchelstown, Cork	Theft
McCARTHY, Charles	55	Ballymurphy. Cork	
McDERMOTT, Thomas	20	Edgeworthstown, Longford	Stealing a pound of tobacco
McGUIRE, James	25	Tinnouse[?], Waterford	Forcible entry
McLEESE, Daniel	20	Belfast, Antrim	Vagrant
MOONEY, Bart	29	Dublin	
MURPHY, John	13	Dublin	
MURRAY, James	23	Drumclan, Monaghan	
NEAL, Patrick	27	Kilkenny City Swindling	
NUGENT, Patrick	40	Omagh, Tyrone	Stealing table cloth
O'BRIEN, Charles	26	Rathfryland, Down	Picking pockets
O'NEIL, John	20	Dublin City	Stealing waistcoats
PALLET, Abraham	20	Crumlin, Monaghan	
PARKER, Peter	20	Carlow	Stealing tobacco & coining
PENDERGRASS, Michael	13	Dublin City	Picking pockets
RIELEY, John	28	Cavan, Cavan	Coining
RYAN, Martin	25	Humewood, Wicklow	Burglary
SHERIDAN, James	40	Cornagall, Cavan	Possession of stolen goods
STEWART, Daniel	19	Baltinglass, Wicklow	
SULLIVAN, Michael	18	Bruff, Limerick	Picking pockets
VANCE, Lansht[?]	40	Shean, Fermanagh	
WALLER, Patrick	19	Dublin	Theft
WALPOLE, William	23	Cashel, Tipperary	
WALSH, John	25	Carrick-on-Suir	Robbing a house
WALSH, Thomas	38	Moyvore, Westmeath	

25 - IRISH-BORN, NOVA SCOTIA CENSUS OF 1770

Upwards of two thousand natives of Ireland lived in the Maritime Provinces in 1770, if early census information is reliable. Unfortunately, much of the early population return has been lost. Since New Brunswick formed part of Nova Scotia until 1784 the loss is even more widespread. The surviving portions of this census record the presence of over 500 natives of Ireland in the region, most of them of Ulster origins. This is not surprising, given the massive emigration from the north of Ireland that occurred in the decades before the outbreak of the American revolution in 1775.

Anyone who runs an eye down the following listings will observe that many families were made up of natives of Ireland as well as members born in North America. There is sufficient anecdotal evidence to indicate that a good portion of the Irish who reached early Nova Scotia had emigrated first to New England and removed to Nova Scotia or the future New Brunswick as part of the greater immigration of New England Planters between 1759 and 1775.

Another characteristic that will become apparent at once is that the Irish person(s) in several of the families were not the party named as head of the household. A few were wives, as records in the several localities tell us, e.g., Nancy, the wife of Jacob Seelig at Lunenburg. Others were servants and farm hands employed by Planters from New England. The presence of such people may be suspected when the number of "men" or "women" is greater than "1", although further evidence would be required to ascertain any particular instance.

Genealogists, and historians more generally, are concerned with *persistence*, i.e., the remaining of families and individuals in a given area for more than a few years. We are fortunate that some of the poll tax listings for the period 1791-93 have come down to us for many of the townships represented in the 1770 census. When a person of the same name appears in both the 1770 return and the poll tax over twenty years later the fact is indicated by an asterisk by his name.

The 1770 census asked people whether they were Catholic or Protestant, but since only a dozen or so were Catholic, I have omitted that as a separate figure from the total in the family, except in those few cases.

AMHERST TOWNSHIP

Head of Household	Men	Boys	Women	Girls	Total	Born in Ireland	Born in America	Others
*Robert BERRY	1	2	1	4	8	6	2	
Patrick CAMPBELL	1		1		2	1		1 Scot
Joseph COCHRAN	1				1	1		
Samuel CRATH	1	1	1	1	4	2	2	
Patrick CRAUFORD	1	1	1	2	5	4	1	
Samuel CREELMAN	1	3	1	3	8	6	2	
Mathew DICKEY	1	4	1	2	8	6	2	
*David FORREST	1	5	1	2	9	6	3	

James FULTON	1	4	1	3	9	6	3	
John GRACE	1	1	1		3	2	1	
James HENRY	1	2	1	3	7	4	3	
*Robert McGOWAN	1	2	1	4	8	7	1	
Robert MUCKLEMAN	1	3	1		5	4	1	
*James ROBERTS	1				1	1		
Mathew SHARP	1	2	1	3	7	7		
John SIMPSON	1	1	1	1	4	4		
John STEWART	1	2			3	3		
TOTALS	17	33	14	28	92	70	21	

ANNAPOLIS TOWNSHIP

John LINSLEY	1		1		2	1		1 Eng.
Archibald MORISON	1	5	1	1	8	8		
TOTALS	2	5	2	1	10	9	0	1

CUMBERLAND TOWNSHIP

John ALLAN	1	1	1		3	1	1	1 Scot.
Anthony BURKE	1	1	2	4	8	2	5	1 Scot.
James LAW	2	1	1	1	5	2	3	
Henry McDONNELL	1	3	1		5	2	3	
Thomas MEE	1	1	1	1	4	2	1	1 Eng.
Mark PATTON	3		4		7	7		
TOTALS	9	7	10	6	32	16	13	3

DONEGALL [PICTOU] TOWNSHIP

James ARCHIBALD	1		1	6	8	2	6	
Robert DICKEY	1	1	1	1	4	1	3	
John HARRIS	6	2	2	1	11	3	6	2
Mathew HARRIS	4	4	2	4	14	2	12	
William KENNEDY	1	2	1	3	7	2	5	
James McCABE	1	2	1	3	7	2 (1 RC)	5	
Charles McCOY	1	3	1	1	6	1	5	

Robert McFADDEN	1	3	1	2	7	1	6	
Barnabas McGEE	1		1		2	1		1 Eng.
Barnett McNUTT	3	2	2	2	9	2	7	
Robert PATTERSON	2	5	1	2	10	1	6	3
TOTALS	22	24	14	25	85	18	61	6

FALMOUTH TOWNSHIP

Malachy CAGAN	1	2	1	1	5	1	4	
Henry Denny DENSON	8	6	5	3	22	4	16	2 Eng.
George FAESCH	3	2	2	2	9 (4 RC)	2	3	4
*Joseph JESS	2	1	1	1	5	1	4	
Peter MANNING	1	5	3		9	9		
Jacob MULLAR	3		2		5	1	1	3
John POTTER	1	1	1	3	6	5	1	
John SIMPSON	1	1		1	3	1	2	
TOTALS	20	18	15	11	64	24	31	9

GRANVILLE TOWNSHIP

Moses BANKS	1		2	2	5	1	4	
Nathaniel BARNS	2	1	1	1	5	1	4	
Widow CAMBEL			1	3	4	2	2	
Edward MacBRIDE	1	1	1	1	4	1	3	
Cormac MacDERMOR	2	3	1		6	2	4	
Thomas McGREGOR	1	1	2		4	2	2	
Ellexander MACKENSEY	2		1	1	4	1	2	1 Scot.
Francis MILLER	1	1	1	2	5	1	4	
Henry MILNER	1		1		2	2		
Hugh MORRESON	1		1		2	2		
John MORRESON	2		1	2	5	5		

John MORRESON, Jr.	1	1	1		3	3		
James RAY	2	1	1	1	5	3	2	
Patrick ROACH	1	3	1		5	2	3	
Moses SHAW	2	3	1	1	7	1	6	
Robert SPROWL	1	5		1	7	1	6	
John STARK	2	3	2		7	6	1	
Peter STARRIT	4		1	3	8	2	6	
Thomas TRAHEE	1	1	1	3	6	2	4	
Andrew WHITE	1	3	1	3	8	1	7	
Capt. Elias WYER	1	3	1	1	6	2		4 Germ.
Job YOUNG	2	4	1	1	8	1	7	
TOTALS	32	34	24	26	116	44	67	5

HILLSBOROUGH [now in NEW BRUNSWICK]

James DEBOY	1	2	2	1	6 (RC)	1	3	1 Eng,
Martyn HATT	1	2	1		4	2	2	1 Acad.
James SMITH	1	3	1	1	6	1	5	
TOTALS	3	7	4	2	16	4	10	2

SACKVILLE TOWNSHIP [now in NEW BRUNSWICK]

George SHEARMAN	2	1	1	4	8	1	7	

HORTON TOWNSHIP

*John HALL	1	1	1	2	5	5		
John MURDOCH	2		3		5	5		
TOTALS	3	1	4	2	10	10		

LONDONDERRY TOWNSHIP

*Thomas BAIRD	2	2	1	3	8	4	4	
*John BARNHILL	2	2	1	3	8	4	4	
Robert CALDERWOOD	1	1	1	1	4	2	2	

*George COCHRAN	1	2	1	1	5	2	3	
*Joseph CROW	1	2	2	2	7	3	4	
*William DAVISON	1		2	1	4	2	2	
*John DENNY	1		3	5	9	6	3	
*Alex[r] DEYARMOND	2	2	1	3	8	6	2	
*Robert FALKNER	2	3	2	1	8	1	7	
*James FLEMING	1	1	1	1	4	2	2	
*Thomas FLETCHER	1	1	1		3	3		
William FORBES	3		2	1	6	6		
*James FULTON, Esq.	2	1			3	3		
David GRAHMS	1	2	1	3	7	4	3	
Archibald KARR	1	2	1	1	5	3	2	
*Anthony McCLANE	2		2	1	5	5		
*Samuel McCLANE	2		2	1	5	5		
*Joseph McCLELLAN	4		2		6	6		
*Michael McCLELLAN	1	1	4	3	9	9		
*Peter McCLELLAN	1	1	1	1	4	2	2	
John McCLENNAN	1	1	4	3	9	9		
*Alexander McCURDY	2	2	1	1	6	6		
*Jasper McKINLEY	1	1	1	3	6	4	2	
*George McNUTT	1	2	1		4	2	2	
*John MAHON, Esq.	1		1	4	6	3	3	
*John MAHON	1		2	3	6	5	1	
William NICHOLSON	1	1	4		6	6		
Francis REED	1	1	4		6	6		
*John RODGERS	3	2	2		7	4	3	
*Robert SPENCER	1	3	1	1	6	3	3	
*David VANCE	1	1	1	2	5	4	1	
Ezekiel WILLIAMS	1		1	4	6	3	3	
*Claud WILSON	1				1	1		

Henry WILSON	2		1		3	3		
James WILSON	2		1	2	5	3	2	
*Thomas WILSON	1	1	1	1	4	1	3	
*William WILSON	2	1	1	1	5	5		
TOTALS	**57**	**40**	**60**	**60**	**217**	**152**	**65**	**0**

LUNENBURG TOWNSHIP

Robert JOHNSTON	1	2	1	1	5	5		
Baptist MOREAU	3	2	1	2	8	1	5	2
Jacob SEELIG	1	2	1	1	5	1	2	2 Germ.
TOTALS	**5**	**6**	**3**	**4**	**18**	**7**	**7**	**4**

NEW DUBLIN TOWNSHIP

John & Wm GIFFIN	2		2	1	5	3	2	
Widow GORTZ	1	4	1	1	7	1	6	
William JOHNSTON	2				2	1		1 Scot.
*Thos. LITTLEJOHN	2	4	1	3	10	1	9	
Mathew McGYER	2	1	1		4	1 (RC)		3
John McLEOD	2	2	1		5	2	3	
Hubert MASON	1	2	2	3	8	8		
*James PARK	2	2	1	1	6	6		
*John PARK	1				1	1		
*Patrick PORTER	1	2	2	1	6	6		
*Joseph WHITEFORT	1	1	1	2	5	3	2	
TOTALS	**17**	**18**	**12**	**12**	**59**	**33**	**22**	**4**

ONSLOW TOWNSHIP

*John BARNHILL	2	2	1	2	7	2	5	
*William HAMILTON	2		2	1	5	5		
Mathew STAPLES	1	2	2	1	6	2	3	1 Eng.
*Hugh TACKLES	1	2	1	3	7	2	5	
William TAKELS	1	2	2		5	2	3	

TOTALS	7	8	8	7	30	13	16	1 Eng.

TRURO TOWNSHIP

*David ARCHIBALD, Esq.	3	2	2	1	8	3	5	
*John ARCHIBALD	1	1	2		4	2	2	
Robert ARCHIBALD	1	1	1	1	4	2	2	
Samuel ARCHIBALD	3	3	3	4	13	1	12	
*Samuel ARCHIBALD, Jr	2	2	1		5	1	4	
*John CALDWELL	1				1	1		
*Charles COX	1	3	2	3	9	3	6	
*Adam DICKEY	1	3	3	3	10	1	9	
*Robert DICKEY	1	1	1	1	4	4		
James DOWNING	1	1	1	3	6	1	4	1 Scot.
William DOWNING	1	1	2		4	2	2	
James FAULKNER	1	3	1	3	8	1	7	
*William FISHER	2	4	3	4	13	1	12	
*John FULTON	1	3	1	3	8	2	6	
*Thomas GOURLIE	3	3	2		8	4	4	
*James JOHNSON	3	4	3	3	13	1	12	
*John JOHNSON	4	1	2		7	2	5	
*John LOGGAN	1	2	1	2	6	2	4	
*William LOGGAN	1	1	1	2	5	1	4	
James McCABE	1	2	1	3	7	1 (RC)	6	
Charles McCAY	1	3	1	2	7	1	6	
*John McKEEN	3		2		5	2	3	
Andrew McKOWN	1		1		2	2		
*Alexander MILLAR	2	3	1	2	8	1	7	
*Hugh MOOR	1		1	3	5	1	4	
Alexander NEILSON	1	2	1	2	6	1	4	1 Scot.
John SAVAGE	2	1	2	1	6	1	5	

*George SCOTT	1		1	3	5	2	3	
TOTALS	45	50	43	49	187	48	137	2 Scot.

KNOWN ORIGINS IN ABOVE LISTS

ANTRIM: Cochran/Amherst, McKeen/Truro, Park/New Dublin.
ARMAGH: Hamilton/Onslow.
BELFAST: Fulton/Londonderry, Millar/Truro.
DONEGAL: Baird/Londonderry, Barnhill/Londonderry & Onslow, Deyarmond/Londonderry,
        McClane/Londonderry, McNutt/Londonderry, Mahon/Londonderry, Spencer/Londonderry.
FERMANAGH: Starrit/Granville.
LONDONDERRY: Archibald/Truro & Pictou, Crow/Londonderry, Fisher/Truro,
        Fleming/Londonderry, Loggan/Truro, McClellan/Londonderry, Moor/Truro.
        Patton/Cumberland.

BIBLIOGRAPHY

Adams, William Forbes. *Ireland and Irish Emigration to the New World From 1815 to the Famine.* New Haven, 1932; repr. Baltimore: Genealogical Publishing, 1980.

Byrne, Cyril J. "The Case of the Schooner "Fanny" from Waterford to St. John's, 1811,"*An Nasc*, 3:1 (Spring/Summer 1990), 19 - 22.

_____. "Irish Baptisms, Marriages and Burials in the Anglican Registers of St. John's, Newfoundland for the years 1753 - 1760." *An Nasc, 5: 1 (Summer 1992), 5 - 11.*

_____. "St. John's? Miramichi? Halifax? Another List of Passengers 1817." *An Nasc*, 3:2 (Fall 1990), 9 - 10.

_____. "Some 18th Century Wills from Canada in Irish Sources." *An Nasc,* 8 (Summer 1995), 14 - 20.

_____. "The United Irish Rising of 1798 and the Fencibles' Mutiny in St. John's, 1800."*An Nasc*, 11 (Fall 1998), 15 - 23.

Byrne, Cyril J., and Margaret Harry, eds. *Talamh An Eisc: Canadian and Irish Essays* Halifax: Nimbus Publishing, 1986.

Cousins, John. "The Irish of Lot Seven." *The Abegweit Review*, 4:1 (Spring 1983), 35-40.

Cushing, J. Elizabeth, *et al. A Chronicle of Irish Emigration to Saint John, New Brunswick, 1847.* Saint John: The New Brunswick Museum, 1979.

Dobson, David. *Ships from Ireland to Early America 1623 - 1850. Baltimore:* Clearfield, 1999.

Donovan, Kenneth, "Mary Grace Barron and the Irish of Ingonish, Cape Breton 1822-1999," *The Nashwaak Review* 6-7 (Fall 1999), 177-237.

Houston, Cecil J., and William J. Smyth. *Irish Emigration and Canadian Settlement: Patterns, Links, and Letters.* Toronto: University of Toronto Press, 1990.

Johnson, Daniel F. *Irish Emigration to New England through the Port of Saint John, New Brunswick, Canada, 1841 to 1849.* Baltimore: Clearfield, 1996.

MacKenzie, A. A. *The Irish in Cape Breton.* Antigonish: Formac Publishing,1979.

Mannion, John J. *Irish Settlements in Eastern Canada; A Study of Cultural Transfer and Adaptation.* Toronto: University of Toronto Press, 1974.

McGuigan, Peter. "From Wexford and Monaghan: the Lot 22 Irish," *The Abigweit Review,* 5:1 (Winter 1985), 61 - 96.

_____. "The Lot 61 Irish: Settlement and Stabilization," *The Abegweit Review,* 6:1 (Spring 1988), 33 - 63.

Mitchell, Brian. *Irish Passenger Lists 1847 - 1871*. Baltimore: Genealogical Publishing, 1988.

Murphy, Peter D. *Poor Ignorant Children; Irish Famine Orphans in Saint John, New Brunswick*. Halifax: Saint Mary's University, 1999.

Murphy, Terrence, and Cyril J. Byrne. *Religion and Identity; The Experience of Irish and Scottish Catholics in Atlantic Canada*. St. John's, NL: Jesperson Press, 1987.

O'Driscoll, Robert, & Lorna Reynolds. *The Untold Story: The Irish in Canada,* 2 vols. Toronto: Celtic Arts of Canada, 1988.

O'Grady, Brendan. "The Monaghan Settlers," *The Abegweit Review,* 4:1 (Spring 1983), 51 - 80.

Passengers to New Brunswick: The Custom House Records - 1833, 34, 37 & 38. Saint John: New Brunswick Genealogical Society, 1987.

Power, Thomas P., ed. *The Irish in Atlantic Canada 1780 - 1900*. Fredericton: New Ireland Press, 1991.

Punch, Terrence M. "Cornwallis's Irishmen 1749." *An Nasc,* 6:1 (Summer 1993), 6- 8.

_____. "Irish Deserters at Halifax, Nova Scotia, during the Napoleonic Wars." *The Irish Ancestor,* 8:1 (1976), 33 - 35.

_____. *Irish Halifax; The Immigrant Generation, 1815 - 1859*. Halifax: Saint Mary's University, 1981.

_____. "The Passengers on the "Polly." *The Irish Ancestor,* 8:2 (1976), 82 -85.

_____. "Ships from Ireland to Nova Scotia, 1765 - 1850." *An Nasc,* 13 (Spring 2001), 3 - 10.

_____. "Some Irish Weddings in Nova Scotia". Covers 1800 - 1845 in a series in *The Irish Ancestor,* 6 (1974), 101-112; 7 (1975), 39-54, 104-120; 8 (1976), 53-69, 124-139; 9 (1977), 133-146.

_____. *Some Sons of Erin in Nova Scotia*. Halifax: Petheric Press, 1980.

Stewart, H. L. *The Irish in Nova Scotia; Annals of The Charitable Irish Society of Halifax (1786 - 1836)*. Halifax: The Charitable Irish Society, 1949.

Toner, P.M., *An Index to Irish Immigrants in the New Brunswick Census of 1851*. Fredericton: the author, 1991.

_____, ed. *New Ireland Remembered: Historical Essays on the Irish in New Brunswick*. Fredericton: New Ireland Press, 1988.

SURNAMES INDEX

Variants have been grouped together whenever possible. Names with the prefixes "Mc", "Mac" and "O" will be found under the substantive part of the surname, e.g., O'Brien under Brien, McGrath under Grath.

INDEX OF SHIPS

"Oh, where's the isle we've seen in dreams,
Our destined home or grave?"
Thus sang they, as by the morning beams,
They swept the Atlantic wave.

– Thomas Moore, *The Coming of the Milesians*[1]

---

[1] The first Celts to come to Ireland were led by Mil, and were called the Milesians.

LaVergne, TN USA
18 March 2011
220677LV00001B/19/P

9 780806 317823